PURPOSE AND POLICY IN THE GLOBAL COMMUNITY

For Dave Kinsella —
Student, colleague, & friend.

October 30, 2014

Advances in Foreign Policy Analysis

Series Editor: Alex Mintz

Foreign policy analysis offers rich theoretical perspectives and diverse methodological approaches. Scholars specializing in foreign policy analysis produce a vast output of research. Yet, there are only very few specialized outlets for publishing work in the field. Addressing this need is the purpose of **Advances in Foreign Policy Analysis**. The series bridges the gap between academic and policy approaches to foreign policy analysis, integrates across levels of analysis, spans theoretical approaches to the field, and advances research utilizing decision theory, utility theory, and game theory.

Members of the Board of Advisors

Published by Palgrave Macmillan

Integrating Cognitive and Rational Theories of Foreign Policy Decision Making
Edited by Alex Mintz

Studies in International Mediation
Edited by Jacob Bercovitch

Media, Bureaucracies, and Foreign Aid: A Comparative Analysis of the United States, the United Kingdom, Canada, France, and Japan
By Douglas A. Van Belle, Jean-Sébastien Rioux, and David M.Potter

Civil–Military Dynamics, Democracy, and International Conflict: A New Quest for International Peace
By Seung-Whan Choi and Patrick James

Economic Sanctions and Presidential Decisions: Models of Political Rationality
By A. Cooper Drury

Purpose and Policy in the Global Community
By Bruce Russett

PURPOSE AND POLICY IN THE GLOBAL COMMUNITY

BRUCE RUSSETT

PURPOSE AND POLICY IN THE GLOBAL COMMUNITY
© Bruce Russett, 2006.

First published in 2006 by
PALGRAVE MACMILLAN™
175 Fifth Avenue, New York, N.Y. 10010 and
Houndmills, Basingstoke, Hampshire, England RG21 6XS
Companies and representatives throughout the world.

PALGRAVE MACMILLAN is the global academic imprint of the Palgrave Macmillan division of St. Martin's Press, LLC and of Palgrave Macmillan Ltd. Macmillan® is a registered trademark in the United States, United Kingdom and other countries. Palgrave is a registered trademark in the European Union and other countries.

ISBN-13: 978–1–4039–7183–8
ISBN-10: 1–4039–7183–8
ISBN-13: 978–1–4039–7184–5 (paperback)
ISBN-10: 1–4039–7184–6   (paperback)

Library of Congress Cataloging-in-Publication Data

Russett, Bruce M.
      Purpose and policy in the global community / Bruce Russett ... [et al.].
            p. cm.—(Advances in foreign policy analysis)
      Includes bibliographical references and index.
      ISBN 1–4039–7183–8—ISBN 1–4039–7184–6 (pbk.)
        1. International relations. 2. Social justice. 3. Poverty. 4. Equality.
      5. Deterrence (Strategy) I. Title. II. Series.

JZ1242.R867 2006
327—dc22   2005049538

A catalogue record for this book is available from the British Library.

Design by Newgen Imaging Systems (P) Ltd., Chennai, India.

First edition: June 2006

10 9 8 7 6 5 4 3 2 1

Printed in the United States of America.

Contents

Chapter 1

Change and Continuity: Four Decades of Research and Policy

This opening chapter introduces each of the following chapters in order. They comprise both essays and research reports, the latter including quantitative analyses chosen so as not to include technical materials inaccessible to an advanced undergraduate. This introduction uses the next chapter, "Rich and Poor in 2000 AD: The Great Gulf," as a thematic focal point for the subsequent pieces, considering their theoretical, empirical, and normative implications as appropriate. It considers how each subsequent chapter carries on themes from "Rich and Poor," how they are developed, and how they may relate to contemporary debates under changed conditions. I also remark on what in those pieces seems to me to be more or less enduring and what was wrong-headed. Each—even the older ones—does I think, have something to say about current issues. I embed the chapters in some discussion of my own intellectual and personal history and conclude this chapter with comments about research and writing in our profession. These include thoughts about where ideas come from; how the study of international relations has changed; the interaction of theory, empirical investigation, and ethical concerns; and the importance of collaboration in research.

The Chapters and Their Origins

• "Rich and Poor in 2000 AD: The Great Gulf" is an exercise in informal theory-guided speculation about the future. I originally wrote it in 1965 as a plenary address to the American Sociological Association, and I sent a revised version off to *The Virginia Quarterly Review*, which was then publishing stimulating articles on foreign policy. My cover letter described the article as developing out of an interest in three related influences that converged here:

> First is a certain malaise with the terribly confident and optimistic predictions my natural-scientist friends frequently make about the world of the future. While perhaps technologically sound, I feel these predictions depend on a very naïve social and political theory. Second is my concern, for some time, with developing the data for some at least moderately disciplined predictions about economic and social conditions that will impinge on politics. This shades into a third influence, which is my theoretical commitment to a macroscopic way of looking at international politics. That is, when we want to understand or predict major developments in international politics we can often do so less by examining the political process per se than by trying to see what the menu of political choice may be, what sets the limits within which political choice must operate.

The chapter lays out several themes, largely around the problem of global inequalities in human life conditions. It is about globalization (before the word was common), including that of communications and the world economy. The most prominent theme is that gross differences in income between the rich and poor have enormous implications for actual living conditions. Closely related to that is the likelihood that these inequalities will stimulate political instability and/or severe repression within poor countries. It also addresses the implications for international peace and stability, including wars between poor countries and whether the governments of rich countries will ally themselves with repression by the governments of poor countries. It mentions some of the possibilities for terrorism, though without using that word and in the context of poverty, rather than of religious fanaticism, which I now see as at least equally important. It emphasizes the vulnerability of a high technology and highly interdependent economy and culture to possible terrorism. A related theme, not developed so thoroughly, considers relations between great powers and the role of nuclear deterrence.

Some of the data and the language (not gender neutral) of this piece reflect its age, but the themes remain central to contemporary theory and policy discourse. Some details look too optimistic (e.g., economical large-scale desalinization of sea water), and it was a little pessimistic about food production not rising much above sub-sistence level, particularly in Asia. While it does not reflect the more recent experience of rapid income growth in much of Asia, especially the large countries of China and India, its pessimism has been borne out in Africa, where per capita incomes typically dropped in the 1990s. Overall, the average citizen of low-income countries has closed the overall income gap slightly, but for those in the poorest countries the gap has widened. (The richest, Luxembourg, has a per capita GDP more than a hundred times that of the poorest, Sierra Leone and Somalia: $55,000 to $500).[1] The chapter correctly antici-pates the rise of expensive high-tech weaponry for use by rich countries in conflict with much poorer ones and the willingness of rich states to spend money on such weapons. Like chapter 3 following, it largely vaults over the cold war issues that otherwise seemed so central at that time. Perhaps for that very reason it seems to wear pretty well in the post–cold war world. There are a lot of consistent patterns and issues in world politics.

• "The Marginal Utility of Income Transfers to the Third World" is an empirical chapter addressing a major normative issue, and it serves as table-setting to much subsequent material in the book. With the help of some simple graphical presentations, it lays out much more deeply than in chapter 2 the human consequences (in health and life expectancy) of poverty and relative deprivation and the relatively small cost at which those differences might be narrowed. Some political implications of this fact left implicit here are developed in subsequent chapters of this book. The high cost-effectiveness of certain measures for poor countries, exemplified by insecticide-treated mosquito nets and inoculations against common diseases, remains true in this century.

I wrote another intellectually related piece at the time[2] as part of a collaboration to study the causes and consequences of dependence and underdevelopment in the third world. That particular article was a measurement exercise intended to produce a surrogate measure of income inequality for the larger project. In it we showed that for those countries with complete data, per capita income was strongly related to high life expectancy and low infant mortality, as expected. But controlling for income level, those countries with a relatively low level of income inequality evidenced especially high achievement on the health measures. We could thus use health and income levels to estimate income inequality in those countries for which direct inequality measures were not available, at the same time gaining insight into possible causal connections.

I offered to do a condensed and nontechnical version of "Marginal Utility" for *Foreign Affairs*, but the Managing Editor turned it down partly from concern that a nontechnical version could not be done. Yet he was equally concerned about the substance. As put in his rejection letter (September 28, 1977), "Finally, there is also the problem of whether or not it is to our interest or even the world's to raise life expectancy among the poor to 65 years old. To say this may imply a certain callousness, but it is again symptomatic of the kinds of questions which your analysis raises." I still wonder how widespread "a certain callousness" is among the U.S. foreign policy elite, for example regarding aid to sub-Saharan Africa where even today the average life expectancy in most countries is below 50, and in many is below 40—about half of that in the rich industrialized world. That's the same ratio as anticipated in chapter 2. U.S. economic development assistance in 2005 amounted to 16 cents per $100 of GDP—less than half the share (36 cents per $100) allocated by European countries. President George W. Bush's *Millennium Challenge Account* for aid to poor countries demonstrating progress in political freedom and improvement in the health and education of their populace could, if properly funded, bring the U.S. contribution up some.

• "Comparative Public Health: The Political Economy of Human Misery and Well-Being" marks a return, about 25 years later with contemporary data and analytical methods, to the concerns of the preceding chapters. I had wanted to do so for quite a while, and a no-strings invitation from Gary King to spend spring semester 2001 in research at Harvard as part of his big project with WHO provided the opportunity. The opportunity was widened when I discovered that Paul Huth, a former Ph.D. student and long-time collaborator (e.g., see chapter 11) would be there, and that he already had been working at Harvard with Hazem Ghobarah, a highly skilled statistical analyst. This chapter asks why most people in some countries enjoy long and healthy lives and most people in others experience neither. It uses quantitative analysis to assess the human costs of poverty, bad government, income inequality, and war on health and mortality. The three of us then collaborated on two other articles, one for a political science audience and a related but improved model for a public health audience, that use a fascinating though controversial WHO cross-national data set on health outcomes to focus specifically on the human health costs of civil wars.[3] We fully expect that our initial efforts will in time be superseded and our results modified as other researchers use more refined theory, methods, and data.

• "Security and the Resources Scramble: Will 1984 be Like 1914?" greatly expands on the theme of economically motivated great power competition alluded to in "Rich and Poor." It speculates about the consequences of scarcity of petroleum, mineral, and other resources, with reference to political conditions within great powers; for example, a "military-industrial complex" supporting imperialism and other forms of economic competition in interaction with other countries. Its specific concern with the Soviet-American rivalry may seem to make the piece dated, but it illustrates the underlying dynamics of international expansion with a theoretical perspective on the period preceding World War I, and that longer-term perspective can be enlightening. It addresses the danger of terrorism and political chaos in producer countries, the matter of alliances with repressive governments there ("unreliable as well as repellent"), which the next chapter addresses in more theoretical detail, the pitfalls of trying to maintain production through military occupation, and alternative policies to reduce dependence through stockpiling and conservation.[4] Although it could not foresee the precise configuration of U.S. involvement in the Middle East and central Asia two decades later, it remains relevant to that involvement and its consequences. It also raises concerns that political leaders will use the risk of losing access to foreign sources of raw materials as an instrument to maintain a sense of national danger among the populace.[5] My use of 1984 in the title of this piece was an illusion to the extreme case of George Orwell's dystopia, which posited totalitarian rule by Big Brother as dependent on the never-ending war of Oceania with Eastasia and/or Eurasia.

• "Conflict and Coercion in Dependent States" picks up the concern in "Rich and Poor in 2000 AD" over possible cross-national alliances of the rich against the poor in underdeveloped countries. It is an analytical chapter using graphical techniques and the dynamic analysis of difference equations to lay out an action–reaction model of spirals of rebellion and repression in third world countries. Contemporary analyses typically use game theoretic models, but this presentation, with the verbal text, gets across the main point that violence by the state and rebels may often intensify each other rather than lead to ready victory by one side. It also situates those dynamics in the global political-economic system whereby poor countries are largely dependent on markets in rich countries whose governments may support repression. Although it is purely theoretical, it fits into a larger framework we used to conduct scientific tests of hypotheses we derived from *dependencia* theory as it was popular in progressive and radical circles at that time. Our project was to have had a large empirical component, but only a single major analysis of the economic effects of foreign penetration reached print.[6]

Dependencia theory, developed by writers from Africa and Latin America, is no longer widely credited. Nevertheless, its questions about the global system—for example, the symbiosis among developed states, multinational corporations, and repressive regimes in countries rich in natural resources—remain relevant and in need of systematic empirical investigation.[7] The dependencia project should also be seen as part of my broader response to the Vietnam War, which involved building and testing scientific hypotheses about the material and ideological sources of U.S. foreign and security policy. These were efforts not to proclaim particular answers that I had already arrived at, but to use social science in the search for answers to policy problems of the day.[8]

• "Islam, Authoritarianism, and Female Empowerment: What are the Linkages?" is a recent quantitative analysis asking whether Islamic states are intrinsically disposed toward authoritarian government and repression of women's rights and what might be the causal interconnections among the three variables in the title. It too goes back to themes of "Rich and Poor in 2000 AD," including the roots of terrorism. A graduate student, Daniela Donno, and I took it up partly because it presented an intellectual challenge to us. Neither of us had previously published systematic research on the possible prerequisites of democracy, Islam, or women's rights, yet we saw an opportunity to bring our skills to bear. Because this chapter is a commentary on, and critique of, a previous article in the same journal, it does not develop new theory. Nevertheless, its empirical analysis and interpretation offers a guardedly optimistic view on the prospects for democracy and human rights in Islamic states and an implicit view on the prospects for discouraging terrorism.

• "The Mysterious Case of Vanishing Hegemony, or, Is Mark Twain Really Dead?" is a chapter picking up on yet another facet of the question about how much the rich countries can dominate the international economic and political system. Here I argue against allegations, common in the 1980s, that U.S. dominance or hegemony in world economics and politics had been declining and was likely to decline further. Rather, I contend that the United States had already, since World War II, consolidated a preeminent position of power in the international system. That position enabled it to establish international institutions—dominated by the United States—to provide military security, political stability, and sustained prosperity to much of the world, and not least to itself. It was and still is a relatively benign hegemony with benefits for many, but also a self-interested one. An essential source of American power was not only its economic and military superiority, but also such cultural elements as the attractiveness of its democracy and market economy. While this chapter certainly did not anticipate the collapse of the Soviet Union and the emergence of a unipolar international system less than a decade later, it suggests that such emergence was more a magnification of past near-hegemony than a total change in the system. Its discussion of the sources of national influence—cultural as well as economic and military—is relevant to contemporary debates about how, and whether, American hegemony can long be preserved.

• "Theater Nuclear Forces: Public Opinion in Western Europe" was one of two articles on public opinion that Donald DeLuca and I collaborated on while we both held responsibilities at the Yale office of the Roper Center for Public Opinion Research.[9] It is an empirical chapter and is the first of four chapters which together explore theoretical, empirical, and normative issues inherent in deterrence policy. The chapter uses public opinion surveys to probe European attitudes toward nuclear and conventional deterrence and the role of the United States and NATO in providing deterrence. It concludes that Europeans were not intrinsically anti-American, neutralist, or pacifist. But they did have major reservations about the wisdom of American leaders (then of President Ronald Reagan) and their policies, including a first-use of nuclear weapons policy that they perceived as excessively risk-prone and especially dangerous to Europe.

The particular conditions in Europe have changed since then, with the threat of Islamic fundamentalism replacing the cold war, but if one substitutes George W. Bush for Reagan, and policies of purported preemptive war for nuclear weapons use, the basic elements are familiar. Now many Europeans, with their huge Muslim "guestworker" populations, understandably are as eager to stay out of the center of terrorists' sights as they were not to provoke the Soviet Union. Underlying reservations about U.S. policy—particularly in members of the generation who were young in 1983 but are now in positions of influence in their countries—still inform contemporary discussions of America's military hegemony, possible preventive war, and ability to maintain the willing cooperation of its allies against a common adversary.

• "Away from Nuclear Mythology" is a short analytical chapter that arose as a commentary on a conference paper and subsequent

book chapter by Kenneth Waltz. Waltz's advocacy of nuclear proliferation as a source of military stability in the international system,
while a minority opinion, was shared by some other analysts at the
time.[10] After summarizing my understanding of Waltz's arguments, I
deconstruct his expected utility analysis on logical and empirical
grounds, thus arguing that nuclear proliferation would be dangerous
and destabilizing. The exercise has clear implications for contemporary concerns about the wish and capability to prevent further proliferation. What may have worked as mutual assured destruction
deterrence during the bipolar cold war may be questionable now for
many nuclear states, with so many contingent linkages of potential
use of force on alert. Consider, for example, an extended chain from
China (on alert against the United States in a Taiwan crisis), to a
combination of India, Pakistan, Iran, Israel, and on to Russia and the
United States. The possibility that nuclear terrorism could deliberately trigger interacting national alerts and launches cannot be dismissed, especially given a debilitated and vulnerable Russian
command system.[11] Also, more nuclear powers provide more possibilities for nonstate actors to beg, buy, or steal them from states.

  • "What Makes Deterrence Work? Cases from 1900 to 1980" is
another empirical analysis with Paul Huth, here investigating the conditions under which a policy of "extended immediate deterrence"—
great power deterrence of an overtly threatened attack on an ally—
succeeded or failed. Our intent was not only to explain how deterrence should be devised so as to work, but equally to identify the
conditions under which a deterrence policy, perhaps including
nuclear weapons, might provoke catastrophic failure. Thus it sought
to avoid undesired war as much as simply a failure to deter an aggressor. It gives a statistical analysis of the influence of relative power and
of great power–small power linkages to 54 cases when deterrence
was attempted and of the 23 cases when deterrence failed and the
state attempting deterrence had to decide whether to fight to defend
the state it had hoped to protect. We found that the linkages between
a defender and its ally were more important in providing deterrence
than were either the overall power balance between defender and
challenger the presence of nuclear weapons. This article provoked a
subsequent controversy about both data and theory.[12]

  Subsequently we developed a research design and empirical
analysis of an intellectually even more challenging problem: "general
deterrence," in which a defender threatens to retaliate against an
attacker, even before an overt threat to attack emerges.[13] The problem

stems from identifying whether the putative attacker really had any intention to attack—if not, its restraint cannot be counted as a case of successful deterrence. This analytical and very practical problem immensely complicated strategic discussions during the cold war (e.g., did the Soviet leaders really intend to attack Western Europe, and, if so should deterrence be credited to NATO nuclear capabilities or conventional capabilities?). It remains in the contemporary era, as in discussions of "preemptive" or "preventive" war against an allegedly undeterrable Saddam Hussein.

• "Ethical Dilemmas of Nuclear Deterrence" is a normative chapter, reflecting on my experience in helping to craft a prominent 1983 statement (a pastoral letter) by the U.S. Conference of Catholic Bishops about the circumstances under which nuclear weapons, or even nuclear deterrence, might be employed. The opportunity arose in a late night conversation with Fr. J. Bryan Hehir who then directed the Office of International Affairs at the Conference and had just lectured at Yale on the morality of deterrence. We found we had much in common. This commentary on the experience, like the pastoral letter, is grounded both in a deductive system of moral logic and in concrete information about nuclear deterrence, including material incorporated in the three preceding chapters. It addresses the deliberative process of producing that statement as well as the wording of the statement itself.

The chapter, like the bishops' letter, ends with a very cautious and nuanced acceptance of nuclear deterrence under the then-existing conditions of the cold war. Both the chapter and the letter conclude that deliberate strikes against civilian populations (as contrasted with some unintended civilian casualties from strikes against military forces) are morally unacceptable. This position derives from just war analyses preceding nuclear weapons, and it continues to apply to conventional weapons as well as to weapons of mass destruction. It has come to be widely recognized in international law, and, contrasting with all powers' behavior in bombing cities during World War II, has substantially constrained U.S. targeting in all its post–cold war uses of military force. The condemnation of deliberate attacks against civilians forms a key peak in the moral high ground over terrorist behavior. In principle it would apply to all countries, but it is evident that several smaller states earmark their nuclear weapons for deterrence as counter-city instruments.

Ten years later, the bishops issued a second letter reflecting on the first one's implications for what had become a world with just one unrivalled superpower. The changed context led them to say, "The eventual elimination of nuclear weapons is more than a moral ideal; it should be a policy goal." They supplemented this with praise for the Non-Proliferation Treaty (NPT) (which proclaims full nuclear disarmament as a goal) and a comprehensive ban on nuclear testing.[14] For a while there was some wider support for total nuclear disarmament, or at least a reduction to no more than a few hundred weapons for the United States, but it faded. A 2004 report listed the United States as still deploying 7006 nuclear weapons, and Russia 7802.[15] The United States may resume nuclear testing, both the United States and Russia have rejected a no-first-use policy, and the NPT is in disarray, in some part because of the big nuclear powers' retention and modernization of their nuclear arsenals. Does nuclear deterrence still have a useful role, and if so what exactly is it now intended to deter, and how? Is it really intended to deter terrorist use of weapons of mass destruction against American civilians? To do so assumes that nonstate terrorists can be identified, and found. (We have not done well with Osama bin Laden and company.) It also assumes there is a target that would be morally acceptable and not practically disastrous. Would the great mosque in Mecca be a conceivable target? The thought is grotesque.

• "Seeking Peace in a Post-Cold War World of Hegemony and Terrorism," with John Oneal, extends some themes from three preceding books.[16] Our collaboration began at the American Political Science Association annual meeting in 1993. John, whom I had not known well, invited me to breakfast and began discussing my just-published *Grasping the Democratic Peace*. In a nutshell, he said it was all very interesting, but had one potentially big flaw: perhaps it was international trade, not shared democracy, that resulted in peaceful relations among the interdependent democracies. I agreed that it was a possibility, but that I could as readily develop a theoretical argument that trade might erode peace as one that it was peace-inducing. Anyway, I added, I just finished, with the help of colleagues, a nearly ten-year long project of data gathering and analysis, and had no wish to add a major new variable. "Not to worry," he said, "I'll find the data and do the computing, and you can do the writing." So I willingly allowed the collaboration to begin, with no idea how it would turn out. Maybe I would be right about democracy, maybe he would be right about trade, perhaps we would both be right.

As it turned out, the terms of the collaboration shifted, of course. I took on more responsibility for data collection than initially anticipated, and he did much more writing. It has been an extremely satisfying collaboration, intellectually and personally.[17] Together, sometimes with additional authors, we have produced a book and 15 articles and book chapters to date. We expanded the concept of the democratic peace to the liberal peace including trade (we were both right) and then to the Kantian peace incorporating international organizations. This chapter summarizes *Triangulating Peace*, but adds a new empirical analysis that confirms what we did in the book and extends its implications to the strong emergence of U.S. military hegemony and to nonstate terrorism. It still finds no evidence for Samuel Huntington's "clash of civilizations,"[18] which in our analyses adds nothing to the explanatory power already contained in realist and Kantian theories. Most centrally, it shows the existence of a system of peaceful international relations, for much of the world if not yet all of it, that is not primarily dependent on military power and deterrence. Peace is an ambitious and often elusive goal, but not necessarily a Utopian one.

• "Bushwhacking the Democratic Peace," the concluding chapter, links research to an explicit and visceral critique of the Bush administration's decision to attack Iraq in 2003. The chapter makes two basic points. First, it disputes both the policy wisdom of invading Iraq ostensibly to lay the foundations for a democratic peace in the Middle East and the veracity of such an *ex post* claim when it was not a significant *ex ante* purpose. Most democratic peace theorists do not endorse democratic regime change by great power military intervention. Success is difficult to achieve (usually at high cost), and the conditions in Iraq were unpromising even had the occupation been carried out competently. Second, it develops a theme left unexplored in *Triangulating Peace*: the ways in which national governments and international organizations can peacefully encourage elites and peoples in countries undergoing transitions to democracy and consolidation of democratic governments. International organizations whose membership is largely composed of democracies are especially likely to succeed in promoting democracy. Carefully considered purpose must guide policy, both normatively and empirically.

Further Reflections

First, on the theme of collaboration: Scientific research in international relations has become highly specialized and compartmentalized by subject, method, and epistemology. That brings obvious benefits, but also liabilities of ignorance. Some scholars cross one or several of these compartmental boundaries in their own heads. Where that is not possible, a division of labor according to comparative advantage is necessary and desirable. It is important to collaborate with others with different perspectives, and especially with different skills. I have been the beneficiary of now-routine free-flowing web-based exchange of data, analysis, thoughts, and drafts with extremely smart and decent colleagues around the globe. I have also been blessed with some extremely smart and decent graduate students—the right kind to have. Three of the chapters in this book (6, 7, 11) were written with people who were graduate students at the time. Many more of my articles and even books had that benefit, both when the individuals were students and often many years later when they were professional colleagues in every sense.[19] Some of those are represented in another collection.[20]

This statement and the preceding commentary make me reflect even more on where so many of the ideas behind the chapters came from. All in one way or another derive from theoretical debates about which I was seeking analytical clarity or empirical evidence. But the theoretical debates did not emerge from trying to solve pure theoretical puzzles "because they are there," as may often be the case in mathematics or physics. All in one way or another have their origins in concerns about the world, and the implications of policy for peace and justice. Many clearly come out of the cold war era of nuclear deterrence and conventional war in the poor countries that were battlegrounds for the war between the superpowers that never escalated to what might have been. During much of the cold war, I was quite pessimistic that the United States and the Soviet Union would in fact be able to avoid deliberate or accidental nuclear war throughout what seemed likely to be a many-decades long confrontation. As it happened, they did avoid such a war that might well have ended civilization. How much to attribute that avoidance to chance and how much to wisdom may be debated for centuries. Whatever one thinks is the answer, the great surprise was that the cold war ended as hardly anyone expected: with the peaceful disintegration of the Soviet Union and its alliance system. And that collapse led to the emergence of many new democracies, of which quite a few across the globe now seem firmly established.

I had previously said that the cold war was unlikely to end peaceably as long as the Soviet Union was ruled as a dictatorship, and I had dismissed the prospects for serious liberalization of that system as incompatible with the leadership's ability to maintain the country's political unity amidst multiple separatist nationalisms.[21] That was not such a bad deduction, except that the Soviet leadership under Mikhail Gorbachev did liberalize anyway, did lose control, and was unable or unwilling to crush the rebels with violence. The result seemed to liberate the world from the threat of a full nuclear catastrophe, and to bring it closer to a substantial (though still importantly incomplete) establishment of a Kantian community of largely peaceful conflict resolution as described in chapter 13 here.[22] That optimism, however, dropped in the face first of 9/11 and then the U.S. government's disastrous decision to invade Iraq. Whereas nuclear terrorism per se does not have the civilization-destroying capability of the cold war confrontation, it could fatally wound a complex interdependent world economy, and it may have some possibility of triggering a large-scale nuclear exchange among the major nuclear powers as I discussed above. In addition, and despite the U.S. administration's spin to the contrary, the Kantian community is weaker rather than stronger as a consequence of the Iraq invasion.[23] At least that's my now less optimistic view as I write this in November 2005. Moreover, I hope that concern with terrorism will not overwhelm concern with other aspects of international relations, many evident in this book, that do and will continue to demand serious attention.

It will be apparent that much of my work represented here, and elsewhere, is inspired by normative concerns. One such normative prior is that war is usually—but not always—a "bad thing" to be avoided if possible, and if necessary to be fought with as much restraint as possible. This is precisely the framework provided by the just war tradition, in contrast with the other ends of the normative spectrum: on one hand, the position of absolute nonviolence, and on the other the conviction that in a Hobbesian world the only justifiable morality for a national leader is to maximize the welfare of her own citizens. I understand and respect both positions, which have deep and honorable roots. I just don't accept them, nor a premise that most of the world is fully Hobbesian.

Another normative theme, discernible though less central in this collection, is with equality. I believe that greater equality of condition, and certainly greater equality of opportunity, over the world and in the United States, is ethically imperative. How much equality, or how to get there, I don't pretend to know. But I can at least try to document the degree of inequality that prevails and to understand its causes and consequences.[24] Yet a third normative as well as empirical commitment is to democratic government, something that in practice is often deeply flawed, but simply better than the alternatives.

To state so baldly that much, probably most, of my work derives from normative concerns may seem to violate the positivist maxim, "Don't mix the "is" with the "ought." I think that's a good maxim, and what science is about is the practice of rigor in theory, data gathering, and analysis so as to maximize other researchers' ability to replicate (or fail to replicate) one's results. It helps at least to be reasonably self-aware and open about one's normative convictions (which are usually present if not active). That, and the scientific method, restrains the temptation to imagine that what we think ought to be in fact is, and keeps us all as honest as possible. Normative theory, positive theory, and empirical investigation are complementary, not exclusive or conflicting. In this respect, the other four "revolutions" mentioned in note 23—the formal theory revolution, the revolution of massively available data (notably on the Internet), the revolution of replication, and the revolution of statistical method— help enormously.[25] None of these conceptual and methodological revolutions is alone sufficient or even primary in importance. But they interact synergistically and, separately and together, have changed for the better the ways we do research and evaluate it.

Chapter 2

Rich and Poor in 2000 AD: The Great Gulf

Affluence and Poverty

Many modern Utopians foresee a coming perfection of social man, stemming from great changes in his physical environment. They see the problem of evil as basically intractable in a world of pain, ignorance, and deprivation, but soluble where the ancient bonds of man's mortality have been loosened. Both the exhortations of the domestic Great Society and Secretary McNamara's conviction that poverty is the cause of insurgency in the underdeveloped world reflect this preoccupation, most apparent in the question, "Who can be interested in democracy when he has an empty belly?" So the apparent prospects of future economic growth lead easily to social optimism.

By many tests, the world of the not-too-distant future will be a far better one than the present. We have confident and compelling predictions of vast automation, greatly diminishing the amount of physical drudgery required in production and freeing members of the labor force either for leisure or for intellectually stimulating and satisfying work. Time and facilities for the leisured pursuit of science and the arts seem within reach for many. We have the prospect of major breakthroughs in medical science, with artificial organs and the control of killer diseases. We are promised supersonic transports to circle the earth at three times the speed of sound and instantaneous electronic communication with data banks and libraries anywhere. A computerized financial system for pay, credit, and tax collection is virtually in preparation. In a recent RAND Corporation survey of scientists who should know, the likelihood of a manned landing on Mars and of a permanent base on the moon by 2000 AD was taken for granted. There is held out to us the image of a new Eden, a stable period wherein many of the most unsettling aspects of modern life may be brought under control and we can more fully reap its great benefits.

But how many of the three billion people on this globe can afford to circumnavigate it? How soon will the Indian villager install his automated farm and devote himself to experimentation in his laboratory? Have *you* paid a hospital bill recently? It is crucial to recognize that the gains from these developments will not apply at all equally to all men. The most dramatic benefits will accrue to those who can afford substantial sums of money to pay for them. A worldview that sees material prosperity as providing the opportunity for the resolution of discord may be attractive, but it will not be very relevant to a society where only a minority possess the necessary wealth.

There has perhaps been a slight widening of the relative gap between the developed industrialized states and the poor underdeveloped nations in recent decades, but not seriously. Though the pattern varies widely, the wealthiest nations of Western Europe, North America, Japan, and Australasia have had an annual per capita income increment of about 4 percent over the past decade and a half. Greece, Taiwan, Jamaica, some of the poor Communist countries of Eastern Europe, and even China help to balance out those poor countries, like India and Indonesia, who have done badly overall. The average for the poor probably comes out to nearly 3 percent, or only a little less than in the developed world.

But the catch in this argument is in its frame of reference—*percentage rates* of growth. While it is hardly fair to expect a poor country to add the same *total* amount to its income each year as does a rich one, the failure to do so nevertheless causes a widening of the *absolute* gap. When the differences between rich and poor are as great as they are in the world today, the cumulative results are very striking. Let us suppose that the poor nations with annual per capita incomes now of around $100 grew at a yearly rate of 3 percent between now and the end of the century. The outcome would be average per capita incomes of a maximum of $275 in the year 2000 AD. About half the population of the world will fall into this category, including India, China, most of the rest of Asia, and Africa. And frankly it is hard to imagine how this performance could be much improved upon, given the shortages of skills, capital, and social incentives for growth in these areas. Except for a few special cases the problem is more than simply one of bottlenecks where the injection of some key component, like money, might quickly trigger self-sustaining growth.

If, however, we assume the same average annual growth rate of 3 percent in the developed countries, the beneficence of compound interest will bring a most impressive absolute level of wealth. Approximately one-fifth of the world's peoples now live in nations where the yearly per capita income exceeds $1000, with an average annual income per head of approximately $2000. This would grow to $5500 in 2000 AD, a figure still 20 times that in the poor half of the globe, and which means an *absolute gap of over $5000 instead of $1900*. With the post-Keynesian understanding of fiscal and monetary policies so well applied in modern nations, this is an entirely plausible projection in the absence of world war. Both the present and the prospective relative difference of rich and poor *between nations* is extremely great by comparison with the income inequalities typical *within nations*. The difference between average income over the entire range of the richest and poorest states currently is on the order of 30 to 1; in the United States the difference between Connecticut and Mississippi, at the extremes, is hardly more than 2 to 1.

Now, as every economist warns, cross-country comparisons of per capita incomes in dollars are treacherous. A dollar will buy much more, fully two or three times as much, of the necessities of life in a poor agricultural nation than in a rich urban one. But, however measured, the gap between rich and poor remains enormous. Furthermore, it is precisely the kinds of things that are expensive in anyone's currency that are some of the most exciting products of modern science and technology. They promise to be produced largely in industrialized societies and by industrialized societies—and because of their cost, for industrialized societies as well.

The Health Gap

What will you be able to buy with money, if you have lots of it? For one thing, there is life itself. Organ transplants and organ banks will become common. We are on the verge of mass use of artificial organs in the United States. Hospitals all over the country now operate artificial kidneys; artificial livers, lungs, and, most importantly, hearts are clearly in the near-term works. Millions of middle-aged and elderly Americans and Europeans will doubtless shortly wear pacemakers—instruments to provide a regular electrical stimulus to the heart, preventing what is by far the most common cause of cardiac arrest. The complete pump for an artificial heart is at present cumbersome, but it will not remain in its now primitive form. Such replacements of natural functions as radar to substitute for the eyes of a blind man are fully contemplated. With all these organs replaceable, it is not hard to visualize the next step—it should be entirely possible to keep a severed head, or perhaps just a brain, alive almost indefinitely if attached to a device for circulating blood (or other fluid) containing nutrients and removing waste products. While it may hardly seem to us a desirable form of near-eternal life, tastes may change. It represents only one of the most dramatic ways in which the degenerations of aging may be postponed or evaded.

Short of this still rather fantastic outcome are the more modest current and prospective achievements of modern medicine. In addition to the artificial organs there is the prospect of an eventual cure for many major diseases, including most manifestations of carcinoma. For more than 20 years, life expectancy in the United States and Europe has just inched forward, with no change at all for almost a decade now. But some of these prospects suggest that another major breakthrough is imminent.

Few of these achievements, however, are likely to be cheap, either in their research and development costs or in their application to particular patients. Major surgery or a series of drug and radiation treatments for cancer are very far from inexpensive; medical care is the fastest-rising item in the cost of living index. The annual cost per user of an artificial kidney machine exceeds the total income of most of its potential recipients even in the United States; where it is never-theless made available, some form of subsidy is required. No doubt the price of such life-giving innovations will come down with further research and mass production of the instruments. Within rich and integrated societies, some form of insurance or burden-sharing doubtless will bring them within reach of virtually everyone. But it is extremely difficult to imagine how they can be brought within range of the price that any but a tiny fraction of the people in Asia, Africa, or even Latin America will be able to pay, and their societies will not be able to afford subsidies on anything approaching a mass basis.

In 1951, the expectation of life for a newborn infant in India was 32 years, less than half that of an American or West European baby born at the same time. By contrast, Ceylon, with a per capita income only about 70 percent higher than India's, had in 1954 an average life expectancy of 59 years, much nearer to that typical of Western Europe and North America (about 70 years) than to India's. Ceylon had been the subject of major public health projects that in a few short years dramatically cut its death rate by more than half. As is implied by the low per capita income of Ceylon, the means for doing this were cheap. Probably the most significant was the use of insecticides, at a cost of only a few cents per person, to kill mosquitoes and eradicate malaria. Some of these measures have also now been introduced in India and the others will be, though there the problems are greater and incomes so low that even cheap public health is not always within their means. But basically the Ceylonese experience is an archetype of the "population problem" in the underdeveloped world, a consequence of the drastic reduction in death rates, and hence life expectancy, which has been achieved rapidly at very low cost.

This near-convergence of life expectancies in the rich countries and in the poor ones may not last long. It takes a great increase in the wealth of a nation to add those additional ten years (between Ceylon and Western Europe) that will equate its life expectancy figures with those currently found in an industrialized country, and only the very rich will be able to afford the technological innovations of the next three decades. Very possibly the year 2000 will see a return to a differential of almost two to one between the number of years a poor man can expect to live and the number to which a citizen of the privileged West may reasonably aspire—a difference between perhaps a little over 60 years in the former case, and more than a century in the latter.

Education and Leisure

Education is a prime example of the desirable aspects of future life that will be available only to those who live in very affluent societies. The United States is notorious in its lavish proliferation of colleges and universities, with almost half the eligible age groups so enrolled. At no foreseeable time will underdeveloped countries be able to afford this, unless possibly as the grossest and most transparent effort to keep young people out of a swollen labor force for a little longer—and in any case only to send them back with higher aspirations but little more in the way of relevant skills.

Furthermore, there is education and education. As practiced in the better Western institutions, higher learning is a very capital-intensive process. The 15 top private universities in the United States, for example, have an average endowment of $25,000 per student—and even so tuition and fees are nearly $2000 apiece for undergraduates at these institutions. Typically the faculty-to-student ratio is one to five, not so very remote from Mark Hopkins' ideal of one to one. The end product is a graduate who has had a good deal of seminar experience, substantial criticism of his writing, and, even in this day of research rewards to faculty, a fair amount of interaction with at least some of his teachers if he desired it. At the same time he has been at a place where exciting, relevant research has been conducted in large scale, and where what he has been taught was not too far removed from the frontiers of knowledge. Such an experience cannot even remotely be approached in an underdeveloped country. (Berkeley students might enroll in Calcutta to discover what anomie is *really* like.) This is not to deny that underdeveloped countries may be able to provide a minimal education for most of their citizens. Whereas the typical rate of literacy in low-income countries is now only about 25 percent, by the end of the century most people will probably at least be able to read and write in a crude fashion—for the past decade or so the literate proportion of the population has grown even in the most hardpressed areas. But the quality of that education, in terms of financial, social, and immediately personal rewards, is very different from that accruing to the graduate of Cornell, or, for that matter, of Manchester or Heidelberg.

Even leisure varies enormously in quality between the two parts of the world. In the developed West, and especially for middle and upper class citizens, leisure is a commodity of great productive value. It is of such value that people may not feel they have much of it, but in terms of time spent away from the office, even the busiest actually have a good bit. Executives are forced to take vacation time whether or not they want it. And though they may have little enough time for strict rest and relaxation, many hours are spent on community or personal activities only tenuously related to earning a livelihood. Education is rapidly becoming a respectable use of leisure hours, if not for some a near necessity. Extensive automation, profoundly affecting every trade and profession by 2000 AD, can but strengthen these tendencies.

The difference between leisure in a rich society and in a poor one involves images that hardly need drawing, though their consequences may require emphasis. For its constructive use leisure demands expensive education and/or facilities of the sort utterly unavailable for the masses of Africa and Asia. In the latter area, the phenomenon of underemployment is already rampant, with millions of agricultural workers occupied only a fraction of the year. On the farm, such a situation may be deplorable because of the human potential it wastes, but unemployment in the cities is far more dangerous for social and political stability. Often amounting to more than a quarter of the labor force, urban unemployment means the existence of a mass of men without income and often without prospects, but located in a part of the country where they can readily be used by demagogues for violent demands on the government.

This pessimistic picture should not be viewed as implying that *none* of the wonders of the future will be of any benefit to the underdeveloped areas. Many of them surely will, including the economical desalinization of seawater; cheap, effective, and widespread fertility control; and the commercial synthesis of protein for food. Another is the profitable "mining" of seawater, probably coupled to the same plants that desalinate for drinking and irrigation. This will make available to states with coastlines the minerals that do not lie in exploitable quantity within the land parts of their domains. Some poor nations, however, are likely to emerge as net losers when this new source provides a cheaper alternative to existing mines. The commercially useful production of tin from seawater, for instance, would demolish the already precarious economy of Bolivia. The cheap manufacture of palatable synthetic food also is likely to be something of a mixed blessing for predominantly agricultural societies. But the trouble with these prospective developments, even ignoring the substitution effects of mineral extraction from the sea or synthetic protein manufacture, is that they cannot upgrade the basic quality of life much above subsistence in the poor areas. They may raise food production, prevent starvation, and put a floor under standards of living that avoids the most utter and abject misery; they may even avoid the further expansion of populations in already densely packed lands while at the same time they improve basic sanitation and prevent high infant mortality and other deaths from the traditional scourges of famine and epidemic. None of these improvements, however, will make available to the poor man the kind of benefits a rich man will be able to buy for himself. One wit characterized the bathtub as the great divider of men, splitting the washed from the unwashed. "Never," he says, "shall the twain meet at table or in the same bed." The technological prospects for the next decades will not remove that division.

The Distribution of Power

This is not to suggest that the consequence of relative deprivation in vast areas of the world, even of an increase in the relative differences that seems so probable, will be successful violent revolution or the decline of the West in terms of sheer power. On the contrary, technological innovations are likely to favor the industrialized nations here too. Among the more exotic probabilities are procedures for manipulating the weather; the perfection of existing biological and chemical agents to destroy the will to resist without causing permanent damage to the organism; and perishable arms for counterinsurgency forces, which would deteriorate rapidly if lost or captured. Surely many of these developments can already be discerned. The United States may not be doing well in Vietnam, considering the road still to be traveled before a military victory can, if ever, be achieved. But the reason the United States has been able to do as well as it has so far is its wealth. Simple calculations show a cost of $250,000 a head for every Viet Cong (or bystander) who shows up in the body count. (The war is currently costing over two billion dollars per month, and Viet Cong casualties run at about 8,000 a month according to official figures.) The enormous weight of wealth and technology that Americans can bring to bear against a small country, even at that distance, makes outright failure in antiguerrilla warfare unnecessary for the determined. The military uses of outer space, if they prove to be significant, will be exploitable only by nations rich enough to pour many billions of dollars into the effort.

Not even the proliferation of nuclear weapons will change this situation. A few atomic or even hydrogen bombs, plus a crude delivery system, make no equalizer for the small state against a superpower. At best a small nation, even if able to deliver its weapons, could not prevent a crushing retaliation capable of utterly destroying it as a functioning social system. The threat to use nuclear weapons against the United States or Russia could be credible only in the most dire corner. More important is that, even ignoring the promise of retaliation, delivery is hard and does not promise to become easier. Currently the American government is in the midst of a most painful debate—whether or not to build an antimissile system. An antimissile would be of some, but marginal, utility for diminishing the damage inflicted by a hypothetical Soviet attack using missiles with the sophisticated penetration aids the Russians undoubtedly can produce. But it would be of much greater use, perhaps to the point of near-perfect success, against the kind of primitive attack that even Communist China will be able to launch for the next decade or two. Getting through a good ballistic missile defense system will require much knowledge of the effects of nuclear weapons and some very clever engineering, plus some extremely fancy and expensive electronics. Underdeveloped countries simply do not and will not have the resources to acquire that detailed and extensive know-how, nor the money to build the equipment if they knew how to do so.

Thus an antimissile system may not in any notable way change the balance of power between the United States and the Soviet Union. It is likely just to cost both powers a lot of money that could be spent elsewhere. Yet it would have the consequence of pricing small or poor nations out of the nuclear deterrence market vis-à-vis the superpowers. They might blow each other up to their leaders' hearts' content, but they could not effectively confront the two great military states that so dominated international politics during the 1950s. An antimissile system would therefore restore the bipolarity and U.S. Soviet preeminence that so recently seemed to be slipping and dash any hopes the small powers may retain of being able to coerce the great states militarily.

Harassment

Thus in the world of 2000 AD, perhaps even more so than now, the poor half of the world will not be able to challenge the rich fifth for control—but it will have the ability to *harass* the rich and bring the entire system into chaos.

The world of the foreseeable future will be one of great inter-dependencies of many sorts; the complex exploitation of material resources that will be necessary to sustain the *living* conditions of the rich will require extremely dense and complicated communications and transportation systems. The whole system, relying as much of it will on very close man–machine interactions (as with artificial limbs and organs), will leave many people extremely dependent, for their very lives, on constant inputs from an extremely artificial man-made physical environment. (What happens, for instance, to the man with radar eyes if he cannot get replacement parts? Or to a system geared to electronic data banks when the power goes off?) Even if an antimissile system could prevent an underdeveloped nation from wreaking major direct physical havoc on the developed world, the hazards of interruption, destruction, and temporary or local chaos might still be very severe. All the more so if the promise of guerrilla-size nuclear weapons for the future should become reality.

Primitive man rarely lived to old age; like the animals he preyed upon, every man, when no longer in his prime, became vulnerable to the abundant natural enemies that before might not have been able to challenge him effectively. Even during the peak of life sudden death from animals, other men, or weather was common enough. Civilization, however, has cut the odds of sudden destruction to a fraction of what they once were. We still are conscious of the hazards of our man-made environment, especially the automobile, but only because other causes of death have for the young and middle-aged become almost insignificant by comparison with their former toll. But the world of the future might well restore the dangers from new sources, and raise the risks of sudden death. Man-made interruptions to the delicate interdependent system would be the new threat, and especially those from the underdeveloped world.

Domestic difficulties have sometimes led to foreign adventures by the heads of underdeveloped states: Sukarno's behavior in West Irian and Malaysia is an example. Wars among poor and frustrated nations may become more common. If nuclear weapons were used in those wars a few would certainly affect rich nations' interests. Or more seriously, the poor states would acquire harassment capabilities to deliver (possibly by individuals rather than governments that might readily be held responsible) nuclear bombs. There are literally hundreds of ways in which a determined, embittered, and perhaps nonofficial minority of people in the have-not areas could prevent the rich from full enjoyment of their prosperity.

Incentives to violence will be there in ample measure. Karl Marx thought revolutions were born from the growing absolute impoverishment of the masses. If he were correct there would be little for the status quo powers to fear, since there is small reason to think many of the poor countries will actually slip downhill. But the evidence of the past century indicates clearly that Marx was wrong in this respect. Alexis de Tocqueville had a contrasting theory derived from eighteenth-century France—that revolutions arise not from increasing poverty, but from an improvement in the fortunes of the poor after ages of hopeless degradation. New expectations aroused—but by no means satisfied by a modest upturn—provide the impetus to revolution.

More recent theories combine something of both Marx's and Tocqueville's. They suggest that the most likely point of revolution is when, after a rather sustained period of betterment for the poor, a fairly sudden stagnation or sharp downturn is experienced. New hopes and demands will be satisfied just enough to control things while the growth continues, but they will not tolerate much of a reversal. None of these theories has been adequately tested, but there is some interesting evidence for the latter in events of the past few years. Ghana began independence with by far the highest standard of living in black Africa, and Indonesia is composed of islands enormously rich in natural resources. From the late 1950s onward, however, each developed serious troubles. Governmental energies turned to various foreign conflicts and prestige-building efforts, which only aggravated their economic problems. Growth turned into stagnation and then into a very serious downturn, creating great unrest and eventually culminating in the overthrow of their governments. If this assessment indicates a more general principle of revolutionary activity, it would seem vital, in their own interests, for the rich nations to help the poor to maintain their growth at the existing rates.

A better evaluation of the political and social potential of economic conditions in the poor half of the world at the end of this century, however, can be gained by remembering some particular aspects of the basically impoverished conditions of life to be expected there. Although not educated to high levels, the bulk of the populations will be literate. They will be heavily if not predominantly urban, with perhaps a third of the population living in cities of 20,000 or more. They will have access to the mass media of communication—their urbanization, literacy, and the cheap transistor radio will see to that. Furthermore, they will have immediate acquaintance with, if not experience of, life in the rich fifth of the world. Communication satellites, television sets in central city and village locations, and all the worldwide paraphernalia of instant communication will assure the breakdown of their previous insulation. Though poor and uneducated, they will not be ignorant of what they are missing. Whereas once they could compare their status only with that of the village landowner, now they will have the example of the whole rich West before them. And they will realize that the structure of the world political and social system makes it impossible for them, *as individuals*, to improve their lot. Barriers to immigration will keep them in their physical places.

In short, Asia and Africa are likely to comprise a huge slum in the social as well as material sense, with close parallels to present-day Harlem. The distinction will be in the degree to which the fate of the privileged will be linked to that of the slum-dwellers, who will be a virtual majority, not a relatively small segment of the population that can be effectively isolated in a ghetto and forgotten. The privileged class will be a distinct minority, and the "middle class" buffer will not be much larger.

Finding a Tolerable World Order

Several courses of action, some of which must be concurrent rather than substitutes for each other, are open to the rich world for the next few decades. One is obvious and attractive to our humanitarian traditions: assistance to the underdeveloped nations to keep the level of income growing at a steady if unspectacular rate. This would have to be achieved not as a simple act of charity, but involving the leadership and activity of the people in the poor world so as to build initiative and confidence in their own abilities. It must also be dependable aid, available over long periods and sufficiently flexible to meet crises and temporary setbacks.

But the prescription of economic assistance is hardly more than a tiresome cliché at this point in our postwar experience and disillusionment with foreign aid as an instrument of development. It is much easier to specify such ingredients than to make them work. Part of the problem is that the doctors have expected too much. The rates of growth that can realistically be achieved will not eradicate unrest, violence, or the threat of violence. One must move from black and white to shadings, hoping not to eliminate the threat of violence but only to reduce its incidence. Aid must be complemented by scientific research seeking to lower drastically the cost of at least some elements of the good life. Certain aspects of education, coupled with teaching machines and communications satellites, may be especially appropriate for cheap mechanization. Others should appear if an intensive effort is made.

At the same time, this is only part of the prescription for a tolerable world order. Another element requires strengthening and multiplying the existing institutional bonds among nations—in effect a *move* in the direction of world government for the sake of political control over the poor states. Of course such a government, in most of the probable and all of the ideologically pleasing forms, would entail control by as well as of the poor world. Any pluralistic variety of political organization for the globe would involve concessions by the rich and some kind of substantial taxation. But this need not conjure up images of utter leveling and loss of privilege—the rich usually manage to retain a power and influence over decisions that is very disproportionate to their numbers. Their skills will give them great advantages in manipulation and an essential ingredient for world growth that can be bartered for a substantial price. Nor should those who fear "world government" on more abstract grounds react too sharply against this part of the prescription. There are, after all, many varieties of "government." Under that label stand historical forms ranging from the most centralized totalitarian regime to the loosest confederation. Modes toward the latter end of the spectrum, as well as the former, can be appropriate models for ultimate world organization.

Efforts to implement these possibilities are vital because the alternative is not so ideologically attractive for Westerners. The threat of violence does not operate merely in an economic and social environment; it is not simply the product of expectations, frustrations, and growth rates. Behavior is also subject to political controls; the resort to violence can be contained by repression. A world government could be a powerful one initiated and firmly controlled by the rich. Or the governments of the developed states could ally themselves with authoritarian or totalitarian oligarchies in the poor world, with regimes that are able, with extant and yet-to-be devised instruments of surveillance and control, to keep the lid on their domestic polities. The price would be privileges for the governing elite in these countries, a sharing in the benefits of 2000 AD material culture that could never be paid to the masses. These oligarchies might continue to mouth the ideology of development and ultimate prosperity for their citizens, and even provide, with outside assistance, the basis for a modest improvement in their peoples' physical condition. Yet they would maintain the ability to control change and suppress dissent, acting in part as agents of the rich world.

This is a repugnant prospect, and I do not advocate it. To do so, especially now before we have made a proper effort with the first two elements, would be a despairing counsel. Until much greater resources have been devoted both to research and practice in development and international organization, a further alliance with the oligarchies would be intolerable. There are more than enough elements of it in the foreign policies of present Western governments. At some point, however, after energetically trying the other ways at substantial sacrifice, the compromise may seem more beguiling. It may come for the simple reason that the world and its civilizations will not, we hope, come to an end in the year 2000 AD. It might be justified by motives other than selfish parochial interest. Men must build for ages to come and construction cannot take place in chaos.

Chapter 3

The Marginal Utility of Income Transfers to the Third World

If the poor will be with us always, how poor must they be? Should we abandon hope of any significant improvement in living conditions for the hundreds of millions of terribly poor people in this world, and, instead, by some desperate notion of "triage," concentrate our limited resources on trying to help those who, while still poor, nevertheless start from something a little better than the bare subsistence level of India, Bangladesh, or poorest Africa? Such questions raise innumerable further questions about morality, about the sources of global poverty, and about the organizational capacity of poor countries ever to cope with their problems. But they also raise some serious empirical questions about what improvement in living standards we can hope for when a minority of people, however rich, give up part of their income or wealth to try to help very much larger numbers of poor people. Recall such old antisocialist arguments in the United States that even if the richest 5 percent of the people were to give up half their income to the poor, that would only be enough to bring the poorest half of the population just one-third of the way toward the average income level for the country. In short, why should so few give up so much to help so many so little?

Much the same argument is now being made on a worldwide basis. Suppose, for example, $100 billion per year were transferred from the 700 million people who live in the world's richest developed countries—in North America, Western Europe, Australasia, and Japan. That amount (almost $150 per capita) would be about seven times the current level of foreign economic assistance from these countries and, speaking realistically, is certainly as much as, or far more than, anyone can imagine these countries *voluntarily* giving up. But distributed to the poorest half of the world, countries with a total population of about 2.4 billion, that would represent a per capita income increment of only about $42—far from enough to relieve their poverty. Is it really much of an improvement to have $292 a year instead of $250?

Although the statistics in this sort of argument are right, the implication is very misleading. Of course it misses all the possibilities that would arise from investing the resources in new productive capacities in the poor countries. Also, it misses the fact that the *welfare* implications of such a transfer would be very different from the proportionate effects implied by the simple money amounts. As economists have long recognized, the marginal utility of $42 to the average citizen of a poor country might well be very much higher, in terms of education, health, or life expectancy, than would be lost to the average rich country citizen by giving up even $150. Intuitively this seems plausible, and it is supported by most of the empirical work by economists under conditions where, as in the modern world, there is a yawning gap between income levels for the rich and the poor. But we have no measurements of the likely effect of such income transfers internationally; by how much the real welfare gains to the poor might exceed the losses to the rich, or for which aspects of welfare the differences might be greatest.

Formidable difficulties stand in the way of making such a quantitative assessment. One must almost begin by making assumptions about how the transfer is made, and whether the overall international economy would be disrupted by the transfer, perhaps with markedly lower incomes everywhere as a result. What would be the effect on incentives for further economic or political actions that would affect the distribution or overall level of income and welfare? One must also make some assumptions about how the income gains and losses would be distributed within countries, both those gaining and those losing. Each of us probably has a different set of preferred strategies for making the transfer. Some prefer government-to-government grants in more or less the standard current form of economic assistance; others would prefer to see the poor countries succeed by greater action of their own, by extracting trade concessions from the rich, by forming cartels to raise the price of the raw materials sold by the third world, simply by expropriating foreign property, or by feats of self-reliance. Each of these would have very different and not readily foreseeable consequences.

Nevertheless, a beginning has to be made. Various assumptions about the origins and means of the transfer can be built into an analysis, and the assumptions can be modified as the analysis continues.

Without concentrating here on just how the transfer might be carried out, I shall outline a strategy for making some crude estimates about its consequences: estimates that can be modified for different assumptions about means. The estimates will be crude, but we now live in a situation of almost totally data-free speculation. Providing the limits of the estimation methods are properly acknowledged, we should be able to reduce our ignorance somewhat.

We may start with some basic data on the *average income level* and on the *average level of various aspects of welfare* that are highly valued, both within and between nations. Here I shall illustrate the approach with data on life itself, that is, the average life expectancy for citizens of various countries and infant mortality rates. In so doing we focus on the most basic need or dimension of well-being, but the approach is nevertheless adaptable, with energy and ingenuity, to literacy and many other dimensions of welfare according to one's favorite schema of values.[1] At least three different specific procedures are possible within this approach, and we shall employ each of them to discover the degree of convergence in the results they give.

Synchronic Cross-National Comparisons

We shall begin with data on the average income level and the average welfare level in most nations of the world in the 1970s. The position of each country is presented in figure 3.1 with the GNP per capita in 1973 on the horizontal axis and the average life expectancy at birth (1970 to 1975 average for both sexes) on the vertical axis.[2]

The resulting pattern is clearly a curve, with decreasing marginal benefits from successively higher levels of income. The slope of the curve (the regression coefficient) indicates the relationship between income and life expectancy at various average income levels. Although there is a fair amount of scatter around the curve, probably indicative both of varying local conditions and of error in data reportage, it is nonetheless apparent that at GNP levels under $600 per capita (1973 dollars), typical of most of Africa, Asia, and much of Latin America, life expectancy varies somewhere between under 40 years and about 60, with a slope at approximately 1 year of life gained for every $28 per year increment in GNP per capita.[3] At the other end of the curve, from about $1,800 upwards, the scatter around the line is more noticeable than is the slope itself, with variations in life expectancy between about 70 years and 75 years without

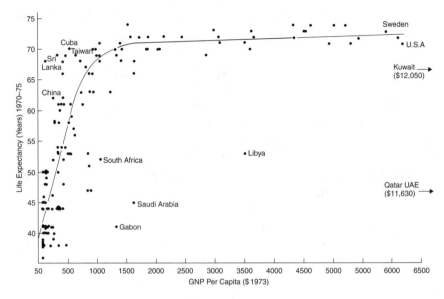

Figure 3.1   The relationship between life expectancy and GNP per capita across nations

too much regard for income levels. Nevertheless, some slope to the line is still discernible, with on the average a year of life being bought by perhaps $2,700 in annual per capita GNP.[4]

The major outliers to the right of the curve are six newly rich OPEC states and South Africa. In each of these states the internal distribution is notoriously unequal. While we have no precise income distribution data on the OPEC states, South Africa shows the lowest percentage of income accruing to the poorest 40 percent of income earners of any of the 66 countries with data. On the assumption that the same sort of convex curve applies internally to these countries, giving decreasing marginal welfare utilities with increasing income, a highly unequal distribution of income within a country would produce a lower average life expectancy for that country than would a more equal distribution. Hence the lower average life expectancy in the United States (71 years) than in more egalitarian Sweden (73 years) despite a slightly lower average income level in the latter in 1973.[5] Also, in the case of the oil-rich states, the achievement of high average income levels is very recent, and it is reasonable to expect that improvements in public health that have been or will be made possible by the new income levels had not yet had their full effect on mortality rates. (Though these 1973 data precede the most dramatic income rises in the oil-exporting states.) Nor should we forget the very heavy expenditures on arms by many OPEC nations.

Without belaboring the point, a similar relationship for infant mortality rates on a global scale can be documented and it is shown in figure 3.2. The curve is concave in this instance, since higher income produces lower infant mortality as well as higher life expectancy. The scatter is somewhat less, perhaps reflecting better data.[6] At the lower end of the income distribution, a point (per thousand) in infant mortality decline is associated with as little as a $6.50 per capita income increment; at high income levels it takes nearly a $350 income increment to bring the infant mortality down one point, on average.

By this crude estimating procedure, we would project a very substantial increase in the expectation of life and reduction of infant mortality rates for the entire world if there were substantial income transfers from rich countries to poor ones. Using our initial example of taking $150 per capita from the 700 million people in the rich

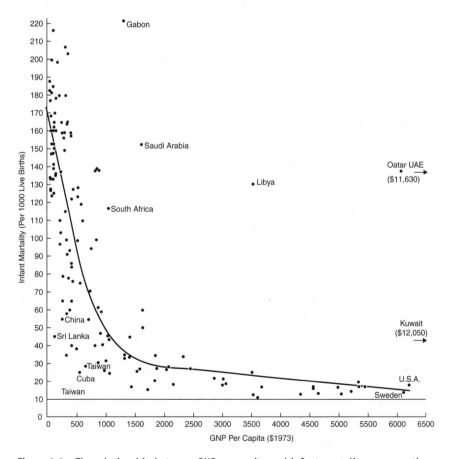

Figure 3.2   The relationship between GNP per capita and infant mortality across nations

countries would correspond (ceteris paribus, and we shall discuss some of these ceteris paribus assumptions below) to reducing average life expectancy by less than a month in those countries (one year = $2,700). Spreading that total equally among the 2.4 billion people in the poorest countries of the world would represent an average income increment to them of about $42, "worth" a year and a half of additional life to each. A rather dramatic effect. But before we take this estimate too seriously, we must try some other estimating procedures.

Diachronic Within-Nation Comparisons

We can take data on several rich nations and several poor ones and look at the changes in income levels and welfare values, like life expectancy, that have been experienced *within each nation over time*. How much rise in life expectancies has been associated with the income growth that has occurred over several decades? This kind of analysis has the virtue of looking at actual changes that have occurred over time in past experience, rather than trying to infer the probable effects of an income transfer merely from a cross-sectional analysis. It has the disadvantage, of course, of being dependent on the particular improvements in medicine and public health already experienced and the patterns of their application in various countries, neither of which may be closely reproduced in the future. Diachronic analysis must therefore reflect both the effects of rising income, and the diffusion of technology independent of income rises.

Figure 3.3 shows the rise in life expectancy and the fall in infant mortality rates in the United States between 1950 and 1973. The vertical axis measures the change in welfare values and the horizontal axis shows the per capita GNP in constant (1958) dollars. The first life expectancy reading (for 1950: 68.2 at $2,342) falls below the subsequent regression line, indicating the unusually great welfare increase associated with the rise in income to 1955 (69.6 at $2,650), but after that we can compute a regression line that falls very close to the remaining points. The result is a slope of about one year added to life expectancy for every $750 of incremental income. Similarly, the regression line for infant mortality rates runs quite close to virtually all the points; its slope over the entire span indicates a decline in infant mortality of roughly one point for every $145. Note that each

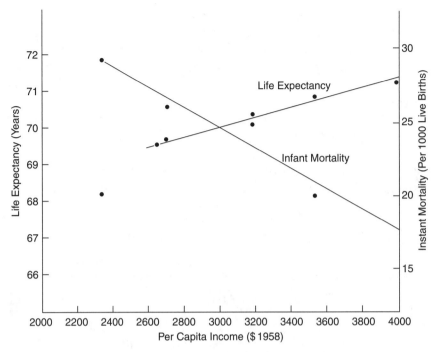

Figure 3.3   The relationship between per capita income and life expectancy and infant mortality in the United States, 1950–73

Source: United States Census Bureau, *Statistical Abstract of the United States, 1975* (Washington: U.S. Government Printing Office, 1976).

of these estimates offers a given welfare increment (one year of life expectancy, or one point on the infant mortality rate) at a cost of about 30 % of those we arrived at for rich countries from the synchronic comparison in the previous section. That is, the slopes computed over time are more than three times as steep as are the slopes computed from comparing countries at the same time. This suggests that of the improvement in life expectancy and infant mortality actually experienced in the United States since 1950, a little less than one-third may be attributed to the rise in the general income level of the country, making all citizens richer and thus able to afford better health care. The other two-thirds (or slightly more) probably should be attributed to scientific progress and the advance of medical and health technology, and possibly in some degree to public efforts to bring health care to previously neglected portions of the population. These latter are not directly the result of rising consumer incomes.

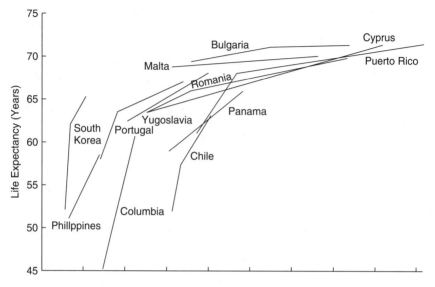

Figure 3.4   The relationship between GNP per capita and life expectancy within selected nations over time

Source: GNP per capita for Latin American Countries from James W. Wilkie, ed., *Statistical Abstract of Latin America, 1976* (Los Angeles: UCLA Center of Latin American Studies, 1976), 231; others from United Nations, *Yearbook of National Accounts Statistics*, 1975, III (New York: United Nations, 1976), 252–270. 1965 comparative GNP per capita data from Charles L. Taylor and Michael C. Hudson, *World Handbook of Political and Social Indicators* (New Haven, CT: Yale University Press, 1972, 2nd ed.), 306–311. Life expectancy from United Nations, *Demographic Yearbook* for 1967, 1974, and 1975.

We may continue this exercise with similar data on income in constant (1965) dollars and life expectancy increases in low and middle income countries. Figure 3.4 shows the situation for 12 such countries, of varying income levels, where some reasonably reliable data seem available. For each, the first (low) reading is from somewhere between 1948 and the middle or late 1950s, depending on data availability; the last or high reading is from sometime in the early 1970s.

While the situation obviously varies a good bit between countries (as indeed was suggested by the scatter around our regression curve from figure 3.1), there are nevertheless important similarities between what we can observe here and what emerged from the synchronic cross-country analysis of figure 3.1. The slopes are clearly steepest for the poorest countries and become flatter as we move to the right toward middle-income nations such as Cyprus and Puerto Rico. At the poorest end of the scale (under $300 per capita GNP in

1965 dollars) a year of additional life expectancy was "bought" for as little as about $10 per capita. At the middle level (around $600 per capita) it took $30 or more increment in income to add a year to life expectancies, and at the $1,000 per capita level the slope approximates one year per $150. Note that the slopes are not appreciably different for the three socialist countries, Yugoslavia, Romania, Bulgaria, than for the capitalist ones.

Again these diachronic figures show a more dramatic welfare-per-dollar gain than was indicated by the synchronic analysis. Here, at the low end of the world welfare and income scale, the diachronic analysis suggests one year for $10; the synchronic analysis showed one year for $28. Thus the poor parts of the world also have benefited more in achievement of basic needs from general progress in scientific and public health technology than from such real income increases as they have experienced.

Synchronic Within-Country Comparisons

Finally, we can look at data on the distribution of income and welfare values within countries at the same time. Unfortunately, adequate data for poor countries are rare, but good studies have been made of the relation between welfare and income within the United States. Kitagawa and Hauser have computed "mortality ratios" (actual deaths for each income group of whites as a proportion of the deaths that would be "expected" for whites over the entire income range). Their data suggest a mortality ratio of 1.09 for those with family income under $2,000 in 1960 ranging down to a ratio of .90 for those with family income above $10,000.[7] Using that slope and converting their mortality ratios back into life expectancies, we can arrive at an estimate of about one year for each $700; if we compute the regression running only from the $2,000–4,000 income group to the over $10,000 income group, the poorest are again here modest outliers: the slope is a little less, closer to one year for each $1,000. But both of these estimates are very close to the estimate of one year per $750 that was derived from the diachronic analysis of the United States in figure 3.3. These estimates remain particularly approximate due to a number of methodological problems carefully pointed out by the authors; nevertheless they later conclude from a further comparison of mortality by educational levels that if mortality levels associated with white men and women having one or more years of

Table 3.1   Differences in U.S. infant mortality
rate by income group

Family Income	Infant Mortality Rate Per Thousand
Under $3,000	31.8
$2,000–5,000	24.6
$5,000–7,000	17.9
$7,000–10,000	19.6
Over $10,000	19.6

college education had prevailed throughout the population, one-fifth of all deaths in 1960 would not have occurred.

Similarly, Kitagawa and Hauser[8] compute infant mortality rates by family income group in 1964–66. These are shown in table 3.1. The flattening, and even reversal, of the relationship in the over-$5,000 groups is strange, and unexplained. But looking only at the lowest income groups, from under $3,000 to the $5,000–7,000 group, the relationship is approximately one point decline for every $300 increment. These low-income groups are, after all, the ones most likely to suffer from the high cost and low availability of basic maternal and infant health facilities. This is near to the diachronic estimate for the United States from figure 3.4. Kitagawa and Hauser conclude (more strongly than we did above) that "there can be little doubt that further reductions in national death rates can be achieved through the reduction of differentials in socio-economic status in the United States. . . . Perhaps the most important next gain in mortality reduction is to be achieved through improved socio-economic conditions rather than through increments to and application of biomedical knowledge."[9]

Some Further Assumptions and Implications

If an international shift of income were to occur so as to raise incomes throughout a poor country, what might be the effect on life expectancies overall and at various income levels? Similarly, what would be the effects of a transfer of income away from a rich country? Our three methods produce different empirical results. Each in different ways taps different aspects of the situation that would prevail in any actual shift. Nevertheless, the convergence among our preliminary analyses is substantial, especially if we make an effort to separate income effects from technological effects.

The synchronic cross-national analysis (figure 3.1) produced a difference between one year of life expectancy for $2,700 at the upper end of the range, and one year of life expectancy for $28 at the lower end: *a ratio of nearly 1:100 in benefits!* The diachronic within-nation analyses (figures 3.3 and 3.4) produced a figure of one year for $750 at the upper end and one year for $10 at the lower end—a ratio of 1:75. The synchronic comparison within the United States basically reconfirmed the one year for $750 estimate, or perhaps a little above $750. While there are problems with these estimates, a conclusion seems inescapable that the marginal utility, in terms of life expectancy, of an incremental dollar at the lower end of the world income scale is *at least 75 times greater* than at the upper end. This is almost as great as the actual income spread (from Bhutan at $60 per capita GNP in 1973 to the United States at $6,200). In figure 3.2 we obtained estimates of a one point reduction in the infant mortality rate for nearly $350 at the upper end of the global income scale and $6.50 per capita at the low end. Figure 3.3 and the subsequent synchronic analysis within the United States respectively produced estimates of $145 and $300, but the former at least was compounded both of income and diachronic technological effects. Using the $300 estimate as something of a midpoint among the three estimates, and retaining the $6.50 figure as our only estimate for the low end of the scale, we again have a great gap in marginal utilities, approaching 1:50.[10]

Of course these estimates are crude; they demand substantial microanalysis of the mechanisms of nutrition, sanitation, and health care whereby income changes are translated into prevented deaths. Of course the governments of many less-developed (and other) countries are corrupt and/or elitist, so that the effects of government-to-government income transfers from rich to poor nations might not be as dramatic as some of our estimates imply. Simple old-style foreign aid transfers, without specific attention to multidimensional patterns of development and the satisfaction of basic needs, might be no more successful in reducing misery than have been some of the inflows of wealth to some OPEC countries. The point nevertheless is that the gap between well-being in rich and poor countries is so enormous, and the multimethod character of our estimating procedures indicates sufficient robustness in the results, that our basic conclusion does not seem challengeable. Even with a large margin for error in the estimates, income transfers from rich to poor countries would produce much greater gains in human welfare in the lower end of the spectrum than they would impose losses at the upper end. We already know that citizens of rich countries are much more likely to consider themselves "happy" than are citizens of poor ones.[11] I am here reminded of John Rawls's comments about the "duty of mutual aid," which requires us to "help another when he is in jeopardy, provided that one can do so without excessive risk or loss to oneself."[12]

So far we have been implicitly assuming the same proportionate income change for all people in a country. To do more one should have more data on income and welfare within poor countries (similar to that discussed for the United States) and one must make some important political assumptions, assumptions that probably would be more realistic than the simple one of proportionate increments/decrements for all. One could assume an elitist government that gave most or all of the increase only to those who were already richest (with results being even more extreme than those observed in some of the oil-rich countries in figure 3.1). Or one might assume that the increase in income for the poor country was distributed so that all citizens had the same absolute increase in income levels. Or one could assume a highly egalitarian government that somehow concentrated the income and especially the welfare increment on the poorest segments of the population. There are a variety of ways in which our assumptions can be varied to introduce more political and social reality into what has so far been primarily an economic and demographic exercise. Furthermore, there are likely to be some special complications, such as unfavorable climatic conditions or stubborn endemic diseases, that might limit the prospective improvement in health unless special efforts were made to raise educational levels.

Herrera et al. emphasize the need for income redistribution within as well as between countries.[13] Note that the left outliers (countries with better life expectancy and infant mortality rates than would be "predicted" merely by their income) in both figure 3.1 and figure 3.2 include China and Cuba and also Taiwan and Sri Lanka. To quote Tinbergen et al., "There is encouraging recent evidence from a number of Third World countries operating under a wide range of systems, that the minimum needs of human well-being can be met for the great majority of the population even under very modest per capita income levels when specific attention is given in development strategies to addressing the needs of the poor majority . . ."[14]

Several recent proposals have set as a goal the achievement of a life expectancy of about 65 years in the poor countries by the year 2000.[15] Let us suppose that goal were to be achieved more quickly, say within ten years. That means 2.4 billion people to be raised an average of 15 years in their life expectancy. Our synchronic analysis in figure 3.1 generated a marginal utility, at the poor end of the income scale, of one year in life expectancy for every $28 increment. But over ten years in the future we can anticipate advantages in medical technology and public health independent of income effects; recall the one year for only $10 estimate generated by the diachronic analysis of figure 3.4. A fairly conservative estimate for transfers occurring over the next ten years might be one year for $20. Thus the arithmetic becomes 2.4 billion × 15 × $20 = roughly $720 billion. Over ten years that is markedly less than the $100 billion per year we imagined at the start of this chapter.

Furthermore, the marginal utilities we used assumed an identical proportionate increase in income for all citizens of the poor countries— an assumption that is very "wasteful" and not in accord with the experience of those countries where life expectancy is relatively high for the income level. Targeting the transfer more pointedly, either through direct distribution within poor countries or through explicit concentration on the public health, sanitation, and nutritional mechanisms necessary to assure basic needs to the poor, would provide the increment in life expectancy for substantially less. An appropriate adjustment to our calculations could bring them into line with "two estimates resulting from different approaches and methodologies," which "suggest that absolute poverty could be virtually ended" in the world for approximately $375 billion.[16] This is not grossly out of line with the $13.6 billion in official development assistance from OECD countries in 1975. (Over 22 years, $13.6 billion would amount to $300 billion.) But of course, current official development assistance still is predominately not targeted to the poorest countries or the poorest citizens.

It might be objected that massive inflows of resources to poor countries would be "squandered" in a consequent even greater population explosion than such countries have so far experienced. Immediate gains might, in the mid-to-long run, produce greater pressure on resources, less satisfaction of basic needs, and more misery. In point of fact, however, dramatic improvements in life expectancy and infant mortality seem to be associated with (cause? or are caused by the same factors as?) *decreases* in birth rates and rates of growth in population. This is especially the case in countries where medical and health assistance has reached deeply into rural and other poor parts of the populace. All of the major outliers to the left of the curves in figures 3.1 and 3.2 (China, Cuba, Sri Lanka, Taiwan) also show birth rates (below 30 per thousand) and population increase rates (20 or below) that are substantially lower than usual for countries at their rather low income levels. Thus *filling basic needs seems to bring the means and/or the incentive to control population.*[17] Also, some observers argue that better health produces higher incomes both from the higher productivity of healthy people and from greater investment, in the form of greater willingness to invest in schooling for the children who are expected to live longer.[18]

One further objection should be considered. Any drastic or forceable transfer of income from one set of countries to another would surely disrupt the global economy; the worldwide recession following the 1973–74 increase in oil prices provides a hint of what might occur. A large decline in total world income resulting from such disruption could wipe out the net welfare gains to be anticipated from the redistribution effect, leaving not only the rich, but the poor as well, worse off than they were before. Okun, for example, expresses the general economic reservation about the effect of income transfers on incentives in noting that a redistribution of income could reduce the size of the total product and everyone's income if higher-producing people earn markedly less than the value of their marginal product.[19]

Exactly what the effects of redistribution would be on incentives, or on the structure of the economic system, are nevertheless extremely hard to calculate and subject to great (and often essentially ideological) debate. Nevertheless, we can extend our mental exercise to offer some insight. Imagine a rather pessimistic scenario where an income transfer of $150 per capita, roughly 3 percent of their GNP, from the rich countries into the poor ones (distributed more widely, to the equivalent of $42 per capita) were to be made instantaneously, and that such a sudden move produced a drop in total world income of as much as 10 percent. For this we should use the marginal utilities generated in figure 3.1. GNP per capita in the rich industrialized countries ran at about $5,000 in 1973, on the average; a 10 percent drop would be $500, equivalent in our estimate to perhaps two months of life expectancy for the average citizen. For roughly 700 million such citizens, the loss is a little over 100 million person-years. For the poorest 2.4 billion people in the world, at an average income of perhaps $250, a 10 percent drop is $25 or a little less than a year of life expectancy—roughly a total of 2.1 billion person-years. And assuming a slope of about a year of life expectancy for $100 lost to each of the 1.2 billion people in the "middle" income range (around $1,000 per capita) gives us another 1,200 million person-years lost. The total thus comes to a loss of around 3.4 billion person-years from the disruption of the world economy. But on the other hand, the net gain from the transfer effect is as follows: 1.5 years × 2.4 billion persons gained at the low end and two months × 700 million lost at the upper end. The arithmetic thus comes to an even trade: 3.6 billion minus 120 million gained from redistribution, to set against the 3.4 billion lost from disruption. But again, this is an extreme disruption because the transfer was postulated to occur all at once. The gradual transfer postulated three paragraphs above would both produce much less disruption and "purchase" a greater increment in life expectancy per dollar because of technological improvements anticipated.

So what? On a prudential level, citizens of rich countries must be aware of these discrepancies in well-being, and of the fact that citizens of poor countries themselves are becoming increasingly aware of them. Rightly or wrongly, poor people's awareness is coupled with growing anger against the rich. Such anger, interacting with perhaps sharp short-term jumps in mortality due to widespread famines we may anticipate, with the proliferation of nuclear and sophisticated conventional weapons, and with the potential for transnational terrorism, raises a "security" threat to the rich. How, if at all, global income redistribution might defuse this threat is highly uncertain, but not a question that prudence can ignore.

On a moral-ethical level, questions of responsibility for the condition of the poor have been debated for millennia, and I will say little about this debate here. On a personal level, though I have worked with data of this sort for 15 years, I find myself shocked by the magnitude of the gaps, a magnitude that I had not anticipated in advance of this inquiry. One must separate any diagnosis of responsibility, if any, for producing the gap, from the responsibility, if any, for doing something to reduce it once it has been identified. With this distinction, to require action one need not blame the rich countries for the poverty of the poor; "From a Rawlesian perspective, one need only show that redistribution would improve the long-run conditions of the poor."[20] It is true that, for most of us, our sense of moral responsibility for others recedes as their physical and social distance from us recedes. Our immediate families get the highest priority; our fellow-nationals may occupy some sort of middle ground, and more distant inhabitants of the globe, about whom we know little, are farthest from our sense of responsibility. Explanations of this vary, from the sense of mutual identification or "we-feeling" that Deutsch et al. some time ago pinpointed for its political relevance, to the sociobiological perspective of preserving one's genes in biologically related populations.[21]

Whatever the reason for a diminished sense of responsibility, these global inequalities are enormously greater than we would tolerate within our own families, or even than we do tolerate within the United States. (The difference between average per capita income in the richest and poorest state is less than 2:1; between the richest and poorest nations, as noted above, approaches 100:1.) Perhaps awareness of this enormity will keep a sense of global responsibility above the null level. Rather than accept a notion of triage, or the simple version of the lifeboat analogy, we might consider the image of a large lifeboat filled by the first-class passengers and all their luggage. The need may be to throw overboard some golf clubs and guns, not people.

Chapter 4

Comparative Public Health: The Political Economy of Human Misery and Well-Being

With Hazem Adam Ghobarah and Paul Huth

The health of humanity varies enormously: by genetic endowment, environmental conditions, and access to health care; by age, gender, income level, and country.[1] Some people live long healthy lives in peace and affluence; many others' lives are briefer and burdened by major disabilities from disease or injury, and often the characterization "nasty, brutish, and short" is all too apt. Our central claim in this chapter is that politics plays an important role in influencing public health conditions, but unfortunately political scientists and other scholars have only conducted limited systematic research on the topic.[2] As a result, the existing literature on the comparative cross-national analysis of the determinants of public health performance is largely based on the work of economists and public health experts in which political processes and conditions are understudied.[3] We believe that political scientists can contribute substantially to a better understanding of why public health conditions vary in systematic ways across countries.

We develop and then test an analytical framework of domestic and international political influences on human misery and well-being. Drawing on newly developed cross-national measures of public health from the World Health Organization (WHO), we find strong evidence that cross-national variation in public health performance is shaped by a variety of political forces, including democracy, civil wars, international rivalries, and political inequalities resulting from ethnic cleavages and disparities in wealth. We hope to help broaden the research agenda of comparative and international relations scholars by encouraging further systematic cross-national analyses of the determinants of human misery and well-being. Indeed, our larger objective is to focus the attention of both social science and public health on these influences, in the hope of stimulating critical analyses to refine the findings we report here.[4]

What Is to Be Explained?

Previous work in political science has concentrated on measures of mortality, as these have been the only data available for most countries. Davis and Kuritsky report that severe military conflict in sub-Saharan Africa cut life expectancy by more than two years and raised infant mortality by 12 per thousand.[5] In a global sample, Zweifel and Navia find democracies have an infant mortality rate about 10 per thousand below that of comparable nondemocracies.[6] Przeworski, Alvarez, Cheibub, and Limongi report the same difference in infant mortality rates, and a gap of about five years in life expectancy.[7] Similarly, Lake and Baum find substantial differences in both measures, as well as in measures of citizens' access to health resources related to both contemporaneous comparison of regimes and changes in regimes over time.[8]

In this chapter, we use new data compiled by the WHO that are more comprehensive and more reliable than information on life expectancy and infant mortality rates. The unit of analysis is the nation-state, since our interest is in the systemic and institutional influences that are characteristic of national political systems. Many of our explanatory variables reflect the characteristics of institutions of the whole society (e.g., regime type, level of expenditure on health, the experience of civil war or international security threats) and in some degree affect virtually all its members. But we also examine the effects on the average level of health conditions in the society stemming from the distribution of income within states, their ethnic heterogeneity, urbanization, and levels of education. Some (e.g., regime type) are obviously political variables, but all reflect the political power—or lack of it—of various groups and their ability to secure better health through public and private resources.

Our principal analysis is to explain outputs of the health system across countries, as expressed by WHO's measure of overall health—Health-Adjusted Life Expectancy (HALE)—for the year 2000. It discounts total life expectancy at birth in each country by the number of years the average individual spends with a major disability as the burden of disease or injury—the gap between total life expectancy and expected years without disability. It is estimated from three kinds of information: the fraction of the population surviving to each age level (calculated from birth and death rates), individual-level data on the incidence and prevalence of various diseases and disabilities at each age, and the weight assigned to debilitation from each type of condition. The result is the proportion of the population suffering from disabilities, giving the average number of years of healthy life that a newborn could expect to live.

The measure taps the concept of years of healthy and productive life, and so is expressed in intuitively meaningful units. It varies substantially by region of the world and income level. In rich countries, more disabilities are associated with chronic conditions of old age— and, at that point, relatively short life expectancies. By contrast, in poor countries infant mortality is far higher and many health problems derive from the burden of infectious diseases such as malaria and schistosomiasis, carried by children who may live a long time with seriously impaired health and quality of life. Empirically, the share of simple life expectancy lost to disability varies from under 9 percent in the healthiest regions of the world to over 14 percent in the least healthy ones.[9] Adjusting life span by time spent with disability comports with psychological findings that people do not simply seek long life, but sharply discount the value of years at the end of life spent with major physical and psychological disabilities.[10]

This information-intensive measure requires not just vital registration data for births and deaths, but expensive health surveys of death, disease, and disability by age and gender. While widely used for monitoring and forecasting in the United States, data only began to be collected on a global basis by WHO for the year 1990, with the most comprehensive report being its 2000 survey.[11] Life tables for 2000 for all 191 WHO members were developed from surveys that were supplemented by censuses, sample registration systems, and epidemiological analyses of specific conditions. WHO experts provided estimates of their degree of uncertainty about the data's accuracy, subjected it to a variety of statistical tests for incompleteness and bias, and adjusted it accordingly. Then they estimated disease-specific disability rates for all countries within each of 14 regions of the world defined geographically and epidemiologically, and used these to adjust available data on death rates at different age levels and life expectancy for each country.[12] The index—of expected healthy life years (i.e., disability-free life)—ranges from 73.8 (Japan) to 29.5 (Sierra Leone), with a median of 58.5 (Syria).

Our analyses must be cross-sectional, as adequate time-series data do not exist on a global basis. Causal inference must thus be somewhat tentative, but still is possible with careful theory and the use of appropriate lags for the independent variables. While limitations of these data must be borne in mind, they are the best that have ever been available and do permit us to make systematic inferences about the influences on health conditions across countries.[13]

Theoretical Framework

To understand why there is so much cross-national variation in human misery and well-being, we build upon existing theory and evidence regarding the influence of a variety of economic and social variables by systematically examining political variables. While the long-term goal of our theoretical and empirical research is to understand the potentially wide-ranging set of complex causal connections that shape public health, in this chapter we take a first step in that direction by breaking down our analysis into two stages.

First, we address *political influences on the allocation and total spending of resources devoted to improving the health of the population*. These are key variables for explaining health conditions in a country and so warrant attention to determine what influences help produce relatively high health spending. The amount of resources devoted to health is determined both by the *total resources available in the economy* and by *public and private allocation decisions* on how much of the resources to spend on health care. Given our focus on political determinants, we pay particular attention to governments' decisions to allocate financial resources to public health expenditures. Then we investigate what affects a health system's effectiveness at using the resources allocated to it, or "productivity." These influences include not only the level of health expenditures, but also social and political factors that influence what particular health conditions are targeted and which segments of the population are the greatest beneficiaries of services provided by the health care system. Figure 4.1 summarizes our conceptual framework.

We begin by discussing the general relationships between politics and health, and then elaborate testable hypotheses for more specific causal connections linking political variables to public health. In

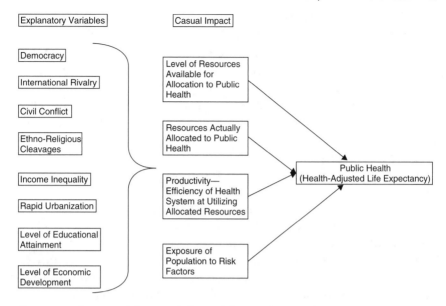

Figure 4.1   Conceptual framework for studying the impact of political, economic, and military factors on public health

broad theoretical terms, we identify four major influences on public health in societies and how political conditions and processes in turn are important causes of each of these major influences on health. In summary, we argue that public health conditions are shaped by the interplay of exposure to conditions that create varying risks of death and disease for different groups in society and the ability of groups in society to gain access to health care and therefore receive the full range of benefits produced. A country's health performance reflects its particular political struggles and competition over investment and resource decisions regarding health care and over the distribution of health care.

1. *The exposure of populations to the risk of death, disease, and disability.* Different populations across and within countries are exposed in different degrees. Geography and levels of development are basic factors to consider. People in tropical climates are at greater risk of many infectious diseases. In poor countries much of the population lives in rural areas where access to good health care is generally lower than in cities. As a result, preventive care is less available and treatment of disease and injury is less extensive and effective. At the same time, health care systems can suffer in large urban areas

experiencing rapid growth with the result that some urban populations are at great risk for many health problems.[14] Political institutions and practices, however, can raise or lower health risks by influencing access to public services. Differential political influence plays a crucial role in determining who has full or limited access to health benefits. For example, income inequalities often translate into political inequalities, with the health needs of low-income groups neglected relative to those of richer groups.[15] When political conflicts escalate to large-scale violence they expose civilians to great health risks due to direct attack, dislocation, and the destruction of public health infrastructure.

2. *The financial and human resources available for addressing public health needs.* Higher levels of income and wealth provide a larger pool of financial and human resources to draw upon. Public and private actors can spend more on health care needs and to develop and purchase more advanced medical technologies. A larger pool of financial resources will enable greater investments in human resources; that is, training more doctors and health specialists. Irregular transfers of political power and political unrest in undemocratic systems reduce growth rates, and hence the pool of financial resources for health care.[16]

3. *The level of resources actually allocated to public health needs by the private and public sectors.* Public health analysts consistently argue that education levels in society affect public health.[17] A more educated population is likely to be more knowledgeable of health risk factors, to support greater investment and expenditure, and to utilize health care services. But claims to resources for public health compete with other demands, and politics can prove crucial in deciding which resources are actually allocated. Below we hypothesize that leaders in democratic countries have greater political incentives to invest in collective goods such as public health care. We also consider how international security threats create pressures for government leaders to allocate more resources to military and defense capabilities, at the expense of nondefense needs such as public health.

4. *The degree to which resources actually allocated to public health are efficiently utilized.* Politics can influence efficiency in two ways. Public health services may not be directed to groups with the greatest need. Poor urban residents, low-income groups, and ethnic minorities are often at greater risk of health problems, yet less effectively represented in the political competition for scarce resources. Health care services for these politically marginalized groups are

skewed in favor of wealthy segments of the population or dominant ethnic groups who on average are healthier and less at risk. Second, health systems often become less efficient during wartime (due to shortages of doctors, displaced populations, and the destruction of the health care infrastructure), and these inefficiencies are likely to persist into the postwar period as well.

The first stage in understanding differences in public health conditions across countries begins with the influences on the level of public expenditures devoted to health care. Since the choice to allocate public resources to health care is fundamentally a political one beyond pure availability of resources in the whole economy, we must know what affects that choice. We then show that allocation decisions concerning public health spending are important to explaining the overall level of resources devoted to the health system on a per capita basis. Total health expenditure per capita, in turn, becomes a critical variable to explain health outputs, notably HALE.

To analyze health expenditures we use WHO data that began with IMF and national sources, supplemented by national accounts data from UN and OECD sources and household surveys and WHO estimates.[18] Since our first step concerns the government decision to allocate budgetary expenditures to health care, the dependent variable for this equation is public health expenditures as a percent of GDP for 1997.[19] It ranges from 0.1 percent in Zaire (Congo) to 8.1 percent in Germany, with a median of 2.7 percent (Albania).

Explaining the Allocation of Resources to Public Health

We begin with hypotheses concerning domestic politics.

H1: *Higher levels of democracy will result in state leaders allocating more expenditures to public health.*

Political leaders want to retain power. They must form a winning coalition among the politically active. To do so they distribute private goods to their supporters and provide collective goods widely for the population. All leaders provide both private and collective goods in some degree. But since democratic leaders must satisfy a wider range of supporters they are less able than authoritarian ones to extract rents for the private benefit of small groups, and must respond more to broad demands for public well-being.[20] They are more likely to invest in public goods such as health services because populations will hold them accountable for failing to address basic and pressing health care problems. For example, famines are much more common in authoritarian states, which spend less to prevent them or to relieve their consequences.[21] Przeworski and colleagues report that the strong effect of democracy in lowering infant mortality operates largely through health expenditures.[22]

Political system type is measured by the Polity IV average score for 1996 and 1997, from (www.bsos.umd.edu/cidcm/polity/). For the 22 countries in our sample with no Polity score we imputed a regime score from Freedom House scores (www.freedomhouse.org/ratings/index.htm), which correlate highly ($r = .95$) with Polity where both exist. Following common practice, we create a 21-point index for each state from a scale for degree of autocracy ranging from -10 (most autocratic) to 0 (least autocratic) and one for degree of democracy from 0 (least democratic) to $+10$ (most democratic), and then produce the composite index by summing the two components.[23] This scale, which we treat as interval, varies from -10 (e.g., North Korea, Myanmar) to $+10$ (e.g., Japan, Norway), with a median of 7 (e.g., Ukraine).

H2: *Higher levels of income inequality in society will result in state leaders allocating fewer expenditures to public health.*

High income inequality indicates a greater ability of economically privileged groups to influence the political system for their own benefit rather than that of the majority. Many public health care programs are directed at basic health services for poor and disadvantaged groups. They are of little direct value to wealthier segments of the population, who rely more on private health care and more specialized forms of public health services. Thus political pressure from economically powerful groups diverts state expenditures away from basic universal health care.

Our measure is the Gini index of inequality of income distribution in 1997. This index, derived from a Lorenz curve of the actual distribution of household income, represents the area between the curve and the 45-degree line for a totally equal income distribution. The data begin with World Bank estimates for 111 countries, supplemented by WHO's multiple imputation estimates using information on socioeconomic development and life expectancy at birth.[24]

Theoretically the Gini index ranges from 0 (complete equality) to 1.00 (one person has it all); in practice our national Gini indices range from a very equal .187 (Slovakia) to .609 (Sierra Leone), with a median of .374 (Uganda).

H3: *Higher levels of racial/linguistic/religious diversity in society will result in state leaders allocating fewer expenditures to public health.*

Differences in the ethnic and racial makeup of a country's population can be a source of political conflict that produces various forms of discrimination and unequal access to political power.[25] Political inequality in turn skews the distribution of resources devoted to public policy programs, including health care. Minorities suffering from discrimination are likely to be in greater need of basic health services but in a weak political position to press for them effectively. Dominant ethnic groups seek to limit public health expenditures for which minorities could be primary beneficiaries and instead try to shift resources into other state programs that are of greater benefit to them. Overall, public health expenditures will reflect the political weakness of groups discriminated against, and thus will be lower than in more homogeneous populations.

We use Vanhanen's index of racial-linguistic-religious heterogeneity.[26] This index, stable over moderate time periods, measures the percentage of the largest ethnic group identified by each of these three criteria, giving each equal weight by summing the three percentages and subtracting the sum from 300 (a completely homogeneous state by all three criteria). It is conceptually somewhat different from that of Gurr (1993), when logged correlating with an *r* of .69 with Gurr's index.[27] But it was created with Gurr's effort in mind and covers more countries. It ranges from 177 (Suriname, very heterogeneous) to a low of 0 (North Korea, complete homogeneity), with a median of 38 (Uzbekistan). The index is skewed, so we use its natural log.

H4: *Involvement in an enduring international rivalry will result in state leaders allocating fewer expenditures to public health.*

International wars are likely to have major short- and long-term impacts on public health spending. We cannot, however, investigate those effects here. By standard criteria, there were only two international wars during the 1990s; that is, the Gulf War 1990–91 and Kosovo 1999. This is not enough to give us reliable estimates of the effect of international wars on national health performance, more so as the human effects were vastly compounded by the economic sanctions against Iraq and Serbia before and after those wars. To provide an international conflict dimension we turn to international rivalries, an indicator of conflict and security threats that may cause states to shift resources from health. We expect that during an enduring international rivalry with repeated threats or use of force short of war, public spending will be diverted from social welfare programs— including health—to military purposes.[28]

An enduring international rivalry is defined as a relationship between two states experiencing at least six militarized international disputes during a 20-year period, and in which fewer than 11 years have elapsed since the last dispute. We code as 1 each of the 25 countries involved in an enduring international rivalry during 1989–97, and all others as 0.[29]

We conclude with two hypotheses about basic economic and social factors used in analyses by the WHO and health economists.[30]

H5: *Higher per capita incomes will result in state leaders allocating more expenditures to public health.*
H6: *Higher levels of education in society will result in state leaders allocating more expenditures to public health.*

The higher the level of per capita income, the more tax revenues that are potentially available to spend on the health of the public without producing acute trade-offs between health spending and other state-funded programs. The more educated the population, the better informed it is likely to be about the potential benefits of various programs and expenditures, and thus to call for and support greater public inputs to the health care system.

GDP per capita is measured for 1998 in PPP-adjusted $ and its range is from $530 (Sierra Leone) to $32,700 (Luxembourg), with a median of $3,500 (Jordan). We use the natural logarithm of GDP per capita to reduce skewness. For the measurement of education levels in society, we follow the lead of WHO analysts, which use the level of educational attainment. WHO regards average level of schooling in the adult population as the most widely available and sensitive measure, logged to correct skewness and to reflect the declining marginal impact of education.[31] For 1998 it ranges from 1.04 years of education (Mali) to 11.5 (United States), with a median of 6.03 (Costa Rica).

Empirical Results for the Allocation of Resources to Public Health

We test these hypotheses using ordinary least squares regression on data for 179 countries: nearly all the 191 members of the WHO, omitting only small states lacking data on one or more of the explanatory variables.[32] Table 4.1 shows the results for *public health expenditures as a percentage of GDP*. The columns show, respectively: (1) the estimated coefficients, (2) the standard errors, (3) the probability levels,[33] and (4) through (7) the actual change in value of the dependent variable and the percentage change from the median value by moving each explanatory variable to the 5th and 95th percentiles.

All political hypotheses are supported, with significant coefficients and important substantive effects throughout the Polity scale democracies spend more on their citizens' health than do autocracies. Controlling for all other factors, a democratic government at the 95th percentile on the Polity scale allocated about 49 percent more to health than did a dictatorship at the 5th percentile on the Polity score. For instance, the relatively democratic Philippine government spent more than twice as much per capita on public health as did Suharto-led Indonesia, despite the two countries' roughly similar income per capita. Income inequality sharply reduces public health spending (a 23 percent drop from the median to the 95th percentile of inequality). Nigeria has high income inequality at .481 and only 0.9 percent of GDP is spent on public health, while Ghana's income Gini is more equal at .317 and 1.4 percent of Ghana's GDP goes to public health.

Table 4.1 Explaining public expenditures on health as a percentage of GDP

Explanatory Variables	Coefficient	Standard Error	p-Value	Movement in Percent of GDP Spent on Public Health When Explanatory Variable Moves from Median Down to 5th Percentile	Percent Change (%)	Movement in Percent of GDP Spent on public Health When Explanatory Variable Moves Up From the Median to the 95th Percentile	Percent Change (%)
Intercept	1.550	1.190	0.10				
GDP Per Capita	0.362	0.131	0.00	−0.54	−16.7%	0.69	21.1
Income Inequality (Gini)	−5.217	1.277	0.00	0.65	20.0	−0.76	−23.2
Education	0.679	0.266	0.01	−0.85	−25.9	0.34	10.4
Ethnic Heterogeneity	−0.148	0.090	0.05	0.37	11.3	−0.16	−5.0
Enduring International Rivalry	−0.776	0.294	0.00	0.00	0.0	−0.78	−23.8
Democracy (Polity Score)	0.066	0.018	0.00	−0.72	−22.2	0.53	16.1

Notes: $N = 179$, Adjusted R-square = 0.50; Sigma = 1.32; Mean of dependent variable = 3.26.

Ethnic heterogeneity also makes a big difference, especially toward the homogeneous end of the scale (the 5th percentile on heterogeneity shows 11 percent higher spending than the median). Bangladesh, ethnically homogeneous but impoverished, allocates 2.2 percent to health while Ethiopia, similarly poor but more heterogeneous, allocates just 1.4 percent. An enduring international rivalry also depresses public health expenditures and the substantive impact is large, producing a 24 percent reduction in public funds allocated to health. For instance, Pakistan and Syria, with relatively high levels of defense spending, allocate less than 1 percent of GDP to public health.

The two control variables from standard public health models have a powerful effect. GDP per capita has a substantial impact, especially among richer countries (21 percent higher in the 95th percentile than at the median). The average level of education also makes a big difference, especially toward the low end, near the 5th percentile.

Overall, we find that domestic and international politics play an important role in shaping government decisions to allocate resources to public health programs. The next step is to use public health spending as an explanatory variable in an equation to explain overall levels of total health care spending.

Hypotheses on Total Levels of Health Spending

Our second equation represents a simple model to account for total health expenditures per capita. Total spending per capita (1998) ranges from $4,055 (United States) to $11 (Somalia), with a median of $197 (Thailand). WHO declares that it is very hard for countries to provide good health outputs below a total expenditure of about $60 per capita, and that it would cost just $6 billion per year to bring up to this threshold the 41 countries with lower expenditures.[34] As these distributions are skewed we use natural logarithms.

The analytical focus is now on the overall level of financial resources committed to the health care system. We draw on standard analyses by economists and public health experts to formulate several hypotheses. In this model the effect of the political influences is captured indirectly by including public health expenditures as a percentage of GDP as an explanatory variable. We had no theoretically compelling hypotheses for why those political variables would exert a strong direct impact on private health expenditures.[35]

> H7: *Higher per capita incomes will result in higher total health expenditures.*
>
> H8: *Higher levels of education in society will result in higher total health expenditures.*

As previously argued, the higher the level of per capita income in society, the greater the tax revenues available for public spending on health by governments. Furthermore, higher levels of income and wealth should also enable individuals and businesses to afford to spend more on private health care. Again following WHO practice, we also expect that higher education levels in society would be associated with greater support and interest in achieving high health standards through support of both public and private spending on various health care programs. For both income and levels of education we use the same measures as in the first equation.

> H9: *Higher allocations of private spending to health care will result in higher total health expenditures.*
>
> H10: *Higher allocations of public spending to health care will result in higher total health expenditures.*

These two hypotheses reflect the straightforward relationship that in societies where both public and private actors make decisions to allocate a larger percentage of available resources to health care, the overall level of total health spending should be greater. Thus while H7 posits that wealthy societies can afford to spend more on health care, H9 and H10 point out that there are always competing claims in society on how to spend available resources. As a result, public and private decisions to spend more or less on health relative to other programs help determine the overall amount of resources spent on maintaining and improving health care. We use the same source for private health spending as for public spending, and sum them. Private health spending ranges from 0.3 percent (Kuwait) of GDP to 8.8 percent (Lebanon), with a median at 1.9 percent (Oman).

Empirical Results for Total Levels of Health Spending

Table 4.2 reports the results in the same format as in table 4.1. All hypotheses are supported with significant coefficients that produce

Table 4.2   Explaining total expenditures on health

Explanatory Variables	Coefficient	Standard Error	p-Value	Change in Expenditures When Explanatory Variables Moves From Median Down to 5th Percentile ($)	Percent Change (%)	Change in Expednditures When Explanatory Variables Moves From Median up to 95th Percentile ($)	Percent Change (%)
Intercept	−3.738	0.165	0.000				
GDP Per Capita	0.937	0.025	0.000	−156.9	−75.4	1,027.9	494.2
Education	0.207	0.052	0.000	−46.9	−22.6	23.1	11.1
Private Spending on Health as of of GDP	0.126	0.014	0.000	−26.3	−12.7	80.8	38.8
Public Spending on Health as% of GDP	0.190	0.010	0.000	−61.4	−29.5	362.4	174.2

Notes: N = 178, Adjusted R-square = 0.97; Sigma = 0.261; Mean of dependent variable = 5.34 ($208).

moderate to large substantive effects.[36] GDP per capita has a powerful impact. For example, the shift from the median GDP of approximately $5,000 per capita to the 95th percentile GDP of $22,700 per capita produces an increase of $1,028 in total health spending per capita. Education also produces strong effects as the movement from 6.5 years of average education to 10.2 years is associated with an 11 percent increase in total health spending per capita. Both these findings converge with standard analyses by economists and public health experts.[37] Finally, higher allocations of public or private resources to health spending are strongly and positively associated with overall total health spending levels. Since public spending usually constitutes a larger portion of total spending, the marginal impact of allocating public spending is greater, as shown in the table.

This second set of results is important. First, as we show below, *total health expenditures per capita* is a powerful variable in accounting for overall health outcomes on a cross-national basis, so we need to understand what affects it. Second, it shows that *allocation of public spending to health expenditures* is a major contributor to *total health expenditures per capita*, and we have already shown (table 4.1) that public spending on health is depends on several political variables. The critical point then is that political variables have important but indirect impacts on health performance through their causal linkage to public health spending.

Theoretical Analysis of the Causes of National Health Performance

We now turn to the centerpiece of our analysis, in which we examine the level of health achievement in a population. Our dependent variable is HALE, the WHO measure for *health-adjusted life expectancy* at age zero, discussed at the beginning of the chapter. We present several new hypotheses about the direct impact of political variables on HALEs, and include variables from basic WHO models as additional explanatory variables. Our first three hypotheses share a common logic about domestic political variables, linking limited access to health services and greater exposure to health risk factors to lower HALE scores.

> H11: *The more unequal the distribution of income, the lower will be the HALE.*

While we have already posited that income inequality indirectly impacts on health performance by influencing allocation decisions on public health expenditures (see H2), we also hypothesize a more direct effect as well. That is, the more unequal the distribution of income, the more unequal will be the distribution of access to both public and private health care facilities. The provision of high quality health care services is thus limited to a smaller segment of the general population, producing lower overall levels of health performance. The rich get more access—at low marginal utility, and the poor get less access—at a level of income at which the marginal utility of greater access would be high. As a result, the poorer segments of the population already at greater risk to disease, disability, and death fail to receive necessary health care services, producing aggregate patterns that produce lower HALE scores.

> H12: *The more ethnically/linguistically/religiously diverse the population, the lower will be the HALE.*

As we argued above, ethnic differences often result in discrimination and unequal access to political power. Once again, group cleavages in society not only indirectly impact on health conditions through the allocation of public spending on health (see H3), but also directly affect health performance by limiting access to the health care system. Access to health services will be biased in favor of politically dominant ethnic groups in society, and politically weak minorities will suffer from limited access to health services. Consequently, minority groups that are already exposed to greater health risks due to discrimination in housing, education, and job opportunities will lack sufficient support from the health care system.

H13: *The faster the pace of urbanization the lower will be the HALE.*

Fast-paced urbanization, particularly in low- and middle-income countries, often brings poor new urban dwellers into slums where they are exposed to new disease vectors and other increased health risks. They will lack adequate access to care as the supply of health service lags behind the surge in need. Surveillance, immunization, and the provision of safe water all become more difficult. Rapid urbanization often reflects an influx of poor and marginalized people from rural areas—people who are politically weak and thus suffer from inadequate access to health care despite great need. New residents of urban slums are unlikely to be well organized in unions to create effective pressure for services either in the workplace or in politics. They are likely to be underrepresented in established political parties that have already developed a base of political support among other urban constituencies. A gap between great need and inadequate health care delivery marks this relative neglect of new city dwellers. Marginal utility analysis predicts that individuals or groups receiving less than an equal share of health care lose more disability-adjusted life expectancy than is gained by individuals or groups receiving more than an equal share of health care. That should be especially true when the disadvantaged group is exposed to the diseases of urban slums.

Our measure of recent urbanization is the average annual percentage change in the urban portion of the population, 1990–95.[38] It ranges from −0.41 percent (Belize) to 7.35 percent (Botswana), with a median of 0.88 percent (Grenada).

H14: *The occurrence and severity of civil wars will reduce the level of HALE.*[39]

We expect civil wars to kill and maim people. But that is more than just a tautology. Wars continue to kill people well after the shooting stops. Civil wars do so by destroying health care system infrastructure that cannot be replaced rapidly, by disrupting normal economic activity and health care delivery, and by slowing down the rebuilding of the health care system in the postwar period due to multiple and wide-ranging reconstruction programs in other areas of society.[40]

Military forces often deliberately target health care facilities in order to weaken the opposition. The result is that the human and fixed capital resources available to support the health care system are depleted. For example, heavy fighting in urban areas is likely to damage or destroy clinics, hospitals, and health care centers; rebuilding this infrastructure is unlikely to be completed quickly in the postwar period as governments face many pressing reconstruction programs. Wartime destruction and disruption of transportation infrastructure (roads, bridges, railroad systems, communications, and electricity) also weakens the ability to distribute clean water, food, medicine, and relief supplies, both to refugees and to others who stay in place. As a result, health care systems suffer shortages in supplies and personnel, inadequate facilities, and a reduced capacity to reach populations outside of major urban centers. These shortages and limited access severely strain the ability of health care professionals to deliver treatment and aid efficiently into postwar periods. Furthermore, severe civil wars may induce a substantial flight of highly trained medical professionals, and this loss of human capital may not be reversed by their prompt return or replacement by newly trained health workers until long after the wars end.

Civil wars often produce huge movements of persons displaced within their own countries. They often lack clean water, food, and access to health care, and these people may remain displaced for years after the end of the civil war. Thus the very people exposed to high health risk factors simultaneously suffer from limited and inadequate access to health services. For example, in many countries ravaged by civil wars, the crude mortality rates among newly arrived refugees were 5 to 12 times above the normal rate. Epidemics of diarrheal diseases, measles, acute respiratory infections, malaria, and other diseases are typical. Malnutrition is common, weakening people's defenses against infection. Civil war has been labeled as the predominant cause of famine in the 1990s.[41]

Even after the fighting subsides, epidemic diseases may become rampant, extending far beyond the displaced population, and immunization and treatment programs are overwhelmed.[42] Nondisplaced populations may also be at greater risk following severe civil wars. For example, diseases that become rampant in camps for displaced populations may easily spread to other regions. Prevention and treatment programs already weakened by the destruction of health care infrastructure during civil wars become overwhelmed as new strains of infectious disease bloom. These spreading diseases may be especially damaging to children, given their greater susceptibility to infection. For example, efforts to eradicate Guinea worm, river blindness, and polio, successful in most countries, have been severely disrupted in states experiencing the most intense civil wars. Drug-resistant strains of tuberculosis can develop and in turn weaken resistance to other diseases, and it is commonly held that the spread of AIDS in Africa has been greatly increased by refugee population movements associated with civil wars.[43] Finally, the risk of physical violence is likely to increase in the aftermath of long and severe civil wars, based on changes in individual and social psychology.[44] Homicide and other crime rates rise during international wars, tending to peak in the first year after the war. The experience of war makes the use of violence within states more common.[45] Gerosi and King report a significant rise in homicides and suicides, transportation deaths, and other unintentional injuries (both of the latter are likely to include misclassed suicides) in the U.S. population immediately following the Korean and Vietnam Wars.[46] If international war has this effect, we should certainly expect the direct and immediate experience of civil war to do the same. These social and psychological changes are magnified by the widespread availability of small arms after many civil wars and the relative weakness of many state police forces compared to private security forces.

> H15: *Civil war in a geographically contiguous country will lower the HALE.*

Whereas many displaced persons stay in their own countries during civil wars, others flee across national borders to become international refugees: their own countries lack the means to care for them, and they often are fleeing political or ethnic persecution from those who have the upper hand in the war. The Rwanda civil war generated not only 1.4 million internally displaced persons, but a total of 1.5 million refugees into neighboring Zaire, Tanzania, and Burundi.[47] Large-scale refugee movements can produce adverse health consequences for neighboring countries in two ways. First, if the refugees must be cared for mainly by the medical resources of the receiving country, those resources may be diverted from care of the host country's own population. Second, they can bring infectious diseases associated with the disruptions of war and the poor living conditions in which they find themselves in host countries. Refugee camps can become vectors for transmitting infectious diseases to the host population.

For H14, deaths from civil war in the years 1991 to 1997 represents a measure of both the existence and severity of civil war, expressed as the number of deaths per 100 people in the country to measure the war's intensity. Civil wars are defined as armed conflicts producing 1,000 or more fatalities per year among regular armed forces, rebel forces, and civilians directly targeted by either. Civil war years and fatality figures are derived from leading data sets on civil war compiled by scholars.[48] For most countries its value is 0; for the 34 countries experiencing civil war during the period it ranges from .02 to 96.9 (Rwanda). For H15, we simply use a dummy variable coded as 1 if any contiguous state experienced a civil war from 1989 to 1998. Contiguity is defined as sharing a land border or separated by no more than 12 miles of water.

The last hypotheses draw on standard WHO models of cross-national health performance.

H16: *The higher the level of total health expenditures per capita, the higher will be the HALE.*

Higher income improves health *through* public and private decisions to spend money on hospitals, preventive and curative care, sanitation, and nutrition. Earlier work by economists showed that "wealthier is healthier."[49] We build on their work with a wider set of countries and a finer-grained argument about *how* total income leads to better health. Per capita GDP does not directly determine the production of health outputs. Rather, it permits a high level of expenditure for health purposes, and though highly collinear with income ($r = .90$), health spending is also influenced by political processes and institutions. For example, above we found that democracy has a strong impact on total health expenditures by raising public health spending. And spending is distributed in a political process that produces actual health outcomes. So our two-stage model, in the economics tradition of production function analysis, treats income as an uncontrollable variable outside the direct process that brings good public health outputs. We follow the WHO in using total health expenditure per capita as a theoretically satisfying variable to incorporate prior political processes that affect spending. It includes health services and prevention, but not the provision of clean water and sanitation that are also affected by levels of education and income.[50]

H17: *The more educated the population, the higher will be the HALE.*

At higher levels of education, preventive and treatment programs become more widespread and effective. Demand for better health care increases as does more knowledgeable and effective consumption throughout the population. Education is strongly associated with the health of both children and adults in rich and poor countries. It is the other independent variable, with total health spending, in WHO analyses of health attainment.[51]

Empirical Results for Influences on Health Performance

Table 4.3 shows the results for the HALE equation in the same format as previous tables. The strongest impact, not surprisingly, is from the level of total health spending—with a shift from the median to the 95th percentile bringing ten years of additional healthy life. The coefficient for ethnic heterogeneity is barely significant, but produces some substantive effect: moving from the median of the heterogeneity index to a quite homogeneous 5th percentile brings HALE more than a year higher. This direct effect reinforces the separate stronger negative impact of ethnic diversity on the allocation of

Table 4.3   Explaining years of healthy life expectancy (HALE)

Explanatory Variables	Coefficient	Standard Error	p-value	Change in Years of Healthy Life Expectancy When the Explanatory Variable Moves from Median Down to 5th Percentile	Change in Years of Healthy Life Expectancy When the Explanatory Variable Moves from Median up to 95th Percent (%)	Percent Change (%)	Percentile Change
Intercept	36.980	3.769	0.00				
Total Health Expenditure	3.921	0.434	0.00	−7.84	−14.2	9.80	17.7
Rapid Urban Growth	−1.426	0.408	0.00	1.00	1.8	−3.57	−6.4
Income Inequality (Gini)	−16.296	4.783	0.00	2.04	3.7	−2.36	−4.3
Ethnic Heterogeneity	−0.489	0.344	0.08	1.22	2.2	−0.54	−1.0
Education	5.044	1.103	0.00	−6.28	−11.4	2.52	4.6
Civil War Deaths 1991–97	−0.085	0.037	0.01	0.00	0.0	−0.98	−1.8
Contiguous Civil War	−2.311	0.817	0.00	0.00	0.0	−2.31	−4.2

$N = 180$; Adjusted R-square = 0.81; Sigma = 4.98 years; Mean of dependent variable = 55.3 years.

public health expenditures. Together, these results suggest that ethnic diversity operates to diminish the overall level of health achievement primarily by reducing overall expenditures, and to a lesser extent also through some discrimination in the distribution of those expenditures and hence access to health care.

The impact of income inequality on HALE is highly significant and substantively strong. A shift from the median Gini index to the 95th percentile reduces average healthy life expectancy in that country by over two years. This is in addition to the separate impact of income inequality on HALE through reducing the allocation to public health expenditures. Together, these results indicate a substantial impact of income inequality on health conditions (HALE) that operates both through lowering public health expenditures and through discrimination in the distribution of those expenditures, and hence on access to health care services. It is important also to recognize that the indirect negative impact of income inequality on HALE through lowering public health expenditures is not adequately compensated by private health spending. Even controlling for total health spending, in unequal societies the overall level of life expectancy is lower and the level of disability is higher.

The United States provides an example for both the above findings. It is moderately diverse in ethnic composition (86 countries are more homogeneous) and distinctly low in economic equality (108 countries are more equal). Despite being the richest country on the globe and the biggest total spender per capita on health care, 27 countries have better HALE.

The impact of education is also strong, especially among poorer countries. If Benin somehow could provide its people with an average of six years of schooling instead of the actual 1.7 years; that is, if it were at the median level of schooling rather than at the 5th percentile from the bottom, we would expect its citizens to gain over six more years of healthy life. Partly that reflects the absence of per capita income in this equation, as education—more highly correlated with income than with health expenditures—likely picks up some effect of income here. Nonetheless, educational attainment was fairly strongly associated with total health spending, and these two results together indicate that education affects both the level of health expenditures and the achievement of better health through greater access and effective use of health services.

A high pace of urbanization also has a strong impact, cutting HALE by over three years in the more rapidly urbanizing countries.

As we argued, this negative impact is likely to be due to the susceptibility of new urban dwellers to disease and the political weakness of new poor urban residents to ensure that the health care system delivers adequate prevention and treatment to them.

Finally, the matter of civil war. First, civil wars within a country have a clear negative impact on health conditions with the loss of a full year of healthy life at the 95th percentile. Not surprisingly, civil wars do kill people, and not just during the course of the war.[52] The damage to life and well-being lingers for years after the war is fought, due to the disruption of institutions and the infrastructure. Truly severe civil wars (rare events to be sure) are even more detrimental. These can reduce healthy life expectancy by nearly ten full years (e.g., Rwanda and Liberia).[53]

Moreover, it is not just civil war in one's own country that matters. A country's HALE is typically depressed by more than two years if a neighboring state recently suffered from a civil war.[54] This relationship is not weakened even if we exclude all countries that themselves experienced a civil war.

Note the cluster of eight countries (Namibia, Zambia, South Africa, Congo-Zaire, Zimbabwe, Malawi, Swaziland, and Lesotho, in declining magnitude of the residual) in southern Africa that are outliers at the left of figure 4.2, with predicted HALES 9 to 16 years above their actual achievement. All but Congo were also in the top ten for per capita HIV/AIDS cases in 1999. It is commonly believed that the incidence of AIDS in Africa has been greatly abetted by civil wars. None of the eight countries experienced major civil conflict in the 1991–97 period, but a few (Namibia, South Africa) had civil

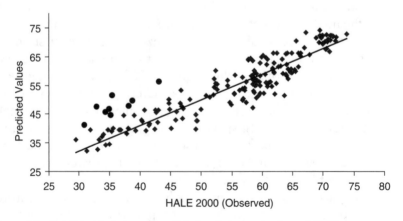

Figure 4.2   Relationship between predicted and observed values of HALE

wars a few years earlier, and the manifestation of HIV infection is often delayed. All of them also border on states that experienced civil wars either in 1991–97 or somewhat earlier.

Many other explanations have been proposed for the prevalence of AIDS in these countries (UN Program on HIV/AIDS, unaids.org/epidemicupdate/report/index.html). No one or two are satisfactory. Public health researchers do not agree on why AIDS is so common in this region. We do not show an equation that includes an HIV/AIDS variable, since to do so would merely put a label on a disease without providing a socioeconomic explanation of its prevalence.[55] This concurs with Evans et al., who decline to use an HIV variable to predict HALE as a measure of efficiency of the health system. Their view, and ours, is that the health system should be held at least partly accountable for the failure to control AIDS.

Conclusions, Limitations, and Future Research

In trying to explain expenditure inputs into the health system, and outputs in the form of the reduction of human misery, we combined variables commonly used by public health analysts with economic, social, and political influences much less commonly studied in this context. The phenomena we tried to explain were measured by newly available cross-national data from WHO. Though preliminary, the results showed the utility of modeling health expenditures and then using those expenditures as an explanatory variable for achievement in health care. Forecasting as well as explanation can benefit. Politics matters, in ways that illuminate the subfields of both comparative politics and international relations as well as public health.

The models we use to explain variation in the allocation of public spending on health care show that, in addition to income and education, several political influences matter. For example, the degree of democracy in a country is strongly associated with higher allocation levels. We also found that ethnically diverse countries and those experiencing great income inequality show significantly lower levels of spending allocated to public health. Furthermore, countries engaged in enduring international rivalries allocate lower levels of public spending to health. Our findings help to quantify these influences and to assess their relative impact.

When we moved to explaining outputs of the health system, the patterns were similar in some respects but importantly different in others. Total health expenditures per capita strongly raise the level of disability-adjusted life expectancy, as does education. As expected, the direct negative effects of civil wars and rapid urbanization on HALE are strong. Income inequality strongly depresses HALEs more by its indirect effect in reducing public health spending than by its direct effect. The primary effect of ethnic heterogeneity works indirectly by lowering public health spending, but also impacts directly on HALE. Working through different causal routes, both show what happens when groups and segments of the population have little political power.

This examination of some of the causes of human misery and its alleviation is still in an early stage. Better time-series information is needed to permit stronger causal inferences. Improved data are essential—and are likely to be forthcoming over the next few years. Certainly we need to better comprehend micro-level political and social processes. For example, variation in the health conditions of women and how politics influences health care opportunities for women require careful analysis. Here we have emphasized health (spending and output) as the phenomenon to be explained, and lagged our explanatory variables accordingly. But poor health conditions surely contribute to economic stagnation, and very likely to civil unrest. Also, democracy may have additional indirect effects on health. We focused on democracy's impact on allocating public spending to health care but there may be further links to educational levels, minority and women's rights, political peace and stability, and economic growth. A more satisfying understanding doubtless requires modeling these reciprocal causal effects beyond what can be done in a single chapter.[56] Finally, while we have considered international security threats in our analyses, another large international influence on health conditions may be the process of economic globalization and its possible impact on societal inequalities.

One possibility for research has been to employ a new data set from WHO on so-called DALYs—that is, disability-adjusted life years lost from various particular diseases and conditions, applied separately to both genders and various age groups.[57] In time this will allow us to better estimate the correct time lags and to focus much more effectively; for example, on the effect of civil wars or income inequality on women and children, and on the burden imposed by particular diseases. Some of these data are discussed in WHO (2000), and more are becoming available. The result should be a far deeper understanding of which groups are especially afflicted, how, and why.

Chapter 5

Security and the Resources Scramble: Will 1984 be Like 1914?

We are about to witness the demise of nonalignment as a viable foreign policy for states with any significant resources. The world market is losing its force as a means of allocating supplies of natural resources. Rather, major powers increasingly will seek assured access to vital raw materials, with that assurance achieved by political means. Access to raw materials will be too important to leave to market forces under conditions of political instability. Unstable or radical third world governments will seem too unreliable. They may be unwilling, or unable, to maintain the large-scale constant supply of vital resources to the industrialized world. The removal of Iran from the world market of petroleum suppliers may be tolerable for a while, as a single case. But many Irans would either paralyze the entire world economy, or set off a scramble for assured access to the remaining raw material sources and economic disaster for all who lagged behind in the scramble. Hence national leaders may feel irresistible pressure to take preventive steps before a crucial supplier collapses.

The Imperative of Growth

The period since World War II has, in a real sense, marked the triumph of capitalism. The OECD countries of the advanced industrial world have experienced an unprecedented era of sustained economic growth, a high level of material well-being, and substantial equality of economic benefits between and within the OECD nations. Even with some slackening of growth during the recent period of "stagflation," the achievement is remarkable. This phenomenon of growth and prosperity has been made possible by modern industrial capitalism—an enormous dynamic force for change.

Of course, not all industrial countries are capitalist, nor are all countries industrial. But in crucial ways almost all try to mimic the behavior of dynamic capitalist states. Beset by fears and historic experience of penetrations, the Soviet leaders see the security of their state as dependent upon the growth of high technology, heavy industry, and expanding production. To accept economic stagnation would be to accept too great a posture of military weakness. Industrial development is essential to survival of the regime in a world where that regime's ideology is seen as a threat to others, and where military power is dependent far less on a large population than on a base of modern industrial capacity and sophistication. If the perceived external threat to the regime's security is not enough (and I suspect it is, given Russia's history of invasion by its neighbors and Bolshevik memories of Western intervention in 1918), then the regime must also be mindful of the internal threat to security implied by any failure to sustain growth. Domestic peace requires an expanding economic pie. Indeed, the Soviet regime has justified its own existence largely on the grounds of its ability to raise the living standards of its populace. Poland's failure to provide sustained growth has washed away that regime's already tenuous legitimacy, and portends a wider crisis of socialism in Eastern Europe unless growth can be restored.

Thus socialists must behave like capitalists in many essentials. Their states must grow to insure their international security and domestic tranquility. Given their lagging productivity and narrow nonmilitary scientific base, their growth requires access to advanced technology and capital goods from abroad. Stalinist Russia could tolerate virtual autarky within its alliance bloc for a time, but the contemporary Soviet Union can no longer do so. It must have Western technology to stimulate stagnant productivity and bureaucratic inefficiency, Western wheat to feed its population, and raw materials—notably in the possible entry of the Soviet Union on to the world petroleum market as a buyer—to feed its industrial and military machine. Even China has ended its era of autarky, forced to obtain Western technology and capital goods in order to provide some measure of military security against the Soviet Union.

All industrial powers—and perhaps all major powers at whatever stage of development—must maintain growing economies. Failure implies falling behind in the industrial and technological base necessary to sustain military power. Without evolving technology for advanced weaponry, and an expanding economic surplus to support a large military establishment, a country invites attack or, at best, atrophy of its international sphere of influence. Failure also implies the risk of overthrow from within. Populations of modern states expect, and demand, rising incomes. Prolonged stagnation, especially with widespread unemployment, loosens popular support for the regime. Most third world governments try to legitimize their rule by fostering economic growth; indeed they often claim the need for growth requires the "temporary" sacrifice of political liberties. They must produce at least some growth if they are to retain the support of the middle classes for very long. Every Western democratic government lives with the specter of the 1930s' Depression; bringing Nazism to Germany and the threat of authoritarian government throughout Europe. Few political analysts seriously contend that "no-growth" economies are easily compatible with stable democratic polities. If continued stagnation or economic decline is politically intolerable, then every threat of denial of access to essential supplies of raw materials becomes a matter of central concern to the state.

The Supply of Resources

The growth of industry and popular consumption requires tremendous quantities of raw materials—to the point where many of the traditional sources of raw materials within the industrialized countries have become much sparser and, in some cases, exhausted. Western Europe imports all its supplies of ten vital minerals; Japan all of eleven. The United States must look beyond the North American continent for more than half its supplies of bauxite, cobalt, chromium, columbium, manganese, mica, platinum, tantalum, tin, titanium, abaca, natural rubber, and industrial diamonds.

Throughout most of the period since 1945, the international trade regime assured more-or-less open access to supplies. The United States was the world's dominant economic and political power. It maintained a stable international reserve currency. By example and by cajoling its trading partners it assured a liberal order of relatively free trade and helped reconstruct the economies of war-torn countries even at the cost of strengthening commercial rivals. It also was ready to intervene politically to ensure the continuance in less-developed countries of governments committed to development plans organized around relatively open economies oriented toward the world market (e.g., Guatemala, Iran after Mossadegh).

From the point of view of its industrialized allies, this hegemonic American regime was not always benign. The British, for example, resented continued American pressure to open up the trade of the Sterling Area and dismantle their system of Imperial Preference. British oil interests were substantially dislodged from their position of predominance in the Middle East, and forced to share, unequally, with American-based multinational corporations. American political muscle supplemented the economic competitiveness of American firms to ensure this.

Nevertheless, the U.S. government was always concerned for the economic strength of its political allies, as witnessed by the Marshall Plan. American insistence on a liberal international order was for the benefit of all (noncommunist) states, and the United States needed militarily strong allies, with underlying strong economies, to participate in the common defense. Great military exertions were not demanded of all the allies, however. Rather, American military strength provided the main umbrella to ward off Soviet penetration and under which all the capitalist industrial states could pursue their global economic interests. Japanese recovery in the 1950s constitutes the most vivid example.

In the past few years, however, these conditions have ceased to apply. American military hegemony can no longer be depended on to resist Soviet penetration of the third world, or to sustain such important allies as the Shah of Iran. Third world governments, even if not significantly Soviet-influenced, cannot so readily be assumed to be open to Western investment activities or so wedded to the large-scale production of raw materials for the world market.

Often they wish to pursue some form or degree of self-reliance and to exert greater control over the extractive activities taking place in their territories. They wish to sell their oil in quantities, at prices, and to customers of their choosing. OPEC, especially AOPEC (the Arab subset), is the most successful grouping of commodity exporters, but other countries and groupings of countries have taken some steps along the same path. U.S. military force would meet greater obstacles, both indigenous and Soviet-assisted, in any attempt to maintain or reinstitute past marketing conditions.

Under these changed political and military circumstances, the free play of international market forces no longer suffices to guarantee access. The threat of politically inspired boycotts—though ever-present since 1973—is secondary to the threat simply of political chaos in producer countries, making them unable to maintain the flow of supplies.[1] A revolutionary government may intend a modest reduction in commodity extraction, but then, in a period of near-anarchic conditions be unable to keep the degree of domestic peace that would ensure even its new and lower level of intended production. Terrorism, the breakdown of domestic order, periods of civil war, or international war between third world commodity producers can readily sever the necessary chain from extraction to international marketing. Industrial importers need assured access; this means third world governments willing and able to keep the mines operating, electricity flowing to the smelters, the railroads or pipelines running to the ports, and the dockside facilities in action. Stability and control, more than ideological orientation or commitment to free enterprise, become the touchstones by which a third world state is judged a reliable ally. To achieve this stability, third world states may have to be generously supplied with military and internal security equipment and training for their forces, perhaps given economic assistance in times of balance-of-payment crisis, and occasionally even bolstered by the presence of military forces from the industrialized countries (viz. the American rapid-response force for the Middle East, or regular French military intervention in Africa).

The need for politically assured supplies of raw materials is most dramatically seen with oil, but is hardly limited to that commodity. Chromium (essential not just for car bumpers, but for most steel) comes almost exclusively from three sources: South Africa, Zimbabwe, and the Soviet Union. Platinum, cobalt, natural rubber, and abaca come primarily from vulnerable or potentially unstable states in Africa or Southeast Asia. More important than access for the United States is access for its natural-resource-poor industrialized allies of Western Europe and Japan. If the United States cannot keep their access, as well as its own, under the American protective umbrella, one or several unpalatable eventualities will occur: its allies will suffer severe economic dislocations; they will seek the protection of some stronger power, if there is one (the Soviet Union?); or they will seek their own military-political associations with third world producers, resulting in sharpened competition among themselves and with the United States. Thus the decline in American hegemony endangers the United States' economic position directly, and Western long-term economic and political security indirectly. A highly competitive struggle for spheres of influence and areas of economic control among the industrialized states—and here we should clearly include the Soviet Union—would imply great dangers of military confrontation and war.

Impetus to World War I

This prospect is more than a little reminiscent of the process that led to the outbreak of World War I in 1914. During the nineteenth century, the major European powers experienced a period of rapid demographic and economic expansion. Their populations, industrial capacities, and technological bases all grew at historically almost unprecedented rates. So too, as a consequence, did their demands for resources to feed their people and fuel their industrial machinery. For much of the century this expansion placed more-or-less tolerable strains on the structure of world order. The Pax Britannica replaced mercantilism with the principles of relatively free trade, defusing some pressure for colonial acquisition. More important, resources and potential colonial territory were abundant. Many areas of Africa and the Far East were still uncolonized, and the major powers could carve out empires or spheres of influence without coming too seriously into competition with one another.

Toward the end of the period, however, competition over the few remaining areas became more intense. The acquisition of a new colony by one power increasingly meant the denial of another's ambitions in that region. Spheres of influence began to intersect, and establishing the borders between spheres of influence became a matter of intense concern, often resulting in political confrontations and military shows of force (e.g., Agadir, Fashoda) and threats of war. During this later period (roughly 1890–1914) tensions grew, alliances and counteralliances formed, and international crises became more common.

These conflicts of interest and political tensions were driven by a variety of forces. The demand for resources, powered by economic and demographic expansion, was supplemented by other internal as well as international influences. Arms races, both naval (e.g., Britain-Germany) and army (e.g., France-Germany) were fed by mutual fears and ambitions, in the now familiar pattern of an upward spiral. Bureaucratic pressures to maintain and incrementally expand military spending were common then, as now. So too were the various economic and societal interests that benefit from increased arms purchases. These entrenched interests provided enormous resistance to any reversal of the dynamics of military spending. Since they operated within growing economies, it was almost always possible to expand the military without seriously infringing on civilian demands—the economic pie as a whole was growing, and greater military spending, representing the same or even a slightly larger share of the total, could be accommodated without an actual reduction in other kinds of expenditure. Moreover, military capabilities, in the form of occupation troops and naval forces, were required to secure the new colonies and maintain lines of supply and communication over long distances. Once these troops and ships were available, however, they then could be used to acquire new colonies or if necessary to fight wars in quite different places. (A substantial number of the "European" troops that fought on the Western Front during World War I were in fact "colonials" brought from India and Africa.) Colonial acquisitions thus gave momentum to the arms expenditure spiral, and were in turn further encouraged by it. Similarly, as the major powers' spheres of influence increasingly collided, these confrontations both fed and were promoted by the expansion of military forces.

By this interpretation, the crisis events of August 1914 followed naturally from the underlying conflicts inherent in the major-power international system. Conflicts of interest inevitably arose as economies demanded new resources, economic and bureaucratic interests supported programs for increased military strength, and in their conflicts national leaders sought reliable friends and feared implacable enemies in an atmosphere of mounting suspicion and hostility. Under these circumstances, major international crises were inevitable. Sometimes, as in North Africa or as late as the Bosnian crisis of 1908, matters might be settled at least temporarily. Perhaps even, with greater wisdom, patience, and objectivity, more prudent decision makers might have managed the 1914 Sarajevo crisis without a general European war. But the underlying conflicts and tensions were so severe that they would have reemerged again within a few years, and ultimately the required combination of luck and crisis-management skill would have broken down. In this interpretation, if by some means the outbreak of general war could have been averted in August 1914, then that would have been not war-prevention but merely a temporary postponement of the almost inevitable.

The events directly following August 1914 may, at terrible cost, temporarily have provided some slack in the system. Three major powers (Germany, Austria-Hungary, and Russia) were dismembered or left militarily almost impotent. The populations of Europe were left disillusioned with war. The biggest colonial powers, France and Britain, kept their empires intact, and indeed expanded them with League of Nations mandates. It took almost two decades for the defeated powers to regain their strength and revive their expansionist pressures. Then World War II, at even more terrible cost, again ultimately released some of the pressure as most major powers were either defeated or economically exhausted, and except for the United States and the Soviet Union had no immediate need or ability to expand. For two or three decades American supremacy served to discourage effective challenge to the new status quo. It took even longer after World War II than after World War I for competitive expansionist pressures to fully resume.[2]

Conflict in the 1980s

Of course the contemporary era is not 1914, but many parallels are apparent. The need for assured access to raw materials, discussed in earlier pages, provides a powerful driving force toward present-day international conflict. When major powers were relatively self-sufficient within their own borders or within their preexisting colonial empires, the pressure to obtain further external sources of supplies was low. Even as the colonial empires were formally disbanded, various tools of political and economic influence would usually maintain the earlier trading patterns and commercial expectations. Where that was unsure, at least American hegemony could be relied upon to maintain a relatively open world economy where raw materials could still be bought and sold as necessary. But self-sufficiency now has vanished for so many of the industrial countries' commodity needs, a victim of the exhaustion of home territory sources, needs for ever-increasing total amounts to supply larger populations and growing economies, and the snowballing loss of colonial and postcolonial controls over third world areas. With all this, the United States' ability to preserve a liberal international economic order, for itself and its allies, has also weakened. Assured access to raw materials is now felt as a pressing need for all states, especially advanced industrial ones.

Partly as a direct response to these needs—for instance, as manifested in the creation of the American rapid deployment force—and partly as a response to general East-West tensions, the arms race has entered a new phase of expansion. Soviet military expenditures seem to ascend each year to ever-higher levels and to give the Soviet Union ever-increasing strategic and tactical military capabilities. American military spending, which had declined for several years under the impact of the late Vietnam War years, began to rise again in real (noninflated) dollars in 1976 and has continued to do so since, with a particularly sharp rise in 1981. Uncertainty about Soviet capabilities and intentions intensifies American fears.

New arms acquisitions are stimulated as much by what the other side does with its military forces as simply by what forces it possesses. Soviet (and Cuban) support for Marxists in Angola, Ethiopia, and elsewhere in Africa contributed greatly to the revival of superpower tensions. It is arguable that former president Carter's decision to seek a larger military budget was provoked as much by the Soviet occupation of Afghanistan—Russia's use of its military forces actually to invade an originally noncommunist neighbor—as by the Soviet Union's growing military capability. In this sense the Soviet Union had acquired military and naval forces that could pose a direct threat to Western access to vital raw material supplies in the third world. Afghanistan or Ethiopia are themselves irrelevant to raw material markets, but their occupation suggested a greater Soviet willingness and ability to move against states that were more important—and of course Soviet control of strategically important places such as Afghanistan and Ethiopia would make it easier for them to move militarily into adjacent areas. We no longer see much imperialism or colonization in the 1914 sense of formal political control, but we certainly see large spheres of influence and many client states.

Finally, once again, as in 1914, the effects of international threat and counterthreat are intensified by domestic bureaucratic and economic interests. (The Soviet Union also has a "military-industrial complex") While the demand for external raw materials' access continues to grow in the West and to emerge in the East because of the decline of domestic reserves, the major powers' economies are not growing as rapidly as they did a few years ago, or as rapidly as in the years preceding World War I. In a sense this may relieve some of the pressure; for example, the recent decline in industrialized countries' imports of foreign oil is due in part to the lack of growth in the world economy. It also imposes earlier limits on the increase of military spending—the trade-offs with civilian needs will be readily apparent in an economic pie of more-or-less constant size. Yet no one should count on civilian demands to be an effective constraint on military spending for some time to come. Military spending in the United States currently accounts for less than 6 percent of GNP; it was about 13 percent during the Korean War, and during World War II exceeded 40 percent—while in Britain, during the same period, the comparable figure touched 60 percent. When people can be persuaded that a clear threat to their security exists they will pay a heavy economic price. Arms races are not readily limited by consumer demands. Rather, both sides are likely to have to pay substantial costs, and make substantial additional sacrifices in the name of military preparedness, before either feels compelled to call an effective halt. Even without wartime urgencies, it would seem that a good deal more could be extracted from the populaces of both Eastern and Western states under the "right" political circumstances.

Those "right" political circumstances, however, include a much greater sense of national danger than existed during the decade of the 1970s, and would have, to be intensified by sustained, consistent communications from political leaders to the general populace. Recall the advice of U.S. Senator Arthur Vandenberg at the beginning of the cold war era: "Scare the hell out of the country." Popular fears and hostilities, once fanned, cannot later be so easily restrained or controlled. Political leaders, once having alarmed the populace about the imminence of enemy threats, may not find it easy, for example, to conclude strategic arms limitation treaties that must inevitably depend in some degree on mutual confidence and trust, or readily to forego apparent (and perhaps illusory) possibilities of achieving strategic superiority.

Protracted economic stagnation is worrisome in another way as well. People have come to expect ever-improving living conditions; the ability to provide those improvements has undergirded the legitimacy of virtually all developed industrialized states, capitalist and communist alike. Rising popular dissatisfactions, with people's anger directed against their governments, add a degree of political instability that must inevitably complicate efforts at prudent crisis-avoidance and crisis-management. Preexisting stagnation and political unrest make any interference with access to necessary raw material supplies even less tolerable than if there were more give in the system.

Competition and War

This discussion has so far closely followed a neo-mercantilist line of argument and eschewed other economic explanations of imperialist or other expansionist behavior. The theories of Hobson, and of Lenin and other Marxists, are of course familiar to readers. Perhaps less familiar are those neo-Marxist writers who see the Soviet Union as epitomizing "state capitalism," beset by stagnation and pursuing a form of international expansionist behavior not readily distinguishable from that of Western capitalist states.

If one were, however, to credit these other economic theories seriously, the result would only be to strengthen my line of argument that emphasizes the pressure of raw material scarcity. For instance, a world of intense political competition, especially a world divided into spheres of influence, would inhibit the now-established patterns of activity by multinational corporations. Both banks and producer corporations need freedom of movement, freedom to shift their investments and to threaten to relocate their activities if host-country restrictions become too binding. Their prosperity, and hence that of their home countries, will suffer if they are shut out of large parts of the world. Indeed, the confluence of Marxist, neo-Marxist, mercantilist, and neoclassical theories suggests even more reason to be alert to the rising dangers of international conflict.

By this analysis the coming years will be more dangerous than any we have experienced in a long time. Conflicts over which third world areas are to be in whose sphere of influence will become more common. It may seem necessary to insure that the vital raw materials' suppliers are in someone's sphere of influence because only then (if then) can access be insured. Hostilities and suspicions among major powers are likely to be corrosive. ("Are they just trying to stabilize the situation, perhaps to preserve their own access, or are they trying to keep or push us out of the area?") It will be hard to reassure leaders or populace of the other side's relatively benevolent intent, or that any benevolent intent can be relied upon once the other has a new base of power.

The absolute level of military destructive capabilities will be higher than ever, and still growing. Thus any outbreak of violence carries enormous risks of devastation. Even more seriously, an arms race implies changing kinds and degrees of capability. It would be foolish to expect changes always to favor the defense, for example. Surely there will be times when offensive weapons systems seem to gain some new advantage over defensive systems, and therefore where the pressures to carry out the first strike, to attack rather than risk being attacked, are intensified. The faster the rates of technological change and weapons deployment, the greater the risk that imbalances may occur.

We know from previous experience that periods of arms races carry high risks of war. One scholar identified 99 "serious disputes" among major powers since 1815. In 71 of those instances, the powers involved were not engaged in an arms race (defined as a three-year increase in the rate of increase in military spending), and the dispute was settled without war in all but 3 of those instances. In 28 cases, however, the dispute occurred between states that were already involved in an arms race—and 23 of those disputes eventuated in war. Similarly, a variety of recent studies, using different methods and differing in detail but not in their overall conclusions, now point conclusively to periods of change in relative strength between major state rivals of nearly equal power as particularly dangerous to peace. Such periods of "power transition" (typically accompanied by arms races) produce great uncertainty in the minds of decision makers, leading to exaggerated estimates of one's own strength or of the rival's hostility and threat. Such uncertainties, fears, and misperceptions frequently lead to large-scale wars.[3]

This is not to say that arms races necessarily, or even usually, cause war. Sometimes they do produce tensions and uncertainties that lead directly to war. At other times an arms race may merely reflect preexisting international tensions. Both the arms race and the war would therefore be caused by those tensions. But whatever the precise causal mechanism—and one would expect it to be different in different circumstances—we do know that periods of rapid bilateral increase in arms spending very often do end in war. A renewed arms race with the Soviet Union may be unavoidable; perhaps we would even invite aggression and war by refusing to compete. That does not, however, detract from the fact that a renewed arms race between the United States and the Soviet Union marks, by historical standards, a period of great danger, and will demand very wise, prudent statesmanship on both sides.

Avoiding and Managing Conflict

How then can we hope to deal with these dangers, to prevent the inevitable tensions and political confrontations from escalating into nuclear conflict? Prescription is harder than diagnosis. One component of any treatment is surely, as suggested, prudent crisis-management: becoming as aware as possible of the risks inherent in crisis situations, particularly of the ways unexpected threats to major values, forcing decisions to be made within short time periods, leave decision makers prone to misperception and miscalculation. John Kennedy is said to have been cautioned, during the Cuban Missile Crisis, by his reading of Barbara Tuchman's *The Guns of August* about 1914. Future decision makers can be cautioned by understanding why and how other crises have, or have not, been managed short of war, and by the scholarship in cognitive and social psychology that illuminates these problems. Crisis-management alone, however, is a thin reed on which to lean. If crises recur frequently, mistakes will almost inevitably occur. Decision makers are, after all, human. Prudent strategy would prescribe efforts at crisis-avoidance as well as crisis-management.

Crisis-avoidance involves reducing the number of conflicts of interest that are likely to occur. To avoid conflicts of interest we might, for example, try to work out prior agreements with our major economic and political rivals as to which parts of the world would fall within whose sphere of influence. Parts of the third world will not, after all, be of great importance to resource-seeking major powers. Some states in Africa and Asia, with large populations and meager resource endowments, are already sometimes labeled the "basket cases" of the world. Obtaining political control over such states would in most circumstances add little to the strength of the acquiring major power—on the contrary, by draining resources, it might actually mean a net loss of power. Exceptions would be states whose population or armed forces might be useful in the role of regional surrogates for military capabilities of the great power, or states whose geographical location gave them special strategic significance.

The most difficult cases will be those states whose natural resources are in demand and whose governments are politically insecure. If there are many such states, with a number of different resources at stake, an elaborate balancing act will be required. How is the value of a state controlling large manganese deposits to be balanced against a major producer of rubber? It would depend, for instance, on the relative share of each state in the world market for the relevant commodity, how politically insecure access from that and from other countries seemed, and how dependent each of the major industrialized countries was on access to that raw material. A major power might be relatively self-sufficient in one but dependent in another, with the situation quite reversed for another power. With virtually all the world's chromium coming from Zimbabwe, South Africa, and the Soviet Union, Western countries obviously could not tolerate hostile control over the African chromium producers to the degree the Soviet Union could. How does one interpret the actions of a rival power in locking up access in a particular country? Are those actions merely those of prudent self-protection, or are they intended as an aggressive threat to sources we need? Calculating equations based on subjective evaluations of so many variables—my need, your need, your intentions, the political stability of this and other suppliers, the size and nature of the resources at stake in a particular case (when world geological knowledge is itself still far from perfect)—sounds extraordinarily difficult. In fact, by comparison the calculations necessary to balance different weapons systems and different geopolitical circumstances in comparisons of strategic "essential equivalence" may seem trivially easy.

Many industrialized countries' interests are at stake. Some allied countries have begun major stockpiling efforts, but there is little evidence of serious intra-alliance planning. One tactic must certainly be to share the responsibility and access with allies, and not to allow the Western alliance to fragment into *sauve qui peut* competition. In important ways allies can serve each other's interests on a mutual basis. It would be curious if Lenin's prediction of sharp competition for "colonies" among states at the "final state of capitalism" should be fulfilled now, driven by forces not fully appreciated by Lenin.

Some sharing with the Soviet Union is also inevitable, as Moscow seeks to secure its own economic and strategic interests. The Soviet leaders have always resisted the vision of all third world states around their border becoming clients of the capitalist world, and now they have the power to make that resistance effective. It is unimaginable that the Soviet Union could be denied access to the world market. Moreover, as American and Soviet experience with third world allies has abundantly shown, local rivalries have their own dynamic. A close political relationship with A (Pakistan, Ethiopia, Israel) is acceptable to A only because of A's needs for external support against a regional enemy B. As a consequence, B (India, Somalia, Syria) then inevitably becomes more hostile toward A's great power ally, and seeks its own great power support elsewhere.

Carving up the third world into spheres of influence and secure access to raw materials is, in plain English, a frankly imperialist policy. There is good if sometimes overstated reason for the repugnance with which the term imperialist is generally regarded. In the contemporary context it means allying with repressive authoritarian regimes, and typically means sustaining regimes that encourage wide inequalities of economic conditions as well as political rights among their citizenry. Jimmy Carter's human rights policies were ineffective in influencing the governments of countries that were regarded as economically or strategically essential to American interests. A realistic policy designed to insure Western security in the coming years probably cannot entirely dispense with such alliances. Nevertheless, in all politics there are matters of degree, and choices available.

Several steps offer promise of significantly reducing the pressures to align ourselves with authoritarian regimes. In fact it is essential to take these other steps, quite aside from moral or humanitarian qualms. The stability of any government with which we ally simply cannot be assured. The very act of concluding the alliance can sharply diminish the regime's legitimacy in the eyes of its population. It may acquire coercive instruments (weapons, police training) from a big-power protector, but that act too sows illegitimacy and dissent. A Western policy dependent on long-term alliances with such regimes is unreliable as well as repellent.

The effectiveness of military force is, moreover, doubtful as a means of insuring continued access and supply. Remember, for example, the widely acknowledged difficulty of insuring a continuous flow of Middle East oil by means of military occupation, or simply the aphorism about the difficulty of sitting on bayonets. Many third world regimes now have highly sophisticated weapons from the United States, the Soviet Union, or France. Gunboat diplomacy, against a state armed with MIG-25s or guided missiles, puts the gunboat at risk. The Soviet Union may on occasion be willing to go in with large-scale military forces and enforce a long occupation: neocolonialism, not "just" imperialism. Americans are less likely to be willing, or able, to use military force that way. Western countries can, instead, supply a volume of food assistance and financial capital to aid development that far exceeds what the Soviet Union can offer.

Reducing Dependence

One timely and substantial step available to diminish the degree of dependence on unreliable sources of commodities—and to reduce pressures for quick military intervention—is stockpiling. The American strategic stockpile of various raw materials, acquired after the Korean War, has since become sharply depleted. The depletion may have been sensible. During the 1960s and early 1970s America's access to most raw materials must have seemed reasonably safe; in any case, a large flow of raw material supplies is irrelevant to the kind of short intense war usually envisaged as the chief military danger. The strategic stockpile has also become something of a political ploy for some domestic producers to maintain high prices and a source of concern to some friendly overseas producers who feared it would be used to manipulate world market prices to their disadvantage. Under the circumstances projected by this analysis, however, stockpiling is again in order. The Reagan administration has assigned this matter a high priority. The United States is no longer concerned with insuring production in wartime. Rather it needs to maintain productive capacity in peacetime against the possibility of reductions in raw material supply resulting from actions like boycotts and from political instability that might cripple commodity production in key third world countries.

The cost of rebuilding the strategic stockpile in those materials chiefly obtained from politically vulnerable third world areas would be substantial but not exorbitant. After all, it was done before. In 1962, for example, the United States held stocks of tin that amounted to more than two and one-half times that year's total noncommunist world production. Even in the mid-1970s America's stockpiles of tungsten equaled eight years of normal domestic peacetime consumption. Current plans to sell excess holdings of these two metals, and especially silver, can largely finance the new acquisitions.

A few metals are of greater importance—perhaps chromium, cobalt, platinum, and, above all, petroleum. The last would be the most expensive. For the one billion barrel reserve currently authorized (enough to replace total oil imports into the United States for about five months) the cost would be, at around $35 a barrel, about $40 billion for acquisition and storage costs combined. The most severe constraint is likely to be not the absolute cost in dollars, but devising appropriate financing means during the next few years when budget cutting and restraint of inflation are primary goals—especially if the stockpiling program becomes a pork-barrel to enrich domestic American producers of noncritical materials. Past strategic stockpiling activities were distorted by politically powerful domestic interests (e.g., silver, lead, zinc; also consider American quotas on imports of oil and sugar).[4] Currently, the "need" for a variety of minerals is also emboldening American mineral companies to demand that national park and other reserved lands be opened up to mining. For some minerals this may be justified; for others fears of a "resource war" provide only a rationalization for private greed.

What is really at stake is the *strategic* stockpile, to be treated as a true instrument of national security. The Soviet Union's leaders may have begun taking steps to avert a similar threat to their country.

Recently the Soviet Union has been importing substantial quantities of nonfuel minerals that are not currently in short supply domestically. This looks like stockpiling behavior.[5] Diversifying suppliers and building the capacity for ocean mining also represent appealing ways to multiply sources of minerals and so to reduce dependence on politically vulnerable foreign suppliers.

What will it take to stimulate the necessary actions? At the moment the United States lacks the institutions and the belief system to operate effectively in a mercantilist world. The prevalent ideology remains that of liberal trade; an ideology and a policy that served the country's interests well in the first decades after World War II. Nor has the United States established the kind of close government-industry cooperation associated with Japan (MITI) or the French government policies of encouraging consolidation and nationalization of industry, and actively promoting arms industry sales abroad. These countries are already well along the way toward the kind of "strong state" that can compete successfully. Efforts to build the institutions of a mercantilist state in America will meet strong resistance.

A change in the belief system may come more readily. At the end of World War II, when American leaders perceived a new and long-term danger from the Soviet Union, a change in the belief system, of both the leaders and the general populace, was achieved speedily. The leaders saw the danger, articulated it as a combination of threat to physical security and to basic American cultural values, and conveyed the message widely. Almost immediately the Soviet Union became seen as an enemy rather than an ally. Isolationism had been a respectable intellectual and political tradition before World War II. Many of its proponents tried to revive the tradition after the war, but within the space of a few years it was utterly destroyed, overwhelmed by the general commitment to the ideology of containment.

It is possible to imagine a similar change in the contemporary belief system, as leaders redefine a sense of national interest away from a narrow preoccupation with military security toward maintenance of a sound economy more resistant to the whims of foreign producers. A dramatic event symbolizing the industrialized countries' vulnerability may be necessary for an effective revision of popular beliefs. The 1973 oil shock, and all subsequent oil price increases, only began the process. The economic damage they did was neither sharp nor sudden enough to have sufficient impact on public consciousness, perhaps already receding during the probably temporary 1981 oil glut. Further shortages and induced economic hardships may be required before the effect is substantial enough. When it does become so, there may be several kinds of political alliances. One is already forming. There is a significant community of interest among domestic minerals producers, arms manufacturers, traditional anticommunists, and covert friends of the government of South Africa. A hard-line ideology of national security, justifying stockpiling, extensive rearmament, and military interventions will frequently be heard. Left unchallenged, the result might well be an adventurous foreign policy of substantial risk.

Seen this way, there is also an opportunity for an alliance between environmentalists and those who take a measured view of national security risks. Conservation and recycling can in this sense become foreign policy instruments, and major components of any strategy to reinforce self-sufficiency in raw materials. This is so in the obvious sense that we benefit to the degree that overall economic growth can be maintained without growth in the use of raw materials, especially those whose supplies are politically vulnerable. Equally important, however, is learning to live with a more modest rate of increase in the GNP. That is *not* to advocate a policy of complete no-growth in the industrialized world (much less in the poverty-stricken third world, for whom a prescription of no growth would be intolerable). It is only to insist that attention to equity, to easing the effects of stagnation on particular groups or industries, and, in general, to cushioning the social and political effects of economic slow growth, is essential. As we know from wartime experience, sacrifices are much more tolerable to the degree they are felt to be more or less equitably levied. If the brakes to economic growth in the industrialized countries can be applied slowly, the restraints should be more acceptable. Over the course of a generation or two, cultural change may significantly reduce expectations of, and demands for, ever-greater material wealth—especially if conditions of equity are given attention.

Another force to defuse the international impact of competition for scarce resources can be found in those resources in which the United States is rich and many other industrialized and less-developed states are poor; namely, food grains. North America now accounts for 80 percent of all grain exports. Others, thus, are dependent on the United States, and the world trade in grain can provide a certain cement to hold the entire system together. Indeed, Russia's reliance on American food resources, in particular, may yet serve to moderate its political ambitions in the third world. We should not expect the Soviet leaders to forego opportunities to secure their own needed supplies of raw materials—for example, oil in the Middle East over the next decade or so. In return for assured supplies of food they may, however, be prepared to be more tolerant of Western needs for industrial raw materials. By this logic the United States should apply political restrictions on food exports to the Soviet Union only for a very limited set of very serious reasons. The Soviet leaders should be assured that they can buy all the food they need subject only to the legitimate needs of the United States and its allies, and subject to Soviet noninterference with Western raw material access. If, however, they attempt to prevent necessary Western access—and only then—they must expect the grain trade to shrink in consequence.

Conclusion

The risks of international great power confrontation stemming from economic causes will be critical in coming years. No government of an industrialized state can tolerate sustained interruption in the supply of vital commodities. Not all commodities are equally at risk; probably the threat is really severe in the case of only a few. But it might require interruption of only a couple—such as petroleum and/or chromium—to create immediate economic and political crisis. To limit the vulnerability, a variety of courses of action must be pursued. They include political arrangements with some third world suppliers, selective stockpiling, learning to live with fewer demands on resources, and strengthening the web of interdependence that already ties all the industrialized states in bonds of common interest. Neither exaggeration of the "resource war" nor ignoring the likelihood of shortages can be done safely. The gravest threat for the next few decades is not contained in the "limits to growth" vision of population explosion, resource exhaustion, and pollution. It is contained in the kind of economic demands that can end in political action—war. Without political vision the world may end in a nuclear bang before it ever has a chance to utter the ecological whimper.

Chapter 6

Conflict and Coercion in Dependent States

With Steven Jackson, Duncan Snidal, and David Sylvan

The "dependencia" tradition offers a new perspective on underdevelopment in peripheral societies. A major premise of this body of scholarship is that the pattern of socioeconomic development in dependent states is, as a result of the states' dependence, fundamentally different from those in advanced industrial states. Recently, this tradition has begun to focus on sociopolitical distortions in dependent states. Our basic argument centers on the proposition that the conditions associated with dependence lead to civil conflict and state coercion. The interaction of these two forces leads to the emergence of the increasingly repressive and authoritarian regimes identified with many dependent states.

Elsewhere we have attempted to describe the conditions associated with dependence, concentrating on their causal interconnections. Basically, the theory argues that external dependence of poor nations on rich nations produces distortions in the economic structures of poor societies. These distortions create a large potential for conflict. Under pressure from external and domestic actors, the dependent state attempts to stabilize the situation by the use of coercion to control conflict. Thus, the interaction of external dependence with latent conflict leads to escalation of the levels of violence used by both the state and opposition.

Most of the research investigating the development of authoritarian regimes under conditions of dependence has been undertaken as part of individual country case studies.[1] There is a need for further systematic examination of the usefulness of dependence theory in explaining the prevalence of coercive regimes in less-developed countries. One approach is to test the theory empirically by examining the impact of dependence on the development of authoritarianism in various less-developed countries. Ultimately this is necessary for a proper evaluation of the theory (and is incorporated as part of the research design for a larger project on dependencia in which we are engaged), but it is not the approach taken in this chapter. Instead, we investigate the relation of conflict and coercion in dependent states by means of formal analysis of the theoretical argument. This allows us to ascertain the significance of particular forms of the propositions and aids us in specifying the exact model for subsequent empirical testing. Furthermore, it complements that analysis by adding to our understanding of the processes underlying the rise of coercive-authoritarian regimes in dependent states.

We begin with a discussion of how a history of dependence leads to a situation where there is a potential for severe conflict in a society. Then we proceed to specify key aspects of the interaction of the state and opposition given the historical context. This requires a discussion of assumptions concerning the motives of state response to manifest conflict and opposition response to the coercive-authoritarianism of the state. Through graphical analysis we explore some implications of a simple model—particularly those conditions under which the system will be either stable or explosive. Finally we use difference equations and phase diagrams to explore more systematically the dynamic implications of the model's underlying assumptions.

We illustrate these results with tentative examples of countries whose experience bears on the model. More systematic empirical analysis is of course required. We are engaged in such analysis, but a report on it would be beyond the scope and permissible dimensions of this article. In any case, it is essential to lay out the logic of the model and to identify implications of a complex specification that could not emerge simply from detailed examination of data.

The analysis suggests that the model we have developed is a valid and useful representation of the rise of coercive-authoritarianism under conditions of dependence. At high levels of coercion, however, the difference equation model is not adequate to explain the interaction of state and opposition. We then consider certain assumptions of our model which must be relaxed in further analysis and speculate on the effects of this relaxation. While increasing coercive-authoritarianism has been the dominant trend since World War II, there have been some conspicuous counterexamples. We end by looking at some ways in which our model and dependence theory might be made consistent with these outcomes.

State and Opposition

The relationship between conflict and coercion in dependent states may be viewed as an ongoing action–reaction process that is embedded in, and structured by, longer-run historical processes. A concise statement of our understanding of the arguments involving these historical processes can be found in another of our publications.[2] Figure 6.1 presents a simple diagram of the set of relations which we will discuss below. The "dashed-line box" is used to highlight the particular submodel upon which we focus in discussing conflict and coercion. These historical processes, as described by dependencia theorists, are too complex to represent fully here.[3] However, for present purposes it is sufficient to observe that a history of foreign penetration of third world economies and societies is seen as leading to an external orientation of economic activity. The trade sector in the less-developed country is enlarged and becomes overly concentrated on a few commodities and in a few buyers. This export-enclave syndrome yields economies vulnerable to the vagaries of the world market and social structures too rigid to adapt to the changing needs of a growing economy.[4] Trade vulnerability, however, is but one symptom (or consequence) of external penetration; more fundamentally, continuing and expanding capitalist penetration leads to severe distortions in the dependent economy.[5] Unbalanced growth and great disparities between sectors accompany the tendency for *dynamic* domestic sectors to become oriented toward the world economy and virtually isolated from the national economy.[6] These self-reinforcing economic distortions lead to increased marginalization and greater income disparities between and within classes.[7] These social cleavages will tend to be exacerbated further by the capital-intensive nature of foreign penetration and by the growing economic role of the government that develops in response to this foreign penetration.[8]

The development of social distortions and inequality in the economic sphere leads to the rise of grievances of class against class and group against group within society. This *latent conflict* will be greater the more unequal the distribution of income and will generally be aggravated by changes in the overall national income. Thus, long-run historical processes lead to grievances between groups (or classes) and to opposition to the *state*, that is, to that part of society that (1) has a legitimate right to a monopoly on the power to make those decisions that have as their object society as a whole, and (2) claims

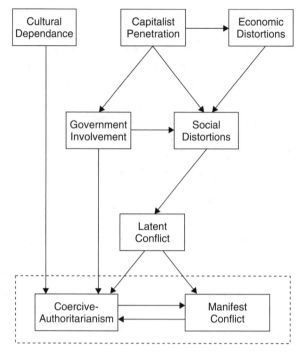

Figure 6.1   Relation of the short-run conflict model to longer-run historical processes

a monopoly on the implementation of those decisions. The mechanisms by which this potential for conflict is translated into *manifest conflict* (MC) can best be understood in terms of the motivations of those engaging in conflict. To explore fully the effects of the interaction of state and opposition, we will also look at the motivations of the regimes in power.

We define those individuals who are engaged in activities the regime considers threatening to the state as the opposition. By regime we mean the set of state agents with authority over a wide range of issue areas. Note that we are not claiming that the opposition sees itself as threatening to the state (although its leaders probably would)—merely that its actions are seen by the *regime* as threatening. Our hypothesis is that the opposition will engage in manifest conflict for two reasons. The first is to manifest its latent conflict. The second is in response to the *coercive-authoritarianism* (CA) of the state, that is, to those patterns of behavior by agents of the state that directly limit or control activities that the regime considers to be political by the use, or threat, of physical force. Three specific arguments apply.

A "signaling" argument is that the opposition is indicating to the regime its latent conflict over particular issues so that at higher levels of coercion the opposition must engage in more violent activity to get its point across. Physical violence by the state also leads the opposition to signal its dissatisfaction with the state's coercion itself.

A second argument is more political. To the extent that a regime is coercive, people feel that the regime itself is hindering the resolution of their latent conflicts, and hence will manifest conflict targeted at the regime as well as at the immediate target of their latent opposition. For example, labor-management conflicts may become targeted at the regime if the latter is seen as intervening on behalf of one party. In effect, the opposition becomes politicized.

A third argument is psychological in nature. The notion that frustration leads to aggression has a fairly distinguished past as an explanation of violence,[9] and given that high levels of coercion are frustrating, one can hypothesize correspondingly high levels of aggression.

These arguments can take two forms. People who were already prepared to manifest their latent conflict decide that a given level of coercion calls for them to manifest an additional amount. Alternatively, people who would have been content to let others demonstrate decide that a given level of coercion requires action on their part. In either case, we would expect a direct relationship between levels of coercion and levels of manifest conflict.

There is, however, a countervailing force. Higher levels of coercion bring with them higher costs, both in terms of pain and suffering and in terms of time foregone by (futile) demonstrations. At very high levels of coercion, the costs are likely to be so high that only very low levels of manifest conflict remain. This can be thought of either as carried on by diehard revolutionary guerrilla groups, or as widespread but very low-level protest.

Thus, the overall shape of the manifest conflict (MC) reaction curve appears as in figure 6.2. (It is worth noting that the height and intercept of the curve will be determined by the preexisting level and history of latent conflict.) This quasi-parabolic shape falls into roughly three zones. At low levels of coercion, in zone I, conflict feeds on government coercion. Moderately severe restrictions on civil liberties serve to stimulate further manifestations of conflict from the opposition. However, at some fairly high level of CA, zone II, each successive "turn of the screw" begins to reduce MC. In the extreme this can be thought of as involving an actual discontinuity in the

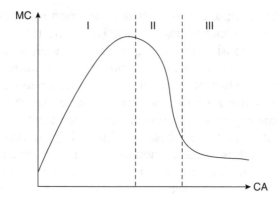

Figure 6.2   Opposition reaction curve

reaction curve: there may be some threshold level of coercion before which the reaction is fury, beyond which it is fear. The last zone, III, is where coercion is so high that only low levels of manifest conflict remain.

Before moving to a consideration of how the regime manipulates coercion in response to manifest conflict, let us consider some of the long-term factors that affect the level of coercive-authoritarianism. When the government is extensively involved in economic affairs, it will have a particular interest in controlling any destabilizing economic conflict. Further, the state can be expected to recognize the potential explosiveness of the long-run build-up of latent conflict and to buttress itself against this by expanding its coercive apparatus. Increasing cultural dependence of the regime on the capitalist center will weaken the traditional class base of the state and increase its reliance on coercion to maintain itself. This increase in coercion will be facilitated by foreign political and military aid.

In the context of these historical developments, there are three main motivations for resorting to coercion as a means of dampening manifest conflict. The first is rational in an instrumental sense: regimes have certain goals—such as limiting political activities and keeping conditions stable for foreign investors—which they want to satisfy, and coercion is one way of doing so. A second motivation is less "rational" in nature—simply that protest per se is disturbing to most regimes. Seen in this way, coercion is less a finely calibrated instrument than an instinctive response to widespread turmoil. Finally, high levels of manifest conflict threaten the regime's tenure in power either because of the threat of overthrow by enraged masses or because persistent high levels of conflict can be seen by aspiring elites as proof of incompetence by the current regime and hence as an excuse for a coup d'etat.

The above considerations imply a direct relationship between manifest conflict and coercion. More precisely, they suggest an accelerating relationship, because the regime is not likely to consider itself seriously endangered until certain levels of conflict are reached. Thereafter, however, the perceived danger—and hence the coercive response—probably grows exponentially. One form this may take is the ascension to power of hard-liners. This may result in a redefinition of the desired level of authoritarianism and hence in a concomitant acceleration of coercion.

As with our earlier discussion, though, there are constraining forces at work. Coercion is not a free activity; it involves significant costs. For one, coercion costs money: police and military forces must be paid, and military hardware is not inexpensive. Other costs, such as information, and loss of efficiency and initiative within the society are equally significant. A second type of constraint, especially relevant to many third world countries, is external in nature. Very high amounts of coercion can be so repugnant as to decrease assistance from both individual nations and international organizations. In short (to put it in economic language), above a certain threshold, the marginal costs of coercion begin to rise.

These considerations suggest a reaction curve of the type shown in figure 6.3. (Contrary to common usage, the dependent variable has been shown along the x-axis to facilitate comparison with figure 6.1. The x-intercept is determined by the levels of the exogenous variables referred to earlier.) At low levels of conflict, the regime responds with coercion in fairly direct fashion. At high levels of conflict, the response becomes exponential and a zone II is entered where the regime feels itself greatly endangered. In extreme cases, this zone can be seen as a discontinuity in the regime's reaction. (Such discontinuities may arise because a regime perceives conflict as dichotomous and thus as either threatening or not threatening to its tenure in power. When the level of conflict reaches this "knife-edge" threshold, the response is likely to be a quantum jump in coercion.) In the last zone, constraints become increasingly operative, and the reaction curve tails off.[10]

The interrelationships of MC and CA, depicted in figures 6.1 and 6.2, are structured and shaped by historical processes such as those

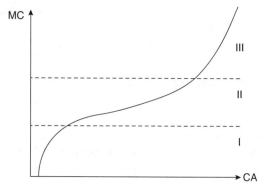

Figure 6.3   State reaction curve

specified in dependencia theory. But although longer-term process determine the shape and location of the respective curves, these processes may be treated as exogenous in the short-term period because of the slow rate at which they change. The rest of this chapter addresses the short-run changes in CA and MC that occur from the interaction of the state and opposition in the context of these historical circumstances.

A Simple Model

So far we have not really stated what each of the actors would "do" in various circumstances, but rather have simply described what circumstances each would desire given the actions of the other. After specifying a mechanism describing how each side alters its behavior in any given situation, we then move toward a model of the dynamic development of the political situation in the dependent state.

Consistent with our preceding discussion, we assume that the regime determines the level of CA and reacts by increasing or decreasing it in order to restore the political situation to a point lying on its reaction curve. (See our discussion of figure 6.5 below.) At points to the left of its reaction curve the regime will feel it is not expending sufficient resources in keeping the political situation (i.e., the opposition) under control and so will increase CA. On the other hand, at points to the right of its reaction curve the regime will tend to feel more secure and able to ease up by reducing the level of CA.

The description of how the opposition acts over time is similar. When members of the opposition find themselves at a point below their reaction curve, they will tend to increase the level of MC; but when they are above the curve, they will tend to reduce the level of MC. This is because a given level of CA in combination with the exogenously determined level of latent conflict will drive the opposition to a certain level of MC determined by the incentives and disincentives to such action. Above the curve, factors dissuading them from MC outweigh factors inducing them.

Earlier in the discussion of the two reaction curves, we mentioned that, in the extreme case, each could be viewed as having a discontinuity lying in middle range. We will temporarily assume that the curves take this extreme form in order to simplify the discussion, and later will relax this assumption. The first presentation also shows the two curves situated so that their "intersection" occurs along the two discontinuities. Although this is reasonable if the discontinuities are of significant size, it will be shown subsequently that this location for the intersection is not required for the model to yield reasonable results.

The final feature that we include in the model is designated to help incorporate the common empirical observation that it appears easier for regimes to expand coercion than to contract it. Once a state has imposed high levels of CA—even if the original intent had been only to deal with a particular "emergency" or threat to the state—it is extremely difficult for that state to ease up and lower the level of CA back to its original level. We crudely include this idea in our model by introducing the idea of a "ratchet" existing around the discontinuity, in the regime's reaction curve. That is to say that once the state passes the threshold implied by the discontinuity, it cannot return to its earlier level of CA, at least not within the context of this short-term model. This is a strong assumption about the step-level nature of the CA function, and in a more realistic and sophisticated model it could be replaced by an assumption about the different rates of speed with which the regime can increase or decrease CA. However, the ratchet effect does capture the spirit of those factors—fear of resurgence of civil strife, the "memories of the generals," and the effect of previous rises in CA in erecting bureaucratic structures of coercion within the state—which make the relaxation of CA so very much more difficult than its imposition.

Using the above assumptions, we can now present a simple model of the interaction of CA and MC in the dependent state. In figure 6.4

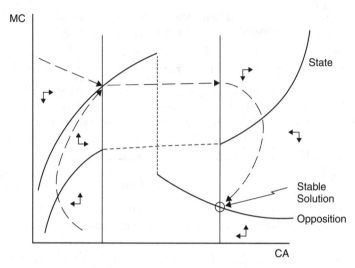

Figure 6.4   Graphical presentation of the simple model

the state opposition curves (with discontinuities) are presented together. The arrows illustrate which way each of the two sides would be moving in each of the "quadrants" determined by the two reaction curves. The two vertical lines represent the boundaries of the regime "ratchets," and the model never operates in the interior space defined by these lines except for the instantaneous crossing of the discontinuity once the regime reaches its "threshold."

The dashed curves illustrate how the system would move were it to find itself in the various locations in our two-dimensional space. The way we have drawn the relative heights of the curves puts the opposition as the determining force in the early parts of the con-flict when the tendency is to move along the opposition reaction curve (i.e., lower levels of CA and MC). However, once its thresh-old level of MC is approached, a "crackdown" occurs and the regime becomes the initiator. Finally a "stable" solution point is obtained at a situation of low levels of MC but very high levels of CA. The ratchet effect prevents the state from reducing CA below this point.

From this point on we will drop the assumption of a "ratchet" and explore the implications of the interrelationships of the two reaction curves. The slope of the two curves tells us how responsive each side is to changes in the actions and behavior of the other. The steeper the opposition curve, the more sharply that side reacts to changes in the regime-determined level of CA. Conversely, the flatter the state reaction curve, the more sharply the regime reacts to increases in the level of MC. The overall "heights" of the two curves reflect the general intensity of the underlying situation. These heights are determined by factors such as latent conflict, external dependence, and state involvement in the economy, which have been discussed as causes of opposition grievances and regime authoritarianism.

To analyze fully the implications of the model, we shall introduce some slightly technical terminology in order to keep our discussion clear. First, any intersection of the two curves may be said to be an equilibrium point, because if the society reaches such an intersection then both sides are on their respective reaction curves and so neither has an incentive to move from that point. However, because we are primarily interested in how the system moves through time, our focus will be largely on the *stability of these equilibrium points*. An equilibrium point is said to be stable if the system tends to return to that point if it is displaced from it. Later we see examples where an equilibrium is stable if the displacement is small (local stability) but where the system will not return to the equilibrium if the displacement is too large. If the system is unstable and values of MC and/or CA tend to become *either very large or very small* through time the system is characterized as "*explosive.*"

It is important to distinguish between the mathematical use of stability and the common notion of "political stability." Mathematical stability refers to the tendency of the system to maintain an unchanging situation through time. Thus, if the model predicted a system to sustain an equilibrium at high levels of both CA and MC, we would characterize this violent situation as a stable outcome. Alternatively, if the model predicts continuously decreasing levels of CA and MC, this represents an "explosive" situation—even though we might normally associate it with political stability.

Since each of the curves presented in figures 6.2 and 6.3 contain three "zones," there are nine possible combinations of zones where the curves may intersect. We can begin a discussion of the nature of these intersections (if any) by first looking at the three other feasible relationships of the zone I sections of the two curves (i.e., the zones nearest the origin on each curve) which, together with the relation shown in figure 6.5, exhaust the possibilities. The reader can verify that in figure 6.4 the result of the opposition curve always being above the regime curve at low levels of CA and MC is that the

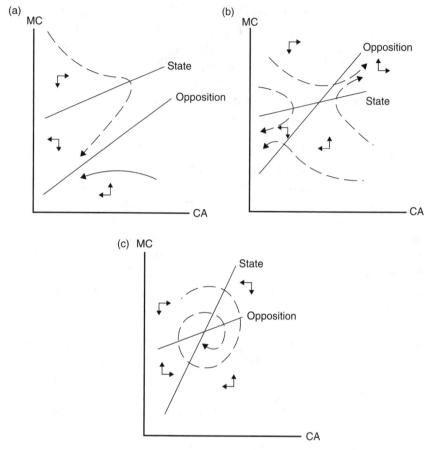

Figure 6.5   "Zone I–zone I" intersection possibilities (a) Case A; (b) Case B; (c) Case C

system moves to higher levels of each. The other relationships are:

Case A: (See figure 6.5a.) If the curves do not cross but the regime curve is higher, then the system moves toward very low levels of both MC and CA. In this situation both sides react more moderately to one another than was the case in figure 6.4, thus preserving lower levels of conflict in the society (e.g., Costa Rica since World War II?).

Case B: (See figure 6.5b.) The opposition curve cuts the regime curve from below. Now the intersection represents an unstable equilibrium point. If the society is able to maintain low levels of both CA and MC it will fare well, but if the two ever approach even moderately low levels of MC and CA there will be a tendency for the society to shoot off toward later stages of the model and the associated undesirable consequences. The instability of this equilibrium is due to the relatively high responsiveness of each side of the other's actions (e.g., Nigeria in the 1960s?).

Case C: (See figure 6.5c.) The regime curve cuts the opposition curve from below. The relatively low responsiveness of each side to the other—reflected in the slopes of the lines—will tend to lead to a stable equilibrium at low levels of MC and CA. This stability results because the slopes of the two curves indicate that the two sides each tend to react moderately to the other's actions. However, it is possible to have the regime curve cutting the opposition curve from below and still have a level of reactivity that makes the intersection itself unstable. A more explicit specification of the slopes of the two curves is necessary to distinguish the two possibilities fully; such a derivation will be presented later in the chapter (e.g., Colombia since the mid-1960s?).

These results can be extended to the eight other possibilities that can arise for the "zone of intersection." But, first it should be noted that if the regime curve is always the higher one then the system tends to move back toward the origin (as in Case A), whereas if the opposition curve is always higher (as in the early parts of figure 6.4) then the system tends to move toward even higher zones of CA and MC. Thus, it is only when the two curves cross that intermediate outcomes—the ones we refer to as "stable, nonexplosive" outcomes—can be maintained.

An examination of the eight other cases confirms our earlier results for the "zone I–zone I" intersection. The comparison of Cases B and C above shows that the responsiveness of the actors is crucial to the stability of the equilibria represented by intersections, and this result can be confirmed in general. *The less responsive the regime is to increases in MC* (i.e., the steeper the state reaction curve) *and the less responsive the opposition is to increases in CA* (i.e., the flatter the opposition reaction curve), *the more likely any intersection is to be stable*. Thus the zones we have earlier characterized as discontinuities separating zones I and II will tend to lead to unstable solutions even when the curves are not actually discontinuous. Other zones will be more likely to lead to stable solutions, but more knowledge of the exact shapes of the curves is required.

Dynamic Models

The "simple model" is inadequate for exploring the dynamic implications of the theory in more than a heuristic manner. Its "ratchets" and "discontinuities" are suggestive, but the underlying linear representation is still a gross simplification of the underlying theory. Direct empirical testing of this model would be inappropriate because: (1) we have not yet specified in a sufficiently precise form the dynamics of how the actors react; (2) we have no criteria for determining the location of the discontinuities; and (3) depending on how we choose to specify the dynamics of the reaction curves, at least one (and possibly both) of the two curves will not be identified and thus estimation is not possible. For these reasons we do not proceed with an empirical test, but instead further develop and explore the analytical model.

First it is necessary to specify the dynamic assumptions more precisely. By so doing, we can begin to evaluate the importance and relevance of various assumptions we have employed in developing our model. We will explore the implications of different shapes of the reaction curves on the stability of the system, the convergence of the system, and the levels of coercion and conflict that will tend to arise under particular conditions.

We choose the mathematical form that allows us to analyze those properties of the model that are of special interest while imposing the fewest demands for assumptions not already contained in the model. We have chosen to place our model in the form of a system of simultaneous difference equations in order to be able to analyze the dynamic properties of the system.[11] Difference equations deal with functions of discrete time periods (as opposed to differential equations, for example, which deal in continuous time). This manner of viewing time is most nearly consistent with our theoretical propositions, especially given the high salience of discrete events of coercion and conflict in the reaction of the state and opposition (e.g., food riots, or Indira Gandhi's mass arrests).

In order to examine this wholly dynamic model, we must first specify the speed with which the state and the opposition respond to the other's actions. In particular, we assume that the state responds to changes in the level of activity of the opposition much more quickly than the opposition reacts to the activities of the state. Of course, in some instances the opposition does respond instantaneously. However, by viewing the level of MC as a pattern of responses over a certain period of time, our assumption of delayed response is reasonable. Regimes usually command superior informational resources and organizational capacity compared with those of the opposition. In addition, in most settings the state operates more in the open while the opposition is restricted to relatively secret, and hence less efficient, means of organizing its activities. We model these different rates of response by assuming that the state response to manifest conflict is instantaneous while the opposition responds to the level of coercion with a one period time lag. This time period is not a constant calendar period but rather a reaction period, which is the rough analogue of the responses referred to in the simple model.

For the moment we use a linear approximation. In essence we abstract from our theory linear predictions of the reciprocal effects of coercion and conflict upon one another. While this is a further simplification, it is appropriate for a first analysis of the system in the neighborhood of equilibrium points. Hence, we model the two reaction curves as

$$CA_t = c + dMC_t \qquad \text{(State)} \qquad\qquad (1)$$

$$MC = a - bCA_{t-1} \qquad \text{(Opposition)} \qquad\qquad (2)$$

The slope parameters d and b are measures of the intensity with which the two sides react to each other, while the intercepts c and a are some indication of the levels of coercion and conflict, respectively. These intercepts are the result both of exogenous factors and of the scaling of CA and MC. This warns us that the precise location of the origin in any graph is partly arbitrary.

In order to proceed, we must solve the two equations in terms of either CA or MC. Mathematically, the choice is arbitrary. We choose to formulate the model in terms of CA because we have a better knowledge of its actual movement over time. Since World War II, increasingly coercive regimes have appeared throughout most of the underdeveloped world. There also have been periods of relatively stable levels of coercion within that pattern. These two observations in the development of coercion over time are stronger than any such statements we might make about the level of manifest conflict.

We solve equations (1) and (2) for CA_t and obtain

$$CA_t = c + da - dbCA_{t-i}. \qquad\qquad (3)$$

Solving this first order linear difference equation,[12] in terms of an initial value of coercion, CA_0, and the equilibrium value of coercion, CA^*:

$$CA_t = (CA_0 - CA^*)(-db)^t + CA^* \qquad\qquad (4)$$

We see from equation (4) that the current level of CA depends on its equilibrium value, on how far the system "started" from the value, on how much time has elapsed since the system started, and on the values of d and b. These last two terms are of greatest interest to us in evaluating the stability and the convergence of the system.

The system will be stable if $| -db| < 1$. This means that as t gets very large the first term in equation (4) approaches zero and the value of CA_t will approach CA^*. *This confirms our earlier conclusion that the model will be stable only in situations where the state and the opposition react moderately to each other's actions.* On the other hand, if one or both of the actors respond very strongly to the other's acts, then the system will tend to explode.

As the magnitude of $(-db)$ determines the stability of the system so its sign determines whether the system will oscillate or converge. The implication of oscillation is that there will be a cycle of alternating high and low levels of coercion, as in Argentina. If $(-db) < 0$, then the system will tend to oscillate. That is, if the quantity being raised to the power t in equation (4) is negative, then the first term in the equation will turn from positive to negative as t goes from even to odd.

A useful way of illustrating these results (in fact, an alternative way of deriving these results) is by use of a phase diagram. A phase diagram allows us to show graphically the time path of a variable in a dynamic system. With the linear approximation, this tool will give the same results as we have already shown. However, in more complex approximations the phase diagram will be used where algebraic analysis is inadequate.

We construct a phase diagram by plotting CA_t against CA_{t+1} as given by equation (3) for an illustrative set of values for a, b, c, and d. In figures 6.6 and 6.7 we have done this for two different sets of values. In figure 6.6, $|db| < 1$, while $(-db) < 0$. Hence, we would expect a stable equilibrium to exist, and therefore the system to converge toward that equilibrium. To show this, we construct a time path on the phase diagram in the following way. First we assume at some time t_0 the level of CA_t is A_0. Our phase diagram (which tells us what value of CA_{t+i} will result from any given value of CA_t) indicates that at time t_1 we will move to point A_1 as indicated on the CA_{t+1} axis. To proceed to the next period, we must locate the point A_1 on the CA_t axis. To do this, we use the 45° line shown in figure 6.6. From this we find A_1 on the CA_t axis and map it onto A_2 at the following time period, t_2. It becomes evident that we are moving

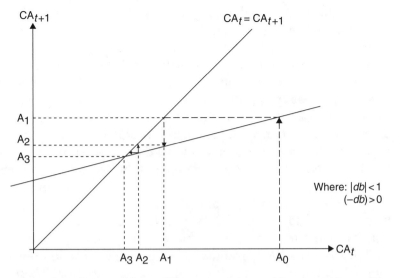

Figure 6.6   Phase diagram of linear difference equation model under stable conditions

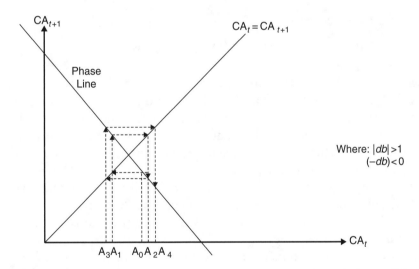

Figure 6.7   Phase diagram of linear difference equation model under explosive conditions

directly (i.e., converging) to the point where the phase diagram intersects the 45° line. Once we reach that point, we are at an equilibrium since a map from A_3 will result in A_3 at the following time period. This equilibrium is by definition stable because no matter what point is chosen at A_0, the time path from that point will lead to the equilibrium at A_3. Analogously, one can construct the time paths in figure 6.7 to demonstrate that the system will oscillate and explode, as a result of the fact that $|db| < 1$, while $(-db) < 0$.

These results are useful and interesting to the extent that, at least with respect to the neighborhood of an equilibrium, the two reaction curves are adequately approximated by linear functions. To examine more general conditions in a slightly more realistic, and complex, form, we turn to nonlinear approximations of the reaction curves. In particular we are now prepared to model the two equations in a non-linear form that allows us to examine stability and convergence conditions more reliably over the whole range of interactions rather than just in the neighborhood of the equilibrium.

If we return to figure 6.2, we recognize in the opposition's manifest conflict reaction curve what can roughly be modeled as a second degree equation (parabola) while the state's reaction function (figure 6.3) can be represented by a third degree equation. These can be expressed in the following form:

$$MC_t = a_0 + a_1 CA_{t-1} + a_2 CA_{t-1}^2 \qquad \text{(Opposition)} \qquad (5)$$

$$MC_t = b_0 + b_1 CA_t + b_2 CA_t^2 + b_3 CA_t^3 \qquad \text{(State)} \qquad (6)$$

where we constrain the parameters in the following ways: $a_1 > 0$, $a_2 < 0$, $b_1 > 0$, $b_2^2 < 3b_1$, and $b_3 > 0$.[13] These constraints do no more than insure that the mathematical forms correspond to the reaction functions we described earlier. Each parameter may be roughly construed as reflecting a line (or set of lines) of argument in our statement of motivations underlying the reaction functions. The essence of all three arguments linking rising levels of CA to increased levels of MC is captured in a_1, while a_2 reflects the "deterrent" effect of coercion. Considering the situation where CA is equal to 0, we see that a_0 represents the level of conflict desired by the opposition in response to forces outside the short-term focus of this analysis. The sensitivity of the regime to the maintenance of a stable order in society for its own sake or for other purposes is captured by b_3. The responsiveness to threats to the regime itself is reflected largely in b_2 while the response to the costs of coercion is reflected in the ratio of b_1 to b_2. Finally, b_0 reflects the maximum level of MC that the state will tolerate without resorting to coercion.[14]

Solving equations (5) and (6) for MC_t yields a first order third degree nonlinear difference equation for CA which is not immediately amenable to analysis of the sort performed above. If we knew the values of all seven parameters, we could construct a phase diagram and analyze its time paths for stability and convergence conditions. Unfortunately, we do not know the values of the parameters in this complex system.

In the absence of sufficient algebraic techniques, and of determined values of the parameters, we use computer simulation to evaluate the impact of different parametric values on the dynamics of the mathematical (and political) system.[15] We begin by setting $b_3 = 1$, which requires that our interpretations of other coefficients be relative to b_3 rather than absolute in any sense. Although the absolute levels of the two constants affect the final *level* of the system, it is only their relationship that affects the dynamics of the system. Thus we combine the two constants, a_0 and b_0, into a composite measure, c_0, of the "average" intensity of the reaction functions, $c_0 = a_0 - b_0$. Finally, using nonzero values for the parameters between -1.5 and 1.5 (incrementing by .5), we construct a phase diagram for every combination of permissible values. For example, $a_1 = .5, 1.0, 1.5; a_2 = -1.5, -1.0, -.5;$ and $c_0 = -1.5, -1.0, -.5,$ .5, 1.0, 1.5. This procedure generates 866 sets of parameters. For each of these sets we draw a phase diagram for CA, and it is from this group that we shall now generalize. Clearly, the results reported below are limited by the assumptions of our simulation. Nonetheless, the results are generally suggestive.

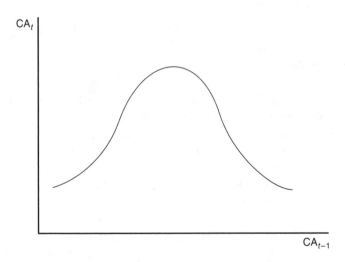

Figure 6.8   The characteristic phase diagram for CA

The first thing we observe is the emergence of a bell-shaped curve as the characteristic phase diagram of CA, as illustrated in figure 6.8. In addition, the typical shape shows a strong tendency for equilibria to be mathematically stable. In other words, the absolute value of the slope of the phase diagrams is almost always less than 1. As we discussed above (in the context of the simple model), mathematical stability implies that a system at equilibrium which is disturbed or shocked by some outside force will tend to return to the equilibrium. This suggests that, at least over the range of parameters used in this simulation, the results of the state-oppression interaction will be largely immune from disturbances caused by other short-run influences as they might arise.

In addition, the bell-shaped phase diagram allows three distinct possible time paths for CA, as illustrated in figure 6.9. As path A shows, there will be a rapid return to an equilibrium if the equilibrium level of CA should be disturbed. This might roughly be interpreted as corresponding to the experience of those peripheral societies (e.g., Costa Rica, Mexico) where low levels of CA have tended to persist. As paths B and C show, a state may reach a high level of CA either by a converging or an oscillating movement, roughly corresponding to the experience of most peripheral countries since World War II.[16] Whether the path is steady or erratic depends upon the location of the equilibrium relative to (i.e., to the right or left of) the "peak" of the phase diagram.

Thus, it is important to analyze the factors in the initial reaction functions that yield an equilibrium of CA at a high or a low level, and that locate the equilibrium in such a way as to produce converging or oscillating time paths. Unfortunately, casual analysis of the more than 800 phase diagrams does not reveal simple answers to these complex questions. Therefore, we randomly select 91 phase diagrams to analyze in more detail. In particular, we use statistical analysis to evaluate the direct linear effects of the parameters of the reaction functions on the time path implied for CA by the interaction. Of course, we miss the nonlinear effects of the parameters and the results of many potentially significant interactions of parameters. Nonetheless, we find significant, interesting results consistent with the simpler analyses above.

The time path of CA oscillates only when the ratio of a_1 to a_2 is larger than some threshold. When a_1/a_2 is relatively large, we have a situation in which the exacerbating effects of state coercion on the opposition outweigh the deterrent effects of that coercion

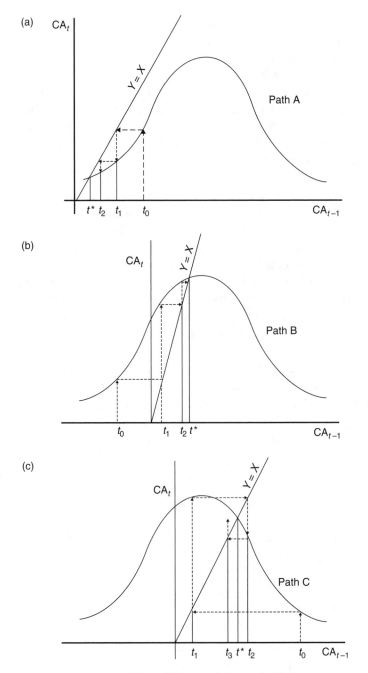

Figure 6.9   Phase diagrams of CA with equilibrium and time path (diagrams not drawn to same scale) Path A: Rapid return to low coercion; Path B: Unstable coercion; Path C: Coercion deters conflict.

throughout the lower ranges of coercion. In this circumstance, we find the politically unstable result of a political system stumbling uncertainly around and toward the equilibrium level of coercion. On the other hand, when the deterrent effects of coercion dominate the exacerbating effects of coercion in the relevant range, the result is a steady time path for CA, one in which, given a disturbance from an equilibrium, the regime will move in the direction of the equilibrium without interruption. Thus, the nature of the equilibrium (whether disturbances result in direct or indirect return) is a function of whether the effects of coercion on conflict tend toward provocation or toward deterrence. While only one cause is important in determining the oscillation or convergence of the mathematical system, three factors appear to influence the equilibrium level of CA. First, the *higher* the average intensity of the reaction (c_0), the *higher* the equilibrium. Second, the *lower* the level of conflict at which the state jumps to a higher level of coercion (b_1/b_2), the *lower* the equilibrium level of CA. Third, when the ratio of exacerbating to deterrent effects of coercion (a_1/a_2) is either *very much larger* or *smaller* than the threshold mentioned above, the equilibrium level of CA will be relatively low.

This final result requires further comment. The case where a_1/a_2 is very large might correspond to those societies in which ideological "hegemony" has led oppressed classes to regard the status quo as legitimate.[17] In these circumstances, any major increase in coercion would threaten to shatter that legitimacy and thus result in massive resistance. In this event, the model developed here implies a low level of coercion. However, where a_1/a_2 is very small, we have the case of repressed societies (e.g., Indonesia and Iran). In this case, the model also implies a low level of CA at equilibrium, which clearly *underestimates* the actual situation. Thus, we find that in the case of societies in which the deterrent effects of coercion predominate the model fails to fully account for the observed time paths of CA in the world.

Concluding Remarks

Recall some of the initial qualifications of this analysis. It is not useful for microlevel investigations. It is neither intended for the prediction of individual events, nor for identifying a specific coup or actors or types of action. Rather, it is concerned with patterns of behavior by the state and by the opposition. Nor is it designed for tracing patterns of behavior over very long historical periods (which are more adequately addressed by our larger project mentioned in note 2). Perhaps even for decade-long periods this model's results may be reasonably satisfactory; but over 25- or 50-year periods some of the excluded variables are likely to change, producing explosion toward high levels of coercion or, occasionally, toward much lower levels. To understand why this is so, we must reexamine some of our basic assumptions.

We remarked earlier that in extremely coercive states (in which the deterrent effect of coercion on manifest conflict is quite strong), the present model appears to underestimate the equilibrium level of coercion. This requires some explanation. In a relatively advanced industrial state, effective coercion can come with the expensive technology and sophisticated security forces that a fairly high income level can maintain (e.g., perhaps Eastern Europe and the USSR). In less wealthy states, however, there can be other ways of supporting an effective coercive apparatus. Here we must reintroduce the *external system*: a less-developed state may support its coercive apparatus through a pattern of dependence. A dependent state may acquire the necessary hardware, technology, and training from a metropole. Additionally (and to some degree alternatively) a state adopting the principles of dependent economic development (e.g., orientation toward the world market or a very rapid growth of GNP per capita coupled with high income inequalities) may produce enough wealth that can be skimmed off to support a state security apparatus of which many components are indigenous. By this reasoning, it is the level of adequate resources available to the state, not the extent of dependence, that accounts for high levels of coercion. With this interpretation we have a general model applicable to both dependent and nondependent states. From another perspective, however, the principal means of attaining a high level of coercion that are available to a relatively *poor* state must be through *some* form of *dependence*, so this factor must still be introduced to the model.[18]

We thus have relaxed our initial assumption that the impact of the external system is held constant. Another assumption was that *latent conflict* is constant. Obviously that is not true over longer time periods. Especially under conditions of moderately high coercion, the strains of nascent development may cause substantial latent conflict to build up. With the deterrent effect of coercion only moderate, and latent conflict rising, the opposition's manifestation of that conflict may go up very sharply—especially in response to some "exogenous" shock such as the death or deposition of a traditional ruler. Such rising levels of manifest conflict may then interact with coercion in a spiral of repression and civil war. (This may capture much of what has happened in Ethiopia, and may perhaps also be seen in earlier stages in contemporary Central America, as basically conservative religious figures become radicalized by the combination of inequality and coercion.) Here again the *external system* matters, for without it there would be no dependent development as a cause of latent conflict.

Another variable included in the causal chain of our larger model, but held constant here, is *government involvement in the economy.* Where statist interests in the economy become large, the state is likely to become less tolerant of manifest economic conflict and readier to apply coercion for the purpose of repressing it. Possibly we see something of this in contemporary Brazil, where reductions in the level of manifest conflict have not brought equivalent reductions in coercion.

This recalls our earlier observations that coercion *responds differently* to conflict when the latter increases from the way it responds when the latter decreases. Our mathematical expressions in the difference equations treated the response rates in each direction as equal, but the graphical formulation of our simple model was expressed to account for a "ratchet" whereby the state could increase its level of coercive-authoritarianism sharply but, once having done so, be unable to reduce CA even after manifest conflict was effectively suppressed. One of the mechanisms we invoked to account for this was bureaucratic inertia: once a large coercive apparatus is built, and draconian methods approved (mass arrests, torture), it is hard to disband or leash the coercers (again, perhaps Brazil or Chile).

In fact, of course, an adequate expression of the relationship would be somewhere *between* the two extremes applied in our modeling efforts. Surely, coercion is easier applied than relaxed, as reflected in our observation about rising levels of coercion in the third world over recent decades. But *shifts downward*—even sometimes sharp and substantial shifts—*do occur*. Such a shift occurred temporarily in Thailand in 1973–75, followed by a reimposition of coercion under conditions that seem to fit our model. One thinks also of the coups and subsequent rapid liberalization of Portugal and Greece in 1974, and the 1977 free elections in India and the subsequent departure of Indira Gandhi. More interesting still is the liberalization of Spain, commencing before but accelerating after Franco's death. While Spain (and perhaps Portugal and Greece) is too "European" and too developed to fit many definitions of a dependent state, the case may nevertheless be instructive both for dependencia theory and for a more general modeling effort. Perhaps much of the latent conflict in Spain had been polarized around Franco himself; with his death the level of latent conflict finally dropped.[19] Also, the new leaders of a rapidly industrializing country probably perceived much higher economic and political costs in coercion. In any case, the level of coercion applied by the state went down fairly far and rapidly despite the fact that manifest conflict rose (strikes, and terrorist acts by separatist and other extreme groups).[20] This, too must be accounted for.

A final point should be mentioned. Thus far we have treated both state and opposition as *reacting* to each other's actions, and have developed the dynamic implications of those reactions. These implications, it should be made clear, are not consequences that are aimed at by either side. Thus, when we speak of systems "stumbling" to equilibrium levels of coercion, we do not mean to imply that either state or opposition is aiming for those levels; rather both sides are reacting to each other, and the way in which they arrive at an equilibrium (and, for that matter, whether an equilibrium is reached) is purely a function of the sensitivity of their reactions (i.e., the values of the parameters).

What we have done, in short, is to put forward an *action–reaction* model, rather than a *strategic* one. The former emphasizes the reactions of each side to the other's actions; the latter concentrates on the goals underlying those reactions. The former treats goals as being satisfied instantly; the latter sees goals as being attained over a period of time. And the former treats goals, for all intents and purposes, as fixed, whereas the latter highlights the possibility of changing objectives.

These differences, it should be emphasized, are not absolute; they are questions of degree, and our model does incorporate some strategic assumptions. We would anticipate, moreover, that our model would yield consistent results, though distinct, from a strategic approach. For example, the high levels of coercion present in Argentina in recent years can be predicted by both approaches. Where they would differ would be their focus. Our model would emphasize the regime's strong *reaction* to guerrilla attacks on army installations. On the other hand, a strategic approach, focusing on the goals of the regime, might emphasize the regime's *goal* (because of the high price of oil) of stable export earnings and its concomitant use of coercion against threats to the business "climate."

We need to explore the conditions thoroughly, both with system-atic empirical investigation rather than the illustrations employed here and with changes in our model. To explain explosive changes in coercion and conflict, we must attend both to changes of the para-meters of the model (e.g., in the deterrent effect of coercion) and to the structure of the system (e.g., in the level of conflict at which a threat to the regime is perceived). To account for these and other changes, our model is presently underspecified; good theory can help us to build a more complete one.

Chapter 7

Islam, Authoritarianism, and Female Empowerment: What Are the Linkages?

With Daniela Donno

Most Islamic countries are governed by authoritarian regimes, and in most Islamic countries women's economic, social, and political rights are significantly less than those of the men of their country. These well-known facts provide the basis for a highly original and important analysis by M. Steven Fish.[1] Fish's major contribution is his suggestion that the relationships at issue are not merely a matter of spurious correlation but rather are indicative of a deep underlying causal pattern. In a sophisticated cross-national quantitative analysis, he shows the following:

1. Even controlling for many other alleged influences on countries' political systems, countries with a largely Islamic religious tradition have significantly more autocratic governments than do non-Islamic countries.
2. Controlling for level of economic development, the condition of women is significantly worse in Islamic countries than in others.
3. In a more limited test, even when controlling for economic development and Islamic tradition, a low level of women's rights may produce lower levels of democracy.
4. More speculatively, Islamic states may be more autocratic so as to repress women's rights more effectively, or autocratic government may permit and even require the repression of a range of human rights, including those of women. This second causal arrow may replace the one just above, or the two may reinforce each other in a feedback loop.

Fish combines his quantitative analysis with a wide-ranging theoretical and factual review of the relationships among Islam, democracy, and female empowerment. We will not significantly add to or modify that part of his contribution. We are, however, skeptical of cultural arguments about why some states are authoritarian. Such arguments, after all, were made about Asian and Latin American cultures, yet democracy now flourishes in many such states. Thus we replicate and modify his quantitative analyses to see whether his findings are robust, and we address the question of complex causation. In doing so we find the following:

1. Islamic countries in general are more likely to be ruled autocratically even when other influences are controlled. But Arab countries in particular are more often ruled autocratically. So, too, are states that have frequently engaged in international military conflicts. However, the effects of culture can change dramatically. Before 1980, countries with large Catholic populations were even less likely than Islamic ones to have democratic governments, but that relationship subsequently turned strongly positive.

2. Islamic countries generally are more likely than others to repress some rights of women. But the effect is much stronger and more consistent for Arab countries in particular.

3. The evidence that autocratic governments systematically repress women's rights in particular is at best inconsistent rather than general and distinctive. Furthermore, we find little indication that female empowerment contributes causally to democratic government as measured by specific indicators.

4. Thus, while Islamic religious tradition and especially characteristics of Arab states or culture do seem to support both autocratic government and the repression of women, our analysis does not support the view that the repression of women is central to maintaining autocratic rule in Arab or other Islamic states or that greater democracy in those countries would greatly improve women's conditions on a broad range of measures. Our analysis of more nuanced equations for female empowerment finds the relationships among regime, Islamic/Arab tradition, and the status of women to be more complex than Fish suggests. In addition, such causal relationships as there are differ depending on the issue-area being considered. Female political rights, economic activity, health, and educational attainment should be treated as distinct measures and not substituted for one another as general proxies for the status of women.

Our contribution, while supporting much of Fish's argument, is thus to greatly weaken major parts of it, especially about any causal role linking women's rights to Islam and democracy. These results leave still largely unanswered the question of *why* countries with a largely Islamic or Arab tradition tend to be more autocratic and to keep their women so little empowered, as measured by conventional criteria of human rights. They also raise fundamental and more general questions about the role of culture and democracy in enhancing the condition of women.

Does Islamic Tradition Discourage Democracy?

We begin with the analysis of determinants of democracy, taking off from Fish's analysis. In numerous regression analyses, he examines the effects of many hypothesized influences, including level of economic development and recent economic growth, sociocultural division, colonial or communist heritage, OPEC membership, and Islamic religious tradition. Of these he finds only three exert a strong and consistent impact: economic development, OPEC membership, and Islamic tradition. We nevertheless suspected that his analysis could be more finely and completely specified.

The correlation between democracy and economic development is one of the strongest and oldest in the literature. Although the particular nature of any causal relationship is strongly contested among scholars, we are inclined to believe in a causal linkage from economic development to the sustainability and perhaps the initiation of democracy, as well as perhaps a reverse arrow from democracy back to development.[2] Since our purpose is not to enter the debate on the reciprocality of the relationship between development and democracy, we simply accept—in the company of Fish and many others—the plausibility of a causal arrow from development to democracy and include development as one independent variable affecting democracy. We also concur with Fish that the independent effects of recent economic growth, sociocultural division, and colonial or communist heritage are inconsistent and at best weak. Consequently we omit them here.

For purposes of replication we conduct our analyses on the same set of countries Fish used, and we use his data whenever we use his variables. When we change or add a variable, we discuss the measure and source and provide details in the appendix available on the web as identified in the unnumbered note. Our reservations concern, first, two of the measures that he finds to have strong and robust effects and, second, possible underspecification in the equations.

OPEC membership is the first of the two measurement decisions with which we quibble. Fish chooses this as a proxy for the theoretical variable of resource abundance, notably its availability to authoritarian actors to buy off large segments of the populace and thus stunt demands for political accountability and its enablement of the state to sustain a large and powerful internal security apparatus. Similarly resource abundance is one of the most commonly and successfully employed variables in examinations of the causes of civil wars.[3] But a dummy variable for OPEC membership unnecessarily loses the potential explanatory power of an interval variable of more or less oil, specifically, the ratio of oil and other fuel income to the economy. It is more plausible to hypothesize a continuous relationship; that is, the greater the relative input of *fuel income* to the total GDP, the greater the ability of an authoritarian regime to sustain itself. Even more relevant may be the ratio of the value of *fuel exports* to GDP, as that more directly measures the regime's potential to import hard-currency consumer goods and security equipment to monitor and suppress dissent.[4]

The other measure we modify is Fish's dummy variable for Islamic religious tradition. He uses "predominance" of Muslims as the "tipping point" for substantial Islamic influence on politics (p. 7). This is especially plausible when considering influences on democracy, since an Islamic majority could in some kinds of democratic systems impose its practices on the entire population. Nevertheless, the binary variable still discards valuable information about the relative impact of small or large Islamic populations on state policy and is at least equally problematic for our later discussion of influences on female empowerment. Thus, for example, the subjugation of women may be largely the result of overt state action or of less formal social practices that may be enabled by state nonintervention in religious cultures. Especially for the latter, the appropriate hypothesis would be the larger the number of *Muslims as a percentage of the total population*, the lower the country's overall level of female empowerment—potentially strengthening Fish's argument.[5]

We identify an additional five possible variables for his equation to explain democracy. First, it is increasingly recognized that a state's political neighborhood matters. In his discussion of conditions producing transitions to democracy, Huntington mentions "snowballing," or demonstration effects, enhanced by international communication, as transitions to democracy serve as models for their neighbors. Similarly, among conditions that favor the consolidation of new democracies, he identifies a favorable international political environment, with outside assistance.[6] The notion of a favorable international environment can readily be extended to a low-threat environment, where the new democracy does not fear attack or subversion by its neighbors and consequently does not need to enhance its military capabilities or suppress civil liberties in the name of national security. It is reasonable to expect that democratic neighbors would be perceived as less threatening. Maoz found that the probability of a transition to democracy was strongly related to the average level of democracy in a state's "politically relevant international environment," defined largely though not exclusively in geographic terms.[7] More recently, Gleditsch establishes strong correlations between the average level of democracy among contiguous neighbors and both the absence of violent conflict by a state with those neighbors and that state's own level of democracy. Pevehouse reports that regional international organizations composed largely of democratic states can ease both democratic transitions and consolidation.[8]

Accordingly, we add a measure of the *degree of democracy in the neighborhood*.[9] This is particularly important for our question here, since most Islamic countries are found in neighborhoods composed largely of undemocratic countries. Any causal relationship could therefore be ambiguous at the very least. Islam and perhaps certain other cultures may be inherently antithetical to democracy, and cultures in turn are largely the product of regional influences (e.g., Islamic countries are concentrated in Africa, the Middle East, and South and Southeast Asia). Or autocracies may in general sustain each other, perhaps deliberately through imitation or inadvertently by mounting threats against one another and thereby providing a reason or excuse for target governments to suppress democratic liberties.[10] Controlling for neighbors' level of democracy will help tell us whether Islam still makes an independent contribution to the likelihood of authoritarian government.

The second variable is the previous experience of democracy in a country. Theories of path dependence and consolidation of regimes are common. Again we cite Huntington, who proposes that "a longer and more recent experience with democracy is more conducive than is a shorter and more distant one."[11] Przeworski et al. discuss the relative staying power of democracy and dictatorship, and Maoz notes the importance of past regime instability to subsequent regime change.[12] From these we draw the hypothesis that the level of democracy in a state will be greater the higher the *average level of democracy in preceding years*. We use every year of independence from 1970 to 1990 to include the most recent and relatively uniform period of experience for all countries.[13] Again this matters for Islamic countries with their largely nondemocratic institutional experience: is the absence of a democratic history a general influence operating to reduce the current level of democracy or, even controlling for such a general influence, are Islamic countries still especially likely to be nondemocratic?

A third potentially important influence on democracy appears in Fish's final equations (Table 9 and 10), where he adds several measures of women's rights but drops OPEC membership. We restore it—or rather, include our alternative measure of fuel export dependence.

We include Fish's measures of female empowerment but also supplement them. We follow him in using the *gap between female and male literacy* rates, the *sex ratio of males to females*,[14] and the *percentage of women in government* as ministerial and subministerial officials. In addition to Fish's measures we use the following: (1) *the percentage of seats held in parliament by women* as a supplement to the percentage of women in government; (2) *the ratio of female life expectancy at birth to that of males*; (3) *the ratio of female to male enrollment in primary, secondary, and tertiary education combined*; and (4) the *ratio of economically active females 15 years and above to males*.[15] Together these seven measures cover major aspects of women's rights (indeed of all people, as recognized by the Universal Declaration of Human Rights),[16] with economic activity and two each for education, health (and life), and representation in politics; this reduces the reliance on a single, possibly misleading measure. The measure for female economic activity may underreport unpaid labor, but it is uncorrelated with per capita GDP and so may be especially influenced by religious and other cultural values.

The fourth addition to the set of explanatory variables concerns whether the lack of democracy is more a phenomenon characteristic of Arab states in particular than of Islamic countries in general. Certainly in the years 1999–2001 no Arab state reached a score of better than 3 (Jordan) on the Freedom House scale or −2 (Yemen) on the Polity scale, whereas a number of non-Arab states with majority Islamic populations did so. The principal cultural explanation is that Arab patriarchal family structure is reproduced in authoritarian government and civil society.[17] Yet a recent analysis offers several perceptive political rather than cultural explanations: low nation-state identity due to pan-Arabism, the weakness of nationalism in states with rather arbitrary borders following the collapse of the Ottoman Empire, and the international security tensions deriving from the extended Arab-Israeli conflict.[18] Another political interpretation stresses historical experience, arguing that the defeat of Arab states in the 1967 war with Israel strengthened radical Islamic movements as the best organized opposition to authoritarian Arab governments—and that this in turn frightened many secular liberals into supporting those governments' efforts to exclude and suppress the Islamists.[19] We cannot sort out these competing explanations for a particular low level of democracy in Arab states here, but we can at least test whether, while controlling for the possible other influences, adding a variable for states that are members of the *Arab League* makes an empirical difference.[20]

For a separate measure of international tensions, we add the number of *fatal militarized disputes* (MIDs) in which each state was involved during the years 1991–2000. Our measure includes all involved countries, regardless of who initiated the dispute, and uses only relatively severe disputes on the principle that sustained multiyear involvement with some casualties is especially likely to place constraints on democracy for the purported goal of enhancing national security.[21]

A final improvement is the use of a lag structure that more accurately captures the possibly causal relationships in question. After first reproducing column 4 from Fish's Table 5 using his measure of democracy for 1991–2000, we then switch to a shorter and later period for democracy, the years 1998–99 through 2000–01, as the dependent variable in the rest of our table 7.1. This change is especially important because the indicators of women's status that Fish (and we) employ are taken from the mid-1990s.

For the dependent variable we follow Fish's use, in his Tables 3 and 10, of Freedom House data with the most free coded at 7 and the least at 1. These data are slightly more complete than Polity's, particularly for the 1990s, and in any case Fish found his results robust to the two indicators. Both Polity and Freedom House essentially measure liberal democracy, with an emphasis largely on institutions in the former and greater attention to civil liberties in the latter. Because neither gives much attention to gender equality per se, we are able to assess how much they are impacted by our independent indicators of women's rights.[22]

Our full set of explanatory variables now includes level of development, OPEC membership, percentage of population Islamic, fuel exports, level of democracy in the neighborhood, previous experience of democracy, MID involvement, and lagged measures of female empowerment. With this more complete specification, better lag structure, and the revised measures, we hypothesized as follows:

H1: *The net effect of the revised and additional variables will be to sharply reduce the explanatory contribution of Islam to regime type, making it no longer statistically significant.*

Table 7.1 presents these analyses, with the coefficient for each independent variable and the standard error directly below it. Statistically significant results are indicated with asterisks. Significance is calculated for one-tailed tests, since our hypotheses and controls indicate the expected direction of association. Model 1 shows Fish's equation with his data (from his Table 5, column 4), and model 2 modifies that with our shorter and later period for measuring democracy as the dependent variable, as well as our continuous measures for Islamic tradition and fuel export dependence[23] and neighbors' democracy and previous experience of democracy. There are some differences in the coefficients for the key variables identified by Fish (economic development, Islam, and OPEC/fuel exports), but all of those coefficients remain quite significant. The added variables of neighborhood effects and previous experience of democracy are also highly significant. Despite the additions, the importance of Islam is only moderately reduced and is still strongly evident. Previous experience of democracy somewhat diminishes the effect of Islamic tradition; but since Islamic tradition surely also affected previous levels of democracy, the difference is not very meaningful.[24] So far our hypothesis is rejected and Fish's is supported.

Model 3 modifies the last equation by adding membership in the Arab League. The only material change is to reduce somewhat the influence of Islamic population in general, but even so the coefficient for Islam is statistically more significant than that for Arab. Arab states are even more likely than other Islamic countries to be governed autocratically, but the additional effect is not strong. The same is true in model 4 when the measure of MID involvement is added. Islamic population retains its significantly negative coefficient, but being Arab and engaged in extended high-level international confrontations adds to a low probability of democracy.

Table 7.1 Regression of freedom house scores on hypothesized determinants

Variable	Model 1: Fish's Table 3	Model 2: New D.V.	Model 3: Arab League	Model 4: MID Involvement	Model 5: Literacy Gap	Model 6: Sex Ratio	Model 7: Women in Govt.	Model 8: Women in Parliament	Model 9: Education Ratio	Model 10: Life Expectancy	Model 11: Economic Activity
Constant	−.319	1.583**	1.340**	1.455**	1.966**	2.554	1.181*	1.455**	1.573**	−.513	1.106*
	(.591)	(.528)	(.538)	(.548)	(.757)	(2.490)	(.560)	(−551)	(.668)	(3.989)	(.613)
Islamic Religious Tradition Dummy Variable	−1.288***										
	(.262)										
Economic Development	1.530***	.750***	.824**	.826***	.695**	.829***	.811***	.826***	.863***	.764***	.820***
	(.163)	(.186)	(.188)	(.197)	(.239)	(.225)	(.197)	(.198)	(.224)	(.237)	(.199)
OPEC Membership	−1.574***										
	(.464)										
Islamic Population		−1.233***	−.912**	−.783*	−.784*	−.782*	−.750*	−.783*	−.812*	−.780*	−.766*
		(.307)	(.371)	(.375)	(.378)	(.378)	(.384)	(.374)	(.385)	(.382)	(.381)
Fuel Exports		−2.976***	−2.723**	−2.624**	−2.489**	−2.479**	−2.507**	−2.620**	−2.618**	−2.620**	−2.464**
		(.935)	(.916)	(1.007)	(1.185)	(1.185)	(1.000)	(1.032)	(1.010)	(1.018)	(1.028)
Neighborhood		.084***	.082***	.078***	.079***	.079***	.056*	.078***	.079***	.075**	.081***
		(.025)	(.024)	(.024)	(.02)	(.025)	(.024)	(.024)	(.024)	(.024)	(.023)
Previous Experience with Democracy		.143***	.135***	.132***	.134***	.137**	.118**	.132**	.130***	.144**	.139***
		(.039)	(.04)	(.041)	(.042)	(.045)	(.040)	(.043)	(.042)	(.049)	(.042)
Arab League			−.599*	−.677*	−.562	−.590	−.530	−.677*	−.669*	−.621*	−.582
			(.341)	(.339)	(.350)	(.369)	(.322)	(.349)	(.337)	(.358)	(.364)
MID Involvement				−.222**	−.200*	−.220**	−.201**	−.222**	−.221**	−.222**	—
				(.086)	(.102)	(.086)	(.084)	(.085)	(.086)	(.087)	(.087)
Measure of Female Empowerment					.010	.011	.039**	.00001	−.244	1.977	.005
					(.012)	(.024)	(.017)	(.015)	(.741)	(3.953)	(.005)
R-Square	.543	.652	.657	.669	.671	.666	.682	.670	.670	.670	.670
N	157	156	156	156	153	154	156	156	156	156	155

Notes: In a one-tailed test, $p < .05$; $p < .01$; $p < .001$; robust standard errors in parentheses. All variables of female empowerment are measured such that higher values indicate a higher status of women.

The next seven columns of table 7.1 (models 5–11) add, one by one, Fish's three measures of women's rights and then our four additional ones. Islamic population and MID involvement always remain negatively and significantly related to democracy. Arab is also significantly negative in three of the equations, and virtually so ($p < .06$) in the other four. This is a reasonably robust result for an effect of Arab culture or political experience, beyond that from Islam in general and the other influences found to affect democracy.[25]

Contrary to the results found by Fish, in our more complete equations the measures for women's rights almost always exert insignificant effects and add little or nothing to the explanatory power of the equations.[26] The one exception is Fish's measure of the proportion of women in government, suggesting plausibly that democratic governments more equitably involve women in the political process. But that still leaves open the question, which we address below, of whether a large female representation at high levels promotes democracy or is a consequence of democracy. Furthermore, in an equation not shown, our measure of women in government, taken from the same source as Fish's but with a slightly different definition,[27] is not significant.

These results mostly confirm Fish's hypothesis about the effect of Islam per se on regime but leave it intensified by characteristics of Arab states and states frequently engaged in serious international disputes. They also challenge his interpretation of the rather bare-bones equations in his Table 10, as *women's rights exhibit virtually no independent influence on democracy.*

As for the effects of culture, Huntington recognizes how cultural attitudes toward democracy can shift markedly. Catholicism was long regarded as a culture antithetical to democracy, until the third wave discredited this conventional wisdom. Reversing vigorous nineteenth- and twentieth-century opposition to democracy by the Catholic hierarchy, in the 1960s the Second Vatican Council joined intellectuals and activists among the ordinary clergy and laity in endorsing democratic structures and the principle of religious freedom for all. From early in his over 26-year reign, Pope John Paul II traveled the world proclaiming the value of democracy as a protector of justice and human rights, most prominently in his 1991 encyclical, *CentesimusAnnus*. The wave swept through Catholic countries beginning in Iberia, then spread widely in Latin America and ultimately, with the collapse of communism, in Eastern Europe.[28]

Table 7.2 Regression of polity scores on hypothesized determinants

Variable	1960s		1970s		1980s		1990s	
	Model 1	Model 2	Model 3	Model 4	Model 5	Model 6	Model 7	Model 8
Constant	−17.523***	−17.644***	−17.181***	−16.058***	−13.040***	−14.231***	−4.789*	−6.621***
	(3.123)	(2.681)	(2.186)	(1.811)	(1.771)	(1.596)	(2.163)	(1.995)
Economic Development	2.484***	2.710***	1.320***	1.398***	1.006***	.907***	1.963***	2.199***
	(.403)	(.342)	(.341)	(.315)	(.287)	(.255)	(.720)	(.705)
Islamic Population	−.652		1.695		−2.187**		−2.707	
	(2.617)		(1.189)		(.911)		(1.692)	
Catholic Population		−3.631*		−3.107**		3.436***		1.845*
		(1.754)		(1.124)		(.939)		(1.034)
OPEC Membership	−3.577	−4.175	−1.520	−1.334	−1.281	−1.538*	−4.091***	−4.623***
	(2.333)	(2.521)	(1.372)	(1.357)	(.933)	(.913)	(1.062)	(1.035)
Previous Experience with Democracy			1.329***	1.297***	1.411***	1.466***	.761***	.756***
			(−.152)	(.152)	(.119)	(.109)	(.134)	(.139)
Arab League	−6.513*	−8.187***	−4.891***	−4.967***	−1.529	−1.740*	−4.047***	−5.365***
	(3.201)	(2.522)	(1.225)	(1.047)	(1.188)	(.996)	(1.542)	(1.194)
MID Involvement	.263**	.204**	.118	.030	.318***	.374***	−.850**	−.867**
	(.103)	(.099)	(.248)	(.250)	(.087)	(.086)	(.363)	(.362)
R-Square	.396	.423	.732	.748	.813	.830	.90	.586
	96	96	104	104	124	124	156	156

Notes: In a one-tailed test, *p < .05; **p < .01; ***p < .001; robust standard errors in parentheses.

To test whether the impact of the cultural variables changes over time, table 7.2 repeats as much as possible the analysis in model 4 of table 7.1, but does it by decades.[29] Model 1 for each of the periods includes our measure of Islamic population. In this table the negative relationship between Islamic population and democracy is statistically significant only in the 1980s (and just short of significance, $p < .06$, in the 1990s). Arab League, however, was always negative and very strongly so in every decade except the 1980s.

Model 2 for each decade repeats the analysis but substitutes for percentage Islamic another cultural/religious variable, *percentage of population Catholic*. The percentages of Catholic and Islamic populations are very highly and negatively correlated ($-.90$, see website appendix table), so both cannot be used in the same equation. Within each decade, the coefficients for all the other variables are extremely similar in both columns. But the Catholic population variable switched from a negative association with democracy in the 1960s and 1970s to an even stronger positive association in the 1980s,[30] while the Arab variable was always negative. Although the Catholic endorsement of democracy was not enthusiastic everywhere, the reversal and resilience of democracy in many Catholic countries leads us to reject a "strongly culturalist" view that Catholic culture is inherently incompatible with democracy, and suggests skepticism toward the application of such a strongly culturalist view to Islamic culture.

Overall, these results support what Przeworski, Cheibub, and Limongi call a "weakly culturalist" view, which holds that while certain elements of a democratic culture are required for democracy to take hold, this political culture is not incompatible with any particular religious tradition, since such traditions are malleable or at least subject to reinterpretation.[31]

Does Islamic Tradition Diminish Women's Rights?

This leads back to the other major focus of Fish's article—his analysis of influences on various measures of female empowerment. Aside from problems with the lag structure, including a measurement of literacy gap in 1990 as the dependent variable, we believed this portion of Fish's analysis also to be underspecified in a way that exaggerates the influence of Islamic religious tradition. In it he uses only two independent variables, Islamic tradition and level of economic development. A more appropriate equation might include at least these additional variables:

- *Average level of education in the population*, rather than ratio of female to male enrollment, on the hypothesis that generally more educated populations are likely to accord greater rights to women.[32]
- *Percentage of the population living in urban areas*,[33] on the expectation that women are likely to have more rights and opportunities in an urban society than in the isolation of rural society.[34]
- *Income inequality*, on the hypothesis that a more unequal distribution of income is likely to reflect inequality of rights across the spectrum of the population, not just gender-specific inequality. For example, the cross-national analysis of Ghobarah, Huth, and Russett finds income inequality to be a significant predictor of such equality-sensitive outcomes as public expenditures on health and the level of healthy life expectancy in the population.[35] As a measure we use the Gini index of income distribution in 1997 they derived from the World Health Organization.
- *Democracy*, on the expectation that in democratic political systems women are more likely to have a wide variety of rights, not only the right to vote and otherwise participate in politics as is now assumed in contemporary definitions of democracy but also the entitlement to economic rights that reduce male exploitation of their labor. Fish himself discusses the likelihood that democracy supports women's rights but does not include democracy in his Table 9 analysis. We do, continuing with the Freedom House indicator averaged over the 1990s.

With these additions we test the following hypothesis:

H2: *The effect of the revised and additional variables will sharply reduce the explanatory contribution of Islam to women's rights, perhaps making it no longer statistically significant. In particular, democracy will emerge as a stronger explanatory variable than Islamic tradition.*

Table 7.3 shows our more fully specified results for each of nine different measures of women's rights (Fish's three, followed by our four and our more appropriately lagged data for Fish's on female literacy and women in government). Each of general education, income inequality, and percentage of urban population makes a significant

Table 7.3 Regression of status of women on hypothesized determinants

	Dependent Variables								
Variable	Fish's Literacy Gap (1990)	Fish's Sex Ratio	Fish's Women in Government	Women in Parliament	Women in Government (2000)	Education Ratio	Literacy Gap (2000)	Life Expectancy Ratio	Economic Activity Ratio
Constant	43.440***	−90.110***	−1.493	12.475*	−8.346	.652***	18.414***	1.074***	115.877***
	(6.369)	(4.271)	(4.472)	(6.744)	(7.100)	(.092)	(4.37)	(.024)	(9.995)
Economic Development	5.029*	−3.962*	−.125	−.015	3.818	−.126	−1.528	−.007	−2.736
	(2.299)	(1.648)	(1.668)	(2.060)	(2.570)	(.034)	(1.834)	(.008)	(3.377)
Level of Democracy	.974*	.660*	1.475***	.506	1.817***	.0006	.359	−.001	.419
	(.578)	(.350)	(.307)	(.523)	(.557)	(.007)	(.443)	(.002)	(.849)
Islamic Population	−1.086	−1.382	−1.152	−4.433*	.504	−.106**	−2.617	−.01	−3.485
	(2.637)	(1.317)	(1.499)	(2.436)	(2.861)	(.036)	(2.520)	(.010)	(4.669)
Arab League	−9.984***	−6.650***	−3.213**	−5.44**	−4.796*	.060	−2.516	−.026**	−24.825***
	(3.110)	(2.068)	(1.499)	(2.156)	(2.558)	(.049)	(2.573)	(.011)	(5.376)
Education Level	.087	.074*	.029	.103*	.089*	.004***	.269***	.0003	−.073
	(.059)	(.035)	(.029)	(.051)	(.050)	(.0006)	(.043)	(.0002)	(.089)
Income Inequality	4.988	−9.170*	10.238*	−19.172*	3.375	.017	−31.176***	−.069*	−71.185***
	(7.144)	(4.375)	(6.145)	(8.463)	(12.063)	(.107)	(6.267)	(.036)	(13.178)
Urbanization	.102**	.019	.003	.004	−.094	.001*	.107**	.0007***	−.123*
	(.043)	(.027)	(.033)	(.048)	(.065)	(.0006)	(.039)	(.0002)	(.072)
R-Square	.607	.329	.347	.348	.283	.563	.654	.262	.447
N	153	153	155	155	155	155	149	155	154

Notes: In a one-tailed test, *$p < .05$; **$p < .01$; ***$p < .001$; robust standard errors in parentheses. All dependent variables of women's status are measured such that positive values correlate with a higher status for women.

contribution in five of the nine equations for explaining women's rights. Islam has a significant negative impact in just two—but Arab is significant in all but our two measures of women's educational attainment and literacy. *Fish's emphasis on the negative impact of Islamic culture is generally supported only for the Arab variant, not for Islam generally.*[36]

Fish makes the valid point that Islamic countries are not necessarily less secular than those deriving from other religious traditions. Nor are they necessarily more patriarchal and antithetic to women's rights than some others. His discussion of the disadvantaged position of women in China and India (pp. 34–36) makes this point well, as might a discussion of the position of women in much of Africa. His comparison (pp. 25–28) of Islamic countries with Catholic ones—many of which are also known for patriarchy and, at least until recent decades, a less than rigorous separation of church and state—also addresses the question of whether the effects of Islamic tradition are especially strong. But he does not use a measure for *Catholic population* in his full equations for all countries, and it is important to do so.

When we substitute Catholic for Islamic in equations not shown here, the results are the same with only three exceptions: Catholic population shows a significant negative impact on the female economic activity ratio (where Islamic population did not) but has no impact on women in parliament or the female education ratio (where Islamic population did). This is an even more underwhelming effect for a cultural variable.

Table 7.3 also shows that the effect of including democracy in the explanatory model is very inconsistent.[37] It is moderately significant in the full equations using Fish's three measures of women's rights (the literacy gap, the sex ratio,[38] and women in government). But for the six we added (all measured in the year 2000)—literacy gap, women in parliament, women in government, life expectancy ratio, the educational attainment ratio, the ratio of economically active females to males—democracy exerts a significant positive effect only in the equation for women in government. Democracy's insignificance is not due to the socioeconomic variables (urbanization, income inequality, general educational level) that we added. Indeed, income level alone is sufficient to render democracy insignificant for the female education ratio, our literacy measure, and life expectancy.[39] And if democracy is dropped from the models, the results for all but one of the rights measures are substantively unchanged; that is, no signs change direction and no variables lose or materially gain statistical significance. The exception is for women in government (2000), where economic development becomes more significant.[40]

To summarize this section, when Islam is in the equations without a separate variable for Arab, it often impacts negatively on women's rights, but when a control for Arab states is in the equation it is that, not Islamic culture per se, which regularly makes the difference. Only for our measures of women's educational attainment (literacy, enrollment in educational institutions) does the Arab variable not exhibit this negative effect. Apparently many Arab states do attend to the education of women, though not necessarily in the same institutions or by providing education of the same quality or type as that received by men.

Democracy sometimes makes a significant independent contribution to the achievement of some rights for women, but not robustly across the range of rights measures. It emerges as such with Fish's three measures, but with our measures shows up only for women in government. Overall, it is important not to generalize too much about the impact of democracy on human rights for women, across different measures and dimensions of political, economic, health, and educational rights: the effects vary greatly across them. This inconsistent result is certainly contrary to our expectations and probably to those of other scholars of democracy who have found a positive effect for democracy on the condition of women but have not controlled for Islamic or Arab tradition.[41] It also seems to conflict with the expectations of Fish (p. 29), though he does not test for it. One possible explanation is the newness of democratic institutions in the 1990s in many formerly authoritarian countries. If democratic political institutions do indeed have a consistent positive effect on the many indicators of women's status included in our models here, it is likely that these "spillover" effects will take years to manifest themselves.

A Continuing Puzzle

The causes and consequences of regime type in Islamic countries are multiple.[42] Fish's conclusion that countries with an Islamic religious tradition are substantially more autocratic and more oppressive of women's rights (as that term is customarily understood in democratic countries) warrants some important qualifications. He has identified a real problem, although it appears to be more of a problem for Arab states in particular than for those with Islamic populations in general. Moreover, authoritarian government is particularly common in states that have frequently been involved in serious international conflict. Our test suggests that international conflict is an important contributor to authoritarian government but that causal interpretation needs to be tested more systematically than we can do here.

An additional surprise, and puzzle, is twofold in our more completely specified equations. The first part is that Islamic countries are more likely to be ruled by autocratic governments whether or not women's rights are heavily restricted. And the second is that Islamic—or more particularly Arab—countries are likely to restrict women's rights whether or not the governments are strongly autocratic. Democracy per se impacts only a few measures of women's rights, making more differentiated theory and empirical research imperative to unpack the nuances of this relationship.

Overall, it does not seem either that Islamic or Arab countries are autocratic because they oppress women's rights or that Islamic or Arab countries oppress women simply because their governments are autocratic. Islam and especially Arab remain key predictive variables, but the particular social and political mechanisms by which democracy or women's rights are repressed in these countries remain enigmatic to us. Figure 7.1 shows our findings schematically.

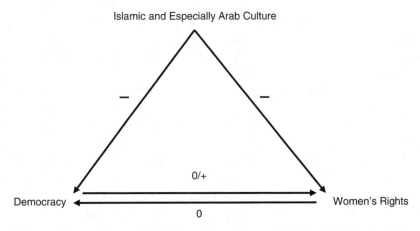

Figure 7.1 Arab tradition reduces democracy and women's rights, and Islamic tradition reduces democracy, but controlling for these traditions the direct connections between democracy and women's rights are tenuous.

If this is correct, democratic institutions alone would not appear to be the key to greatly improved status for women in Islamic and especially Arab societies, nor would improving the status of women alone promise much by way of subsequent greater democracy in those countries. Both democracy and female empowerment may be highly valued—they certainly are by the authors of this analysis. But the goal of achieving one by means of the other may prove elusive. Recall also our results in note 40 using the interaction of GDP per capita and regime to explain women's rights. They suggest that a high level of women's rights could be a "Western" phenomenon (i.e., typical of those countries with high levels of democracy and income). Thus, some of the unsettling results showing an insignificant relationship between democracy and women's rights might best be understood as depending also on income levels. Democracy alone— which in many developing countries may have little substantive meaning beyond holding elections—cannot solve such social problems as the low status of women.

These results are not exactly what we had hoped or expected to find. We began with hypotheses that the apparent effect of Islamic culture in sustaining both autocracy and female subordination would prove to be largely an artifact of other social, political, and economic influences. Perhaps these influences would themselves be more malleable to political intervention, and Islamic or Arab culture would not be "the real problem." Our results do suggest that Islamic culture in particular may not be a major impediment to achieving women's rights, but something about Arab states is, at least in the set of explanations tapped by the variables in this analysis. Our results in table 7.2, however, do reinforce the fact that countries characterized by what many viewed as an inherently antidemocratic religious tradition—Catholicism— have proved remarkably amenable to the emergence and survival of democracy. They suggest that the most fruitful direction for future research is not to focus on the intractability of religious and cultural traditions but instead to continue to identify potential paths of change in Arab and Islamic societies.

We suspect Fish knew well that he was writing a ground-breaking and provocative article that would be built upon and modified by subsequent scholars. We expect the same to follow from our analysis here. Very possibly our still-parsimonious models omit other important variables or oversimplify their functional relationships. More detailed analysis of the relationship between religious groups and the state could be productive. How secular is the state and how autonomous is it from organized religion? How radical are the country's dominant religious organizations? Do the tenets or practices of different sects of Islam have different implications for state–society relations and female repression? In addition to examining culture, the effects of other variables—international and civil conflict—on both democracy and women's rights need to be probed more deeply. Is it possible that peace is easier to achieve than is deep cultural change? Are oil-exporting Arab countries more likely than are other resource-rich countries to be authoritarian rentier states? Much more theory and research, including intensive focused case studies, is necessary.

If these results withstand further scrutiny, we expect Fish to share our dismay. He says, "Nothing could be less heartening to democratic idealists than the notion that a particular religion is inimical to democracy. Religious traditions are usually constants within societies; they are variables only across societies" (p. 37). At this stage some effect of Islamic and especially Arab culture or institutions in discouraging democracy and suppressing female empowerment seems real, and the causal mechanisms are more puzzling than ever—but the idea of culture as a constant is less solid.

Chapter 8

The Mysterious Case of Vanishing Hegemony, or, Is Mark Twain Really Dead?

Has American hegemony greatly declined over recent years? Much of the recent literature on "hegemonic stability" has been devoted to explaining the effects of a decline in American hegemony on the international system since the high point immediately after 1945. In a variant of the theme, scholars have searched for ways in which to maintain an international regime established during that lost hegemony. Others have perceived an ethnocentric bias in some of this angst.[1]

The very premise of a major decline in American hegemony has, however, gone largely unexamined, and it is to such an examination that this chapter is devoted. I shall first make the familiar but crucial distinction between power base and power as control over outcomes. I am much readier to concede decline in America's position in the former—though it too can be exaggerated by choice of baseline for evaluation—than in the latter. Simple versions of hegemonic stability theory predict that control over outcomes will decline as power base deteriorates. Collective goods theory, moreover, a key component of the hegemonic stability literature, seems to predict both that the achievement of these goods will decline and that the goods will be achieved only to a suboptimal degree. I question those predictions.

Turning to control over outcomes—the achievement of various "goods" in the global system and the regimes by which those goods are achieved—I distinguish between security goods and economic goods. A sensitivity to demands and achievements in the domain of international security helps to temper assessments, based primarily on political economy, that the decline of American power has been great. I evaluate the degree to which achievement of those various goods has in fact declined in the past three or four decades. The decline has been substantially less than would be expected had they been collective goods, and less than many variants of hegemonic stability theory would predict.

This substantial continuity of outcomes must be explained. Some variants of hegemonic stability theory emphasize institutionalization as a partial explanation. But, as I shall argue, many of the gains from hegemony have been less collective goods than private ones, accruing primarily to the hegemon and thus helping maintain its hegemony; this applies to short-term as well as to long-term gains; the hegemon has not really borne the costs of achieving these goods (both collective and private) as unequally as might have been the case had they been relatively pure collective goods; and one very important kind of gain, cultural hegemony, has proved a major resource to the hegemon in maintaining its more general hegemony.

These gains have helped the United States both to maintain its power base in ways not readily measured by standard indicators and to continue to control outcomes. Specifically, the international system has been structurally transformed, largely by the United States. This transformation of preferences and expectations continues to produce the goods (e.g., free trade) that the United States and the dominant elements of the rest of the world (especially in the other industrialized, noncommunist states) need to maintain a compatible international system. Since the transformation took place, the United States has not had to exert such overt control over others in order to maintain control over outcomes.

Power Base and Control

The perception of a significant decline in American power over the last two decades is widespread, indeed virtually universal. Many observers, writing from diverse perspectives, characterize the decline in strong terms. Richard Rosecrance, for example, says the American "role as maintainer of the system is at an end," Kenneth Oye speaks of "the end of American hegemony," and George Liska repeatedly applies the word "dissolution" to the state of the "American empire."[2] The perception is particularly common, however, in the literature on international regimes and most straightforward in that part of the literature identified with "hegemonic stability" theory. Strong characterizations of decline are frequently associated with the work of Robert Gilpin, Stephen Krasner, Charles Kindleberger, and even Robert Keohane.[3]

To be sure, most of these characterizations are nuanced, and they change in a literature and a world that are rapidly evolving. Nearly everyone recognizes that the United States retains great power and, in the economic sphere at least, greater power than any other state. These same writers typically remind us of a continuing degree of American preeminence. The decline, then, is relative—relative to past American power or perhaps relative to what a hegemon needs to maintain essential elements of the world economic order. My purpose is to point out the assumptions and consequences of this emphasis on decline rather than continuity, for there is a great deal still to be said for the latter perspective.

The standards against which to measure the American decline are seldom made clear. Part of the difficulty stems from a lack of agreement about how much power is necessary to produce "hegemony." Unless there is some rather sharp step-level jump at which hegemony comes into existence or is lost (a level that has never been specified), relative power is necessarily distributed continuously. The theoretical problem is basic: there is always room for argument about whether a given degree of superiority is enough to produce particular (and also rarely well-specified) results.

A second and related difficulty stems from a lack of agreement on the relevant dimensions and indicators of power. In some amorphous manner, of course, our senses do not deceive us. American power, as measured by various power base indicators, surely has declined. The litany is too familiar to require full recitation, and some examples will suffice: loss of strategic nuclear predominance; decline in conventional military capabilities relative to the USSR, especially for intervention; diminished economic size in relative gross national product, productivity, and terms of trade with some commodity producers (principally of oil); loss of a reliable majority in the United Nations; and loss of assured scientific preeminence in the "knowledge industries" at the "cutting edge" and even in the numerical and financial base that enabled U.S. scholars to dominate global social science.

Even with these power base indicators, however, it is not quite a case where "all the instruments agree" that it is a dark, cold day. President Reagan's rhetoric about "a definite margin of superiority for the Soviet Union" had to be corrected the next day by his own director of the Bureau of Politico-Military Affairs of the State Department, his talk of a "window of vulnerability" by his own Scowcroft Commission. Reasonable (if, on both sides, rather ideological) people can debate the relative importance of warheads versus throw-weights versus "kill ratios," the proper exchange rates for comparing Soviet with American military expenditures, and the true balance of conventional forces between NATO and the Warsaw Pact. U.S. economic/industrial predominance in the world looks slightly less impressive if one takes its share of world GNP rather than its share of world energy consumption. While virtually all power base measures show a clear decline in American predominance over the past 40 years, they do not agree on the rate or the depth of that decline. Some show the United States slipping to second place in the world, but many more show merely a shrunken lead for the front-runner.[4]

When in time one begins measuring the power base indicators also makes a great difference. If one begins with 1945, all indicators show a significant, though never precipitous, decline in American power base over the subsequent four decades.[5] But 1945 represents the absolute peak of American strength. The old powers of Europe and Japan were physically and economically devastated; the United States unscathed. That situation could not continue, the United States hastened its passing, and by 1955 the former powers had significantly recovered. The first decade, with the sharpest slope of decline in American predominance, represented a substantial "return to normalcy." The immediate postwar years look even more peculiar if one starts with 1938 or earlier. America's military preeminence dates, without question, only from World War II. Its predominance in 1945 over the existing military capability of any other state (even, at that point, the Soviet Union) could be matched by no state since at least the time of Napoleon. Since 1945, the Soviet Union has achieved parity, but the dominance of the two states over all other powers, including those of the Western alliance, remains. The name of the Soviet-American military game is duopoly.

A long time-perspective on economic power makes clear the unusual degree of American superiority in 1945 in that power base as well. Table 8.1 provides a historical perspective on hegemons' ability to dominate three of the most commonly used dimensions of national power base. Gross national product is the most fungible of resources, usable to exert many kinds of influence; it also represents market size, the attraction of which can give important advantages in international trade negotiations. It represents the basis of structural power, that is, the ability to define the context within which others must make decisions. Military expenditures give a good if hardly perfect indication of relative military strength. Manufacturing production is a basic source of both economic and military strength.

Table 8.1   Four leading powers indexed to "hegemon"[a] 1830–1983

Year	Largest		2nd Largest		3rd Largest		4th Largest	
Country and percentage of "hegemon's" value								
Gross National Product								
1983	U.S.A	100	USSR	41	Japan	35	W. Germany	20
1950	U.S.A	100	USSR	29	U.K.	19	France	13
1938	U.S.A	100	Germany	37	USSR	37	U.K.	27
1913	U.S.A	306	Russia	123	Germany	113	U.K.	100
1870	U.S.A	117	Russia	117	U.K.	100	France	86
1830	Russia	132	France	105	U.K.	100	Austria-Hungary	87
Military Expenditures								
1983	U.S.A	100	USSR	100	China	19	U.K.	16
1950	USSR	106	U.S.A	100	China	18	U.K.	16
1938[b]	Germany	657	USSR	481	U.K.	161	Japan	154
1913	Germany	129	Russia	125	U.K.	100	France	99
1872[c]	Russia	127	France	119	UK.	100	Germany	68
1830	France	148	U.K.	100	Russia	92	Austria-Hungary	54
Manufacturing Production								
1980	U.S.A.	100	USSR	47	Japan	29	W. Germany	17
1953	U.S.A.	100	USSR	24	U.K.	19	W. Germany	13
1938	U.S.A.	100	Germany	40	U.K.	34	USSR	29
1913	U.S.A.	235	Germany	109	U.K.	100	Russia	26
1870	U.K.	100	China	75	U.S.A.	51	France	37
1830	China	319	India	185	U.K.	100	Russia	59

Notes:
[a] There was no hegemon in 1938, but I have arbitrarily used the U.S. values as the base.
[b] United States ranked fifth.
[c] 1872 data used, as figures for French and German (Prussian) military spending were inflated in 1870 and 1871 by the Franco-Prussian War.

Sources: GNP data 1983 from OECD, *Main Economic Indicators* (Paris, May 1984), 182; USSR total is estimated. Other GNP data from Paul Bairoch, "Europe's Gross National Product, 1800–1975," *Journal of European Economic History* 5:2 (1976), 273–340, and U.S. Bureau of the Census, *Historical Statistics of the United States: Colonial Times to 1970* (Washington, DC: U.S. Government Printing Office, 1975). Military expenditures 1983 from *World Armaments and Disarmament: SIPRI Yearbook, 1984* (London: Taylor & Francis, 1984), 117–18. SIPRI lists USSR military expenses as 74% of the U.S. figure, but U.S. government sources (CIA. and DIA.) gives USSR expenditures as exceeding those of United States I have set the two countries as equal. The estimate for China, given by SIPRI and used here, may be somewhat low. Military expenditure data for previous years are from the Correlates of War national capabilities data provided by Professor J. David Singer. Manufacturing production data from Paul Bairoch, "International Industrialization Levels from 1750 to 1980," *Journal of European Economic History* 11:2 (1982), 269–333. Data for 1870 are interpolated between Bairoch's figures for 1860 and 1880.

These data make several facts apparent. First, the United Kingdom was *never*, even at its peak in the nineteenth century, the dominant power as measured by either GNP or military expenditures. The wealth provided by its industrial strength was always overwhelmed in terms of GNP by the demographic base of its sometimes less wealthy but more populous chief competitors; its military expenditures were always markedly below one or more of its continental rivals. Only in manufacturing production, and then only rather briefly, did it lead the world. (For purposes of this analysis, however, we should probably discount the surprising manufacturing capacity of China and India, as they were hardly great powers in the world system.) These data should encourage a cautious interpretation of Britain's "hegemonic" power. Britain's commercial power, reflected in trade or financial indicators, is not evident in other very important indicators of power base. Second, despite slippage since filling the void immediately after World War II, the United States retains on all these indicators a degree of dominance reached by the United Kingdom at no point, and one that compares well with the U.S. position in 1938. (U.S. military expenditures for 1950 do not reflect the Korean War and are artificially low for the cold war period.) The basis of American hegemony may have declined, but it has hardly vanished.

Other indicators are imaginable, but many data are not available for a long time span, and length of historical perspective is essential to the argument. Moreover, the meaning of some potential indicators is not entirely clear: for example, does a large volume of foreign trade indicate market dominance or vulnerability?[6] Nevertheless, any truly scientific assessment will require more, and more rigorous, measurement than table 8.1 provides, as well as some agreement on appropriate baselines for temporal comparison. With conceptual and theoretical clarity, one could establish appropriate rules for measuring certain kinds of power base decline. Until that time it would be well to remember Galileo's experiment with falling bodies: if one would explain the velocity of those bodies, one must first determine what the velocity is! The hegemonic stability literature, to be persuasive, demands better measurement than it has enjoyed so far.

The more important question, however, is "so what?" In what ways has decline produced (or, perhaps, been reflected in) a decline in American power as control over outcomes—that is, "ability to prevail in conflict and overcome obstacles"?[7] Surely it is this control over outcomes that really interests us. If we are to have a matter worth investigating, we must identify hegemony at least with success in determining and maintaining essential rules, not merely with power base or resource share. Hegemony is a condition, as Keohane and Nye recognize, in which "one state is powerful enough to maintain the essential rules governing interstate relations, and willing to do so." We must avoid making a tautology out of Krasner's statement that, "The theory of hegemonic leadership suggests that under conditions of declining hegemony there will be a weakening of regimes."[8] Rather, we should ask whether, when predominance in the power base declines, the basic regime (the network of rules, norms, etc.) weakens or the ability of the preponderant state to determine rules lessens. The former, a weakening of the network, is difficult to investigate empirically though good efforts have been made, especially with aspects of the trade regime. Here, however, I address the latter, the influence of the preponderant state. I emphasize the distribution of *desired outcomes* as a result of the rules, in conformity with Krasner's formulation of a causal chain from "basic causal factors" to regimes to outcomes and behaviors.

It is widely acknowledged that the United States did occupy a position of hegemony in the international system immediately after World War II. Its enemies were defeated and its allies exhausted. The productive base of the American economy alone escaped wartime devastation; indeed, it was enormously expanded by the war effort. The United States was the world's foremost military power, and only it had the nuclear "winning weapon." While U.S. preponderance was not so overwhelming as to enable it to set all the rules for the entire world system, it did permit it to establish the basic principles for the new economic order in the over 80 percent of the world economy controlled by capitalist states and to organize a system of collective security to maintain political and economic control over that 80 percent. While U.S. power was not complete, virtually all analysts of the regimes school agree that the United States in about 1946 came closer to meeting the criteria of global hegemony than has any other state in world history. Indeed, as Timothy McKeown and Keohane have argued, one should have important reservations about the "supposed hegemonic leadership" of nineteenth century Britain and must wonder whether Britain was hegemonic in any meaningful sense.[9]

One can also have reservations about the scientific status of a theory derived in large part from a single case and attempting to explain behavior in that same case. Proponents of hegemonic stability theory frequently acknowledge this problem, which does not greatly concern me here. One can appropriately seek to extend insights and test propositions by looking at various "issue-area" regimes within the overall set of rules and by looking at the behavior and outcomes of actors in various kinds of arenas (as in small groups of individuals or in coalitions within organizations) where degrees of hegemony may be examined, compared, and even manipulated.

Empirical tests of the theory of collective goods have been made in just such arenas; with care their findings can, and because the questions are important should, be extended to the global situation. Nevertheless, in these arenas global conditions are but crudely approximated, and we should look very closely at some key assumptions about the goods provided by a regime (do they truly meet the definition of collective goods?),[10] about behavior by unitary actors,[11] and about "fairness" in the distribution of costs and benefits.[12] I shall return to these matters below.

Achievements, Goods, and Regimes

In the years immediately following World War II, the United States emerged as a hegemonic power, perhaps following in the path George Modelski characterizes as occurring at roughly 100-year intervals.[13] The United States provided the world with a variety of "goods," some of them collective goods, of security, international organization, and a framework for international economic relations. The idea that a hegemon provides collective goods to permit peace and prosperity within a wider area is an old one; Karl Deutsch's work on integration anticipated much of what emerged in the regimes literature of the 1970s.[14]

But there is more than one way of looking at the provision of goods in the postwar international system. A radical perspective exists. Recognizing the existence of a Pax Americana, it identifies achievements that are not necessarily collective goods.

> The pacification of capitalist interstate relations and the imperial guarantee against nationalization created a reliable world legal framework which reduced the risks of transnational expansion; decolonization opened up the entire periphery to primary transnational expansion based on comparative advantage rather than on the monopolistic privileges and restrictions with which rival metropolitan states had increasingly enmeshed their colonial possessions; the gold-dollar standard restored the possibility of capitalist accounting on a world scale, thus enhancing secondary transnational expansion, which depend decisively upon reliable calculations of the cost advantages of alternative locations of production.[15]

Giovanni Arrighi recognizes two kinds of achievements or goods: security (peace) and economy (prosperity). Each can be broken down further, and we can ask what conditions or regime made possible those achievements.[16] Arrighi speaks of the "pacification" of relations among capitalist states, and indeed there have been no wars between capitalist states, at least between developed (capitalist) industrial states, since 1945. Whether this absence of war is attributable more to the spread of advanced industrial capitalism or to the spread of representative democracy in the world is hard to say, because the two potential explanatory variables are so closely correlated. Various arguments do not necessarily agree on the direction of causality, and indeed, all the correlations may be spurious.[17] Nevertheless, the absence of interstate war is indisputable, and by fairly early in the postwar era even preparation for, and expectation of, war among capitalist states had diminished nearly to the vanishing point. By the end of the 1950s, one could say with reasonable confidence that a "security community" or "stable peace" had been established nearly everywhere in the OECD area, even between traditional enemies.[18] Nor have there been any civil wars (involving 1,000 or more deaths) within any of the advanced capitalist countries, nor hardly any serious expectation of such. (Violence in Northern Ireland and the Spanish Basque country could possibly escalate above this threshold.) One could argue that the absence of war between democracies has been a fact of life since the end of the Napoleonic era,[19] but the recent extension of stable democracy and also (therefore?) a "zone of peace" to various industrialized countries where it was previously fragile—Germany, Italy, Japan—is surely a major achievement. It is, moreover, an achievement that can be credited in some degree to the United States, either as a result of enforced suppression of hostilities[20] or, in Arrighi's terms, by provision of a "cohesive political and ideological framework."

Stable peace has not been achieved to anything like the same degree in the third world and between its capitalist states. Virtually all post-1945 wars have been fought on the territories of third world states, between or within third world states or between third world states and intervening first or second world states. Open insurgency has often been avoided only because of the threat of direct foreign intervention or because of the establishment of powerful coercive states within third world countries, usually with strong external support. It is all too often a "peace" based on threats, either the mutual threats of deterrence or the one-sided threats of dominance.

From the point of view of third world peoples, this sort of peace may well be no great achievement. From the point of view of the

United States, however, the judgment will be less certain. Wars have been fought in third world countries, civilian casualties have been incurred there, and it is third world peoples who have borne most of the costs of maintaining coercive states. The result has been sufficient "pacification" to provide a "reliable legal framework" for transnational corporate expansion and to discourage most large-scale nationalizations without "fair" compensation. Some parts of the third world (some countries, some classes) have shared in the resulting prosperity, others have not. But by historic standards, even compared with the colonial era of direct control, the overall results show not a bad ratio of costs and benefits for the United States.

If stable peace has been achieved among and within many capitalist countries, it has surely not been achieved between capitalist and communist countries. Instead, we can speak only of containment or deterrence and the ability of American hegemony to maintain stable boundaries between the capitalist and communist worlds. The United States was able to erect around the Soviet Union, in the first decade after the war, a *cordon sanitaire* that held from the "loss" of China to the accession of Castro. It is a "peace" maintained by deterrence. Initially somewhat one-sided (Soviet conventional superiority in Europe gave some compensation for American nuclear monopoly), it has become increasingly based on a system of mutual threat. Although there are many flaws and dangers in this system, the substantial success for "containment" and the avoidance of superpower war should not be dismissed.

Is it appropriate to refer to these achievements as "regimes"? If we use Krasner's definition ("principles, norms, and decision-making procedures around which actor expectations converge"),[21] it seems reasonable to do so, at least for "stable peace." Stable peace is built on a set of norms and rules for regulating, limiting, and resolving conflict. While not necessarily embodied in organized institutions, they do involve a set of stable expectations about others' behavior and principles to guide one's own—what acts and demands are appropriate, permissible, or unacceptable. Students of international political economy miss insights into the regimes directly of interest to them when they ignore the regime of stable peace.

Whether one can use "regime" to characterize superpower deterrence is less certain. Robert Jervis is not inclined to, yet admits that "the subject is so complex that I lack confidence in this judgment."[22] Certainly the element of pure threat, as contrasted with established norms for resolving conflict and pursuing mutual reward, is much greater. As Jervis notes, the restraints have been, in large part, shifting, narrow, and short-term. Still, norms and rules for behavior were built up, embodied both in formal arms control treaties and in various implicit understandings about what kinds of acts (e.g., military alerts, weapons procurements, troop deployments beyond one's borders) may be legitimate to achieve certain ends or to signal intentions, what kinds may be too provocative and threatening. The element of building rules and norms was especially important during the era of détente; and then, it seems to me, the term fits as well as it does in its wide application in political economy.

The second gain that Arrighi identifies from establishment of the Pax Americana is decolonization and the consequent entry of the United States into previously closed markets and sources of supply for raw materials. The price of American assistance for postwar reconstruction was the demand that former colonial powers accede to demands from their colonial peoples for independence. Clear-cut examples include the experience in 1949 when the threat to cut off American economic aid halted the Dutch military operation to restore control over the Dutch East Indies, American pressure in 1962 that helped impel the Dutch effectively to cede West New Guinea (Irian Jaya) to Indonesia, and the American refusal to approve an urgent IMF loan that forced the British and French to retreat from their effort to reoccupy the Suez Canal in 1956.[23]

The American goal was more than mere nominal independence for colonies; to follow was the dismantling of the formal and informal barriers that had largely restricted colonies' trade to their metropoles. Britain, for instance, was strongly pressured to give up Commonwealth Preference and the Sterling Area, which had provided it with a relatively closed, secure market. Britain was also forced, most notably as part of the settlement of the Anglo-Iranian Oil nationalization in 1953, to give American-based multinationals a dominant share of Middle Eastern oil supplies. Decolonization as an ideology was attractive to Americans; it cost them almost nothing (the only American colony was the Philippines) while creating enormous economic opportunities. With its dominant technology and industrial organization, the United States was ready and able to move into hitherto closed markets. Decolonization meant acceleration of the introduction of advanced capitalism into the third world, and the United States was the most efficient capitalist. The postwar regimes in international trade and finance brought worldwide prosperity, not least to the United States.

Continuity and Distribution of Gains

These achievements, often embodied in regimes, are very important products of American hegemony. Moreover, they represent a continued achievement of outcomes desired by the United States, even at a time of discernible decline in standard indicators of the American power base. If one looks not at narrow issue-area regimes but at broader aspects of the international environment after World War II, one has to be impressed by the degree to which perceived American interests, not just the interests of all states, were served. Strong elements of continuity, and of sustained reward, characterize these achievements. These two elements—important gains to the United States and the continuity of gains—are interlinked.

Over the past decade we have seen a breakdown in détente: a breakdown in the rules and norms governing Soviet-American behavior. "Prompt hard-target kill" weapons have been acquired, in numbers and capabilities formerly avoided; troops have crossed some of the implicit boundaries between East and West; and continued adherence to formal agreements, among them SALT and the ABM treaty, is in doubt. Yet the rules and norms built up over the decades have not been entirely abandoned. Some vestige of a regime in East-West relations survives.

More dubious is the continuity of containment, but even there the argument of drastic decline is readily exaggerated. American strategic nuclear predominance is gone (forever, in my opinion, though members of the Reagan administration may disagree). Most of us now feel less secure about maintenance of the balance of terror than we did formerly, especially about the risks of low-level political or military conflict spiraling into Armageddon. But the risks of deliberate Soviet nuclear attack still seem remote and are likely to remain so indefinitely, barring either gross American provocation or gross American negligence in providing a secure nuclear deterrent.

Despite some breaches, the *cordon sanitaire* around the Soviet Union still looks quite effective. Counterbalancing Soviet gains in Afghanistan, Vietnam, and parts of Africa has been the Soviet loss of China, once its foremost ally. By any standards of resources or population, the reentry of China to the world economy and the reorientation of Chinese foreign policy more than compensate for losses to the "free world" elsewhere. American losses in the Middle East (e.g., Iran) have by no means translated into Soviet gains.[24] The biggest real switch in that part of the world was Egypt, from "them" to "us." Soviet penetration into Latin America since Cuba still remains more of a threat than a reality (and the Soviets "acquired" Cuba despite the American nuclear predominance of the time).

Continuity also applies in America's relations with the industrialized countries. The hegemonic stability literature does not give precise predictions about whether, and particularly how much, the achievement of goals will decline as the relative power base of the hegemon declines. Except in its vulgar form as what Keohane calls "crude theory," it emphasizes the mediating and conditioning roles of, for example, international institutions and the characteristics of domestic political systems.[25] Nevertheless, some decline, particularly in light of the sharp decline in American military power, might be expected. It has not happened. By no reasonable criterion has stable peace declined among the advanced capitalist countries. They are hardly able to solve all their common problems, but—and it is no small achievement—war among them is now less thinkable than ever. War among them, moreover, became no more thinkable during the 1970s, when the apparent common threat, the Soviet Union, became less threatening. And while wars in the third world remain common, they do not tend to happen more frequently than they did in the past.[26]

If American predominance (hegemony) vis-à-vis the Soviet Union is gone, American nuclear predominance (hegemony) over all other states remains, perhaps stronger than ever, and there is little sign that it will erode in the future. Western Europe seems unable to put together a substantial deterrent of its own, and any Soviet-American success in constructing space-based antimissile systems will only reinforce their nuclear duopoly by drastically reducing the effectiveness of smaller and less sophisticated forces. In a nuclear world American military hegemony over its allies may never end. That kind of hegemony gives the United States some fungible resources with which to maintain a degree of hegemony in other areas. ("Open up your domestic market more, or Congress may tire of keeping our military commitment.")

In economic matters the structure of a relatively open world economy (the GATT, various rounds of trade liberalization, etc.) remains substantially intact. Despite the spread of such measures as "voluntary" export restraints and many observers' anticipation of a major relapse into protectionism, the sky has not fallen. It is significant that world trade fell only in 1982, and by only 1 percent, after a decade of increased protectionist efforts. The inflation-adjusted increase in world trade between 1973 and 1983 was between 6 and 7 percent, as contrasted with a 28 percent drop from 1926 to 1935. Progress in opening up Japan, the best-protected capitalist economy outside the United States, continues to creep forward.[27] Currencies remain convertible. The United States can use the attractiveness of its financial markets, with high interest rates, to finance its military buildup with other people's money.

It would be perverse to deny that there has been some demonstrable (if less easily measurable) decline in recent decades in America's ability to get others to do as it wished. That decline has been well documented in the regimes literature, though it is often exaggerated. Arrighi, whom I quoted earlier on the gains achieved by the United States by its world predominance, also considers both the persistence and the decay of those gains:

> In general, the U.S. government has simply exploited, in the pursuance of national interests, the core position that the U.S. national economy still retains in the "world-economy." Its internal reserves of energy and other natural resources, the sheer size of its internal market, and the density and complexity of its linkages with the rest of the capitalist world imply a basic asymmetry in the relation of the U.S. economy to other national economies: conditions within the U.S. state's boundaries influence, much more than they are influenced by, conditions within the boundaries of any other national economy. This asymmetrical relation, though independently eroded by other factors, has not yet been significantly affected by the undoing of the U.S. imperial order. What has been affected is the *use* made by the U.S. state of its world economic power: while in the 1950s and 1960s the national interest was often subordinated to the establishment and reproduction of a world capitalist order, in the middle and late 1970s the reproduction of such an order has been subordinated to the pursuit of the national interest as expressed in efforts to increase domestic economic growth.
>
> In such a sense, this redeployment of U.S. world political-economic power in the pursuit of national interests has been a major symptom of, and factor explaining, the state of anarchy that has characterized international economic relations since 1973. It is important to realize, however, that at least insofar as the advanced capitalist countries are concerned, this state of anarchy in interstate relations has been strictly limited to monetary and budgetary policies and that it has yet to undermine the two main "products" of formal U.S. hegemony: the unity of the world market and the transnational expansion of capital.[28]

As will shortly become apparent, I disagree with several counts of Arrighi's assessment. I contend that the U.S. national interest *was* served, even in the short run, by the policies of the 1950s. I also regard his characterization of a "state of anarchy"—even applied only to monetary and budgetary policies—as much too strong. A literal "absence of government" is not necessarily synonymous with chaos, as Hedley Bull and others have urged.[29] (It is worth emphasizing that, with the world capitalist order once established, the tasks of maintaining and reproducing it are far easier.) Nevertheless, Arrighi's emphasis on asymmetries rather than simplistic uses of "interdependence," and hence the remaining power of the United States to influence others, is of major importance.

If significant continuity in the ability of the United States to get what it wants is accepted, then it must be explained. The explanation starts with our noting that the institutions for political and economic cooperation have themselves been maintained. Keohane rightly stresses the role of institutions as "arrangements permitting communication and therefore facilitating the exchange of information."[30] By providing reliable information and reducing the costs of transactions, institutions can permit cooperation to continue even after a hegemon's influence has eroded. Institutions provide opportunities for commitment and for observing whether others keep their commitments. Such opportunities are virtually essential to cooperation in nonzero-sum situations, as gaming experiments demonstrate.[31] Declining hegemony and stagnant (but not decaying) institutions may therefore be consistent with a stable provision of desired outcomes, although the ability to promote new levels of cooperation to deal with new problems (e.g., energy supplies, environmental protection) is more problematic. Institutions nevertheless provide a part of the necessary explanation.

Collective or Private Goods?

The nature of the institutions themselves must, however, be examined. They were shaped in the years immediately after World War II by the United States and they, and the regimes of which they are a part, have significantly endured. The American willingness to establish those regimes and their institutions is sometimes explained in terms of the theory of collective goods. It is a commonplace in the regimes literature that the United States, in so doing, was providing not only private goods for its own benefit but also (and perhaps especially) collective goods desired by, and for the benefit of, other capitalist states. (Particular care is needed here about equating state interest with "national" interest.) Not only was the United States protecting its own territory and commercial enterprises, it was providing military protection for some 50 allies and almost as many neutrals. Not only was it ensuring a liberal, open, near-global economy for its own prosperity, it was also providing the basis for the prosperity of all capitalist states and even for some states organized on noncapitalist principles (those willing to abide by the basic rules established to govern international trade and finance). While such behavior was not exactly selfless or altruistic, certainly the benefits—however distributed by class, state, or region—did accrue to many others, not just to Americans. Coupled with this commonplace argument is the implication that the United States paid substantial costs in the immediate postwar period to set in place the basis for it and others to accrue long-term benefits.[32]

If this were a case of providing a collective good, several conclusions would follow. First is the prediction of collective goods theory that, in the absence of a strong central authority able to coerce members to pay appropriate contributions, a collective good will be supplied to only a suboptimal degree. Second, the costs of providing the good will be borne unequally and disproportionately by the hegemon. Usually implicit in the assessment of inequality in burden sharing is an assumption of inequity or unfairness, implying that while the hegemon bears disproportionate costs, the nonhegemonic powers desire the good as much as, or almost as much as, the hegemon does. (This proposition should alert us to the normative implications of the prior assumption that the principal goods provided are truly collective. If the goods largely benefit the hegemon, it is hardly fair to berate smaller states for an unwillingness to pay an equal share of the costs.)

Finally there is an implication not so common in collective goods theory per se as in many of its applications to problems of hegemonic stability: costs must typically be incurred in the short run whereas benefits are primarily gained in the long term. Most collective goods, after all, involve a significant investment that, once in place, will pay returns for a long time. Deterrence, stable peace, a liberal trading order that undergirds prosperity, all fit this characterization.

Serious doubt about the willingness and even the ability of the hegemon to continue to pay the costs is a corollary to this last conclusion. The short-term costs were so heavy, the argument holds, and the benefits distributed so widely to those who never paid the costs that a weakening of the United States and a loss of its hegemony were inevitable. Equally inevitable, except as retarded by such factors as institutionalization, mentioned earlier, was a weakening of the regimes that the United States had established and sustained.

Collective goods theory, so applied, predicts the very weakening whose existence I have contested. Yet the absence of that weakening can itself be understood by a different application of collective goods theory. This interpretation requires a careful examination of the goods provided and an awareness of the degree to which they were not collective, but private. To the degree that they were private goods— benefits to the United States itself— they have brought important if sometimes obscured resources to the United States, resources that help it to maintain regimes and to obtain further private goods for itself.

A "collective good" must meet the two standard criteria of nonrivalness and nonexclusiveness. By the first is meant that one's enjoyment or consumption of a good does not diminish the amount of the good available to anyone else; by the second, that it is not possible to exclude any party from enjoyment of the good, as a result of which many actors may be "free riders" unwilling to pay any of the costs for providing the good. Few goods ever fit these criteria perfectly; one can usually find some possibilities of rivalness and exclusion, but judgments of less and more are perfectly feasible.[33]

None of the major goods identified earlier primarily meet the criteria for collective goods, I shall argue. In many ways they represent private goods accruing as much to the United States as to others. The conclusion that the exercise of hegemony necessarily weakened the United States does not follow. If the United States has not been severely weakened, moreover, we need not be surprised at its continued willingness and ability to secure these goods.

The first of the goods at issue is stable peace, particularly among the industrialized states. It probably satisfies the criterion of nonrivalness, though some radical critics contend that peace within and among the industrialized states is achieved only at the price of exploiting (through dominance, military threats, and military intervention) the third world. Whatever one thinks of that assessment, peace clearly does not meet the criterion of nonexclusiveness. It certainly is feasible to exclude various countries or areas from stable peace, if one so wishes, by attacking or invading. Even for "peace" by dominance one can choose boundaries to the area one pacifies.

Many Western observers would probably judge containment to be largely a collective good. It was desired by *most* of the citizens of all the countries protected, not just by the United States. The unanimity of this desire has weakened recently, however, as many of its beneficiaries, notably in Western Europe, have come to doubt the reality of a Soviet military threat to their security or way of life. Containment is achieved both by deterrence and by a willingness to defend. It is neither entirely nonrival nor entirely nonexclusive. As the distinction in the alliance literature makes clear, deterrence satisfies the criterion of nonrivalness well and that of nonexclusiveness reasonably well, but defense is another matter.[34] Fortifying one area may require the adversary to concentrate troops there, actually enhancing the defense of other areas; or, by drawing the hegemon's resources away from other areas, it may indeed prove to be "rival" by leaving weak spots elsewhere in the perimeter. (In the Korean War, many American analysts feared that too great an involvement would divert needed forces from the European theater.) One may attempt to exclude "unimportant" countries or uncooperative governments from one's defensive or deterrent umbrella, though as South Korea in 1950 suggests, it is not always possible to stick to the resolve to exclude them. Since defense is significantly a private good, small and large states have strong incentives to provide substantial military capabilities of their own. Other important goods can also be derived from military forces, among them technological knowledge, prestige, and internal security.[35]

Prosperity, as provided by an open world economy, is also to be found somewhere on the continuum between private and collective goods. It is partly nonrival and partly rival. General gains accrue from prosperous and expanding markets, yet a capitalist economy lives by competition, and one sells at the expense of a competitor. (The mixed-motive game characterization is appropriate.) States can be formally excluded from the most-favored-nation system—the system that provides much of the basis of international prosperity—as the Soviet Union has been.[36] Within the system, the rules of the international trade and finance game prohibit many kinds of discrimination (exclusion from benefits), but many loopholes can be found, as in various preferences, restrictions, and common market arrangements.

I have already argued that the United States was in the immediate postwar years well positioned to reap *at least* a proportionate share of the collective and private gains to be obtained from the prosperity induced by decolonization and a more open world market. In some sense there were costs, as the United States, in accordance with the liberal free-trade regime it was sponsoring, had to open its own previously protected markets. But these costs were, during the first decades after World War II, recouped many times over from the prosperity stimulated generally by a relatively open world market and specifically by American access to others' previously closed markets. These markets, of course, included those of the metropolitan countries of Europe as well as of the third world. The United States mitigated EEC discrimination against American trade by insisting that EEC trade and investment barriers be low and, save for agricultural products, it succeeded in gaining access on terms not much worse than those accorded to intra-EEC enterprises.

The gains from an open global economy surely exceeded the costs to the United States. Despite what ultimately proved to be heavy burdens that the United States shouldered to maintain the open economy, the balance sheet for Americans looks favorable when compared with the costs that other powers accepted in decolonization. (The costs associated with maintaining the dollar at a fixed price in gold, for example, eventually became too great, but for a long time they were substantially balanced by the gains from seigniorage and autonomy.) Indeed, gains from decolonization helped shield the United States from what might otherwise have been a *rapid* deterioration of its relative economic position resulting from the disproportionate economic burden (the Marshall Plan as well as high military expenditures) it carried in the interests of containment. The two defeated powers, Germany and Japan, did quickly close much of the per capita economic gap with the United States—as a consequence of deliberate American policy to build strong pillars of containment at either end of the Soviet Union. But the major power whose decolonization occurred after rather than during the war, Great Britain, was in no way able to close the gap.

A careful understanding of the kind of goods provided to various actors tells us that the picture of hegemonic America largely supplying others with collective goods is simply misleading. Earlier, I also argued that the image of a gross long-term deterioration in benefits enjoyed by the United States was a serious distortion of reality, ignoring much continuity of gain. To recognize that distortion, however, is not to argue that the benefits to the United States were necessarily weighted in the direction of the long term. In fact, gains began to accrue rather quickly while many of the costs emerged only in the longer term; in the 1970s. The Western alliance system to contain the Soviet Union was created quickly and was especially effective in the first decades. Stable peace was established among and within the OECD countries quite early, and it too was a quick as well as an enduring benefit.

The prosperity that both supported and was maintained by peace likewise began early, with the immediate rebuilding of war-torn economies, and it extended unbroken until the oil shocks of the 1970s. True, the postwar reconstruction entailed immediate large-scale costs to the United States, in the Marshall Plan and in trade concessions to Japan that in large part substituted for heavy grant assistance, but the United States had large amounts of surplus productive capacity after World War II, making the costs of overseas economic assistance not really very onerous. Furthermore, that excess capacity made postwar American prosperity dependent on foreign economic expansion in worldwide prosperity. Had the European or former colonial economies been allowed to stagnate, almost surely the American economy would have done likewise. Most major currencies had become convertible by the mid-1950s and at stable exchange rates, reducing, in Arrighi's words, "the risks to capital of, and so favoring, the expansion of international trade and investment."[37] Again, the United States was superbly positioned to capture its full share of those gains. It is also worth remembering that this open world economy did not, especially in the first decades, include the communist countries. When those states began to seek partial global economic integration, however—Eastern Europe in the 1960s and the Soviet Union and China somewhat later—the terms were largely the initial American specifications.

It is no more correct to describe the costs of obtaining noneconomic goods as disproportionately borne by the United States. Even in the instance most often cited, the cost of containment, the argument fails. It is true that in purely economic terms (i.e., share of GNP, a cost that the wealthy United States could most easily bear) the burden fell more heavily on Americans. But non-Americans have consistently provided the real estate and the manpower. For example, America's formal allies alone, in Europe and Asia, have maintained twice as many soldiers under arms as has the United States. They did so immediately after the war as well as in recent years, many of them with compulsory national service.

The balance sheet of costs and benefits to all parties, coupled with a rigorous application of the criteria for collective goods, casts a

good deal of doubt on the proposition that the United States provided disproportionate benefits to others. The major goods provided
by American postwar hegemony—"stable peace" within much of the
industrialized world, a *cordon sanitaire* around the major perceived
security threat, a relatively open, expanding, and largely predictable
world economy—were obtained in degrees that were not markedly
suboptimal from the American point of view. The burdens were
not grossly unfair to the United States relative either to the gains to
the United States or to the burdens borne by many other noncommunist countries. Nor did the United States incur especially large
short-term costs for its own or others' long-term benefit. True, there
were short-term costs, especially economic costs that the world's
largest, richest economy could readily bear, but the benefits came
pouring in quickly too.

This assessment fits with what is, after all, conventional wisdom
about governmental decision makers, perhaps especially those in an
elected system. Decision makers experience incentives to incur long-
term costs (payable after election) to show short-term gains, or at
least to avoid short-term losses.[38] It is possible that after great
disruptive wars politicians are more likely to become statesmen,
concerning themselves with a long-term institutionalization of a
"structure of peace." Certainly there was a great deal of action after
1945 based on long-term vision, but at the same time the short-term
gains were very far from trivial. Indeed, from many radical and even
liberal perspectives American aid and rearmament expenditures—
both in themselves and as stimulants in a wider and open world
economy—prevented a postwar repetition of the Great Depression.
For Americans it was the ideal outcome: one could do well by
doing good.

Cultural Hegemony

How do we explain the U.S. ability to achieve and to maintain a
rather favorable balance of costs and benefits? One answer, found in
a few versions of the hegemonic stability literature, asserts that in the
early years, at least, the United States was such a powerful hegemon
that it could skew the division of private goods in its favor and
enforce "adequate" burden sharing for collective goods by other noncommunist states. The United States, according to this interpretation,
in effect provided something functionally equivalent to the coercive

mechanism of central government that insures the provision of collective goods within nation-states.[39] In this sense American hegemony was essentially imposed and maintained by political-economic coercion, though not largely by the threat or fact of physical violence. Certainly other countries were in a weak position to resist American demands in the immediate postwar era, and relatively strong international institutions—at least by comparison to those of the period before World War II—were created, dominated by the United States. But the qualification of "strong" as relative to what went before is an important one. I find it hard to believe that the institutions provided the basis for coercive, tax-collecting power necessary to enforce what was from an American point of view a near-optimal provision of collective goods at a distribution of costs that was not unfair to the United States. Coercive hegemony provides at best a challengeable answer.[40]

A final major gain to the United States from the Pax Americana has perhaps been less widely appreciated. It nevertheless proved of great significance in the short as well as in the long term: the pervasive cultural influence of the United States. This dimension of power base is often neglected. After World War II, the authoritarian political cultures of Europe and Japan were utterly discredited, and the liberal democratic elements of those cultures revivified. The revival was most extensive and deliberate in the occupied powers of the Axis, where it was nurtured by drafting democratic constitutions, building democratic institutions, curbing the power of industrial trusts by decartelization and the rebuilding of trade unions, and imprisoning or discrediting much of the wartime leadership. American liberal ideas largely filled the cultural void. The effect was not so dramatic in the "victor" states whose regimes were reaffirmed (Britain, the Low and Scandinavian countries), but even there the United States and its culture was widely admired. The upper classes may often have thought it too "commercial," but in many respects American mass consumption culture was the most pervasive part of America's impact. American styles, tastes, and middle-class consumption patterns were widely imitated, in a process that has come to bear the label "coca-colonization."

Altogether, the near-global acceptance of so many aspects of American culture—consumption, democracy, language—very quickly laid the basis for what Gramscians would call cultural hegemony. It paid immediate benefits, in markets and in a willingness of many people to bear significant burdens in order to establish and maintain the *cordon sanitaire*. In the longer term it shaped people's desires and perceptions of alternatives, so that their preferences in international politics and economics were concordant with those of Americans. (The rationalization of hegemony is itself part of this process.) Pervasive American cultural influence was part of a structural transformation of the international system. It meant that in many cases Americans would be able to retain substantial control over essential outcomes without having to exert power over others overtly.[41] Rather, others' values were already conditioned to be compatible with American wishes in ways that would benefit Americans as well as themselves (antiauthoritarianism and, within limits, acceptance of free-market economics).[42]

Gramscian ideas of influence are notoriously difficult to operationalize because by definition they leave no traces in events; overt persuasion is usually unnecessary, much less coercion. But they should not be dismissed.[43] Evidence of the mushroom expansion of American television, film, and printed matter in the world, often in spite of other governments' efforts to reinforce cultural boundaries, supports a Gramscian interpretation. It is truly a worldwide phenomenon, not limited to the industrial states of Europe and Japan. The internalization of Western (but especially American) norms by the rulers and middle classes of the third world forms a constant theme in *dependencia* writing. Nor has it noticeably diminished over the years. De Gaulle and Mitterrand offer but ineffectual resistance in an industrial country, and only the draconian measures of Khomeini bring much success in an underdeveloped one.

The international institutionalization associated with regime building, noted earlier, helps spread common cultural and political norms, especially among governing elites, helping to achieve consensus on what problems must be solved and how. Norm-creating institutions broaden individuals' self-images; institutions may change the "decision criteria—members may become *joint* maximizers rather than just self-maximizers."[44]

The spread of American culture (democratic, capitalist, mass consumption, anticommunist) has laid the basis for innumerable American economic and political gains. The spread of American culture has been a collective good in the sense of being nonrival. (We can state this observation more strongly: to the degree one state in the global system becomes more Americanized, others are influenced to become more, not less, so.) It also is not readily capable of being excluded. If one regards it normatively as a "good," then all parties are beneficiaries, but even then the private benefits to the United States itself can hardly be ignored. Many peoples who would have liked to exclude American culture were unable to do so, and certainly to them it was hardly an unalloyed "good."

It was appropriate that Americans, who have reaped so many gains from cultural dominance, should pay whatever extremely modest costs it may have entailed. Cultural hegemony provides long-term influence that persists, and persists deeply, to this day. It is among the primary reasons why a decline in dominance over material power has not been reflected in an equivalent loss of control over outcomes.

Conclusion

These observations begin to untangle a central puzzle of the hegemonic stability literature. Two empirical assumptions at the "hard core" of the hegemonic stability research program depart so far from reality as to have seriously misleading effects. First, the characterization of hegemonic America as predominantly supplying itself and others with collective goods is inaccurate. Even for those goods that can correctly be called collective, the United States has not paid at all disproportionate costs. Second, the description of American hegemony itself as having declined is a gross overstatement, particularly when one looks at the military and cultural as well as at the economic elements of hegemony.

The puzzle stems from trying to explain a phenomenon that has not really occurred. Mark Twain did die eventually, and so will American hegemony. But in both cases early reports of their demise have been greatly exaggerated.

Chapter 9

Theater Nuclear Forces: Public Opinion in Western Europe

With Donald R. DeLuca

Despite the outcome of the March 1983 West German election—favorable from the point of view of the Reagan administration—it is clear that many Europeans do not support the deployment of a new generation of American theater nuclear weapons in their countries. Some observers imagine that this reluctance is based on a new "war scare," an upsurge of pacifism, or a new wave of anti-Americanism. None of these explanations, however, can be supported by closer analysis. There was a "war scare" around 1980, but it has now passed; no upsurge of pacifism ever existed; and anti-Americanism is present, but in no significantly greater degree than the postwar norm. The problem is both more specific and more general—a new loss of confidence in the current political leadership of the United States combined with a long-standing popular reluctance to rely as confidently as do their governments on nuclear deterrence. Suspicion and distaste are directed toward the American government, not toward American citizens. These attitudes are more widespread in Britain than in West Germany, and they are concentrated in the young, those voters who will be in the electorate for decades to come. Unless the implications of these attitudes are faced constructively, the recent crisis in the NATO over West European defense will not be the last of its kind. An undercurrent of fear and mistrust will remain, surfacing periodically with unpredictable and profoundly dangerous implications.

These assertions can be documented with a wide range of public opinion survey material from the major nations of Western Europe. Many surveys contain similar questions asked in many countries throughout the region, or similar questions repeated periodically over years or even decades. While there are many pitfalls for the unwary in analyzing such survey data, analyses across countries and time can provide some crucial information about the relative depth of popular concern.[1] It is, of course, another matter to move from statements about the nature of public opinion to statements about the probable impact of that opinion on governmental policy. Even democratic governments often can long insulate themselves from the popular mood. But in the long run, no government, especially a democratic one, can depend on resisting the deeply felt will of its people.

Fears of War

As figure 9.1 shows, there clearly was a sharp upsurge in "the fear of a world war within the subsequent ten years" in all the major countries of the European Community (EC) between 1977 and 1980. We cannot be sure just when that surge became strong, but it is likely to have been after the Soviet invasion of Afghanistan at the end of 1979. People in most countries calmed their fears by late 1981, though the West Germans—in a position to be most alarmed by President

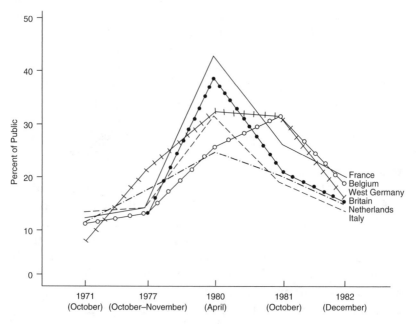

Figure 9.1   Assessment of risk of war in next ten years. Percentage of those expressing an opinion who considered war "certain" or "more than 50/50 chance"

Sources: *Eurobarometre* 16 (December 1981) 9, and 7:8 (1980), 145; and *Gallup Political Index* (Britain) No. 269 (January 1983), 15–18.

Reagan's and Secretary of State Alexander Haig's offhand remarks in the spring of 1981 about fighting a "limited" nuclear war in Europe—remained quite worried. Significant relaxation is apparent in all countries by the end of 1982, although the level of fear was, in most instances, still a little higher than it had been in 1977. Longer-term data suggest that recent fears of war in West Germany and Britain have been at a level that is a little above the average for the 1960s and the early 1970s, though lower than during the Berlin crisis of 1961.[2]

Expectations of war are not significantly linked to specific segments of the population. For example, they are about as common among men as among women, and equally prevalent among the various age groups. Nor are they related to political opinion, either on a standard "left-right" political spectrum or on a scale of foreign-policy preference ranging from pro-NATO through neutralism to a pro-Soviet orientation.

Instead, they are closely associated with personal life conditions. Those who "cannot or only just about make ends meet," for whom, at work, "things are going rather badly," or who, in regard to their lives in general, are "not at all satisfied," are much more likely than others to think there is a better than even chance of war.[3] In other words, the "expectation of war" question becomes something of a projective test indicating the overall state of an individual's psychological mood, rather than the person's considered evaluation of the state of world affairs. In times of international political tension, the number of people expecting war may increase, but their susceptibility to fear depends more on their personal experiences than on their political convictions. It also is worth noting that the fear of war is notably less severe in Western Europe than in the United States. Indeed, it is greater among Americans than anywhere else save among white South Africans (who occupy a global pariah status). Table 9.1 shows the average probability of war (on a 0 to 100 scale) assigned in various countries, in December 1982, with the United States at the top.

Two further aspects of European fear of war emerge in another set of data, given in table 9.2. First, several years ago there was a serious expectation of Soviet attack, but that expectation has since dwindled to a very low level. Second, the Europeans are nearly as afraid of American adventurism ("the United States will attack Eastern Europe") as of Soviet adventurism, though neither fear is very great.[4]

Table 9.1   Average estimates in selected countries of the probability of a World War, December 1982

Question: "Here is a sort scale." [Show card, with percentage gradations from 0 to 100, by tens.] "World you, with the help of this card, tell me how you assess the changes of a world war breaking out in the next ten years?"

Country	Average (%)
United States	45
South Africa (White)	44
Canada	38
France	35
Netherlands	34
Ireland	33
Switzerland	32
West Germany	32
Belgium	32
Norway	31
Luxembourg	30
Sweden	29
Great Britain	28
Italy	26
Finland	26
Denmark	26
Greece	18

Source: *Gallup Political Index* (Britain), No. 269 (January 1983), 15–18.

Table 9.2   Perceptions of the likelihood of an attack

Question: Russian attack: "How likely do you think it is that Russia will attack Western Europe within the next five years—very likely, fairly likely, not so likely, not at all likely?" (Percentage is of those answering "very likely" or "fairly likely.")

Question: U.S. attack: "How likely do you think it is that the United States will attack Eastern Europe within the next five years—very likely, fairly likely, not so likely, not at all likely?" (Percentage of those answering "very likely" or "fairly likely.")

	Russian Attack (%)			U.S. Attack (%)
Country	May 1979	March 1981	February 1982	February 1982
France	62	42	—	—
West Germany	71	55	15	11
Britain	—	48	21	21

Sources: Kenneth Adler and Douglas Wertman, "West European Security Concerns for the Eighties: Is NATO in Trouble?" paper prepared for the Annual Meeting of the American Association of Public Opinion Research, Bucks Hill, PA, May 1981; Gallup International Survey reported in *Newsweek*, March 15, 1982, 9.

Anti-Americanism

West Europeans are less confident than they once were in the basic prudence and reliability of the United States. This downturn in European evaluation emerges in many surveys in all the major countries. Figure 9.2, for instance, shows a clear drop in "overall opinion of the United States" since the 1960s, and table 9.3 a shorter-term drop even since the early 1970s (during the Vietnam War), in "confidence in the ability of the United States to handle world problems." The perception was worst in Britain, and has become more so. Opinion of the United States was at an all-time low in February 1982. A year later, 33 percent of Britons gave positive answers to this question, with 64 percent reporting they had little or no confidence.[5]

These doubts are focused especially on the personage of President Reagan. A British survey in June 1982 found only 31 percent

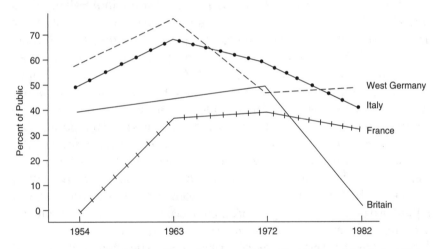

Figure 9.2   Net predominance of favorable over unfavorable opinion of the United States

Question: "What is your overall opinion of the United States? Do you have a very favorable, somewhat favorable, somewhat unfavorable, or very unfavorable opinion of the United States?" In the interest of brevity, only the net predominance of favorable over unfavorable opinion is shown. (Two favorable categories combined, minus two unfavorable.) As an example of how to read this graph, in Great Britain in October 1954 there was a 40 percent predominance of favorable opinion (49 percent) over unfavorable opinion (9 percent) toward the United States. This is the latest question wording; earlier wording varied, but still permits comparison of net approval.

Sources: Leo P. Crespi, "Trends in U.S. Standing in West European Public Opinion," USICA Report R-4-82, February 1982; February 1982 Gallup International Survey reported in *Newsweek*, March 15, 1982, 9.

Table 9.3   Confidence in United States ability to handle world problems

Question: "In general how much confidence do you have in the ability of the United States to handle world problems—a great deal, a fair amount, not very much, or none at all?" (Percentages are the sum of "a great deal" and "a fair amount.")

Survey Date	Britain (%)	France (%)	West Germany (%)	Italy (%)
1972[a]	65	41	57	58
1982	4	33	49	42

Notes: [a] Data for 1972 are an average of three surveys (January, March, and June).

Sources: Leo P. Crespi, "Trends in U.S. Standing;" February 1982. Gallup International Surveys reported in *Newsweek*, March 15, 1982, 9. The survey question varied somewhat in the 1970s but, according to USICA, "not so much as to preclude a broad comparability."

believing that President Reagan "is proving a good president of the United States," with 29 percent saying their opinion had "gone down recently," and only 10 percent saying it had gone up. Lest it be imagined this evaluation is merely a response to lukewarm American support for Britain during the Falkland Islands conflict in April and May of 1982, it may be noted that opinions were even lower in November 1982, with only 23 percent saying he is a good president and 29 percent saying their opinion had gone down recently, and with only 3 percent reporting an improvement.[6] A decline in a leader's popularity after he or she has held office for a while is of course common. All recent American presidents have had the same experience, and the approval rating in the United States of "the way Ronald Reagan is handling his job as president" fell from 49 to 41 percent during the course of 1982.[7] West Europeans particularly may have begun the Reagan term with excessively high hopes out of frustration with aspects of the Carter presidency. If so, some decline is hardly surprising. More informative is the specific content of some West European attitudes, as revealed by the example of West German attitudes. Table 9.4 reports the decline in German opinion of President Reagan, as given by the use of various adjectives to describe his character.

Doubts about the ability of the United States government to deal responsibly with world problems must not, however, be confused with simple "anti-Americanism." On the contrary, at the same time that indications of confidence in American leadership has waned, indications of positive personal feelings toward Americans have waxed. West German citizens are much more likely than at any time since the mid-1960s to say they "like" the Americans, as shown in figure 9.3. Moreover, while doubts about American leadership are

Table 9.4   How west Germans view Ronald Reagan

Character Profile	Percent(%)		
	November	July–August	October
Calculating (berechnend)	29	34	37
Imprudent (rucksichslos)	15	24	28
Aggressive	19	16	23
Educated (gebildet)	30	21	19
Far Sighted	32	30	24
Trustworthy	27	23	19
Intelligent	45	38	27

Source: EMNID surveys, reported in EMNID Informationen 10 (1981), 17.

greatest among the young, so, by a small margin, are positive attitudes toward individual Americans.[8]

Neutralism

West Europeans may question the prudence and judgment of the U.S. government, but as yet they show little sympathy for a neutralist foreign policy. West Germans in particular welcome the presence of American troops on their soil. They consider them "a welcome protection," and would "regret" their departure. They prefer a close alliance with the United States to one of political equidistance between America and Russia, and show virtually no interest in a close political relationship with the Soviet Union. Most West Germans see their security as inextricably bound to the NATO alliance in general, and to the United States in particular. As figure 9.3 shows, this German reliance on the American connection has become stronger, not weaker, in recent years.[9]

If the question is asked in terms of "security," that is, in the context of military relationships and fears of war or invasion, the overall level of commitment of West Europeans to NATO is strong. It is not an unequivocal commitment, containing as it does frequent demands for more control and consultation in forming NATO policy. Furthermore, the French prefer their partial association with NATO—allied, but not under the NATO unified military command— to a closer association. But nowhere is there substantial support

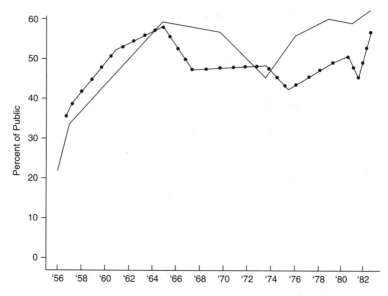

Figure 9.3   German attitudes toward Americans and American troops

Question I: "Generally speaking, do you like the Americans, or don't you like them particularly?" ("Like Americans" is the dotted line.)

Question II: "If you read in the paper tomorrow that the Americans were pulling their troops out of Europe, would you welcome that or would you regret it?" ("Would regret troop withdrawal" is solid line.)

Sources: Elisabeth Noelle-Neumann, ed., *The Germans*; Noelle-Neumann, "Are the Germans 'Collapsing' or 'Standing Firm'?" *Encounter* (1981), 76–81; and German Information Center, *Focus on the Federal Republic of Germany* 2 (April 1982), 6. In this same issue, the German Information Center presented similar trends on whether "Foreign troops constitute an 'unavoidable necessity,' 'a welcome protection,' or an 'undesirable burden.' " An increasing number—now a slight plurality, 44 percent—describe the troops as a "welcome protection," and only a small number—12 percent—take the highly negative "undesirable burden" stance.

for military neutrality or accommodation to the Soviet Union ("Finlandization"), or even for creation of a European military force independent of the United States. Nor is NATO seen simply as a mechanism to avoid bearing what West Europeans see as a reasonable share of the burdens for their defense. Many at least say they would pay more in return for "more say in NATO." Those who prefer the NATO option turn out to be those who are most willing to spend money on defense; certainly there is virtually no sentiment for armed neutrality, with Western Europe balancing between East and West.[10]

However, one should not accept this reassurance too readily. As can be shown in the answers to many other questions, sharp differences emerge among age groups. The majority of older people everywhere in the Atlantic Alliance are firm in their adherence to NATO and in their rejection of neutralism. Among the young, especially those

Table 9.5   Percentage of university-educated people who favor NATO or neutrality, March 1981 (NATO/neutrality ratio)

Question: "All things considered, do you think it is better for our country to belong to NATO, the Western defense alliance, or would it be better for us to get out of NATO and become a neutral country?"

	Age		
Country	*18–34*	*35–49*	*50 and Older*
West Germany	59/28	63/25	95/5
Britain	62/27	70/21	86/5
France	53/33	61/34	79/18
Italy	56/39	82/18	81/14

Source: Kenneth Adler and Douglas Wertman, "Is NATO in Trouble? A Survey of European Attitudes," *Public Opinion* 4 (1981), 10. Similar data appear in Noelle-Neumann, ed., *The Germans*, 418.

under 35, this adherence is less in evidence. There are signs of a serious "generation gap" among Europeans on this issue, a gap that is most serious in the ranks of the well-educated and therefore in the ranks of those who are likely over time to be most politically influential. Table 9.5 shows this situation clearly.

Citizens of the other major West European countries are less wedded to NATO and the United States than are the Germans. If asked to express a very general preference regarding "international policy," neutrality attracts substantial support.[11] This support seems to represent a desire for good political and economic relations with both superpowers and probably more than a small wish to distance themselves from recent American hard-line policies toward the Soviet Union and its allies. Most West Europeans, for instance, had little sympathy for the Americans' policy of imposing sanctions on Russia following the Afghanistan invasion and the crackdown on Solidarity in Poland.

Furthermore, there is an increasing belief that "the Russians are today basically sincere in their desire to negotiate with the West." Whereas most West Germans still do not believe that this is the case, the trend is definitely toward greater belief in the sincerity of the Soviets.[12] Surveys of attitudes toward placement of the new generation of nuclear-armed missiles on West European soil repeatedly show strong preferences for arms control rather than missile deployment. If asked to choose between the missiles and arms control, the typical preference in West Germany, Britain, the Netherlands, and Italy is about two-to-one in favor of arms control. The preferred "solution" is the official NATO "double-track" option: tentative plans to deploy the missiles while pursuing arms control negotiations that would make them unnecessary. In West Germany, Britain, and the Netherlands, a majority can be mustered in favor of the new weapons only under hypothetical circumstances in which arms control talks failed. In Italy, a majority for the weapons cannot be found even then.[13] Arms control is widely popular, coupled with a sense that a reasonable agreement with the Soviet Union is possible if the NATO countries really want it.

Pacifism

If most West Europeans cannot correctly be described as neutralist, neither can they readily be labeled pacifist. Table 9.6 shows that a solid majority of citizens in all the major countries (except Italy, and a clear plurality there) declare it "would be better to fight in defense of your country than to accept Russian domination." West Europeans are not pacifists. They say they are prepared to fight, and surely they would not welcome Soviet occupation.

At the same time, there are cracks in this seemingly solid determination. When the specter of nuclear war is evoked, the response is quite different. Despite the stated West German willingness to fight, when the questions are asked differently the results are quite different. Another variant, for instance, is the following: "If we are one day faced with the choice of either letting Europe become Soviet or

Table 9.6   Russian domination versus war

Question: "Some people say that war is so horrible that it is better to accept Russian domination than to risk war. Others say it would be better to fight in defense of your country than to accept Russian domination. Which opinion is closer to your own?"

	Percent in Favor in Each Country			
Opinin	*Britain* (%)	*Germany* (%)	*France* (%)	*Italy* (%)
Better to Accept Domination	12	19	13	17
Better to Fight	75	74	57	48
Don't Know	13	7	30	35

Source: Gallup surveys as reported in *Newsweek*, March 15, 1982, 9.

defending ourselves against such a fate by every means, which is more important—to defend democratic freedom, even if it means a nuclear war, or to avoid war at all costs, even if it means living under a Communist government?" When this question was presented in July 1981, the split was 45 percent to avoid nuclear war at all costs, only 30 percent to defend democracy, and 25 percent unable to decide. Not surprisingly, nuclear war raises the ante. Also, among young people (under 30), the proportion wanting to "avoid nuclear war at all costs" is 10 percentage points higher than among their elders.[14]

The Soviet-American Military Balance

West Europeans live in the shadow of Soviet military might and many of them regard their strategic position as significantly inferior to that of the Soviet Union. West Germans have been asked, "Supposing the Russians were to start a war, do you think that we, together with NATO, have enough troops and would be sufficiently well armed to stave off an attack from Russia and prevent them from entering our country, or don't you think that we could defend ourselves against a serious Russian attack?" In May 1981, 41 percent answered that they could not expect to defend themselves, whereas only 25 percent thought they could do so. Ten years earlier the comparable figures had been 37 percent and 27 percent. The results indicate an overall negative evaluation at both times and a drop in confidence in West German military security, though not a precipitous one.[15] In fact, West Europeans have always felt uneasy about their defensive capabilities, and the current skepticism is only a little greater than usual. Table 9.7 shows the trends from 1957 to 1981 in the four major countries in perceptions of which side, the United States or the Soviet Union, is ahead in total military strength. The data are not fully comparable over time because of a change in question wording between 1969 and 1977. The earlier wording did not offer "neither" or "equal" as an option (though some people volunteered it). The presence of this option in 1977 seemed to cut especially into the proportion (already a minority) who would otherwise characterize the United States as ahead. Nonetheless, the change in question wording does not obscure some basic conclusions that emerge from table 9.7.

First, perception of American relative military strength has clearly declined in all countries since the 1960s. This shift corresponds

Table 9.7 Perception of United States and Soviet military strength, 1957–81

Question (1957–69): "All things considered, which country do you think is ahead in total military strength at the present time—the US or the Soviet Union?"

Question (1977–81): "How do you think the US and the USSR compare at the present time in total military strength—US considerably ahead, US somewhat ahead, US and USSR about equal, USSR somewhat ahead, USSR considerably ahead?"

Country and Date	U.S. Ahead (%)	USSR Ahead (%)	Neither Ahead (%)
Britain			
1981 (October)	10	51	29
1977 (March)	10	50	19
1969 (October–November)	33	34	13
1957 (November)	19	50	6
France			
1981 (October)	15	34	33
1977 (March)	16	34	27
1969 (October–November)	40	26	19
1957 (November)	17	25	20
West Germany			
1981 (October)	15	38	29
1977 (March)	15	34	35
1969 (October–November)	41	26	25
1957 (November)	38	23	20
Italy			
1981 (October)	24	29	41
1977 (March)	22	20	34
1969 (October–November)	44	13	25
1957 (November)	34	22	23

Sources: Kenneth P. Adler and Douglas A. Wertman, "West European Security Concerns for the Eighties;" Leo P. Crespi, "Trends in U.S. Standing." "Don't Know" answers are omitted from the table.

roughly to the changing overall strategic balance as perceived by most military experts, from American superiority to a situation of no more than rough "parity" or "essential equivalence." Second, perceptions differ significantly in different countries. Italians consistently have had the most favorable impression of American military strength; the British have had the worst.

Furthermore, even in the 1950s and early 1960s, the British, the French, and often the West Germans regularly perceived the Soviet Union as militarily superior. This is notable because it happened at a time when the Soviet Union clearly was not ahead—behind in strategic weapons, and probably not measurably superior even in the European theater.[16] Many NATO military and civilian leaders, however, have regularly proclaimed their fears about Soviet military superiority for the purpose of spurring further defensive efforts by the Western allies. They seem to have been successful in conveying their stated perceptions, if not in bringing about the desired level of military effort.

Finally, in their perceptions of the relative military balance, the Europeans are not discernibly more pessimistic than Americans have been. The American public also lost confidence in American military capability, increasingly so during the late 1970s. Fully 41 percent of Americans said that they felt "the military defense system of the United States is weaker than that of the Russians" in February 1980, as compared with only 27 percent in December 1976.[17] West Europeans thus are not victims of a peculiarly West European wave of "panic."

"Panic," in fact, is hardly the correct term. Quite to the contrary, most Europeans feel more comfortable in a world of approximate military parity between the superpowers. Since the middle of the 1960s, repeated samplings have almost always shown a clear preference for parity, not for American superiority. Table 9.8 demonstrates this beyond doubt for both elite and mass population samples.[18] The reason for this result is simple: parity implies mutual deterrence and caution; superiority implies the possibility of recklessness and adventurism. Europeans prefer that neither side has confidence it can "win" a world war or a European war.

Table 9.8   Preferred power alignment: United States versus Soviet Union, 1974

Question: "Whatever you think may actually happen, which would you personally like to see more powerful ten years from now, the United States or the Soviet Union—or would you rather see them about equal in power?"

Sample by Country	U.S. More Powerful (%)	USSR More Powerful (%)	About Equal (%)	Don't Know (%)
Elites				
British	37	1	61	1
French	25	5	62	8
German	35	2	61	2
Italian	30	5	60	5
Public				
British	49	1	47	3
French	21	6	62	11
German	39	4	51	6
Italian	28	6	54	12

Source: United States Advisory Commission Information, 28th Report to Congress (Washington, DC, 1977), 123.

Another aspect of West European fears about provocative military postures can be seen in table 9.9. Here, as in figure 9.3, there appears evidence of the welcome that West Europeans give to American troops on their territory. Except in Britain, the troops are seen as a deterrent that provides protection. American nuclear missiles, however, are another matter. For the British, the missiles are seen as making an attack more likely, not deterring it. In Belgium the split in perception is about even, and in West Germany the missiles would, on balance, be preferred. But in every case the missiles are far less welcome than the troops.

This perception is especially significant in light of plans to deploy Pershing II missiles in Western Europe. These new missiles will be capable of striking at or near Soviet command and control centers in Moscow, in a time of only about five minutes from launch to impact, with greater accuracy than anything yet deployed. Since they will be only clumsily mobile, by many experts' judgment they both threaten Soviet territory and invite a preemptive Soviet strike. West Europeans, whether or not they are familiar with all the technical details, can nevertheless be pardoned for wondering whether such weapons "increase chances of an attack." As the distinguished British military historian Michael Howard has put it, weapons not only must provide deterrence of one's enemies, they must also provide reassurance to one's friends.[19] Not all American weapons systems can easily do so.

Table 9.9   Perceived effects of American nuclear missiles or troops stationed in Western Europe, February 1982

Question: "What is the effect of having American nuclear missiles (troops) stationed in Western Europe?"

Perceived Effect	Britain (%)	France (%)	West Germany (%)	Belgium (%)
Increases Chances of an Attack				
Missiles	42	24	27	24
Troops	25	—	15	22
Provides Greater Protection				
Missiles	29	31	41	25
Troops	24	—	48	25
No Effect/Don't Know				
Missiles	29	45	32	51
Troops	51	—	37	54

Source: February 1982 Gallup International Surveys, reported in *Newsweek*, March 15, 1982, 9.

Nuclear weapons are relatively cheap. In the words immortalized by Secretary of Defense Charles Wilson during the Eisenhower administration, they provide "more bang for the buck." American officials have seen nuclear weapons as providing "affordable" deterrence, in contrast to the heavy expenditures thought necessary to defend Western Europe from a conventional (nonnuclear) attack purely by conventional means. Nuclear weapons provide an "equalizer" for the technologically superior West against the Eastern "hordes." West European governments typically have shared this judgment; indeed in 1983 both France and Britain were cutting back their conventional forces so they could buy a new generation of nuclear weapons. The preference for nuclear deterrence has been thought, furthermore, to be politically popular—certainly more popular than would be bigger defense budgets for conventional forces.

But there is reason, in public opinion sources, to wonder whether that preference is really so widely shared. The British public has at least given hints to the contrary. One question read as follows: "It is often said that if we gave up nuclear weapons we would have to increase total expenditure on conventional forces because conventional forces would be more expensive. Would you prefer to keep nuclear weapons, or spend more on conventional forces?" The answers split 42 percent for nuclear weapons, and 45 percent for spending more on conventional forces. (The remaining 13 percent had no opinion.) Similarly, another survey asked, "If the money to spend on arms alone could not be changed, would you prefer the Government to spend more on non-nuclear forces and less on nuclear arms, maintain the present balance, or spend more on nuclear arms and less on non-nuclear forces?" A plurality (38 percent) choose "the present balance." But of the others, 31 percent would spend more on nonnuclear forces, and only 17 percent more on nuclear arms.[20] It is of course not clear that the public would be so approving when it actually came time to reallocate expenditures. Nevertheless, one fact is clear: nuclear arms may be accepted in Britain, but they are not loved.

NATO has long maintained a posture of "flexible response" in Europe. That is, any Soviet attack would be met with whatever weapons were necessary to try to contain it. An attack with tactical nuclear weapons presumably would be met with nuclear weapons, either tactical or, very possibly, with strategic weapons launched against the Soviet homeland. A conventional attack might be resisted with only conventional weapons, or, especially considering the widespread image of NATO conventional inferiority in Western Europe, with nuclear weapons. The argument has been that the possible or probable resort to nuclear weapons is necessary if deterrence is to be reliable. No one imagines that either conventional or nuclear war in Europe would be anything but immensely destructive; but the nuclear threat is supposed to deter, and thus prevent, either.

The West European populace, however, has long-standing doubts on the wisdom of using or of threatening to use nuclear weapons in Europe. Indeed, these doubts have mounted over the years. Repeated surveys in all major European countries found extreme skepticism toward fighting a nuclear war even two and three decades ago.[21] Except for the first two surveys in Britain, in virtually no case was there a net approval (percentage approving minus percentage disapproving) for a first use of nuclear weapons even if NATO forces were being overrun. The longer NATO has relied on a "first use" posture, the more negative attitudes have become.

West European doubts about the wisdom of nuclear "first use" have hardly been assuaged by more recent developments. Table 9.10 gives the results to a similar survey question in July 1981. The options presented ranged from the complete rejection of the use of nuclear weapons under any circumstances, through purely retaliatory "nuclear in return for nuclear" use, to the standard NATO posture of "flexible response" (i.e., use of nuclear weapons if a Soviet attack by conventional forces threatened to overwhelm NATO forces). The latter statement ("threatened to overwhelm") actually is

Table 9.10   Attitudes about use of nuclear weapons in Europe by NATO, July 1981

Question: "There are different opinions about the use of nuclear weapons in Europe by NATO. Which one of the following opinions is closest to your own?"

	Britain (%)	France (%)	West Germany (%)	Italy (%)
NATO should not use nuclear weapons of any kind under any circumstances.	24	44	29	42
NATO should use nuclear weapons only if the Soviet Union uses them first in attacking Western Europe.	47	32	37	39
NATO should use nuclear weapons to defend itself if a Soviet attack by conventional forces threatened to overwhelm NATO forces.	19	17	17	12
No opinion.	10	8	17	8

Source: Leo P. Crespi, "West European Perceptions of the U.S.," paper presented at the convention of the International Society of Political Psychology, June 1982, Table 4.

a fairly strong proposition, one that would seem to encourage assent. But the striking conclusion is that few people did in fact give that assent; fewer than 20 percent of any country's populace approved NATO first use of nuclear weapons. The same question has been repeated in subsequent surveys with similar results.

Implications for the Future

Many observers over the past 30 years have periodically declared NATO to be "in crisis." So far, the Alliance has weathered such crises. The fact that disaster has always been averted must not, however, obscure the major problems and differences of opinion among NATO members. West Europeans, and particularly the West Germans, are exposed to possible Soviet occupation in a way that Americans have never been. Moreover, West Europeans have already twice in this century experienced disasters of "conventional" wars to a degree unknown in the United States. As a result of these two facts—exposure and experience—West Europeans desperately want to deter the initiation of any war on their soil. "Limited" nuclear war has little meaning in one of the most urbanized and densely populated areas in the world; a full-scale conventional war would be little better. West Europeans therefore want to be reassured that war in general can be deterred, and overwhelmingly have chosen to rely on an alliance with the United States, through NATO, to provide that deterrence. They are not anti-American, neutralist, or pacifist. But neither are they confident in the good judgment of contemporary American leaders, nor are they reassured by talk of fighting a limited nuclear war in Europe, or convinced that a new generation of theater nuclear weapons—the 464 ground-launched cruise missiles and 108 Pershing II ballistic missiles—will truly deter an attack.

The immediate danger to NATO cohesion raised by the new weapons deployment issue may be resolved, either by conclusion of an arms control agreement or by a determination by the governments to go ahead with deployment in the absence of arms control. The underlying problem of retaining Alliance cohesion will not, however, so readily be put aside. The people of Western Europe will remain deeply disturbed by the risks inherent in their security predicament. They fear the risk that, for one reason or another—inadvertent crisis escalation more likely than deliberate assault—they will again suffer devastation. As a result, continued reliance on nuclear deterrence will continue to evoke ambivalence. Proposals for lessened reliance on nuclear weapons will retain great attraction, especially for the younger generation of the West European populace and periodically for their governments. Proposals to avoid a first use of nuclear weapons, or at least to avoid an "early" first use, will have wide appeal. Arguments will continue to rage about the feasibility of alternative defense postures, and this chapter is hardly the place to try to resolve them.[22] At the minimum, however, steps toward tighter command and control of battlefield and theater nuclear weapons in Europe, and to move vulnerable nuclear forces back from the front lines, make much military sense. They also make excellent sense in the context of West European politics. If the NATO alliance is to survive, it cannot do so with weapons and military postures that ignore legitimate popular fears.

Chapter 10

Away from Nuclear Mythology

The chapter by Kenneth Waltz[1] is courageous, stimulating, and utterly wrongheaded. I sincerely admire several aspects of the chapter. It addresses the security issues that are central to the *political* decisions states make to acquire or abstain from acquiring nuclear weapons. That is, it takes seriously security and other political motivations and thus avoids the common fallacy of imagining that nuclear acquisitions can be affected primarily by manipulating technical conditions of access to nuclear material or know-how. It is forthright about asking what happens if, or when, the nonproliferation regime substantially fails. That is, unlike much of the earlier writing on this topic, it leaves us with some hope and some direction for policy in the event of failure. Finally, it is courageous in taking an unpopular position. It argues forthrightly, developing a line of reasoning that, until recently at least, has risked ostracism for its proponent.[2] Waltz's readiness to dare opprobrium by challenging conventional wisdom deserves respect at the same time that it deserves vigorous rebuttal. I want to move to that rebuttal, but in the context of a real appreciation for what the author has done and risked.

Waltz's fundamental thesis is that the spread of nuclear weapons will enhance deterrence and make the destruction of war less likely. I deliberately say "the destruction of war" less likely rather than merely "war" because, as we shall see, Waltz fails fully to appreciate the latter as contrasted with just the likelihood of war. Rather, especially in the nuclear case, it seems more likely that wars, even if infrequent, would be so destructive as to leave us worse off on any combined (in)frequency times severity measure. Nevertheless, Waltz is not very concerned about that problem, and states that a gradual spread of nuclear weapons should be welcomed more than feared.

Nowhere does Waltz tell us how nuclear proliferation is actually to be kept measured or even whether or not it is likely to be so. Almost everybody (Waltz perhaps excepted) wants to keep nuclear weapons out of the hands of leaders like Muammar Qadhafi and Idi Amin, but no one has been very persuasive about how that prevention can be accomplished once every other national leader has nuclear weapons. If we really want to keep nuclear weapons out of those hands, surely a more promising route is first to keep them out of the hands of the tenth, eighteenth, and ninety-third "responsible" states as well as out of the hands of terrorists or international gangsters.

A more serious reason that Waltz's thesis should be suspect is that it is not actually a thesis—in the sense of a conclusion—at all. Rather, it is more of a premise. The structure of the chapter hints that Waltz started with the premise that nuclear deterrence is not such a bad thing after all, and then went backward, seeking those assumptions that would support his case for nuclear proliferation.

It is also hard to follow Waltz's argument because not all the assumptions are essential to the conclusion. It is not always clear which assumptions are necessary and which are superfluous. So many of those assumptions are either dubious or demonstrably in error or in direct contradiction with each other that the conclusion must necessarily fall. Nevertheless, his chapter does deserve a responsible effort to show why its thesis must be rejected.

Uncertainty and Expected Utility

One proposition appears several times early in the chapter: "Certainty about the relative strength of adversaries . . . makes war less likely . . . Miscalculation causes wars." (p.118) It would be tempting to treat this proposition as a variant of the familiar argument that great disparity in power relations produces peace: both sides can anticipate who will win a war between them and hence do not need to fight to determine the outcome. Relative equality of power, to the contrary, produces uncertainty about the outcome of a war and hence contributes to war by causing one side or both to overestimate the chance of success.

This argument has been subjected to systematic empirical testing in several forms, with "certainty" about power relations depending on the power of alliances and strength of alliance bonds as well as on the power of individual states. More studies seem to support the proposition that disparity (certainty) equals peace[3] than support its converse;[4] but others claim no consistent support for either.[5] Serious theoretical or methodological problems impair most of these studies, however, so it probably would be most prudent simply to say that the evidence on both sides is unconvincing.[6] Waltz cannot claim significant support either for uncertainty equals peace or for uncertainty equals war in this literature, nor does he even refer to it.

Rather, after raising the proposition, he brushes it aside in this form as relevant only to a world armed with conventional weapons. Instead, nuclear weapons induce caution in the behavior of the states that possess them and in those faced by states that possess them.[7] This caution (hesitance to go to war) results from a combination of "[u]ncertainty about the course a nuclear war might follow, along with the *certainty* that destruction can be immense. . . ." (p.123) "In a nuclear world, one is uncertain about survival or annihilation. . . . [T]hat is not the kind of uncertainty that encourages the use of force." (p.119) The Russians, despite their superiority over the Chinese, must deal with the possibility that, if they attack China, some Chinese bombers or missiles nevertheless may get through in retaliation. Waltz approvingly cites Thomas Schelling's principle of "the threat that leaves something to chance" as a sufficient deterrent— and of course that is precisely the principle on which NATO's deployment of tactical nuclear weapons in Europe rests.[8] Even better, says Waltz, if there are many nuclear powers, then one must worry about the possible actions of all of them if war should ensue: "Such worries at once complicate calculations and strengthen deterrence" (p.122).

In fact, Waltz's argument is less about uncertainty than about expected utilities. He says that it is not certainty about who will win that is a force for peace, but uncertainty about the costs the war maker may incur and the real possibility of terribly great costs. Whatever gains might conceivably be achieved in a war, the possibility (probability) of very high losses (disutilities) is enough to give the war option a negative expected utility. More precisely, nuclear weapons are alleged to have restraining effects not because of the uncertainty of their consequences, but simply because they greatly raise the possible costs of war. They deter, in the language of the stock market, by opening up an enormous downside risk and making it likely that heavy costs will be paid if one actually chooses to run the risk. This deterrent (substantial probability of very high disutilities, therefore a low expected utility for anyone contemplating a war) is overwhelmingly strong, and reliable. In the U.S.-Soviet deterrent equilibrium, Waltz argues, since one side cannot destroy enough of the other side's missiles to make a retaliatory strike bearable, the "balance of terror" is maintained.

This argument is quite an oversimplification. Of course, for the superpowers another leg of the triad may survive even if land-based missiles become vulnerable; and indeed the whole thrust of modern deterrence theory (and most U.S. strategic-weapons policy) is to maintain at least the strong appearance that the balance of terror is indestructible. To assert indestructibility as *a fact*, however, is an exaggeration at best. Elsewhere we are told that deterrent balances are stable because it is easy to thwart a first strike. Many observers would say that this is factually wrong, as evidenced by the current concern about the vulnerability of U.S. land-based missiles imposed by new Soviet MIRVs of improved accuracy. The basic assumption of reliably stable deterrence becomes still more dubious when it is applied to small powers, as we shall see.

Nuclear Deterrence Has Worked—Or Has It?

The proposition that nuclear weapons induce caution is supported by several subordinate propositions, many of them dubious at best. One is the assertion that we need not worry much that nuclear powers may come in hostile pairs and share a common border. Of course hostile pairs do not necessarily fight, even when they have common borders. States often do fight states directly on their borders, however, as has been shown by Starr and Most.[9]

Waltz gives as an example that nuclear weapons have made China and the USSR deal with each other cautiously (p.126). This is empirically dubious. The major incident in which caution prevailed in the midst of Sino-Soviet hostility was the Ussuri River clash in 1969—at a time when Chinese nuclear capabilities were minuscule.[10] If the USSR was restrained at that time, it was by the prospect of a protracted conventional war with China, not by the nascent Chinese nuclear deterrent. Waltz also notes that the USSR and the United States, though bitter, have not gone to war. This observation is true, and Brito and Intriligator make a similar comment.[11] The implication, however, that war hasn't occurred because the states are deterred by each other's nuclear weapons does not necessarily follow.

The implication that nuclear deterrence has worked is part of conventional wisdom for many people. How else can we explain 38 years of peace between the superpowers? We hear this argument, for instance, as a defense of a strategy of mutual assured destruction (MAD). It is essential to say, however, that the argument that nuclear deterrence has prevented war is not really testable, at least until it is proved false by the occurrence of war. Nonoccurrence is not proof of the statement's truth. A counterfactual proposition is that we would not have attacked the USSR, or vice versa, even if we and they did not have nuclear weapons.

Although there is no fully satisfactory way to test this counterfactual proposition, there is some evidence to support it.[12] The first two major superpower crises—those that, until the Cuban missile crisis of 1962, seemed most to threaten war—were the Berlin crisis of 1948 and the Korean War. In 1948, the United States defended its stake in West Berlin, but in doing so carefully avoided initiating military conflict. Surely it was not deterred by Soviet nuclear weapons, which then did not exist.

In the Korean War, U.S. forces invading North Korea were pushed back, almost to the point of military disaster, by Chinese intervention. When the United States finally recovered, it had to settle for a disappointing and costly negotiated draw. Was the United States deterred from using nuclear weapons against China by Soviet or Chinese nuclear capabilities? Of course not—Soviet armed forces at that time (1951) still had *no* operational nuclear weapons. If the United States was deterred, it was by the prospect of a still larger-conventional war. *The myth that nuclear weapons bring peace is precisely that: a myth*. It probably holds important elements of truth, but those elements are so embedded in mystification that we can rarely be sure what we should firmly believe.

For most contemporary states the deterrent relationship between probable destruction (cost) and probable gain looks like a rapidly flattening curve. Both nuclear and large-scale conventional capabilities in the hands of an opponent provide adequate deterrence, putting the expected damage from massive and extended modern warfare clearly disproportionate to the gains that most states could hope to achieve. This relationship is illustrated in figure 10.1. For any given intensity of warfare, the probable level of destruction is shown on the horizontal axis and the probable gains on the vertical axis. The 45° line extending to the upper right marks the break-even line of zero expected utility; no leader would choose to fight at an intensity to the right of that line.

At quite low levels of (conventional) violence, gains may well exceed costs. Even such low-level and potentially beneficial military actions, however, are deterred by the prospect of escalation. The gain/cost point of intersection for the highest level of escalation—large-scale nuclear war—is indicated by A, and that for a small or

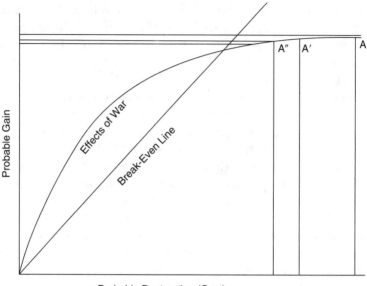

Figure 10.1   Probable costs and gains of various wars
A″ = sustained, large-scale conventional war.
A′ = small, limited nuclear war.
A = full-scale nuclear war.

very limited war is located only moderately below it in A′. This corresponds to the famous remark by McGeorge Bundy that the explosion "of even one hydrogen bomb on one city of one's own country would be recognized in advance as a catastrophic blunder."[13] Waltz appears to agree.

I contend that the argument applies as well to the cost of a protracted *conventional* war against a well-equipped state capable of sustaining a war effort, or a state that is supplied and sustained by a powerful ally. This point is represented by point A″, slightly below the point for a "small" nuclear war (A′) in figure 10.1; but it is arguable that points A″ and A′ should be reversed. Surely the current mood in Western Europe reflects a fear of conventional war on that continent (on the order of World War II, or worse) almost as much as a fear of nuclear war.

Few leaders of contemporary states would willingly pay any of those costs for the available gains. One of the reasons for what Waltz identifies as the gradual spread of nuclear weapons is precisely that many states feel they have sufficient deterrent capability already, without adding nuclear weapons. Most world governments have decided their security is better served without nuclear arms than with them.

Antiproliferation measures deserve some credit for that restraint. So should governments' good sense in seeing—Waltz's theories not withstanding—the extremely modest (or negative) increment in their security that nuclear weapons could bring to most of them.

Limited Nuclear War

Waltz varies his expected-utility argument when it suits him to do so. Most of the time he wants to tell us that nuclear deterrence works because of the high (significant? nontrivial?) probability that any nuclear war would be terribly destructive. Many people looking at this equation, however, would say that the combination of probability times destructiveness makes for intolerable expected utilities. Waltz admits that one may nevertheless oppose nuclear proliferation because nuclear weapons would make war, though perhaps unlikely, intolerably intense. To reassure us, he must argue that nuclear war *is* unlikely, or that the chances of limiting (controlling) nuclear war are really very good.

Waltz tries to do both. For the latter, we hear that the chance that if any nuclear weapons go off, many will is the least likely of unlikely possibilities and that even if deterrence fails, rapid deescalation is likely, as "a few judiciously placed warheads . . . produce sobriety in the leaders." (p.132) Indeed, at one point he tells us that nuclear weapons may actually lessen not only the frequency but also the intensity of wars among those that possess them (p.132).

This leads Waltz to some complacency about fighting tactical nuclear war in Europe. "Early use of very small warheads may stop escalation. . . . The chances of deescalation are high if the use of nuclear weapons is carefully planned and their use is limited to the battlefield." (p.119) This "if" clause begs all the important questions. It *may* be true that nuclear war can be kept limited, but many of the best-informed observers stand in disbelief. These include academic analysts; former national-security advisers; and according to General Collins, the former deputy commander, U.S. Army, Europe, "From my experience in combat, there is no way that this escalation of nuclear capability can be controlled because of the lack of information, the pressure of time, and the deadly results that are taking place on both sides of the battle line."[14]

Elsewhere in his discussion, Waltz wanted to tell us that the expected utility of a devastating war among nuclear powers is low enough (nontrivial probability, very great disutility) to deter war. Here he wants to tell us that the expected utility of limited nuclear war is high enough (substantial probability of only moderate disutility) that we should be willing to initiate—in a defensive and "controlled" fashion, to be sure—nuclear war in Europe. It is hard for him to be persuasive all the time.

At another point waltz tells us that even if new nuclear powers should use their weapons, we need not worry about the danger of catalytic war because the superpowers are unlikely to be drawn into other nations' nuclear wars. Brito and Intriligator similarly tell us that should a nuclear war among local powers arise, the major powers would actively ensure that it would not escalate to a regional or global war.[15] Nevertheless, the assumption that great powers can contain, rather than be drawn into, a local nuclear war is basically just that— an assumption supported only by those passages about the secure stability of superpower deterrence that the reader finds plausible.

More Reasons Not To Worry

In fact, according to Waltz, we need not worry much even about the likelihood of the new nuclear powers using their weapons. First, he claims, the probability of a preemptive strike against a nascent nuclear power by its regional opponent is low. Here Waltz must contend with the awkward fact that such a strike has already occurred (Israel against Iraq in June 1981); but after considering it, he declares that such preventive strikes are hard to imagine. (The April 1982 version of his paper said simply, "The forces of all the present nuclear countries necessarily developed unevenly in relation to each other, and nobody has struck so far." Brito and Intriligator regard the risks of a preventive strike much more seriously.)

Second, Waltz says, we need not worry about the difficulties of command and control (C^3I) in small or poor states: many states have the ingenuity to hide nuclear weapons and keep them under control. Here he neglects all the problems of "nuclear decapitation," which in important ways are more severe for small states than for superpowers.[16] True, there may not be much that needs to be commanded and controlled. The chief of state of a politically unstable underdeveloped country, however, is not likely to have great confidence in his subordinates. He will distrust other fingers on the button; rival button pushers might be, in his view, "irresponsible," or even turn the weapons against him. If no one else has the means to push the button, however, then the state is subject to nuclear decapitation. One bomb (or bullet) directed not at the state's nuclear-armed aircraft, but at the leader, would suffice. Given the leader's dilemma, the control over retaliation so necessary to stable and credible deterrence is *not* assured.

Third, Waltz assures us that we need not worry much about the irresponsibility of new nuclear states, even those in the third world. True, there is some inherent racism in the notion that only developed, big states will be responsible. Yet not just the matter of responsibility, but also the implications of political instability are involved. Less-developed countries are, on the average, politically less stable than developed ones. For example, of the 50 nations experiencing the most deaths from political violence over the period 1948–1977, all but two—Hungary and the United Kingdom (i.e., Northern Ireland)—were less-developed countries. Of the 233 irregular executive transfers (changes "outside the conventional or customary procedures") in that period, all but two occurred in less-developed countries.[17] Waltz sensibly argues that political instability need not lead to loss of control over nuclear weapons—but should he be complacent with the implications of *this much* instability?

Finally, Waltz says, we need not worry much about arms races: "Deterrent balances are inherently stable ... [T]he logic of deterrence eliminates incentives for strategic arms racing." (p.130) Is this a description of the current U.S.-Soviet situation? Clearly it is not, admits Waltz, with the explanation that too many Soviet and U.S. officials have been unwilling to settle for deterrence and instead have sought war-fighting capabilities. Small countries, he says, will have no illusions about the impossibility of achieving such capabilities. We can listen to his arguments but should wonder whether, after an enormous effort of 38 years to create the stability of superpower mutual deterrent expectations has worked poorly, we can expect other rival pairs of states to arrive more readily at the supposedly inherent stability of a deterrent balance.

The Frequency and Intensity of War

In the latter part of his chapter, Waltz tries to reassure us that nuclear war is not so probable, nor its disutility so great, that we should fear it excessively. He must counter the argument—a powerful one—that, even though nuclear weapons *might* make states more cautious and more effectively deterred, we must reckon with the consequences if deterrence *does* fail under nuclear conditions. Though the probability of that may be low, the cost (disutility) could be catastrophic. His response is basically a recapitulation of the points we have discussed earlier, with an emphasis on the improbability of the event.

Waltz's discussion simply ignores some serious counterarguments. One, for example, concerns the probability of war between any pair of states. He says this probability is lower for a pair of nuclear-armed states than for two conventionally armed states—presumably low enough to compensate for the heavier damage that a nuclear war might inflict. This argument might be acceptable if the probability really was low and if it bore some constant linear relationship to damage. Waltz forgets, however (as do Brito and Intriligator), that the probability of a nuclear war occurring is a function not of the number of nuclear-armed states, but of the number *of pairs* of nuclear-armed states. If there are only two nuclear-armed states in the world, there is only one pair of states that can fight a nuclear war. If there are 20 nuclear-armed states, then there are 190 pairs of states between which nuclear war is possible. (The formula is $n(n-1)/2$, where n = number of nuclear-armed states.) Is the (alleged) diminution in the likelihood of war occurring between nuclear states (from the likelihood of war between them when they were conventionally armed) enough to compensate for this exponential increase in the number of possible nuclear wars?

Waltz never really does come to grips with the fact that in a nuclear world the downside risk is the end of civilization in the Northern Hemisphere—Schell says, perhaps hyperbolically, the end of human life.[18] That kind of disutility will have to come with a very low probability attached if we are to find the further spread of nuclear weapons desirable.

In the end, Waltz's position is only as strong as the propositions we have analyzed. That is, it is a house of cards.

Chapter 11

What Makes Deterrence Work? Cases from 1900 to 1980

With Paul Huth

The use of military force to achieve foreign policy objectives is an enduring feature of international politics. Force, or the threat of force, may be used either to change the status quo or to maintain it. Threatening the use of force to maintain the status quo often takes the form of deterrence, defined by Patrick Morgan as "the threat to use force in response as a way of preventing the first use of force by someone else."[1] Deterrence sometimes succeeds and sometimes fails. Failures are attested to by numerous international wars of history. In the nuclear age, a failure could cost us our lives. The conditions of successful deterrence thus require thorough logical and empirical analysis.

Deterrence may seek to prevent an attack on oneself, or an attack on some other party—in international politics, an ally, a client state, or a friendly neutral. Deterrence as practiced by major powers is most commonly deterrence of an attack on another party. This is known as "extended deterrence." For the United States since 1945, it has meant deterrence of attack on American allies in Western Europe, Asia, and the Middle East. It is a more precarious and demanding task than that of deterring a frontal attack on oneself. "Extended deterrence" will be the focus of this chapter.

Deterrence may also be classified as either general or immediate deterrence. Morgan identifies general deterrence as relating to "opponents who maintain armed forces to regulate their relationship even though neither is anywhere near mounting an attack." Immediate deterrence concerns a relationship "where at least one side is seriously considering an attack while the other is mounting a threat of retaliation in order to prevent it."[2] The success or failure of general deterrence is difficult to evaluate. As most observers have long recognized, the absence of an attack does not necessarily attest to the success of deterrence: perhaps the potential "attacker" never really had any intention of attacking. If so, the "attacker" was never deterred. Lacking access to the archives and minds of the Kremlin, for instance, analysts can argue indefinitely as to whether the Soviet Union in fact has, or has not, been deterred from invading Western Europe.

Situations of immediate deterrence are somewhat easier to identify and to analyze. They may also be more important. If we do not know how deterrence works when it is most needed (in a crisis when there is a relatively high probability of war), policies designed to assure general deterrence are likely to be based on incomplete or misleading notions of how deterrence works, and deterrence theory will be weak. Even with immediate deterrence, however, there remains a problem in identifying precisely why an attack does not materialize. It is always possible that the reason has little to do with the threat of retaliation, and that the failure to attack is due to a change of priorities by decision makers, or a change of decision makers. But it is a reasonable presumption, permitting empirical analysis, that the threat was the primary reason for success. If the deterrent threat fails, then we may ask whether the threat was not perceived, or not perceived as likely to be executed, or not perceived as, even if carried out, bringing consequences severe enough to warrant abstention from the attack. Most commonly, the perception may combine some element of low expected probability of execution with not-too-severe consequences—in other words, attack carries an acceptable "expected utility," at least as compared with the perceived alternatives available to the prospective attacker.

In this chapter, we lay out an expected-utility model of deterrence and test that model on a set of cases of extended, immediate deterrence from the period 1900 to 1980. We shall conclude that successful deterrence is very much more than just a matter of having a favorable military balance, and very much a matter of the nature and extent of ties between the defender state and the state it wishes to protect.

The effort derives in part from an exercise first carried out more than two decades ago.[3] That exercise, although it reached some potentially important conclusions, needs to be refined and extended in a number of ways. First, it considered only 17 cases of deterrence, from the period 1935 to 1961. The set of cases can now be extended both forward and backward in time. Second, the definition used to identify the cases needs to be made more rigorous—an explicit use of the concept of immediate deterrence, with overt threat of retaliation, will enable us to identify the universe of applicable cases and to protect against the inclusion of cases in which deterrence was not demonstrably applicable at all. Third, we can extend the theoretical model with additional variables and more rigorous empirical measures. Finally, expansion of the universe of cases will permit formal statistical analysis in a way not possible with only seventeen cases.

The problem, then, is one of immediate deterrence. We will employ Morgan's criteria[4] to identify the relevant cases:

1. The officials in a state (which we shall call the "attacker") are considering attacking a state ("protégé") that is formally allied to or deemed important by a third state ("defender").
2. Key officials in the defender state realize this.
3. Recognizing that an attack is a distinct possibility, the officials of the defender state, either explicitly or by movement of military forces, threaten the use of retaliatory force in an effort to prevent the attack.

The threats of the attacker and defender states must be overt and clearly entail the use of military force, and the target of the attack (protégé) must be clearly identifiable. We are concerned only with the period before substantial interstate violence begins. Subsequently the defender's task becomes one of compellence—stopping an action already undertaken—which is more demanding than deterrence.

The expected-utility model we shall be applying in our efforts to explain decisions to fight requires some further assumptions. An expected-utility model involves analysis of inference about the utilities decision makers attach to outcomes, and the probabilities they attach (however crudely or vaguely) to achievement of those outcomes. It is customary to assume that the decision making systems of attacker and defender operate essentially as unitary actors. Although there is a vast literature on bureaucratic politics that disputes the applicability of such an assumption, it remains a common one in studies of peace and war decisions. In this instance it only requires assuming that the key decisions (to attack or not, to respond to the attack with force or not) are made by single decision makers or by small groups operating as units. For such key security decisions it remains a justifiable assumption.[5]

Similarly, we must assume that decision makers are rational expected-utility maximizers. This too appears at first to be a strong assumption, but it is reasonable as required here. We use "rational" in the sense of being able to order one's preferences, and to choose according to that ordering and perceptions of the likelihood of various outcomes. A rational decision maker may be risk-averse, or risk-acceptant. The assumption of rationality does not require that perceptions be accurate, or that a given decision maker's preferences be the same as other people's.

It does require that a decision maker choose the option with greatest expected utility at the time, but in this context it does not mean the choice has to be made from a search through a near-infinite set of possible options, as in the ideal model of rationality. It requires only a choice between two options so clear as almost surely to be among those considered. For the attacker, the options are holding back or pressing ahead with military force against the protégé. For the defender, the choices are accepting the consequences of the loss of the protégé or meeting the attack with substantial military force. Permutations within these options doubtless exist but need not be considered here. As to whether the decision maker's search of options yields the optimal plan of action, we cannot know, but we do assume that the search is intense enough to yield a "satisficing" version for each of the two basic options, and that the satisficing version will not be so different from the optimal one as to distort our results significantly. For decisions of great import, usually taken over a period of some weeks or months, this assumption appears reasonable.[6] With these assumptions we are much closer to an image of the bounded rationality of the "sensible" decision maker than to the unattainable ideal of full rationality.

An Expected-Utility Model

Deterrence can be viewed as a game of strategic interaction, in which a "rational" opponent assesses the potential costs and benefits of its actions based upon expectations regarding the likely behavior of its adversary.[7] By this view, a deterrent threat is effective to the extent it can produce cost-benefit calculations on the part of the potential attacker in which the expected utility of an attack would be less than the expected utility of foregoing the attack. The expected gains from an attack must be so small, or the expected losses so substantial, that abstaining from attack will produce a more favorable outcome (greater gains or, more likely, smaller losses).

In the standard formulation, expected utility is the product of the utility of a given outcome times the decision maker's estimated (subjective) probability of achieving the outcome. The attacker, in estimating his prospective gains from an attack, must consider the gains he can achieve from attacking (occupying, perhaps, or otherwise forcing major concessions from) the protégé if the defender does not provide active military assistance to (fight for) the protégé, and the gains (or very likely net losses) to be accrued if the defender does fight. Furthermore, he must weight each of these outcomes by the estimated likelihood that they will occur (the probability that the defender will indeed fight or not). Then he must compare the value of this term (expected utility of attack) with the utility (which may or may not be high) of not attacking. If the value of the first term is more than the second, he will attack; if less, he will be deterred. Finally, in making estimates of the probability that the defender will fight, the attacker must expect the defender to make a calculation of the utility the protégé provides to the defender, as compared with the costs the defender would incur from fighting. To the degree the attacker thinks the defender's losses would be less from fighting than from letting the protégé go without a fight, the higher should be the attacker's estimate of the probability that the defender will fight.[8]

Most attention in analyzing deterrent situations is usually given to the balance of military capabilities between attacker and defender. The attacker must assess whether it has sufficient military power to win a war with the defender, and at what cost. That assessment affects the attacker's calculations in two ways. First, it affects the raw utility of attacking and fighting the defender. Second, it affects the attacker's estimate of the probability that the defender will in fact fight, since the defender presumably will make a similar assessment and, other things being equal, be more likely to fight the more favorable it considers the military balance. This kind of consideration is standard in contemporary political assessments, from arguments about the need to close the "window of vulnerability" to debates about whether NATO conventional forces can be adequate to support a policy of no first use of nuclear weapons. Both strategic weapons for general war and the balance of capabilities for local war in the region of the protégé are said to matter. In the nuclear era, debate is further complicated by arguments as to whether nuclear weapons are so destructive that the mere prospect that substantial numbers of them might be used is sufficient to deter the attacker, regardless of the relative balance.[9]

Deterrence is a much more complex problem than simply weighing military balances, however. As George and Smoke point out, "[T]he requirements for implementing deterrence are much less a matter of acquiring, proving possession of, or using raw military capabilities than a matter of demonstrating concern, motivation and commitment."[10] This is especially true in the case of deterrence of attack on a third party, since the costs of failing to meet an attack on the third party are rarely as great as the costs of failing to defend one's home territory. Bargaining power is a product of resolve as well as of capability, and resolve is in turn a function of the interests at stake and of "inherent" resolve (that is, risk-proneness). Presumably (again, other things being equal) the willingness to run risks or pay costs to defend a protégé will be greater the greater the objective or intrinsic value of the protégé, perhaps as measured by wealth, population, or strategic importance. But that value may not be very helpful in analyzing a deterrent situation, since the greater the value of the protégé, the higher the costs and the greater the risks the attacker will presumably be willing to accept in order to acquire it. The "objective" value of the protégé thus appears on both sides of the equation.[11]

Motivation, commitment, and resolve are in some part a matter of the "psychology" of the decision maker. Some decision makers seem to be determined, others irresolute. Or, in decision making terms, some may be risk-acceptant (Hitler in 1938) and others risk-averse (Chamberlain). An attacker (whatever his own attitude toward risk) must try to assess the behavior of the defender in previous international crises, if any are relevant. Ideally one would look at the behavior of the particular decision maker(s) in charge of the defender state; lacking that example one might look at the behavior of previous decision makers in charge of the state.

What conclusions can be drawn from such considerations? The obvious one would follow from an assumption that risk-acceptance or risk-aversion are inherent to a decision maker (or state). If he was unwilling to take the risk of fighting the last time, the odds may be that he will be risk-averse once again. An alternative assumption, however, would be that attitudes toward risk-taking are determined more by political context than by personality or "character." Context may be determined so randomly (e.g., variations in the intrinsic importance of the protégé in each case) that past behavior will provide little or no guidance for predicting future behavior. Or it may operate perversely, leading to an opposite prediction. For example, Chamberlain's acquiescence in the dismemberment of Czechoslovakia may have made him less willing to acquiesce in the case of Poland a year later. Some research suggests that the defender's previous behavior does not systematically predict either way to subsequent behavior,[12] but we still must take it into account in our analysis. Certainly the "need" to demonstrate resolve (to avoid falling dominoes) was a key rationalization for America's experience in Vietnam and throughout the post-Munich era.

Motivation and resolve are also affected by aspects of the relationship between the defender and its protégé. Resolve may be communicated by establishing a formal military alliance between the two—and once established, it may serve to strengthen a defender's resolve by raising the stakes it has to lose by failing to honor its alliance commitment (weakening its credibility the next time it is challenged). Motivation may be strengthened by a variety of economic, political, and military ties between defender and protégé, such as trade, investment in the protégé's economy, economic assistance or military equipment and advisers to the protégé from the defender, and a host of less tangible forms of political or cultural affinity. Again, holding other elements of the calculation constant, the defender should be more willing to take risks in defense of a third party when the more tangible and intangible interests there are at stake. The immediate role of tangible interests such as trade and investment is obvious. Additionally, they, and other less tangible ties, may widen the defender's image of itself, providing an emotional stake in the well-being of politically or culturally related peoples. There also is some evidence from systematic comparative analyses to this effect.[13]

We shall test hypotheses about conditions favoring deterrence on a set of historical cases of attempted deterrence of attack on third parties. The cases include all those we were able to identify in the international system in the period since 1900. We limited ourselves to that period because reliable information on earlier cases is too difficult to acquire, and because even with reliable data the utility of some of the measures (the significance, for instance, of certain military forces) shifts as one moves into earlier historical epochs. Even so, we were able to identify 54 relevant cases including examples from both the nuclear and prenuclear eras. Thus we can test whether nuclear weapons make a difference.

The universe of cases is delineated in terms of overt threat and counterthreat. Military or political acts that constitute such threats include threats of force (threat to use force, threat to blockade, threat to occupy territory, threat to declare war) and displays of force (alert, mobilization).[14] We studied diverse primary and secondary sources to establish that the cases chosen fit our criteria, and to obtain information on the variables.[15] Table 11.1 shows a list of the cases with dates, the states involved, and the outcomes. Some historical events are "unpacked" into separate, sequential cases. For example, in the Agadir crisis, France first must decide whether to defend its interest in Morocco, and then the United Kingdom must decide whether to defend its ally France; in August 1914 there were 4 separable cases.[16] We judged deterrence to be successful in 31 (57 percent) of the cases.

We have attempted to identify the conditions under which deterrence will succeed or fail. Thus for explaining the attacker's decision we simply code that decision as "attack the protégé" (0) or "no attack" (1). A military attack is defined as a government-sanctioned engagement of its regular armed forces in combat with the regular armed forces of the protégé and/or its defender resulting in more than 250 fatalities. Once this level of combat and casualty has been reached, subsequent events become a matter of "intrawar" deterrence. We also include as "attacks" (failures of deterrence) instances in which the attacker gained its principal goals even though fatalities

Table 11.1   Deterrence cases, 1900–80

Case	Year(s)	Attacker	Protégé	Defender	Outcome
Cases of Attempted Deterrence					
1	1902/3	Germany	Venezuela	United States	Success
2	1904	Russia	Korea	Japan	Failure
3	1905/6	Germany	Morocco	France	Success
4	1905/6	Germany	France	Britain	Success
5	1908	Turkey	Persia	Russia	Success
6	1908/9	Russia/Serbia	Austria-Hungary	Germany	Success
7	1908/9	Austria-Hungary/Germany	Serbia	Russia	Failure
8	1911	Italy	Tripoli	Turkey	Failure
9	1911	Germany	Morocco	France	Success
10	1911	Germany	France	Britain	Success
11	1912	Serbia	Albania	Austria-Hungary	Success
12	1912	Austria-Hungary	Serbia	Russia	Success
13	1912	Russia/Serbia	Austria-Hungary	Germany	Success
14	1913	Rumania	Bulgaria	Russia	Success
15	1913	Bulgaria	Greece	Serbia	Failure
16	1913	Serbia	Albania	Austria-Hungary	Success
17	1914	Austria-Hungary/Germany	Serbia	Russia	Failure
18	1914	Russia/Serbia	Austria-Hungary	Germany	Failure
19	1914	Germany/Austria-Hungary	Russia	France	Failure
20	1914	Germany	Belgium	Britain	Failure
21	1920	Soviet Union	Iran	Britain	Failure
22	1927	Yugoslavia	Albania	Italy	Success
23	1935	Italy	Ethiopia	Britain	Failure

Table 11.1   Continued

Case	Year(s)	Attacker	Protégé	Defender	Outcome
24	1936	Japan	Outer Mongolia	Soviet Union	Success
25	1938	Germany	Czechoslovakia	Britain/France	Failure
26	1938/39	Italy	Tunisia	France	Success
27	1939	Japan	Outer Mongolia	Soviet Union	Failure
28	1939	Germany	Poland	Britain/France	Failure
29	1940	Soviet Union	Finland	Germany	Success
30	1946	Soviet Union	Iran	United States	Success
31	1947	Soviet Union	Turkey	United States	Success
32	1948/49	Soviet Union	W. Berlin/W. Germany	United States	Success
33	1950	United States	North Korea	China	Failure
34	1955	China	Taiwan/Islands	United States	Success
35	1957	Turkey/United States	Syria	Soviet Union/Egypt	Success
36	1957	Egypt/Syria/Soviet Union	Turkey	United States	Success
37	1958	China	Taiwan/Islands	United States	Success
38	1961	Iraq	Kuwait	Britain	Success
39	1961	India	Goa	Portugal	Failure
40	1961	Soviet Union	W. Berlin/W. Germany	United States	Success
41	1962	India	Nepal	China	Success
42	1962	North Vietnam	Thailand	United States	Success
43	1963/64	Indonesia	Malaysia	Britain	Failure
44	1964	Turkey	Cyprus	Greece	Failure
45	1964/65	North Vietnam	South Vietnam	United States	Failure
46	1965	India	Pakistan	China	Failure
47	1966/67	Turkey	Cyprus	Greece	Failure
48	1967	Israel	Syria	Egypt	Failure
49	1970	Syria	Jordan	Israel	Success
50	1973	Soviet Union	Israel	United States	Success
51	1974	Turkey	Cyprus	Greece	Failure
52	1975	Morocco	Western Sahara	Spain	Success
53	1976/77	Guatemala	Belize	Britain	Success
54	1978/79	Tanzania	Uganda	Libya	Failure
Cases of Failed Deterrence					
2	1904	Russia	Korea	Japan	Yes
7	1908/9	Austria-Hungary	Serbia	Russia	No
8	1911	Italy	Tripoli	Turkey	Yes
14	1913	Bulgaria	Greece	Serbia	Yes
17	1914	Austria-Hungary/Germany	Serbia	Russia/France	Yes
18	1914	Russia/Serbia	Austria-Hungary	Germany	Yes
19	1914	Germany/Austria-Hungary	Russia	France	Yes
20	1914	Germany	Belgium	Britain	Yes
21	1920	Soviet Union	Iran	Britain	Yes
23	1935	Italy	Ethiopia	Britain	No
25	1938/39	Germany	Czechoslovakia	Britain/France	No
27	1939	Japan	Outer Mongolia	Soviet Union	Yes
28	1939	Germany	Poland	Britain/France	Yes
33	1950	United States	North Korea	China	Yes
39	1961	India	Goa	Portugal	No
43	1963/64	Indonesia	Malaysia	Britain	Yes
44	1964	Turkey	Cyprus	Greece	No
45	1964/65	North Vietnam	South Vietnam	United States	Yes
46	1965	India	Pakistan	China	No
47	1966/67	Turkey	Cyprus	Greece	No
48	1967	Israel	Syria	Egypt	Yes
51	1974	Turkey	Cyprus	Greece	No
54	1978/79	Tanzania	Uganda	Libya	Yes

were minimal (e.g., Czechoslovakia in 1938, case no. 25; Cyprus in 1964, no. 44; Goa in 1961, case no. 39), and instances in which the attacker occupied territory of the protégé for several years.[17]

We have also analyzed the cases in which deterrence failed: can we explain the defender's decision whether or not to fight? Attackers often misjudge the defenders' resolve. As Lebow remarked, describing his results, "Perhaps our most striking finding is the extent to which crisis strategies in the cases we studied were based on unrealistic assessments of how adversaries would respond when challenged. In every instance brinkmanship was predicated upon the belief that the adversary (defender) in question would back down when challenged."[18] Therefore we shall also try to see whether our model and analysis can successfully discriminate between cases where the defender ultimately fought (coded i) and where it did not (o).

Our general hypothesis is that an expected-utility model will provide a better-than-chance explanation of defenders' and attackers' decisions. But much more important than that, we wish to test various hypotheses about which elements of an expected-utility analysis provide the most powerful explanations. Our hypotheses, tapping aspects of the variables in the model, come under three general categories: those emphasizing relative power, those concerning the role of past behavior in signaling current intentions, and those stressing the contextual importance of communitarian ties between states. By including variables of all three types in our equations we can test their relative explanatory power. The hypotheses and independent variables are as follows:

H1. *The relative balance of military capabilities will help explain the results.*

H1a. *Attacker will be more likely to fight (deterrence to fail) to the degree that attacker's overall ("strategic") military and economic capabilities (a measure of military potential) exceed those of defender.*

H1b. *Attacker will be more likely to fight to the degree that attacker's* overall existing *military forces exceed those of defender.*

H1c. *Attacker will be more likely to fight to the degree that attacker's* potential local *(in the area of the protégé) military capabilities exceed those of defender.*

H1d. *Attacker will be more likely to fight to the degree that attacker's* existing local *military capabilities exceed those of defender.*

H1e. *Attacker will be less likely to fight if defender is known to possess nuclear weapons.*

To measure overall military and economic capabilities (military potential) we used the composite national capabilities index developed by the Correlates of War Project. This index measures three theoretically distinct dimensions of national capabilities: military, industrial, and demographic.[19] The military dimension includes each state's military personnel and military expenditures (weighted equally) for each year. (This is the measure we use for existing military capabilities for hypotheses H1b and H1d.) The industrial dimension consists of each state's production of ingot steel and industrial fuel consumption and measures the potential of a state to support a military effort. The demographic dimension includes each state's population and urban population and indicates the state's potential to increase its power by drawing on its civilian population during extended war. In the index of military potential for hypotheses H1a and H1c, the three dimensions are weighted equally.

For local capabilities, the military dimension is adjusted to reflect the impact of distance. If both defender and attacker share a border, or share one with the protégé, then no adjustment is made. Otherwise the indices of military capabilities are adjusted for the distances between the attacker's and defender's loci of power and the protégé, and for the principal military transport capabilities of the day (expressed in travel days).[20] Ideally it might have been desirable to measure actual locally available military forces (divisions, gunboats, etc.) but that would have required a level of information not easily accessible, and in any case still would not have evaded decisions about forces that, although not immediately on the scene, could be brought in within a "reasonable" time. The procedure we did use seems less arbitrary, and adequate to the purpose. In all cases, the power of the protégé is added to that of the defender. As noted earlier, military capability should affect both one's own utilities and one's subjective probability that the other will fight.

Reciprocal hypotheses apply to the behavior of the defender in those cases in which the potential attacker has actually attacked:

H1f. *Defender will be more likely to fight to the degree that defender's overall military potential exceeds attacker's.*
H1g. *Defender will be more likely to fight to the degree that defender's overall existing military capabilities exceeds attacker's.*
H1h. *Defender will be more likely to fight to the degree that defender's potential local military capabilities exceed attacker's.*

H1i. *Defender will be more likely to fight to the degree that defender's existing local military capabilities exceed attacker's.*
H1j. *Defender will be more likely to fight if defender possesses nuclear weapons.*

This last hypothesis cannot really be tested because there were only three instances in which an attacker pressed an attack against a nuclear-armed defender.

H2. *The second set of hypotheses concerns the effect of the defender state's previous behavior in deterrent situations (if any are applicable). This variable measures the extent to which the defender has a record of strongly supporting a threatened protégé and suggests the likelihood that the defender will fight (its degree of risk-proneness).*
H2a. *Attacker will be more likely to fight if defender has not fought in the past when its protégé was attacked.*
H2b. *Attacker will be less likely to fight if defender has not fought in the past. This is the alternative hypothesis, suggesting that a defender who earlier demonstrated "weakness" will be considered less likely to do so again.*

In the statistical analysis, we assigned a series of "dummy variables" to three different possibilities: whether the defender had fought on behalf of a protégé in the past, whether it had not fought, and whether it had a record of successful deterrence. In all of these cases a "no" could indicate either the opposite historical experience or simply no relevant experience. (For example, a success would be coded 1 for the last dummy variable and 0 for either no past experience or a failure.) We tested the hypotheses by examining the defender's behavior in the most recent past case of attempted deterrence. Similarly, we have corresponding hypotheses to explain the behavior of the defender if attack occurred.

H2c. *Defender will be more likely to fight if it has fought in the past.*
H2d. *Defender will be more likely to fight if it has not fought in the past.*

H3. *Third, we have a set of hypotheses concerning the effect of ties between the defender and protégé, with more or stronger ties raising the value of the protégé to the defender and thus raising the probability that defender will fight rather than allow protégé to be overcome.*

H3a. Attacker will be less likely to fight if defender was linked to protégé by a formal military alliance prior to the emergence of the immediate deterrence situation.

For our purposes, a military alliance was defined as a written agreement, bilateral or multilateral, between sovereign states. Both defense pacts and (rare) ententes were coded as 1, and the absence of either as 0.[21] Five cases in this study were instances in which the threatened protégé was a colony. Although a formal military alliance between sovereign states could not, by definition, exist in those cases, we assumed that there exists an unwritten but internationally recognized alliance between a colony and its metropole. Thus we treated a colonial relationship as one of formal military commitment.

The corresponding hypothesis for the defender is:

H3b. Defender will be more likely to fight if it was linked to the protégé by a formal military alliance prior to the emergence of the immediate deterrence situation.

Two similar hypotheses apply to the role of economic linkages:

H3c. Attacker will be less likely to fight, the stronger the economic linkages between defender and protégé.
H3d. Defender will be more likely to fight, the stronger the economic linkages between defender and protégé.

We measured economic linkage as the protégé's share of defender's total merchandise exports and imports. These figures were calculated as the average level over a two- to three-year period, depending on the availability of data prior to the outbreak of the dispute.[22] This variable attempts to estimate the extent to which the defender has developed an important and direct material interest in its relationship with the protégé. Exports to the protégé represent the interest of those firms and industries selling abroad; imports suggest commodities for which the defender's economy may be "dependent" on reliable supplies of goods of a known quality or at favorable prices. Norming the volume of trade by the size of the defender's economy is thus appropriate. Although the decision makers of the attacker are unlikely to calculate the exact amount of the defender's trade accounted for by the protégé, they are likely to be aware of the general level of commercial activity between the two states. Greater refinement for measuring this variable might result from analyzing exports and imports separately, but the high correlation between the two prevents their separation in statistical analysis. Data on the defender's private foreign investment in the protégé would be desirable but are not available for enough of the cases.

Two further parallel hypotheses apply to political-military linkages:

> H3e. *Attacker will be less likely to fight, the stronger the political-military linkages between defender and protégé.*
> H3f. *Defender will be more likely to fight, the stronger the political-military linkages between defender and protégé.*

We measured political-military linkages by the amount of military assistance provided by the defender to the protégé—specifically the percentage share of major weapons systems (aircraft, ships, missiles, armored equipment) imported by the protégé from the defender. Because available data were incomplete, and imprecise, we coded this variable on a four-point scale rather than on strict percentages: 0–25 percent = 1, 26–50 percent = 2, 51–75 percent = 3, 76–100 percent = 4.[23]

Finally, we have two further hypotheses about power that apply only to the defender's decision whether or not to fight if an attack does materialize. The defender must decide on the basis of the protégé's value; this includes both values as reflected in linkages and "intrinsic" value as represented by the protégé's strategic, military, or industrial potential. The utility of "peace" under circumstances in which the protégé is lost will depend in some degree on that intrinsic value. We tapped this in two ways. One was to use the measures earlier employed for potential military capability (the composite national capabilities index) and existing military capability, and to calculate the ratio of the protégé's capability on each to that of the defender. As a partial measure of the protégé's strategic importance to the defender we also included a dummy variable for whether they shared a common border. Both defender and attacker will have to take these considerations into account in estimating the defender's utility for not fighting, and thus into account in deriving subjective probabilities for each other's actions. The relevant hypotheses therefore are the following:

> H1k. *Defender will be more likely to fight the greater the ratio of protégé's existing or potential military capability to its own.*

H1l. *Defender will be more likely to fight if its territory borders directly on that of protégé.*

This reminds us that one element of a full expected-utility model is necessarily missing from the analysis that follows. We should also have a term for the expected utility of peace to the attacker; that is, the attacker's utility for not actually pressing ahead with attack on the protégé. Peace, of course, includes the utility of possible prosperity and the avoidance of the costs and casualties of war. The utility of peace may be lower if a state must otherwise deal with severe domestic political discontent. Peace also includes the benefits of normal commercial exchange among nations. Most of us assume, most of the time, that the expected utility of peace is high enough to discourage military attacks. We assume, for example, that the Soviet Union probably would not, in "normal" times, have sufficient incentive to make it worthwhile to incur the costs of attacking Western Europe. But this condition might change drastically under circumstances of high-level political and military crisis. Should the Soviet Union suddenly be faced with widespread open revolt in Eastern Europe, the benefits of peace suddenly might look much less attractive. Under those circumstances, its calculation of expected utilities might change entirely and, under the further danger of actual military upheaval in Europe, it might well decide to attack. A previously unattractive balance of military capabilities suddenly might not look so bad.

Because these considerations are much more subjective than most of the others we have discussed, and especially because they can change so drastically in a short period of time, we are not able to incorporate them. To the degree that they are important, they will reduce the explanatory power of our empirical investigation. But partly because they can change rapidly, we do not expect that they will be correlated with the more stable variables in the model. In particular, we do not expect them to be related to the military balance.

Conditions Affecting Deterrence: Some Empirical Results

We analyzed the data through probit analysis, which is analogous to multiple regression analysis for situations in which the dependent variable is dichotomous (yes–no, 1–0). Table 11.2 gives the results of the best (most powerful explanatory) equation. It employs the best (most powerful) indicator for each of the theoretical concepts specified earlier. The equations have been simplified to eliminate variables that did not reach the 0.10 level of statistical significance— a useful cutoff criterion even though we are dealing with the universe of cases over the relevant time period, not a sample.[24] The coefficient's statistic, in parentheses, indicates the significance level, and the relative explanatory power, of each independent variable. The coefficients (b) indicate the amount of difference in the dependent variable for which each independent variable accounts. These coefficients are not readily interpretable, but we present below a further display that will give this information in understandable form. In probit analysis the best measure for the power of the whole equation is the "percentage of predictions correct," which we provide, but for those interested in the R-squared we provide that too. The cross-tabulations show the proportion of deterrence failures, and successes, that are correctly explained by each equation.

Table 11.2   Conditions promoting effective deterrence

Success = -1.57 + .18 Trade + .60 Arms + .16 Local Military Balance $-$ 1.02 Alliance
    (-2.93) (1.94) (2.84) (2.35) (-1.93)

	Predicted	
Failure	18	5
Success	7	24

Contributions to Probability of Success

	Value %	Probability of Success
Trade	0	.49
	1	.56
	2	.63
	4	.76
Arms	0–25	.28
	26–50	.35
	51–75	.58
	76–100	.79
Local Military Balance	0.1	.26
	0.5	.28
	1.0	.32
	2	.37
	3	.43
	5	.56
	10	.83
Alliance No	Yes	.39
		.77

Note: Percentage of predictions correct = 78; R^2 = .31; N = 54.

The first point to be made about these results is the fact that a majority (78 percent) of the outcomes are correctly predicted by the model. No social science model can explain every case, and this rate compares very well with chance, or with the simple prediction that deterrence will always work. (It did in 57 percent of the cases.) It also is a very robust result in terms of consistency when various cases are added to or deleted from our set, as, for example, in earlier analyses before events such as August 1914 were "unpacked" into discrete cases or before our list of cases had been thoroughly checked for appropriate inclusion by historians and other authorities. The results from all these analyses are very robust in that the proportion of correct predictions remains very stable; the same three variables (trade, military assistance, and local military balance) consistently make significant contributions to the equations, and only these variables consistently do so. Finally, our findings here compare well with the results derived from a set of expected utilities computed by Bruce Bueno de Mesquita for *The War Trap* and kindly provided to us by that author. Of the 49 cases for which Bueno de Mesquita has data, his model correctly predicts 71 percent and ours, 76 percent. Bueno de Mesquita has since revised his method of computing expected utilities.[25] By that new method, his results would give correct predictions for 72 percent of the 18 cases to which those data apply, and we correctly predict 83 percent of those cases.

But our model here, in addition to showing substantial credibility for our expected-utility model in the aggregate, provides a means of disaggregating components of the model to show which variables are the most effective predictors to deterrence success. Turning to look at the individual variables, the equation shows strong effects for economic linkage (the share of defender's trade with the protégé, hypothesis H3c), arms transfers from defender to protégé (hypothesis H3c), and the military balance, in the variant of existing local capabilities (hypothesis H1 d), and a negative effect for military alliance (hypothesis H 3a). Military assistance and the local military balance are of about equal importance and are significant at the level of .02 or above, and trade is at the .05 level. Trade and military assistance testify to the importance of economic and political linkages: deterrence is more likely to be effective the greater the defender's visible and symbolic stake in the protégé.

The presence of a negative relation between alliance and successful deterrence is a surprise, just the opposite of the standard hypothesis (hypothesis H3a). The relationship is not very strong,[26] but nevertheless is strong enough to require explanation. An attacker may threaten a protégé that is formally allied to the defender, fully realizing that the risks are very high precisely because of the formal alliance relationship. In such a situation, the potential attacker has made a firm decision to force the opponent to back down or to go to war. Successful deterrence is therefore much more difficult to achieve. Russia in July of 1914 (case no. 18) was determined' to protect Serbia against Austria-Hungary in order to avoid humiliation like that over Bosnia in 1908–09 and realized the risks of a confrontation with Germany in doing so. Similarly, Hitler in September of 1939 (case no. 28) pressed ahead with the attack against Poland, accepting the possibility that Britain and France would declare war.

It is also important to note the variables that do not enter into the equation. For example, the defender's past behavior in crises seems to make no systematic difference. Neither do the other kinds of military power indicators, such as power potential or overall ("strategic") military superiority by the defender (hypotheses H1a–H1c), make a significant contribution.[27] We also tried a dummy variable for either local or overall military superiority on the basis that *either* might suffice to deter an attack, but found that effort made no greater contribution to our results.

One other power variable—defender's possession of nuclear weapons—also is absent, perhaps surprisingly, from these results. We cannot entirely dismiss a possible effect for nuclear weapons, because that dummy variable did approach ($P = .12$) our cutoff level for statistical significance, and it does appear at an acceptable significance level if the case of Vietnam (no. 45) is deleted from the analysis. Although the Vietnam case does not fit our analysis very well (and will be discussed below) it is not so deviant that it should be dropped as an "outlier" from the statistical examination. We do not delete this case but merely point out here that this result at least is sensitive to the treatment of Vietnam.

The effect of nuclear weapons is nonetheless marginal, not one on which to put much weight. Moreover, the possession of nuclear weapons is sometimes irrelevant (spurious), as in the British successful effort to deter Guatemalan seizure of Belize (case no. 53).

With probit analysis it is possible to compute the change in probability that the "1" value of the dependent variable will be achieved for a given change in any one of the independent variables while holding the other independent variables constant. This is the more readily interpretable measure of the impact of each independent variable, better than the probit coefficients at the top of table 11.2. The lower half of table 11.2 shows those impacts. We see that if the protégé takes 25 percent or less of its arms imports from the defender the probability of successful deterrence is just .28, but if the proportion of military imports from the defender exceeds 75 percent, the probability of successful deterrence rises to .79. Similarly, with no trade between defender and protégé, the chances of successful deterrence are just about even, but if as much as 6 percent of the defender's trade is with its protégé, the chances of effective deterrence rise to about seven out of eight. Trade and arms sales can be considered relatively susceptible to policy manipulation by the defender, perhaps more so than are relative power bases. Local military superiority likewise shows a wide range of effect, from a 26 percent chance of successful deterrence even if defender and protégé have only a tenth of the attacker's power, to a very high probability if together they have a ten-to-one advantage.[28]

The importance of local but not overall capabilities, coupled with the absence of much explanatory power for nuclear weapons, has profound import for contemporary superpower deterrence. It suggests that rhetoric about "windows of vulnerability" is off the mark. Local military capabilities (of the defender and protégé combined) seem to have more to do with successful deterrence than do strategic ones, and both may be less important than having a dense network of political and economic bonds between defender and protége.[29] Israel, for instance, arguably is better protected by its own local, conventional military strength (possibly augmented by that of the United States) than it would be by American strategic superiority (now declined) or by its own overt possession of nuclear weapons. It also, in terms of our results, is better protected by its dense network of political and economic linkages with the United States than it would be by a formal military pact (e.g., in the Yom Kippur war of 1973, case no. 50).

Certainly the mere fact of a military alliance between defender and protégé makes no positive contribution by itself, as the existence of more tangible interests does. Just as the formal alliances provided little deterrence for Czechoslovakia and Poland, they did not suffice either for various "protégés" who had them in 1914 (although the alliance system did insure that war, once begun, would cascade to include most of the great powers). Insofar as United States foreign policy decision makers continued to fight the Vietnam War for almost a decade in order to preserve the credibility of America's "pledged word," they may have missed the real point. The operative ties that drew the United States in were not those of the formal commitment represented by the Southeast Asian Treaty Organization (SEATO) pact, but rather the close links of economic and military assistance, and political commitment, to the South Vietnamese government. Moreover, our results indicate that the effect of honoring that commitment was not central to the credibility of American deterrent threats in the face of subsequent challenges: the defender's past behavior against a threat does not predict whether the defender will be able to succeed in deterring a later attack.

Mention of the Vietnam War is important because it does not fit standard theories of deterrence. The United States had nuclear weapons, overwhelming total superiority over Vietnam, and clear local military superiority if its forces were fully engaged, and it provided virtually all of South Vietnam's military capabilities. Up to that point the United States had no record of having failed to come to an attacked protégé's defense, and, indeed, it had come to South Korea's defense in 1950 even without having first made any prior deterrent threat.

Substantively and theoretically, the Vietnam case shows the limitations of many extant theories of deterrence. Those we have tapped here would not have predicted the true outcome. The reason lies in the element of a full expected-utility model of deterrence that we have not been able to incorporate in this empirical test—the value of "peace" to the would-be deterree was not sufficiently high. That is, the government of North Vietnam valued very highly its campaign to eliminate the vestiges of colonial rule in all of Vietnam and to reunify the nation. To that end it was prepared to suffer great costs rather than be deterred. Its goals in the war far exceeded those of the Americans and sustained them despite the latter's apparent advantages.[30] If American deterrence of North Vietnamese intervention in South Vietnam epitomizes the limitations of our empirical test, the successful earlier American deterrence of North Vietnamese intervention into Thailand (case no. 42) exemplifies the strength of our model. All the conditions that applied there applied in the subsequent case—except for much more important goals held by the North Vietnamese.

Two other cases where our model erroneously predicted successful deterrence are those of Austria-Hungary against Serbia, and Germany against Belgium, (cases nos. 17 and 20. We correctly predicted the other two 1914 results.) The events of "the guns of

August" illustrate what can go wrong in a deterrence crisis—the limits of any "rational" model. The complex array of alliance commitments and quasi-commitments of the many powers made it unusually difficult to predict behavior. Mobilization plans made it virtually impossible to make a military threat, or even to take defensive measures, without provoking the other side. Shifting power relationships made the value of continued peace uncertain, and few expected the costs of war to be as catastrophic as they proved to be.

What Happens After Deterrence Fails? Empirical Results

Predicting the attacker's decision whether to press ahead or to be deterred is important, but so too is the matter of what happens after deterrence fails. The attacker's move is known, and the defender has to make a choice: whether to allow its bluff to be called or to resist the attacker's move against the protégé. The defender must decide whether it will lose more by going to war or by not resisting. Table 11.3 shows the results of our analysis of the cases in which a defender faced this choice.

Our equation correctly predicted 18 of the 23 decisions (78 percent). This record is the same as that obtained when predicting whether

Table 11.3   Conditions promoting defender resistance

Fight $= -.50 + 3.91$ Protege Power $+ 1.37$ Alliance
$\quad$ (−1.11) (1.36) $\qquad$ (1.87)

		Predicted	
		Not Fight	Fight
	Not Fight	6	2
Actual			
	Fight	3	12

	Contributions to Probability of Resistance	
	Value %	Probability of Resistance
Protégé Power	5	.61
	10	.69
	20	.81
	30	.89
	40	.95
Alliance	No	.69
	Yes	.97

Note: Percentage of predictions correct = 78; $R^2 = .29$; $N = 23$.

deterrence would or would not succeed, and it compares favorably with the success rate using data from Bueno de Mesquita's *War Trap* (80 percent success for us in the 20 cases for which his data are available, and 50 percent success using his method).

In 15 out of the 23 cases the defender chose to fight. A decision to fight is more likely where the protégé's military capability is fairly substantial compared with the defender's own capability (hypothesis H1k). That is, the defender will fight to retain a "big" protégé. To fail to do so would be too costly, materially as well as perhaps to its reputation. The value of "peace" without trying to defend the protégé would be too low, even as compared with the costs of war. The cutoff point comes fairly quickly with increments to power. By the time the protégé's existing military power (protégé power) reaches even 10 percent of its defender's, the probability the defender will fight becomes better than two to one, and by 40 percent the probability virtually reaches unity. Sharing a common border with the protégé did not, however, significantly increase the probability that the defender would fight (hypothesis H1l).

In this exercise too, the defender's past behavior proved to have no power in predicting whether it would fight on the subsequent occasion. However, the existence of a formal military alliance does contribute substantially to a defender's decision to fight (hypothesis H3b). Without an alliance, the chances the defender would fight were only about two in three; with an alliance, virtually unity. We predicted all but two of the eight instances in which a defender was not willing to use military force on behalf of a protégé. One of those cases dealt with the Indian seizure of Goa (no. 39). Despite the fact that Goa was juridically part of Portugal, and thus protected by a formal bond even stronger than a mere alliance, the Indians took Goa without resistance. Doubtless they were emboldened by their own overwhelming local military superiority, and by their knowledge that the Portuguese Empire was moribund and unable to offer effective resistance. The other such case is Czechoslovakia in 1938, when Hitler correctly assessed the relatively greater importance of his own local military capabilities as compared with the substantial overall capabilities of his opponents and—more crucially—the absence of his opponents' political will to honor the alliance between France and Czechoslovakia.

Perhaps more important, we correctly identified 12 of the 15 cases in which the defender *did* fight. Very often these cases, in which large-scale violence did transpire, had very costly consequences that all parties would have done better to avoid. The most notable of those for which our model did not predict resistance by the defender were Russia over Serbia and Britain over Belgium in 1914. Our earlier comments about decision making in 1914 are apropos. Also, in both the Russian and British decisions the absence of a formal military alliance is deceptive. Russia was deeply committed to maintaining Serbia's independence, and Britain was drawn into World War I as much to prevent Germany from defeating France and dominating the continent as it was by the catalyst of the invasion of Belgium.[31]

Note that the influences associated with a defender's decision to fight once deterrence has failed are not the same as those associated with successful deterrence. Only formal alliance plays a role in both—and in opposite directions. An alliance made it more likely that the defender would fight if deterrence failed but was negatively associated with the success of deterrence. A military alliance not backed up by more tangible linkages—linkages that perhaps give the defender some control to prevent adventurism by a protégé—thus may *increase* the danger that a defender will be drawn into war. Local military superiority clearly made a contribution to effective deterrence, but, in the defender's decision to fight, military power was relevant only in the sense that the defender was more likely to fight on behalf of a protégé with substantial existing military strength. Trade ties and arms transfers, which were important for deterrence, did not appear in the second analysis.

Perhaps there is a serious and potentially dangerous mismatch between attacker's and defender's calculations. But that is not a necessary conclusion from our results. Since deterrence usually succeeds where the defender and protégé have close economic and political ties, it may well be that the attacker is correct in assuming that the defender will fight on behalf of such a protégé, and thus it rarely presses its challenge to a full military attack. (For example, where the protégé accounts for 6 percent or more of the defender's trade, deterrence almost always is successful.) In cases where those ties are weaker the attacker is more likely to press forward, and other influences predominate. Another consideration, contained in our analysis of the defender's calculation, is missed entirely in the one for the attacker. Sometimes a war, even with the high probability of intervention by the defender, may look like a reasonable option to a rationally calculating attacker. The attacker may expect to win the war at a tolerable cost. Such a reasonable calculation could apply even if the attacker believed it might very well lose, if the other options looked worse. North Vietnam's decision to push ahead with its attempt to unify the Vietnamese nation may be a case in point.

Conclusion

We have developed and tested an expected-utility model of deterrence and its immediate consequences. Writing about the deterrence literature, Lawrence Freedman has judged that "much of what is offered today as a profound and new insight was said yesterday."[32] We may not have offered striking new insights, but we have uncovered some notable empirical findings that help discriminate among alleged insights. We have produced these results without analyzing the process of bargaining and threat that goes on during a deterrence crisis. Very likely, additional explanatory power could be found by such analysis, perhaps especially by looking at the ways bargaining may serve to call attention to the very elements of capability and interest we have identified in this macrolevel analysis.

For deterrence attempts, we found that in our sample, success was most often associated with close economic and political-military ties between the defender and its protégé. Local military superiority for the defender and its protégé helped bolster deterrence, but a military alliance was associated with deterrence failure.[33] Only a marginal contribution was made by the possession of nuclear weapons. Other elements of national power and the history of the defender's earlier deterrence behavior played no significant role. Existence of a formal military alliance played no positive role, and, if not backed up by more tangible ties, actually worked against the success of deterrence. We want to caution the reader that these findings apply only to cases of immediate deterrence; that is, to instances in which an overt military threat from a potential attacker has already become manifest. Perhaps this kind of case understates the value of military strength in general deterrence. If military power were overwhelming, possibly no aggressor would ever rise to the level of making the overt challenge that characterizes these cases. But in the world of the cold war, for example, U.S. military power has never been so dominant as to prevent the ten challenges we have listed here.

The problem of immediate deterrence touches on many of the most dangerous opportunities for the outbreak of war. These are portentous occasions, and our conclusions have important implications for policy, especially in an era when overwhelming military superiority is not available to either superpower. Our conclusions suggest that a definition of deterrence as primarily sensitive to strict calculation of military capability is both mistaken and profoundly dangerous. A quest for strategic nuclear superiority is unlikely to be the most effective means for providing security to America's friends and allies in a crisis, or to America itself. Nor does success in deterrence follow merely from establishing a record of "standing firm" in the past. Insofar as military strength is critical, local military forces—in some combination of forces of defender and local protégé—are likely to prove more effective than overall or "strategic" forces. Finally, an important contribution to effective deterrence may emerge from achievement of a goal that is usually sought for other purposes— maintaining and strengthening the ties of mutual interest among nation-states in an open global economic system.

Chapter 12

Ethical Dilemmas of Nuclear Deterrence

For the first time in the nuclear era, normative and practical issues have become explicitly intertwined in widespread public discussion of deterrence. Previously, "main-stream" strategic analysts typically avoided overt attention to normative questions, preferring to concentrate on the alleged psychological or military foundations of deterrence theory. Public commentators who did raise normative issues all too often did so only at the fringes, debating the virtues of pacifism or the implications of simple "red vs. dead" declarations. Of course there had long been analysts who insisted on raising more subtle and complex normative issues, but their impact was limited. In the past few years, however, normative issues have been brought front and center and knitted inextricably into the traditional political and military context. In this chapter, I shall address these issues by explication of the choices faced, and the conclusions adopted, by the Catholic bishops.

The Drafting Process

The National Conference of Catholic Bishops of the United States issued its Pastoral letter on War and Peace in May 1983. The letter is detailed, complex in its reasoning, and remarkably progressive for a group often—and not always justly—regarded as cautious and politically rather conservative.[1] The letter throws down some fundamental challenges to contemporary American military policy, significantly contributes to a de-legitimization of nuclear weapons as an instrument of war-fighting or even in some ways of deterrence, and demands far-reaching changes in thought and action.

For many years the American Catholic Church rarely took a public stand in opposition to the state's foreign policy. Rather, it emphasized the unquestioned patriotism of the institution and its members. Partly this was because it was initially a church of immigrants, and often of immigrants (Irish, Italian, East European, Spanish-speaking in this century) at the lower end of the socioeconomic scale. In recent decades, however, this situation changed. Catholics moved into the mainstream of American social and political life (viz., the emergence of a body of American Catholic lay-intellectuals, and the election of John F. Kennedy as president) and no longer felt insecure. Furthermore, as they became able to shape foreign policy actively, they began to feel more responsibility for it. Many Catholic laypeople and clergy (the Berrigan brothers being the most prominent example) were active in opposition to the Vietnam War, and by 1971 the U.S. Catholic Bishops' Conference as a body concluded that continuation of that conflict could not be morally justified.[2]

Toward the end of that decade, as concern about the dangers of nuclear war grew more pervasive, Catholics were again among the more prominent critics of established perceptions and policies. Some bishops even began to make strong public statements not only about the immorality of the arms race but also about the immorality of nuclear deterrence itself, and calling for disengagement from the production or deployment of nuclear weapons. While calls for unilateral nuclear disarmament or pacifism were by no means the norm in the American Catholic community, they were too widespread and forcefully articulated to be ignored. Moreover, there was a long-standing moral-theological critique of the kind of counterpopulation strategy that was inherent in American declaratory deterrent policy. Indeed, in 1944 Father John Ford had published an analysis of strategic bombing during World War II that clearly demonstrated, in terms of traditional Catholic thinking, that deliberate bombing of population centers was morally utterly unacceptable. This analysis—written before the first atomic bomb—exhibits a cogency of reasoning yet to be improved upon.[3]

Responding to the generally rising concern, several bishops introduced resolutions calling for a formal statement on the topic by the entire conference. These resolutions were supported vigorously not only by "doves," but also by other bishops who hoped to see some consensus replace the increasingly discordant cacophony of ecclesiastical voices. As a result, the Ad Hoc Committee on War and Peace was established in 1981, and chaired by then-archbishop Joseph Bernardin of Cincinnati. Archbishop Bernardin was already widely respected for his good judgment and ability to encourage consensus even in the presence of heated initial disagreement. His skills had been recognized in his election several years earlier for a term as president of the Bishops' Conference, and would be recognized again in his subsequent appointment as archbishop of Chicago and elevation to cardinal. Other members of the committee were Bishops George Fulcher and Daniel Reilly (perceived as "centrists" on this issue, with no substantial record of public pronouncement), Bishop Thomas Gumbleton (president of *Pax Christi*, an organization dedicated to nonviolence), and Bishop John O'Connor (second in command of the Catholic Military Chaplains, with a Ph.D. in political science, regarded as somewhat of a political and theological conservative). The committee was supported by a five-member staff including a representative each from the nation's men and women religious (monks and nuns), Father J. Bryan Hehir (director of the Conference's Department of International Justice and Peace in Washington, and a Ph.D. in Government from Harvard), Edward Doherty (also from the Department of Justice and Peace, and a retired U.S. Foreign Service Officer), and myself as "principal consultant."[4]

Choice of a committee that covered most of the American foreign policy spectrum was no coincidence. The Bishops' Conference is constitutionally prohibited from adopting a Pastoral Letter by less than a two-thirds majority of all members. Moreover, the bishops are extremely uncomfortable in taking public positions on the basis of sharply divided votes. The informal, but very real, decision rule is more like 85–90 percent of all members present and voting; if the draft appeared unlikely to garner that many votes, it would probably have been returned to the committee for further revision. Thus the process guaranteed that all sides would be heard, and that the committee would report a draft letter that seemed to reflect a broad range of views. The majority of the bishops could be expected to be somewhere near the "center" of the American spectrum on this issue, but enough could be located near either end that the "center" alone could not carry the vote. The document would have to be acceptable to a significant share of *both* "hawks" and "doves" to achieve the necessary majority. Furthermore, it would not be enough simply to write a document full of glittering generalities about the virtues of peace; too many bishops wanted a statement with specific evaluations, touching central issues in the nuclear debate, for a platitudinous statement to be acceptable either. In consequence, the committee's task was a formidable one.

The committee proceeded with many days of discussion, along with hearings at which about 50 experts (including theologians, biblical scholars, political scientists, present and former government officials and military officers, and peace activists) were heard and questioned. After circulation and intensive criticism of various portions proposed by many members of the committee and staff, the committee's first public draft was released early in June of 1982. This draft immediately became the subject of widespread discussion. Reactions varied greatly, as could be predicted. The committee then, on the basis of the public commentary and numerous private communications, produced a second draft that was distributed in October 1982 and discussed at length by all the bishops in their annual meeting in November. The committee took the latest set of comments into consideration and produced a third draft at the beginning of April 1983. This third draft became subject to the bishops' formal process of amendment, with the committee preparing formal recommendations for disposition of the over 200 proposed amendments. Final action was of course the responsibility of the entire conference. In the end the letter, as amended, was adopted by a vote of 328 to 9 (96 percent)—better than virtually anyone had dared anticipate.[5]

Both the drafts and the full meetings of the conference had been subjected to enormous public scrutiny, with the debate at the final meeting conducted under the eyes of scores of television cameras from around the globe. The process, then, had become one of full involvement by the lower clergy, the laity, and the public in general. In so doing, it served a major purpose of those who in the first place proposed that the letter be written: It brought great public attention to the issues of nuclear weaponry, and established those issues not as esoteric technical matters best left to the "priesthood" of civilian and military strategists, but as fundamentally political and moral issues that were the proper province, and indeed responsibility, of ordinary citizens. This, as much as the letter's substance, may ultimately constitute its most enduring achievement.

As for the substance, first it is important to repeat what was said at the outset of this chapter: the letter is severely critical of accepted policy in a number of highly significant ways. Second, despite changes through various drafts of the document, the changes occurred within quite a narrow range of substance. The basic thrust and substance of the letter, rooted in a very substantial degree of consensus on the committee as to what constituted the constraints of established Catholic teaching on peace and war, endured from the first draft. Although the document did go through refinement of tone, and some limited shifts in substance and applications, its underlying principles did not change.

"Acceptable" Deterrence

The consensus was forged around the long-established principles of "just war" analysis. It is thus not written from the point of view of an advocate of nonviolence. The bishops did take the nonviolent position seriously. That has a long and honored position in the tradition, from the early days of the Church through St. Francis of Assisi and modern witnesses. In this letter, it is accorded a prominence that is really unprecedented for official Church documents. It is presented as a legitimate and often laudable option for individuals, even in the face of injustice—an option that should be respected by governments. Nevertheless, it is not required of individuals, who have a right to defend themselves and perhaps a duty to defend others. In this world of conflicting states, governments too have a right to self-defense, and even an obligation to defend their people and their allies—although, as for individuals, that does not always include a right to exercise lethal violence. The bishops did not want to *prescribe* nonviolence because most of them sincerely believe in that right of self-defense, and that there are major values—liberty, justice, human rights—which are endangered in the world, and should be defended.

Another constraint was an unwillingness to demand of people an obedience they were not yet ready to give as a matter of conscience. A specter that always hung over deliberations was the response to *Humanae Vitae*, the papal encyclical on birth control. No one wanted to put individuals under that kind of moral burden. Neither did anyone want to fragment the institutional church by making non-violence, or even some form of "nuclear pacifism," mandatory.

A final constraint, emerging after release of the first draft but both consistent with that draft and defining the terms of subsequent debate, was Pope John Paul II's June 1982 statement to the United Nations. It said, in part, "In current conditions, 'deterrence' based on balance, certainly not as an end in itself but as a step on the way toward a progressive disarmament, may still be judged morally acceptable."

The letter appropriately calls this a "strictly conditioned" acceptance of deterrence. We must realize how little it explicitly accepts. It cannot be used to indicate a blanket acceptance of all, or even many, forms of deterrence.

Most obvious, and noted by virtually all commentators, is the condition that deterrence must be "a step on the way toward a progressive disarmament." Deterrence cannot be considered "an end in itself," nor can we resign ourselves to an indefinite future whereby we are condemned, in the pope's next words, to be "always susceptible to the real danger of explosion."

Another element of his statement is the phrase "based on balance." It implies a need, as recognized by most strategists and policymakers, to maintain some sort of "parity" or "essential equivalence" to the capability of one's opponent. American analysts have taken that need to mean not necessarily matching an opponent one-to-one in every weapons category, which would make little sense given the great asymmetries of technology, geography, and interest between the two superpowers. Many analysts would concede even that it need not imply being able to do as much damage to the opponent as he can do to you, but only enough, reliably, to make the costs of beginning a war far too high for a rational opponent to contemplate. But a further implication of the "based on balance" phrase is a willingness to concede such a capability to the opponent. In other words, one can reasonably read the pope's words as rejecting notions of seeking "superiority" or means to "win" or "prevail" in nuclear wars. Such notions can lead to a continuing upward spiral of the arms race as one power tries to establish such a capability and the other seeks to avoid being under such a threat, or to establish its own "winning" capability. At worst, attempts to achieve a "winning" capability would produce first-strike forces and "use it or lose it" situations of extreme danger in crisis.

There are other limitations implicit in the pope's words. He refers very generally to "deterrence," not to particular implements or strategies of nuclear deterrence. In the French original of his United Nations address, the operative words are "une dissuasion"—a deterrent, some deterrent, not any and all deterrents. He does not even explicitly endorse nuclear deterrence. What we have here, in explicit words, is no more than a recognition that in competitive international relations states require, at least "in current conditions," some means to deter other states from aggressive action. The specific form of that deterrent is not specified. Moreover, deterrence "may still be judged" morally acceptable. Again, this is hardly a blanket endorsement of everything that is said, done, or planned in the name of deterrence.

The vague, general, and ambiguous content of Pope John Paul's words must be fully appreciated. Possibly he would explicitly accept various specific aspects of American or Soviet deterrent policy. The fact remains that he has not done so. The very restricted nature of his overt "acceptance" impels the kind of further normative analysis articulated by the bishops in their letter.

A Just War Analysis of Deterrence

The just war tradition, developed from St. Augustine onward, has been the predominant strain of Catholic thought concerning any resort to violence on behalf of political units. That tradition, rightly understood, constitutes a strong presumption against violence, and establishes very strict constraints both on the circumstances under which a resort to violence may be considered "just" and on the actions that can morally be taken in the course of exercising that right. Three analytical categories of that tradition are especially relevant.

First is the requirement of *discrimination*, or observing the principle of noncombatant immunity. This requirement forbids direct attacks on civilians: "Under no circumstances may nuclear weapons or other instruments of mass slaughter be used for the purpose of destroying population centers or other predominantly civilian targets. . . . No Christian can rightfully carry out orders or policies deliberately aimed at killing non-combatants."[6] This is a strong statement. It implicitly condemns the bombing of Dresden, the firebombing of Tokyo, and of course the atomic bombing of Hiroshima and Nagasaki. (No matter that the destruction of those cities may have helped shorten the war, and even have reduced the total number of civilian casualties from what they might otherwise have been. The direct killing of innocents—making them means to achieving some good end or avoiding some great evil—can never, by this reasoning, be morally permissible.)

The wording of the presentation is very important, in light of the letter's distinction between general principles of moral theology (those principles are not open to question by the reader) and applications on specific matters of policy. Applications are matters of opinion, on which a Catholic—though he or she must "give serious consideration and attention" to the judgments reached in Church teaching—may nonetheless still disagree in good conscience, and obedience is not demanded. (Note the comments above about prudence in demanding such obedience.) Most of the policy recommendations in the letter are clearly identifiable as applications, judgments. But the prohibition of deliberately killing noncombatants is not, nor did the committee or the bishops in plenary session ever consider any other possibility. It is a basic principle of Christian ethics that one may not directly and intentionally kill innocent human beings. Its relevance to nuclear deterrence follows from the same premise as does the Catholic condemnation of abortion. The fetus is innocent, and may not be deliberately killed, even to avert some great evil or achieve some good end. The same reasoning applies if children or adult civilians are deliberately killed in a bombing raid—and there can be no question but what individual human beings are at stake. In the words of Cardinal Bernardin's opening address to the Chicago May 1983 meetings, such an action is "murder."

The condemnation of direct attacks on civilian population centers as such removes a great deal of deliberate ambiguity from past American deterrent policy. "Collateral" damage must be limited, not intended, and "bonus effects" of civilian casualties may not be sought. American *operational* policy has at times fluctuated in the relative attention to counterforce and counterpopulation targeting. Military targets often have been broadly defined to include "economic recovery" capabilities and even the civilian labor force. *Declaratory* policy for many years stressed the potential destruction of the attacker "as a viable 20th century nation," defining that destruction as some portion of the enemy's population and general industrial capacity. Secretary of Defense Robert McNamara's well-known 1962 attempt to move toward a counterforce declaratory policy failed, but was resurrected in the subsequent decade. In 1973, Secretary of Defense Elliot Richardson testified, "We do not in our strategic planning target population *per se* any longer."[7] This kind of statement has subsequently been repeated, most frequently in the last two years in obvious response to the evolving position of the bishops' letter. However one judges the sincerity of official disavowal of an intent deliberately to strike civilians, achieving its expression has to be considered a major achievement, one with many implications for the direction of future policy.[8]

The second just war category, of equal importance, is the principle of *proportionality*. By some (inevitably subjective and uncertain) calculation, the harm done by an act, even unintentionally, may not be disproportionate to the good intended to be achieved or to the evil to be avoided. The principle of discrimination forbids counterpopulation warfare; the principle of proportionality puts sharp limits on counterforce warfare. The latter principle recognizes that in almost any war some civilians will unavoidably be killed if military targets are hit. This is clearly a case of "double effect," and admits that some civilian deaths can be accepted as a by-product of striking a military target. But just because civilians are not killed intentionally does not mean they can be killed without limit. Specifically, the Pastoral Letter expresses very grave reservations about the massive civilian casualties that would surely occur in any nuclear exchange, even one directed deliberately only to military targets. The section on deterrence is filled with references to the way military facilities and civilian living and working areas are interspersed, to the fact that the number of civilians who would necessarily be killed is "horrendous," and cites admissions by the Reagan administration that "once any substantial numbers of weapons were used, the civilian casualty levels would quickly become truly catastrophic." The principle of proportionality thus says that discrimination alone—merely limiting a nuclear strike to counterforce targets—is not enough to make that policy "morally acceptable."

Many strategists and government officials—especially, but not only, members of the current administration—have maintained that improvements in strategic weaponry are movements in the direction of greater moral acceptability. Specifically, improvements in accuracy, coupled with elimination of the very large warheads placed on older missiles like the Titan, will have the effect of limiting collateral damage. The number of (supposedly greatly reduced) civilian casualties sustained when military targets are hit could therefore be judged appropriate to some aims of war or deterrence. Nuclear deterrence could then be said to be both discriminating and proportionate.[9]

Modernization of the strategic arsenal, with more accurate weapons like the MX, is therefore morally permissible and even required! Similar claims are made for "small" battlefield tactical nuclear weapons.

On first encounter, it is hard to disagree with this assessment. A reduction in unintended civilian deaths would be consistent with traditional moral principles. But on examination the problems are immense. One problem is the fact, as already mentioned, that any large-scale nuclear exchange, even of "discriminating" weapons, would inevitably produce millions or tens of millions of civilian casualties. Numerous studies, drawing on private and government material, reach this conclusion. The combination of immediate casualties from blast and radiation, with longer-term casualties from fallout, disruption of the medical, sanitation, transportation, and communication systems, ecological devastation, climatic effects, and so forth, would be very great—even from attacks that were "limited" to such "strictly military" targets as the 1052 American and 1398 Soviet land-based long-range missiles ICBMs. Actually, the Defense Department's list of military and militarily related industrial targets (40,000 of them, including 60 in Moscow alone) encompasses industry and utilities essential to the economic recuperation of the Soviet Union.[10] If the Soviet (American) economy is destroyed, tens of millions of Soviet (American) citizens will die of hunger and disease. To "prevail" in such a war would have little meaning, and there are not many causes to which such deaths would be "proportionate."

One problem is therefore the illusion that any large-scale nuclear exchange could in any real sense be "limited" in its consequences. The other problem is with the expectation that nuclear war could be fought in some precise fashion of strike and counterstrike, that in any substantial nuclear exchange the war could be restricted to a limited number of strictly military targets. There are people who imagine it could be done, with acceptable consequences. The majority of analysts, however, consider the likelihood of such limitation, under wartime conditions of anger, confusion, ignorance, and loss of control, to be extremely small. One cannot definitively rule out the possibility, but neither should one bet the future of civilization on it. Two of the most knowledgeable experts on this matter are Desmond Ball and John Steinbruner, who offer nearly identically skeptical views. In Steinbruner's words,

> Once the use of as many as 10 or more nuclear weapons directly against the USSR is seriously contemplated, U.S. strategic commanders will likely insist on attacking the full array of Soviet military targets. . . . If national commanders seriously attempted to implement this strategy (controlled response) in a war with existing and currently projected U.S. forces, the result would not be a finely controlled strategic campaign. The more likely result would be the collapse of U.S. forces into isolated units undertaking retaliation on their own initiative against a wide variety of targets at unpredictable moments.[11]

In a nutshell, limitation of nuclear war fails a third principle of the just war tradition: *reasonable chance of success.*

So much for what could—or could not—morally be done in war. Is *deterrence*—as contrasted with what one actually *does* in war—different? After all, the purpose of deterrence, as we are so often reminded, is to prevent war.

The bishops have two answers to this. One is the fact that, whatever our good intentions, deterrence may fail. If we make plans—build weapons, construct strategic programs, proclaim doctrines, instruct commanders—on the basis of principles we would not be willing to act upon, we just may be called to act upon them anyway. Many things happen almost automatically in any war or defense establishment. In the 1914 crisis, the powers had competitive mobilization plans that worked automatically, making World War I almost unavoidable. Or, we may contemplate recent talk about launching nuclear weapons on warning. Plans adopted in the name of deterrence may come to fruition in action, whatever our desires at the time. If war should come as the result of some uncontrollable crisis, or a physical or human accident, plans calling in the name of deterrence for morally unacceptable acts would very likely be *realized* as morally unacceptable acts. The second answer is the traditional principle of Catholic moral theology that says one may not intend what one may not do. An intention to commit an immoral act in a particular event (even if one is confident that the triggering event will not transpire) is itself immoral. For the bishops, the argument from "mere deterrence" will not fly.

Another aspect of recent strategy that the bishops probably would reject is brinkmanship, or what Thomas C. Schelling called "manipulating the shared risk of war."[12] Schelling recognizes that a would-be deterrer might well threaten to do something that, in the event deterrence failed, he would not in fact want to carry out. The United States might *threaten* to go to all-out nuclear war if the Soviet Union occupies West Germany. In the event the Soviet Union *did* occupy West Germany, the U.S. government might not want to execute its threat. In fact, a government fully in control of its military forces probably would *not* want to initiate all-out nuclear war. One way to deal with this situation would be to build some variant of a "doomsday machine": commit oneself irrevocably and automatically to an act of mutual destruction that one would not want to carry out if one retained a choice at the time. Almost everyone rejects the "doomsday machine" solution as grossly imprudent and disproportionate.

But a less drastic solution would be to build into a situation an element of unpredictability and uncontrollability. In practice, a Soviet invasion of West Germany might very well trigger all-out nuclear war whether or not the American government wished it to do so. American nuclear weapons would be widely dispersed, to low-level commanders who would very likely have operational control over the weapons. (The PAL [Permissive Action Link] codes that prevent unauthorized use in peacetime very likely would be released to low-level commanders in a time of high crisis in Europe.) One of those commanders, in the "fog of war" with his troops under siege, might very well use the weapons.[13] Or the Soviet Union, fearing they would be used, might stage a preemptive attack on them. Use of a few tactical or theater nuclear weapons would be very likely to escalate into a strategic exchange between the American and Soviet homelands, as several military analysts cited in the Pastoral Letter have testified. The threat of unintended use of nuclear weapons in the event of a conventional war or even a high-level crisis in Europe provides a powerful deterrent to the deliberate initiation of war, of any kind, in the center of that continent. No rational Soviet leader would deliberately run such a risk.

If we believe that political crises (unlike military events) are always fully controllable, then perhaps such a deterrent seems prudent. But if we believe that political crises are not always controllable or avoidable (1914 again, or a revolt in Eastern Europe that somehow attracts support from the West, or a political breakdown in Yugoslavia that draws in regular or volunteer fighters from East and West), it does *not* seem prudent. In the apt words of Michael Howard, military forces must serve two purposes: they must deter enemies, and they must reassure friends.[14] Nuclear "deterrent" systems that depend on their uncontrollability are not reassuring to one's friends. The bishops termed "the deliberate initiation of nuclear war" to be morally unjustified. I believe they would similarly declare a deliberate posture of probable loss of control to be an unjustifiable moral risk. As they have said, "Non-nuclear attacks by another state must be resisted by other than nuclear means."

Use, Threat, and Possession

The just war tradition demands that the means used to defend must themselves be at least morally neutral. They may not be indiscriminating, nor used in a disproportionate manner. They must offer a reasonable chance of success. The bishops say they are extremely skeptical whether any use of nuclear weapons could pass these tests. Deterrence, in the sense of what one prepares to do, must pass the same tests.

Yet another question is whether one may threaten to perform acts which one could not licitly do or intend. The broad question of "bluffing" as a theological issue is not, I understand, settled. The bishops avoid it in their letter. On more narrowly pragmatic grounds, we can ask whether making deterrent threats of indiscriminate or disproportionate use of nuclear weapons would be a prudent national policy. The answer, I believe, is clearly "no." For one thing, if the threatener were known to adhere to other aspects of the Christian just war tradition, it would be an obviously empty bluff—the threatener simply would not be believed. If the threatener were not a known adherent to the just war tradition, the threat would gain greater credibility. But to be credible, the threat would have to be supplemented by public orders and plans for the contingent use of nuclear weapons if deterrence failed. Declaratory policy would have to be contrary to operational policy, with only a very small circle of policymakers aware of the difference. It is very unlikely that such a policy could succeed. On the one hand, the fact that the threat was only a bluff probably would become known, through leaks or espionage. Or, if the secret were held tightly enough, the automaticity inherent in strategic nuclear planning very possibly would take over in the event of war, especially if war included (as it very likely would) a "decapitating" attack that removed the commander-in-chief. The use of nuclear weapons would then probably follow the lines of the declaratory policy rather than the secret operational policy—and nuclear weapons would be used in a morally unacceptable manner. The circle cannot be squared.

To encourage belief in the probability of "morally acceptable limited nuclear war" would play into the hands of the war-fighters, the "prevailers," those who think "victory is possible." It would encourage those who want to continue to rely on a threat of first use of nuclear weapons to deter a wide range of acts in Europe, the Middle East, and elsewhere. It would encourage brinkmanship and crisis risk-taking at the expense of building up alternative, nonnuclear means of defending ourselves and our allies. The bishops prudently avoid that trap.

The trap on the other end of the spectrum lies in the position that a nation may continue to possess nuclear weapons but with an explicit policy that it will not use them under any conceivable circumstances. This becomes the "you can have it but you can't use it" position. It is easily parodied.[15] It falls under much the same objections as apply to expressing a threat one could not licitly execute. If it is known that the weapons would not be deliberately used under any circumstances, then the weapons lose most of their deterrent power. If—as is in fact virtually unavoidable in a complex military establishment—one leaves open the possibility that the weapons will be used despite the commander-in-chief's intention not to use them, the result is hardly better from a moral standpoint. "Leaving something to chance" inescapably involves moral responsibility for those who leave it to chance, and intend to benefit from the chance. Again, the circle cannot be squared.

Some critics, including several conservative columnists, *The New York Times* in a May 6, 1983 editorial, and Albert Wohlstetter in his article cited earlier have accused the bishops of adopting just such a "you can have it but you can't use it" position. It is true that the second draft (October 1982) of the Pastoral Letter was ambiguous—deliberately so—on this matter. While it contained no passage explicitly saying *no* use would be permissible, it was imbued (properly) with a strong rhetoric of "saying no to nuclear war," and contained a few passages whose full meaning was obscure.[16] The ambiguity was intended to mollify critics who chose to interpret some passages in the first draft—notably, "If nuclear weapons may be used at all, they may be used only after they have been used against our own country or our allies, and, even then, only in an extremely limited, discriminating manner against military targets"—as the bishops' giving some "Good Housekeeping Seal of Approval" to limited nuclear war. In context it certainly was nothing of the kind. Predictably, the ambiguity of the second draft opened the bishops up, from the perspective of conservative critics, to ridicule or mischievous charges that the bishops, despite their disclaimers, were "really" adopting a stance of unilateral nuclear disarmament. Fortunately this ambiguity was removed in the third draft and the form adopted in the final Chicago meeting. In fact, a proposed amendment by Archbishop Quinn, of "opposition on moral grounds to any use of nuclear weapons," was not adopted.[17]

A Dilemma Without Easy Resolution

These two traps—the extremes of counterforce as nuclear "war-winning" and of "possession without use"—frame a fundamental dilemma that cannot easily be resolved. There is *no* perfect practical solution to the problem of nuclear deterrence. Moral considerations further complicate the problem. The bishops' position in the final letter is not so ambiguous as it is frankly torn between desirable ends.

One proposed deterrent has been through advocacy or adoption of an extreme version of MAD (Mutually Assured Destruction) that is expressly and solely a counterpopulation deterrent. But practically, it would mean abandonment of almost all forms of extended deterrence, since no state would initiate its own sure destruction in order to "defend" another. And morally, most Christians reject strategies of counterpopulation warfare.

A possible way to ease, though not escape, the moral dilemma would be through adopting a posture of "tolerating" nuclear weaponry as a means to a good end (deterrence, or ultimate disarmament). There were hints of this kind of reasoning in the first and second drafts of the letter. But critics labeled that reasoning "consequentialist" and feared it would lead to much wider application of "bad means justifying a good end" variants of moral theology. Consequentialist reasoning is widely condemned by traditionalist Catholic theologians. While it is not entirely clear that the early drafts depended on such reasoning, and there are respectable Catholic theologians who do not reject consequentialism, it was not a supportable basis for the bishops' letter. To avoid totally rejecting nuclear deterrence, the bishops had to find some strategy that at least had a chance, in some hypothetical circumstances, of being morally neutral (discriminating, proportionate) rather than intrinsically evil. The need to clarify their position helped increase the bishops' determination to make a variety of specific applications in other parts of their letter. They lay out the reasoning against vulnerable "prompt hard-target-kill" weapons, and specifically mention MX and the Pershing II as candidates for this category. (The first two drafts mentioned MX in the text, but as part of a compromise in the final versions the specific identification of MX was moved to a footnote but supplemented with reference to Pershing II.) They call for "sufficiency" and reject any quest for nuclear superiority. They oppose "proposals which have the effect of lowering the nuclear threshold and blurring the difference between nuclear and conventional weapons" (probably including the neutron bomb). Furthermore, they recommend a variety of measures, including a comprehensive test ban treaty, removal of nuclear weapons from border areas where they might be overrun in war (thus forcing early decisions on their use), and "immediate, bilateral, verifiable agreements to halt the testing, production, and deployment of new nuclear weapons systems." This last was widely, and correctly, interpreted as meaning support for a freeze.[18]

The central problem for the bishops' analysis is not deterrence of attack on the United States, but of attack on allies or neutrals under American protection. This of course has also been the central function of American nuclear deterrence since its inception. Nuclear deterrence, furthermore has been extended to deterrence of *conventional* attacks on our allies, a policy promoted by the relatively inexpensive nature of nuclear weapons (more "bang for the buck") and the difficulties of raising adequate conventional defense forces against the "Eastern hordes." Thus a key element of some acceptable resolution of the bishops' dilemma is their strong advocacy of a "no first use" posture. It is not quite an unequivocal rejection of first use ("We do not perceive any situation in which the deliberate initiation of nuclear warfare, on however restricted a scale, can be morally justified"), but it comes very close. In doing so, the bishops oppose the idea of using nuclear weapons for extended deterrence, and require that nonnuclear attacks be resisted by other than nuclear means. If so, a purely counterforce deterrent has no need for prompt hard-target-kill capabilities, or any other seemingly first-strike forces that could endanger crisis stability. The risks of escalation are high under the best of circumstances. If the opponent should begin nuclear war, *some* of those risks would already have been taken. To deter that act, and to bring the war to a negotiated halt just as soon as possible, we may plan certain very restricted forms of retaliation. But the risks of first use of nuclear weapons are too high to justify our ever setting the process in motion.

While understanding that "development of an alternative defense position will still take time," the bishops insist that NATO "move rapidly" toward such a position. They are willing—clearly if unenthusiastically—to consider that "some strengthening of conventional defense would be a proportionate price to pay, if this will reduce the possibility of nuclear war." This is an essential piece of realism. While many military experts differ as to whether nonnuclear defense of Western Europe really is possible, there are many cogent and informed arguments for its feasibility.[19] The hurdles really are political rather than economic or military, and the lack of current political will in America and in Europe need not be taken as a given for all eternity. Furthermore, there are also other ways to help defend Western Europe than by nuclear *or* nonnuclear forces. A general lowering of international political tensions would help, as would a structure of rewards implicit in the extension of East-West economic interdependence. And if the United States were to abandon nuclear deterrence of nonnuclear threats, the act would contribute greatly to a worldwide de-legitimization of nuclear weapons. It would help persuade potential nuclear powers that nuclear weapons "buy" more insecurity than security.

The bishops' normative and factual assumptions thus lead them, in terms of the familiar policy debates over deterrence, to the conclusion that, while the need for military deterrence cannot be evaded in a world of conflicting states, relatively lower levels of threat are adequate and a shift to lower levels is required.[20] Lower but adequate levels of threat mean no "city-busting" and no first-strike capability; extended deterrence of conventional attack can succeed without reliance on nuclear threats; and rewards, as well as punishments, must play a key role in any acceptable deterrent posture. A shift to lower levels is required because of the ever-present and not fully controllable chance that deterrence may fail, bringing our threats to reality. Their position is not perfect, but it is reasonable, logically coherent, and fully comprehensible in the language of secular discussion. While the bishops derive their conclusions in large part from their normative assumptions, others can share the conclusions without sharing all those assumptions.

I repeat, there is no perfect, or maybe even good, solution overall. Every possibility contains practical and moral dangers. No one can be optimistic about the chances of surviving decades or generations of continuing reliance on nuclear deterrence in any form. People are prone to error, and machinery to accidents. An indefinite future of nuclear weapons seems intolerable. The bishops correctly insist on a new way of thinking for the long run. They have not totally de-legitimized nuclear deterrence, but they have stimulated and "are prepared and eager to participate . . . in the on-going public debate on moral grounds." Meanwhile, the extremes of unilateral disarmament and even of *nuclear* pacifism seem undesirable, and full mutual nuclear disarmament really does seem improbable. Pope John Paul II's statement that deterrence "may still be judged morally acceptable" still somehow rings true. That statement is in no way authoritatively binding even on Catholics, and it is full of ambiguities. But there is no path other than one of continued wrestling with the ambiguities and contradictions inherent in any deterrent policy.

Chapter 13

Seeking Peace in a Post–Cold War World of Hegemony and Terrorism

With John R. Oneal

The world is full of testimony to tragedy. Governments oppress their own people and attack their neighbors. Countries and groups perfect the techniques of terrorism. Realists say that every country is potentially an enemy of every other—intentionally or not, a threat to their security and very existence. This tradition, like the anarchy that underlies it, has a history from Thucydides, Niccolo Machiavelli, and Thomas Hobbes and shapes the perspective of many policymakers. Centuries ago rulers threw off any remaining authority above the state, affirmed their sovereign autonomy, and in so doing accepted a system in which that autonomy would be at risk from the acquisitive designs by their fellows. With no world government to impose security, states are caught in this precarious condition of freedom and risk.

The possibility of violence is always present. Yet there is order in the anarchy. States do not fight all others even when purely realist principles dominate; they are constrained by geography, shared national interests as expressed in alliances, and the balance of power. In the realist system, deterrence is the essential basis of survival, but deterrence really is a miserable way of avoiding war, and a miserable way to live. Treating all international politics as unending struggle, and everyone as a potential enemy, risks becoming a self-fulfilling prophecy.

A competing perspective on international politics, sometimes labeled liberal-institutionalist, is associated with such classical analysts as John Locke, Hugo Grotius, and Immanuel Kant. Kant proposed that "republican constitutions," commercial exchange, and a system of international law and organizations could give the basis for sustained peace. The alternative would be peace of a different sort: "a vast grave where all the horrors of violence and those responsible for them would be buried."[1]

Often the realist and Kantian perspectives are characterized as antithetical. That is an error. While Kant accepted Hobbes's description of conflict among many of the nations, he went far beyond it. He was convinced that among liberal republics a genuine peace could be developed. This *positive* peace would rest more on the three Kantian supports than on power politics. The pacific federation he envisioned is not a world state. Its members remain sovereign, linked only by partially federal institutions as in Europe today or collective security alliances. The difference between the two traditions is that Kant sees democratic governance, economic interdependence, and international law and organizations as means to supercede the security dilemma of the international system. Among states not much linked by these ties, the threat of violence remains.

Kant argued that the three elements of his pacific federation would strengthen over time to produce a more peaceful world. Individuals desire to be free and prosperous, so democracy and trade will expand, which leads naturally to the growth of international law and organization to facilitate and regulate these processes. Kant did not believe that peace within this system depends upon a moral transformation of humanity: even devils can calculate on the basis of their self-interest. That peace would develop as a natural consequence of individuals desire for freedom and prosperity was, for Kant, a child of the Enlightenment, evidence of an ordered universe. Yet the achievement of a durable peace was not a mechanical process, nor was the outcome fully determined. Reason would not necessarily prevail; states and individuals do not always act as their enlightened interest might suggest. Human agents would have to learn from experience, including the tragedy of war. A more peaceful world could be built, but human intelligence, choice, and effort were required to bring it about.

The Kantian tradition is alive and well, not just as a prescription but also as a description of much of contemporary world politics. Kant was not a wishful thinker. Though he lived in a time and place (Konigsberg, Prussia, 1795) that was no republic, and international law was weak, he did know something of actual republics, and his city had been a trading state of the Hanseatic League. While he took his theory far beyond his experience, it was empirically informed.

What is astonishing is how accurately it fits much of what we can now discern on the basis of social scientific analyses of how nations behave toward one another.

The Epidemiology of War and Peace

It is useful to compare the way medical scientists seek to understand the causes of disease and the way social scientists now seek to understand the causes of conflict. We show how this epidemiological perspective can be used to evaluate the realist and Kantian perspectives on international relations. Our previous work addressed these issues, but with information extending only up to 1992—too soon to adequately consider the post–cold war era with its emergence of U.S. hegemony and the terrorist threat that is widely viewed as validating fears of a clash between Western and Islamic civilizations. Here we focus on replicating key analyses from our past work data that now extend through 2001; assessing the ability of the most powerful state in the international system to provide security to its allies and testing whether interstate conflict is exacerbated by a clash of civilizations.

By a combination of theory and research, medical researchers try to identify conditions that promote or prevent disease. Much of that research is *epidemiological* in character. That is, researchers look at large populations and try to discover why some individuals contract a disease while many others do not. Computerized databases—about who dies of various diseases and about the behavior, experience, and genetic heritage of those individuals—help researchers to uncover the causes of illness and ultimately to devise regimens for prevention or treatment. Often these databases include records on hundreds of thousands of individuals. A skilled researcher with keen intuition or a sharply honed hypothesis can perform statistical analyses to discover some of the conditions that are correlated with disease. If the theory is sound, the researcher may be able to move beyond correlations to suggest the causal mechanisms by which something in individuals' heredity or their environment actually produces the disease. Causal mechanisms must of course be confirmed by controlled experiments and studies of individual patients. But good epidemiological work can suggest where to look for plausible causal mechanisms, and even before the individual-level mechanisms are fully understood can provide practical advice. Practical experience in turn, with medical theory, can help inform epidemiologists about what to look for next.

Consider the kind of results that might emerge in an epidemiological examination of the causes of death from heart disease. One would be that the risk increases as a person ages. A second would be that one's chances of a heart attack are greater if one or both parents died of heart disease. Also, men are more likely than women to die of heart attacks when other influences like age and heredity are held constant. This first list comprises influences over which no one has much control. One cannot keep the years from advancing or change parents, for example. So far, a physician can do little more than advise patients at high risk to keep their life insurance paid up. For some patients that could be valuable—if unwelcome—advice.

But neither patient nor physician will stop there. Smokers run a much higher risk of heart attack than do nonsmokers. So too do those who consume a diet high in saturated fats or who engage in little physical exercise. Each of these influences operates largely independently of the others. That is, smoking by itself increases the risk of a heart attack whether or not one has a family history of heart disease and regardless of diet. And each can be modified by a sufficiently motivated patient.

None of the risk factors is a perfect predictor. Many people who do not smoke, or give it up, nevertheless have heart attacks. Many smokers live a long time without a heart attack, ultimately dying of something else. The predictions are probabilistic, about greater and lesser risks, not about certainties. Moreover, estimates of the different influences may change on the basis of subsequent research or better data. But at some point physicians and patients decide that the science is reliable enough to act upon.

What Do We Know About War and Conflict, and How Do We Know It?

As with the medical studies, large-scale statistical analyses do not avoid the need to closely examine the experience of particular individuals or countries. But a similar analysis on the causes of serious military disputes constitutes the basis for this report. We omit most of the technical discussion of the sources, definitions, and decisions necessary to turn concepts and hypotheses into measures and statistical models suitable for analysis.[2] The database we have examined is like the life histories of individuals used by medical epidemiologists. It consists of information on relations between virtually all countries in the world in each year over the period from 1885 to 2001.

Countries can in principle fight any other country, but in most instances they are constrained from fighting particular countries, so our data are organized by pairs of countries, or *dyads*. For example, we are concerned not with Germany in general, but with relations between Germany and Austria, Belgium, Japan, and so forth. Thus we consider the questions of greatest interest to policymakers and citizens alike: which pairs of states are prone to conflict and which are apt to remain at peace? This gives us more than 460,000 cases, where a case is the experience of *a pair of countries in a year*. From them we can compute the likelihood that a pair of countries sharing a certain constraint on conflict (e.g., a common alliance, or both being democratic) experienced the onset of a militarized dispute or a war in a particular year, and how much lower their risk of conflict was than for a pair of countries not having that constraint.

For conflict we use data on militarized interstate disputes (MIDs). Wars are fortunately rare events and, as with rare diseases, it is hard to find general patterns in where and why they erupt. Casting our net more widely, to include all organized uses of violence between countries, gives us a better chance to discern those general patterns. Here we focus our attention on the analyses of *fatal* MIDs: those in which at least one combatant died. These incidents are much more common than wars, but they often have the potential to escalate to war. We also report key results for all militarized disputes and for wars. These analyses show that the influences and constraints that affect the probability of interstate conflict do not differ much from one level of conflict to another, but it makes sense to focus on fatal disputes because they are more numerous than wars and generally more serious than disputes that do not involve the death of combatants.

Here are the influences we consider, and how we measure them:

Realist Influences

Power Ratio. One obvious way to reduce the likelihood of war is to deter it by military strength. But is conflict best avoided simply by matching the other state's power, so that both sides are more or less equally deterred? This is the basis for the school of thought that stresses the value of a balance of power. In this view, an even balance inhibits conflict because both states will be uncertain whether they can win a military conflict, and thus will be reluctant to start one. But militarized disputes are often tests of national power and arise when the two sides have different expectations about what the outcome of a military contest will be. So other theorists claim that conflict is better constrained when one state is clearly predominant. The weak state is deterred from attacking the strong one, though the reverse is not true. Often, however, a powerful state need not actually demonstrate its strength; the weak may acquiesce to avoid a war they know they will lose. In Thucydides' words, "[T]he strong do as they will and the weak do as they must." A preponderance of power may constrain the resort to violence, but at the risk of dominance and exploitation. We examine the evidence to determine whether a balance of power promotes peace or whether preponderance does.

To assess the effect of power on the likelihood of conflict, we use information on states' material capabilities. A standard composite index of national power includes iron and steel production, population, military manpower, and military expenditures. Together, these tap a combination of elements that can be used immediately for military purposes and longer-term military potential relevant in a protracted conflict. No measure of power is perfect, but this one is reasonable and widely accepted. The power ratio is the logarithm of the stronger state's capability index divided by that of the weaker member of the dyad.

Allies. Another way to constrain military conflict is to ally with another state. Allies share important strategic and security interests. If they have military disputes among themselves, they risk weakening their common front against a country each perceives as an enemy. But being allied provides no guarantee that countries will avoid military conflict. Several times during the cold war, the Soviet Union invaded or threatened its allies to keep them from changing their governments and leaving the Warsaw Pact. The United States acted similarly on occasion. To investigate how important an alliance really is in reducing the risk of militarized conflict, we identify whether the countries in each dyad were allied by a formal treaty.

Two other realist influences, presenting opportunities as much as constraints are geographical distance and great power status.[3] It is difficult and expensive to exert military power far from a country's homeland. States that are geographically proximate, especially those with a common border, can readily fight. They also are more likely to have competing interests regarding territory, control of natural resources, or common ethnic groups—any of which may provoke conflict. Great powers can exercise force at a distance, and they have wide-ranging interests for which they may be willing to fight. But distance and the ability to be a great power are matters over which most states have little control. They are givens, like individuals' age, family history, and sex in our medical analogy. Forming an alliance and devoting resources to the military, like diet and exercise, are matters over which national decision makers can exercise a good deal of control. The fundamental determinants of power, population and level of development, are less amenable to quick, dramatic manipulation.

Kantian Constraints

Kant and other liberal institutionalists, however, insist that the realist influences do not exhaust the list of constraints, especially those over which states can exercise significant control. States do not always fight others when and where the realist constraints are weak. To the realist influences we add the three Kantian ones: democracy, economic interdependence, and international organizations. Since the modern international system is still far from being a "pacific federation" of democratic states linked by strong economic bonds, we expect both realist and Kantian factors to affect interstate relations.

Democracy. Kant suggested that democracies will rarely fight or even threaten each other and may also be more peaceful with all kinds of states. Two reasons for this have been proposed.[4]

First, democracies operate internally on the principle that conflicts are to be resolved peacefully by negotiation and compromise, without violence. Democratic peoples and their leaders recognize other democracies as operating under that principle in their internal relations, and so extend to them the principle of peaceful conflict resolution. Violence is illegitimate as well as unnecessary. Dictatorships, by contrast, operate more on Hobbesian principles, making threats, exploiting weak resolve, and using force. Thus in their relations with dictatorships, democracies, will not exercise the same restraint.

Second, democratic institutions hold leaders responsible for the costs and benefits of war. Many of the costs are borne by the general public. Democratic leaders who fight wars—especially if they lose or the war is particularly costly—risk being voted out of office. In anticipating this political judgment, democratic leaders will be reluctant to engage in militarized disputes. When facing another democracy, both sets of leaders will be restrained. Dictators, however, are better able to repress opposition and to stay in power after a war; and by repression they can keep more of the benefits of war and impose more of the costs on their peoples than can democratic leaders. Consequently they will be less hesitant to fight.

The first explanation of the democratic peace is a normative constraint based on notions of right behavior in democratic societies. The second is straightforwardly rationalist: Peace can be maintained by leaders who pursue their own self-interest in both domestic and international relations in order to stay in power. Kant's understanding of devils who, by the creation of appropriate institutional incentives can be made to behave like angels, captures this argument. In addition, democracies are apt to be more peaceful in their relations with one another because they have little to fight about. Their views of national and international politics will be more compatible than those of autocratic states or mixed dyads.

The measure of democracy we use (Polity) incorporates (1) institutions and procedures through which citizens can express their preferences for alternative political policies and elect or reject leaders, (2) institutional constraints on the exercise of executive power, and (3) the guarantee of full political participation to all citizens. No democracy is perfect, nor are even the most totalitarian governments totally without restraints on arbitrary rule. Many states combine some mixture of democratic and authoritarian features. So we use a scale of +10 to −10 to test the effect of domestic political institutions on the likelihood of military conflict. For each pair, we first measure the degree of democracy in the less democratic state. When that is not very low (both states are quite democratic), we expect to find a low risk of an MID. Then we measure the level of democracy in the more democratic state. If that is not very high (both states are quite autocratic), we expect a high risk of violent conflict, as we do when the gap between the two is great (a mixed pair of one state very democratic and the other very autocratic).

International Trade. According to liberals, sustained commercial interaction gives a means of communicating information about needs and preferences across a broad range of matters well beyond the specific commercial exchanges. This can bring greater mutual understanding, empathy, and mutual identity across borders. A complementary view stresses the self-interests of rational actors. Trade depends on expectations of peace with the trading partner. Violent conflict threatens access to markets, imports, and capital. Wars and militarized disputes, if they do not make trade between disputing states impossible, certainly raise the risks and costs. So, the larger the contribution of trade between two countries to their national economies, the stronger the political base that has a material interest in preserving peaceful relations between them and the more extensive is the exchange of information that accompanies trade.

We measure the importance of trade for each state as the sum of its imports from and exports to the other state in a dyad, divided by its gross national product.[5] A given volume of trade will exert greater economic and political impact on a small country than on a big one. A militarized dispute can result from the actions of either state; but it is likely that conflict is primarily influenced by the degree of constraint experienced by the less constrained state in each dyad. In effect, that state is the weak link in the chain of peaceful relations. The state that is less dependent on trade should be the greater risk to peace: the more economically important its trade is for this state, the more constrained from engaging in a dispute it is likely to be. We have consistently found that asymmetric commercial relations, that is, trade between a large and a small state, do not increase the danger of war if their trade is economically important to the larger state.

International Organizations. They include both quasi-universal organizations like the United Nations or the International Monetary Fund and those whose membership is restricted to particular types of countries or a single region. They may be multipurpose or "functional" agencies devoted to military security, international commerce and investment, health, environmental concerns, human rights, or other purposes. Intergovernmental organizations (IGOs) vary widely in effectiveness and in the means by which they promote peace. These measures range from coercing norm-breakers, mediating among conflicting parties, reducing uncertainty by providing information, expanding members' material interest to be more inclusive and longer-term, shaping norms, and generating narratives of mutual identification.

Our measure of international organizations is the number of IGOs to which both members of the dyad belong in a particular year, divided by the average number of joint memberships among the dyads in our sample in that year; normalizing by the international average eliminates the distinct increasing trend in the number of IGOs over time.[6] This is a crude index, equating all types and strengths of IGOs in a simple count. Others are developing more refined measures, taking into account different organizational functions and purposes, but these data are not yet generally available. Using a simple measure like the normalized number of joint memberships for each dyad means that we are likely to underestimate the conflict-reducing benefits of IGOs.

Analyzing the Global Experience of More Than a Century

To uncover the relative importance of these various influences on the risk of interstate conflict we use logistic regression analysis to estimate the independent effect a change in any one variable while holding the effect of all other variables constant. In most of our analyses, we control for the number of years that have passed since the dyad's last conflict in order to minimize the danger of imputing a causal role to an influence that is itself a consequence of previous conflict.[7] For example, we expect that peace will promote trade as well as trade enhancing the prospects for peace. Without taking into account past conflict, we could not be confident that the current level of trade really influences the prospects for peace, rather than being spuriously correlated with the probability of conflict. We also control for the growing number of states in the international system when estimating the probability of conflict for pairs of states that are not contiguous or include a major power.[8] For these cases, the dramatic increase in the number of states in the system over time makes conflict in any specific dyad less likely.

Table 13.1 shows the influences of the three Kantian variables taking into account the realist influences, the number of years since the last conflict, and the size of the international system. We report three analyses: all militarized interstate disputes; fatal disputes, in which there was the death of at least one combatant; and wars. The first entry in each cell is the regression coefficient, and below that is the standard error which, to the degree it is smaller than the coefficient, indicates how statistically significant the effect of the coefficient is.

The results provide strong support for the separate peace among democratic states. Two democracies are at less risk of becoming involved in a dispute, a fatal dispute, or a war than are two autocracies, while the incidence of conflict between a democracy and an autocracy is particularly great. Two autocracies are more prone to conflict than a democratic pair of states.

Economically important trade reduces the likelihood of militarized disputes, whether all MIDs or just fatal ones are analyzed, though

Table 13.1   Models of the onset of militarized interstate disputes, fatal disputes, and war, 1885–2001

Variable		All MIDs	Fatal MIDs	Wars
Lower Democracy	Coef.	−.0710***	.0880***	−.142***
	S.E.	.0075	.0148	.030
Higher Democracy		.0388***	.0405**	.0459***
		.0066	.0112	.0240
Lower Trade-to-GDP Ratio		−27.6***	−80.1**	−25.8
		8.2	25.8	22.5
Joint Memberships in IGOs		.0460	−.119	−.363**
		.0477	.116	.131
Allies		.0403	−.0954	−.356
		.1024	.1964	.371
Capability Ratio (Log)		−.271***	−.419***	−.816***
		.033	.057	.098
Contiguous		1.10***	1.02***	1.05***
		0.15	.25	.36
Distance (Log)		−.272***	−.488***	−.472***
		0.055	.088	.154
Major Power		.934***	1.01***	2.56***
		.141	.27	.45
Constant		−.615	−.420	−2.51*
		.417	.624	1.18
Wald Chi^2 (df)		3869.2 (14)	1307.2 (14)	471.0 (14)
p of Chi^2		.0001	.0001	.0001
Pseudo-R^2		.37	.27	.26
N		463,644	463,400	463,644

Notes: $p < .05$; ** $p < .01$; *** $p < .001$ (two-tailed tests). The estimated coefficients of the statistical controls (the years-of-peace spline and the number of states in the international system) are not reported to save space; with few exceptions all are very significant.

interdependence is not significantly related to the incidence of war in this test.[9]

Joint memberships in intergovernmental organizations significantly reduce the risk of war, but are not associated with a reduction in the probability of a militarized dispute or a fatal one. These results, however, use Beck, Katz, and Tucker's (1998) correction for duration dependence. Two other methods are also appropriate.[10] Using either to estimate effects on fatal MIDs produces coefficients with exactly the same sign and significance levels as in table 13.1— with the exception that IGOs become negatively associated with fatal MIDs at a high level of statistical significance ($p < .001$). Further research is in order, with better measures of the capacity of IGOs to resolve conflict peacefully.[11]

To estimate the effects for the post–cold war era, we expanded the basic model to include interactive terms identifying the effects of the

Kantian variables in the years after 1989. This analysis, which is not reported separately in a table, indicates that the pacific benefit of democracy has been greater than ever; interdependence constrained conflict more, though the change from the cold war era is not statistically significant, and IGOs were somewhat less influential.

The realist influences in this analysis generally perform as expected. A preponderance of power is associated with peace, and states that share a border or are geographically proximate are more likely to fight. Allies are not significantly less likely to fight than other states—a result consistent with many previous analyses. Also as expected, a recent conflict predisposes a dyad to fresh violence, and the risk of conflict between two small, distant states has fallen as the number of states in the system increased.[12]

It is easy to tell from the signs of the estimated coefficients in table 13.1 whether a particular variable constrains or encourages interstate conflict, and the magnitudes of the coefficients relative to their standard errors indicate the reliability (statistical significance) of this effect. What we are most concerned with, however, is the magnitude of these influences. In the case of heart disease, we want to know how much the average patient's risk of a heart attack would be reduced if her blood cholesterol level were 20 points lower or if she were not a smoker. Analogously, we now ask how much lower the risk of conflict would be if two countries are both democratic, highly interdependent, and so on.

Table 13.2 reports this information for all the years of our analysis, 1885–2001, and for the post–cold war years in particular. We give the risk of a fatal militarized dispute for a typical pair of states and show the percentage change in the risk associated with a change in each variable plausibly subject to policy intervention. The first row of table 13.2 shows the probability of a fatal militarized dispute for a typical pair of contiguous states in a year, where all variables are set at their median (or mean) for this war-prone subset of cases or to zero for the indicator of an alliance and major-power status. We then changed each variable one by one, either increasing it to the 90th percentile or decreasing it to the 10th percentile.

The results in table 13.2, especially those in the last two columns which show what happened in the post–cold war era, provide strong support for Kant's vision for perpetual peace. As shown in those two columns, two democracies are 58 percent less likely to have a fatal MID than the baseline case. Two autocracies are 65 percent more likely to be involved in conflict, and a mixed pair of states—one

Table 13.2   Annual probabilities of the onset of a fatal militarized dispute, for 1885–2001 and post–cold war period

	1885–2001 Based on Table 1, Column 2		1990–2001 With Interactive Terms for Post–CW Period	
	p	Change (%)	p	Change (%)
1. Democracy scores, trade-to-GDP ratio, IGOs, and capability ratio set at median for contiguous dyads; allies equals 0; Distance, years of peace, and system size at mean for contiguous dyads	.0059	0	.0059	0
2. Increase both democracy scores to 90th percentile	.0033	−43	.0025	−58
3. Decrease both democracy scores to 10th percentile	.0081	+39	.0098	+65
4. Decrease lower democracy score to 10th and increase higher to 90th	.0174	+197	.0219	+269
5. Increase trade-to-GDP ratio to 90th percentile	.0026	−56	.0007	−88
6. Increase IGOs to 90th percentile	.0040	−31	.0046	−22
7. Increase both democracy scores, trade-to-GDP ratio, IGOs to 90th percentile	.0004	−83	.0002	−96
8. Allies equals 1	.0053	−09	.0054	−09
9. Increase capability ratio to 90th percentile	.0022	−61	.0023	−62

democracy and one autocracy—are 269 percent more likely than the typical pair to experience the onset of a fatal MID in the years since the end of the cold war. Economic interdependence lowers the risk of a fatal dispute by 88 percent, and a dense network of intergovernmental organizations reduces it by 22 percent. Two democracies with a high degree of interdependence and extensive ties in IGOs are 96 percent less likely to fight. The results for the entire period, based on the basic equation without interactive terms and presented in the first two columns of table 13.2, are similar.

By estimating the Kantian benefits for the post–cold war era, we confirm that the liberal peace is not just a phenomenon of the bipolar nuclear era, when the democratic capitalist states were united against their communist rivals. Indeed, the benefits of democracy, interdependence, and IGOs are also evident in the pre–cold war era as well, both before World War I and in the interwar years.[13]

The preponderance version of realist theory—not the balance of power—is also strongly supported. Disproportionate power generally deters weak states from challenging strong ones, and the strong usually get what they want without resorting to force. If the relative power of the stronger state is increased to the 90th percentile, the chance of a fatal militarized dispute drops by 62 percent. But that demands a ten-fold growth in relative power. Such an increase, especially in the basic elements of power, like population and industrial production, is beyond the capacity of any nation. The other realist influence, alliance, has only a modest effect (−9 percent).

Or Is It Hegemony That Reduces Violence?

The enormous imbalance of power needed to impose peace suggests an important role to be played by the leading state in preserving the peace. Hegemonic-stability theory holds that the strongest state will constrain weaker ones from resorting to violence because it is in its interest to do so.[14] Both schools suggest that after a major war the leading state creates and operates a new international system from which it disproportionately benefits. Satisfied with the status quo, it adopts conservative policies designed to maintain the system as it is.

The hegemon has an incentive to maintain peace because wars are disruptive, breaking beneficial economic ties, for example. Consequently, the leading state uses its power to suppress wars within its own sphere of influence and, through its network of alliances, in the spheres of influence of powerful allies. In addition, the hegemon deters potential adversaries from using military force in a way that would be detrimental to its interests. Whether through domination or deterrence, the ability to preserve the peace depends upon the hegemon's power relative to others. A simple measure of its relative power is the hegemon's share of the world's militarily relevant capabilities. In making this assessment, we use data on states' armed forces and their population and industry—indicators of immediately available military capabilities and the potential to develop greater military force over time.

Most scholars agree that in the 30 years before World War I, the United Kingdom was closer to being hegemonic than was any other country, although its power relative to both Germany and the United States declined as time passed. During the interwar era, the United States had greater economic strength and military potential than Britain. But their actual military capabilities were about equal, and the geographic position of the US and its isolationist policy limited its involvement in the central European system. Consequently we accept Organski and Kugler's judgment that Britain was more nearly hegemonic during the interwar period. If any country can be said to have been hegemonic in the post–World War II period, it is the United States.[15] So we use the proportion of the capabilities held by the United Kingdom through 1945 and that of the United States subsequently to estimate the strength of the hegemon for each year, 1885–2001.

Proponents of power-transition theory have also emphasized the role of states' satisfaction with the status quo in explaining the resort to violence. States rising in power will challenge the hegemon only if they are dissatisfied with the international system that the hegemon dominates. Lemke and Reed extended this argument in an effort to subsume the democratic peace under power-transition theory.[16] Democracies have fought less historically, they contend, because the hegemonic power since 1816 has been a democracy. First Britain, and then the United States, structured the international system so as to benefit itself and its mostly democratic allies. Thus, democracies' satisfaction with the status quo is said to account for the separate peace they have enjoyed.

Like Lemke and Reed, we assess this argument using a measure of each state's satisfaction with the status quo based on the correspondence between its portfolio of allies and that of the hegemon. The more similar a state's alliance ties are to the hegemon, the more that state should prefer the status quo. They should be satisfied with the international system because they enjoy the ability of the hegemon to preserve the peace. To create a measure appropriate for dyadic analysis, we summed the two states' satisfaction scores; thus, two states closely allied to the hegemon will be highest on this scale, two dissatisfied states will be lowest, and a mixed pair will fall in between. This ranking is consistent with the expectation that the hegemon should be most motivated and able to maintain peace within its sphere of influence, should have the ability and interest to deter many attacks against its allies, and will be indifferent or even welcome conflict among rivals. This measure of joint satisfaction will show whether it is satisfaction with the status quo and not democracy per se that accounts for the democratic peace.

Table 13.3 adds three variables to our basic model, which includes the Kantian and realist variables and the statistical controls for years of peace and the size of the international system. We show only the

Table 13.3   Effect of hegemon's power and states'
satisfaction with status quo 1885–2001

Hegemon's Power	Coef.	5.08
	S.E.	3.21
Satisfaction w/ Status Quo		.104
		.284
Hegemon's Power*		−1.54
Satisfaction w/ Status Quo		1.38

Notes: *$p < .05$ (two-tailed tests). The estimated coefficients of the Kantian and realist variables and the statistical controls (the years-of-peace spline and the number of states in the international system) are not reported to simplify the table. The results for these variables are little changed from what is reported in column 2 of table 13.1.

effect of the new variables, since the others are little different from what we showed in column 2 of table 13.1. To assess the central claim of both hegemonic-stability and power-preponderance theories—interstate conflict becomes more likely as the power of the leading state declines—we add the measure of the relative power of the leading state to our basic model. Our results show clearly that the relative power of the leading state has no effect on the likelihood of dyadic disputes. A powerful hegemony does not reduce the resort to violence in the international system. There is no evidence here of a Pax Britannica or Pax Americana.

The second new variable is a measure of the joint satisfaction of each pair of states for the international system. If the hegemon can regulate the level of conflict in the international system, then its influence should be greatest with those states with which it is most closely allied. Moreover, the advantages for a state of aligning itself closely with the hegemon should be greatest when the leading state is most powerful, and thus best able to confer benefits on its supporters. But the measure of states' satisfaction with the status quo is not significant, while the direct benefits of democracy remain strong.

The third measure is an interaction between hegemonic power and joint satisfaction. This is appropriate if the ability of the leading state to protect its allies is conditional on its having sufficient power and if the benefits of its power are conditioned by states' satisfaction. But the interactive term is also far from statistical significance. The character of states' political institutions and culture accounts for the separate peace among democracies, not the satisfaction they are said to have with the international system.

These results, plus our findings about the post–cold war period in particular, clearly refute the assertion that the cold war era of peace between democracies was merely an artifact of the global alliance system or U.S. domination during that era.[17] The power of the leading state, the so-called hegemon, has little effect on the incidence of dyadic conflict. Power-transition theory is correct that a preponderance of power leads to peaceful dyadic relations; all our analyses indicate that a preponderance of power increases the prospects for peace. But power-transition theory errs in believing that this dyadic effect has important systemic consequences, that a powerful state is able and willing to pacify interstate relations throughout the system. Hegemonic-stability and power-transition theories exaggerate the ability of the strongest state to shape the international system for its benefit and the benefit of its allies. In short, the contribution of a hegemon to keeping the peace is highly overrated, and should not be relied on even with the present-day imbalance.

Is Islamic Terrorism Symptomatic of a Clash of Civilizations?

Samuel Huntington's *The Clash of Civilizations* has become one of the most influential books on international relations. He offered it as "a more meaningful and useful lens through which to interpret international developments" than any alternative perspective. Huntington's core claim is that "clashes of civilizations are the greatest threat to world peace" and that "[i]n the post-Cold War world the most important distinctions among peoples are not ideological, political, or economic." "Culture and cultural identities, which at the broadest level are civilizational identities, are shaping patterns of cohesion, disintegration, and conflict in the post–Cold War world."[18] His claim cannot be dismissed. Fear and hatred of those who are different is all too familiar, within societies as well as internationally. Huntington's greatest worry regards the great divide between the West and all other civilizations—"the West and the rest," as he puts it, with particular danger for the West from Islamic states.

Yet different ethnic populations coexist peacefully in much of the world, and mix freely. Huntington bolsters his case with illustrative examples, but he does not subject his thesis to scientific tests. Since his perspective is probably the most prominent alternative theoretical perspective to the realist and Kantian ones we have examined, a social scientific test of it in competition with these frameworks is essential.

For the first time, given the recent availability of data for years through 2001 (including the invasion of Afghanistan after 9/11), we can test Huntington's thesis over a significant number of years in the post–cold war era, the period for which the theory was explicitly formulated. For the sake of the argument we use his grouping of almost all states into eight civilizations: the Western, Sinic, Islamic, Hindu, Slavic-Orthodox, Latin American, Buddhist, and African. We create a new variable, labeled "split," to indicate whether the two states in a dyad come from different civilizations or not. It is coded 1 if a dyad is split culturally; and 0 if the two states are from the same civilization. To make this determination we relied primarily on Huntington's map (pp. 26–27). Classifying countries on this basis is usually straightforward, but not always. Russett, Oneal, and Cox address the particular difficulties, so we need not repeat that discussion.[19]

The first column of table 13.4 compares the incidence of conflict for split dyads to the average rate for pairs located within a single civilization. We limit our analyses to the years after World War II so as to ease comparisons of the cold war and post–cold war eras. We estimate the effect of civilizational differences for 1990–2001 using an interactive term. The table gives no evidence that civilizational differences explain interstate conflict. The effect of being split across a civilizational boundary for the years after the end of the cold war is given by the sum of the coefficients for split and the interactive term and is very nearly zero ($0.301 - 0.278 = 0.023$). Neither of the

Table 13.4   Effect of clash of civilizations on the onset of fatal militarized interstate disputes, 1950–2001

Split between Civilizations	Coef.	.301	
	S.E.	.223	
Split * Post–Cold War Era		−.278	
		.188	
West versus Rest			.369*
			.168
West versus Rest * Post–cold war era			−.311
			.208
West versus Islam			.230
			.235
West versus Islam * Post–cold war era			−.314
			.307
Israel versus Islam			.790*
			.365

Notes: * $p < .05$. The estimated coefficients of the Kantian and realist variables and the statistical controls (the years-of-peace spline and the number of states in the international system) are not reported to simplify the table. The results for these variables are little changed from what is reported in column 2 of table 13.1.

coefficients for the indicator of split dyads is statistically significant: civilizational differences do not contribute to our understanding of the causes of war either during the cold war or afterward.

Next, we evaluate Huntington's hypothesis that the Western states would find themselves in conflict with other civilizations after the end of the cold war. We identified those pairs of states that are composed of one Western state and one state from any other civilization and estimated the relative frequency of conflict for these dyads. Again we pay special attention to the post–cold war era, when the clash of civilizations is said to apply with particular force. The second column still gives no support for Huntington's thesis. Even the apparent effect of civilizational differences during the cold war, given by the coefficient of the West versus Rest, reflects the familiar political and economic conflict across the iron and bamboo curtains, not a clash of cultures per se. The cold war was a clash between capitalist democracies and communist states, not between the West, on the one hand, and the Orthodox and Sinic civilizations, on the other.

Finally, we ask whether there is particular animosity between Western and Islamic states. The last column shows that the current war against Islamic terrorism is not a symptom of a general clash between these two civilizations. As before, the sum of the coefficients of the West versus Islam variable and the interactive term for the post–cold war years is close to zero ($.230 - .314 = -.086$), indicating that Western and Islamic states really have not fought at a higher rate than other pairs, either before 1989 or afterward. The popular perception to the contrary perhaps captures the conflict between Israel and the Arabs. Whereas we feel that Israel may well be classified as a Western state, Huntington (90, 150, 186) calls it non-Western. So we analyzed Israel's conflicts separately, and of course found evidence of the animosity between Israel and its neighbors. But it did not spread into a general West-versus-Islam confrontation.

Here we have assessed the clash of civilizations systematically, focusing for the first time on 12 years from the post–cold war era when the theory should be most applicable. Civilizations represent a highly aggregated form of human cultural characteristics that would be difficult to alter. Policies adopted over the course of a few years could not be expected to change the nature of civilizations that have evolved over centuries. Fortunately, national leaders need not attempt such a Herculean task. Knowing whether a pair of states is split across civilizational boundaries does not improve our ability to predict whether their relations will be marked by violence beyond what we know from realism and Kantian theory.[20] Civilizations do not define the fault lines along which international conflicts occur.

Some Conclusions About This Order in Anarchy

This analysis has implications for an important pair of countries: the United States and China. In the mid-1960s the risk factors for a fatal dispute were rather high. The two countries were of course not geographically close, reducing the risk. America was reasonably predominant in power over China, but not hugely so, implying a moderate risk. Yet none of the Kantian influences were in operation. Mao's China was all the way to the totalitarian end of the political scale (-10); U.S.-China trade was nil (illegal for Americans), and they shared no IGO memberships (China was not even in the UN).

By comparison, some influences at the beginning of the twenty-first century were still unchanged. But with the much more rapid growth of China's economy relative to the United States, the power ratio moved closer to equality and was on a trend toward an equal balance: a dangerous development by our analysis. However, all the Kantian influences had come into play. China had liberalized politically somewhat, moving from -10 to -8 on our scale, and our analysis finds that changes near either end of the scale have a much greater effect on the risk of conflict than do changes of the same number of points nearer the middle of the scale. Chinese-American trade was flourishing. Finally, China is in virtually all the universal organizations, and in many smaller functional and regional organizations to which the United States also belongs. Even with the more dangerous power balance the risk of a fatal dispute dropped by more than 50 percent from what it was in the 1960s. Engagement is working.

Many countries do learn to live peaceably with each other despite a centuries-long history of desperate, violent competition. They may still have sharp economic and political disputes, but those disputes rarely become militarized, risking the use of force. The European Union—created deliberately by leaders and citizens—testifies to this possibility. A similar if weaker effect is evident in much of South America. Countries can support the emergence of democratic government in other countries, build economic ties with them, and construct international organizations.

The stability in our results over time suggests another perspective—that of the international system. Changes in the average level of democracy, interdependence, and IGO involvement capture not just dyadic phenomena but elements of the norms and institutions of the international system. For the first time in history, by the 1990s the majority of the world's countries were at least somewhat democratic. Since democracies fight well—winning about 75 percent of their wars—as the proportion of democracies in the international system grows, autocracies must worry more about the security costs of weakening themselves in war, either with democracies or with other autocracies. If most great powers become democratic, peace among them would reduce the incentive for wars involving nondemocratic states across great power spheres of influence. If liberalization spreads and stimulates economic growth among interdependent states, nonliberal states will need to fear they will be punished by global markets for being the instigators of international violence that disrupts trade and investment; even antagonistic dyads with little mutual trade may find it prudent to abstain from violence. If international norms and institutions for resolving disputes grow, even nonliberal states may be impelled to use regional or international organizations to help settle their disputes rather than accept the political, military, and economic costs the liberal community might impose for using force.

Furthermore, Kant's vision was not of a set of three independent influences on peace. Rather, he saw a dynamic system with reinforcing feedback loops. The various elements of Kant's prescription for peace enhance one another in *virtuous circles*: interstate relations can evolve toward a peaceful "federation" of republics linked by mutually beneficial commercial relations under international law. Theory and systematic global evidence for connections among the three Kantian elements continue to mount since our previous research reports.[21]

There is order to be discerned and nurtured within the anarchy. It is the assumption that everyone is a potential enemy, not anarchy itself, that drives the Hobbesian security dilemma. An order of cooperation and reciprocation broadly consistent with basic precepts of moral behavior does not demand a moral transformation of humanity so much as it requires a careful structuring of relationships to channel self-interest in directions of mutual benefit.

Of course, not all states are yet part of this order. Those not bound by mutual ties of democracy, economic interdependence, and international institutions have a much weaker basis for cooperation. Afghanistan under Taliban rule gave haven to al Qaeda terrorists. Where Kantian linkages are still weak, the Hobbesian dilemma remains. That is the condition when one or both states lie largely outside this order. Power and deterrence dominate their relationships. The challenge is to find how to overcome the anarchy of relations with the likes of Iran or North Korea. (It seems to be happening with Libya.) They may strive to create more stable relationships, often stumblingly, as in U.S. relations with China. On the other hand, it is possible to make a so-far failed prediction like Huntington's about the clash between Islam and the West come true if we believe it enough and use military power unwisely against Islamic states.

In the contemporary world, the United States enjoys great power. Its hegemony brings burdens, benefits, and temptations. It does not always behave as a Kantian state. With a military budget as big as the combined total of the next 20 military spenders of the world, it is tempted to rely on the armed force that money and high technology create. But our results indicate that the importance of hegemony for world peace has generally been exaggerated. In any event, it will not last forever. Unilateral reliance on military instruments is the surest way to prod other states, not only undemocratic ones, into balancing against the United States. The Kantian perspective does not dismiss the importance of military power; it does emphasize its inadequacy. It recommends promoting democracy but not imposing it by force except in response to clear aggression, deepening linkages of international trade, and extending the multilateral network of international organizations. This depends less on military power than on soft power, on the justice of our efforts and perceptions that we are acting on legitimate principles and following international rules. This will serve American interests and those of other states and peoples.

All good things do not necessarily go together. Democratic liberties can be debased, the inequalities of capitalism may run wild, a global authority could become a leviathan, peace does not always mean justice. Yet the roots of world peace lie less in force than in structured freedoms. The evidence for Kant's alternative and now partially realized conception of international relations speaks of behavior that is self-interested and other-regarding. We are not condemned to a choice between victimization and endless cycles of violence. We have the capacity to discover constructive patterns of behavior and to act accordingly. Even after 9/11, when viewing a world in which war and terrorism are all too frequent, there are grounds for optimism.

Chapter 14

Bushwhacking the Democratic Peace

President George W. Bush concluded his final 2004 debate with John Kerry by declaring his faith in "the ability of liberty to transform societies, to convert a hostile world to a peaceful world." Such affirmations then became part of his rhetorical repertoire, as in his 2005 State of the Union address and his claims about building democracy in the Middle East as a result of his invasion of Iraq. For example, "By now it should be clear that decades of excusing and accommodating tyranny in the pursuit of stability have only led to instability and tragedy . . . It should be clear that the advance of democracy leads to peace, because governments that respect the rights of their people also respect the rights of their neighbors."[1]

This rhetoric of course incorporates a core principle of what is widely known as the theory of democratic peace. Most versions of that theory do not insist that democracies are necessarily peaceful in general—a proposition that is supported by less evidence, is weaker, and requires substantial qualifications.[2] But the last decade of social-science research has produced abundant strong evidence, as well as theory, that democracies almost never go to war with each other.[3] Sentiments like this have issued from the White House ever since the last year of the Reagan administration. Yet what our current president neglects to mention is that most of us who helped formulate and test the theory of democratic peace have consistently argued for a second core principle: "The model of 'fight them, beat them, and make them democratic' is irrevocably flawed as a basis for contemporary action."[4] So used, the democratic peace proposition emerges only post hoc as a primary justification for invading Iraq. Many advocates of the democratic peace may now feel rather like many atomic scientists did in 1945. They had created something intended to prevent conquest by Nazi Germany, but only after Germany was defeated was the bomb tested and then used—against Japanese civilians whose government was already near defeat. Our creation too has been perverted.

Democratic Regime Change as a Motive For Invading Iraq

It is always dangerous to attribute a major act of a large bureaucracy to a single purpose or goal. Such caution should certainly apply to an analysis of why the United States invaded Iraq. Some who justified the attack on the grounds of eliminating weapons of mass destruction doubtless sincerely believed—however misguidedly—that Iraq had such weapons. Iraq of course did not, as everyone can see and the administration subsequently admitted. Nor, despite assertions, is there any evidence that Saddam Hussein intended to give such weapons to al Qaeda. A further justification was that the threat of the use of Weapons of Mass Destruction (WMDs) by Iraq, against the United States or less implausibly against our allies in the region, was so immediate as to warrant a preemptive strike. The conditions for preemptive war derive from the cold war, during which it always remained controversial. They were that a massive nuclear attack was imminent (in days, hours, or minutes), could not effectively be defended against, and virtually certain.[5] Despite using the concept, the Bush administration never spelled out its proper implications because the conditions never applied. It also dismissed the whole cold war doctrine of deterrence, which had not failed against Josef Stalin or his successors.

Some observers have asserted that George W. Bush was principally avenging Saddam Hussein's attempt on his father's life, but evidence for that assertion is lacking. I believe it highly improbable that any U.S. leader would make such a commitment of American blood and treasure to such a purpose. Other reasons for going to war, held in various parts of the administration, included a wish to establish bases to secure American military and economic interests; a general goal of combating "terrorism";[6] concern for the safety of Israel; a conviction that Saddam Hussein was a tyrant oppressing his own people (true of course, but he was hardly alone); and the view that regime change to democracy would make the Middle East more peaceable.

All those considerations helped produce an intergovernmental coalition that could converge on a decision to go to war despite the different reasons for arriving at that decision. But only WMDs and preemption played more than a minor role in the public rhetoric. Only after the WMD threat was found to be nonexistent, and the costs to the United States and Iraq began to mount, did promoting a democratic peace emerge front and center as a post-hoc justification for war.[7] Whether it will succeed, or if so be worth the costs cannot be determined now, and is not my topic here. Rather, my purpose is to establish that there was no informed basis for assuming it would succeed, and so to invoke the model of external intervention to produce democratic regime change in Iraq is inconsistent with most of what we know about democratization as well as with the theory of democratic peace. Most democratic peace adherents opposed the war, as did as many realists who would not accept promoting democracy as a foreign policy goal.[8]

If in fact the decision to invade Iraq was taken for multiple reasons, and perhaps was even overdetermined, we should look for more general explanations of conditions under which certain kinds of democracies, or of democratic leaders, may choose to use force. Since the vast majority of democracies' use of force is against autocratic states, such explanations would help to illuminate why the monadic democratic peace proposition (democracies are less likely in general to use force than are autocracies) is only contingently supported.

One certain qualification is that major power democracies, by virtue of their widespread interests and intervention capabilities, are more likely than smaller ones to exhibit higher frequencies of international conflict.[9] Moreover, if democracies are more successful in war than autocracies, by better mobilization of resources or soldierly initiative, then their success may prime them for further efforts to exert their military power.[10]

David Sobek derives a distinction from Machiavelli and applies it to the modern international system with components of the Polity index.[11] He identifies highly "Machiavellian" potentially expansionist regimes as those with high competition within the elite and low levels of executive constraint, and relatively low values for regulation and openness of executive recruitment and for regulation and competitiveness of participation. These are intended to characterize states where elites compete, but have institutionally weak executives and limited participation by the middle and lower classes.[12] He expects them to be expansionist, with a big selectorate unable to push for the redistribution of goods, but which may see itself benefited by imperial acquisition. By this conceptualization, many Machiavellian expansionist states will be autocratic regimes, but may also include some democratic regimes with very mixed levels on the various components, notably with constrained executives but only moderate levels of popular participation and recruitment, as in nineteenth century Britain and United States.[13] Indeed, he finds that while democracies low on the Machiavellian scale are very unlikely to initiate a militarized dispute, those democracies at the highest level on the Machiavellian scale are almost as likely to initiate disputes as are the most autocratic regimes whatever their Machiavelli score.

Similarly, John Ferejohn and Frances Rosenbluth argue that a regime based on a wide franchise in general reduces the expected net gains from war for the elite who, in an oligarchic state, would be better able to externalize the costs of war. Yet that same wide franchise allows them to mobilize human and material resources more fully than oligarchies can. Although that capacity gives them no advantage over other popular regimes (and hence is a disincentive to fight them), the mobilizational difference does encourage expansionist or imperialist wars against oligarchies, raising both the probability of winning and the expected benefits to both elites and wider population. The net effect of cost and benefit varies, but under some circumstances it may be attractive enough to encourage wars of expansion and imperialism. They find some evidence for this in ancient Greece, Rome, Renaissance Italy, and more recent history.[14] Nonetheless, most democracies do not adopt, or long sustain, policies of imperial expansion.[15]

A different kind of contingent influence may lie at the often-neglected level of leaders' attributes and personality characteristics. One intriguing recent study by Jonathan Keller posits a we-versus-them leadership style of a "constraint challenger" characterized by distrust, nationalism, task emphasis, and need for power. He applies a measure originally developed by Margaret Hermann to the behavior of heads of state from a wide variety of political systems in 154 foreign policy crises—all but one of which are between autocracies, or between an autocracy and a democracy.[16] He finds that while "constraint respecting" leaders of democratic states form the least likely combination of leaders and regime type to use force in a crisis, constraint challengers in democracies are much more likely to use force than are all other leaders, including constraint challenger heads of autocratic states.

The recent studies just discussed are not conclusive. Nevertheless they suggest some underexamined differences between democracies, and why generally (i.e., monadic) pacific behavior by democracies may be hard to identify without probing into more subtle characteristics of democratic institutions and leadership styles.

Democracy By Military Intervention: The Record

Prominent examples of "fight them, beat them, and make them democratic" can be invoked on both sides of the argument about applying it to Iraq in 2003. Some members of the Bush administration, publicly and privately, pointed to the post-1945 experience of the Western allies in Germany, and of the United States in Japan. Their goal at the beginning of the war was just to avoid defeat, not regime change per se. But as early as the Atlantic Charter in August 1941, before the United States was actually at war, Churchill and Roosevelt declared that their vision of peace in a postwar world included self-government for all peoples.[17] Certainly their postwar policy was built on the principle that the former German and Japanese governments could never have been peaceful, and that democratization of their systems was essential. To this end they devoted enormous material and intellectual resources (for Germany alone more than an order of magnitude in dollars than any subsequent effort). Their success served as an example to those in the Bush administration who hoped to achieve a similar result in Iraq.

The difficulty in applying this experience to Iraq, as so often when making policy by analogy, was that Germany and Japan were poor analogues. Not only had the allies been willing and able to carry on a long occupation and provide massive economic assistance, Germany and Japan met most of the conditions for successful transitions and consolidation that political analysis has since identified. In Iraq, the negative influences included many of those most prominent in the comparative politics literature, including low per capita income (at least after years of wars and sanctions), no previous history of democracy, the "resource curse" of a society dependent on petroleum exports (which allow dictators to keep themselves wealthy and in power), and the alleged authoritarian character of Islamic and especially Arab culture, about which I am more skeptical.[18] This is a simple short list, but Iraq falls short on many other domestic factors commonly cited in the comparative politics literature on democratic transitions.[19] Also working against democratization in Iraq are its geographic situation at the center of a neighborhood populated largely by dictatorships who do not wish democracy well, and its history of militarization and violent international conflict. So it was a hard case from the start, even had the post-invasion occupation and reconstruction not been bungled: executed on the cheap and with stunning incompetence.[20] Thomas Carothers's earlier warning[21] should have been heeded:

> The limitations of democracy promotion . . . are still there in best-case situations where a peaceful, stable country is attempting democratization and is open to influence from the outside. Even military intervention—a tool useful only in a narrow range of circumstances—is no guarantee of democratic results. Interventions only sometimes get rid of the dictators they are directed against. Even when a full-scale invasion is mounted to ensure that the strongman is ousted, the underlying political pathologies are difficult to heal. . . .

I am not indifferent to the difficult just war question of whether, and if so when, regime change in a sovereign state should be engineered by force. When applied to the invasion of Iraq, the just war criteria produce at best mixed results.[22] Here, however, I address the empirical question of when it may have a good chance of success. To think about the utility of war in establishing democracy in the twenty-first century, the history of the previous century—carefully analyzed with appropriate theory—provides the best evidence available. If the odds of success are bad from the start, much of the empirical part that needs to go into a moral calculus is already available. The following survey is done in a broad sweep, and the research cited is illustrative but neither conclusive nor exhaustive.

A study of 90 U.S. military interventions from 1898–1992 found that in only two instances did a democratic government become nondemocratic, while 14 became democratic in the year after the intervention—and almost all remained democratic ten years later.[23] This modest record leaves 85 percent of the interventions not promoting democracy. Democracy building was not usually part of the intervention agenda, however, so a simple correlation between military intervention and subsequent democratization would be deceptive.

More recent study distinguishes among 92 United States, British, and French interventions between 1946 and 1996, with a further distinction between friendly interventions intended to prop up a favored local government, and hostile interventions to produce regime change.[24] It reports that British intervention, whether supportive or hostile, never produced political liberalization, and indeed often resulted in less democratic governments. French interventions were usually in support of endangered and undemocratic clients, though some of the later actions produced more liberal governments, notably in Comoros when in 1989 French troops ousted a French mercenary who had led a coup, and democratic elections followed shortly. As with the other powers, U.S. supportive interventions had no systematic effect, but unlike the others U.S. hostile interventions in this period were associated with liberalization. This statistical result, however, depends almost entirely on the sustained democratic transition in Panama after 1989, and the short-lived restoration of Jean-Bertrand Aristide in Haiti in 1994.

Most relevant is what happened following those interventions in which political liberalization was one of the explicit goals of the intervention. Of the 14 countries in Peceny's initial study that became democratic, 13 were ones in which the United States "actively supported pro-liberalization policies."[25] Democratization failed in 6 other cases where it started as an American goal but was abandoned by the end of the intervention (South Vietnam is an example), and in 10 instances even a sustained liberalization project failed. So the count is 13 successes for a policy of democratization, and 16 failures. When democratization was not an explicit goal it virtually never happened.

Selection effects may be at work here, making the record look better than it should. That is, democratization may have been tried largely in cases that were more promising in terms of the comparative politics criteria. Even so, two relevant influences are that (1) states with no previous experience of democracy were less likely to become democratic after intervention, and (2) states that experienced a civil war, either before or after the intervention, were much less likely to democratize. Moreover, and related to the civil war problem, when the United States made a major push to strengthen the country's military establishment, democratization often failed.[26] Democracy and militarization make bad barracks-mates.

Another study, by John Tures, confirms that the experience of combat increased the likelihood that a more autocratic state would emerge, even though ousting the target tended to produce a more democratic government. This study reports on 228 U.S. "military operations," including a wide range of actions covering war, peace-keeping, humanitarian missions, interdiction, border control, and military training. In 42 percent of the cases there was no change in the target country's political regime, in 30 percent it became less democratic, and in 28 percent more democratic.[27]

All this does not mean that democratization by forcible intervention cannot work. It sometimes does, but no systematic analysis of the costs and benefits—or even just the costs—has ever been done. I doubt that the prospects of success in Iraq are now favorable, but we will not know for at least another decade how stable and how democratic a regime will emerge. The probabilities and costs of failure, as in a full-scale civil war and incubator of terrorism in Iraq, are huge.[28] We can and should hope for the best, but this review suggests why the American effort was at best unpromising even before its flawed execution.

Military Intervention By Intergovermental Organizations (IGOs)

Military intervention by the United States was more likely to make democratization a key goal, and achieve its objective, after World War II than before. UN military intervention in civil wars and failed states is largely a phenomenon of the post–cold war years, coinciding with an explicit commitment to promoting democracy.[29]

Simplistic views of UN peacekeeping efforts emphasize the failures and ignore many of the successes. Traditional UN peacekeeping, largely evolved to mitigate international conflicts (as between India and Pakistan in Kashmir, or between Israel and its neighbors), was almost exclusively an impartial operation designed chiefly to separate warring parties. These interventions were contingent on the mutual assent of the warring parties, and limited to lightly armed forces authorized to shoot only in self-defense. But the end of the cold war lifted the lid on many civil conflicts. This led UN practice, and then its doctrine, to evolve into more muscular forms of peacekeeping. Sometimes termed peace enforcement, these efforts were designed to resist vigorously efforts to interfere with the UN's humanitarian mission, while still not taking a partisan position between the parties. These more muscular efforts, in turn, led to a greater willingness to intervene in an overtly partisan fashion to prevent one side from conducting massive ethnic cleansing and/or committing other major human rights violations. And such vigorous interventions inevitably led to major efforts to build a peace by helping actively to disarm the participants and put together the pieces of the warring country.

These peace-building actions became multidimensional operations, both imposing and maintaining the peace militarily and rebuilding the physical and administrative structure of the country.

And that rebuilding virtually always involved a major effort to reconstitute, or create, the institutions and practices of democratic government. East Timor is an example of such a multidimensional intervention. Generally they developed a record of substantial achievement, especially as the UN and associated IGOs and nongovernmental organizations (NGOs) learned over time from their mistakes as well as their successes. Michael Doyle and Nicholas Sambanis do a very sophisticated and exhaustive analysis particularly sensitive to selection effects.[30] They find that multidimensional operations by the UN usually are successful in keeping the peace and establishing reasonably democratic regimes for about five years from initiation of the operation. After that, there remains some residual beneficial effect. But unexpected shocks, such as natural disasters and economic collapse, may disrupt the established order. This would seem a pretty good record, and it is superior to similar efforts mounted solely by single countries or regional organizations or coalitions.[31] And in joint operations, UN involvement strengthens the effect of the non-UN actors. This too provides an interesting reflection on the U.S. experience in Iraq, where neither NATO nor the UN has been eager to risk soldiers or civilians in a unilateralist peace-building operation controlled by the United States.

Nonmilitary Interventions By IGOs to Support Democratization

An emphasis on military actions cannot do justice to all the ways in which international organizations foster democratization. The concern among many IGOs with democracy is a reflection of the desires of their member states. Democracies have vested interests in having stable democratic neighbors. Fellow democracies are likely to provide larger and more reliable markets, to be more politically stable and less likely to fight their democratic neighbors, and to avoid human rights abuses and civil wars with consequent cross-border spillovers of refugees. Democratic neighbors are also more apt to form a mutual protection society against unconstitutional usurpation of powers at home, as well as join in collective security endeavors against common external foes. Many regional international organizations are formed among neighbors largely for these purposes. Those IGOs composed mostly or exclusively of democratic governments are especially likely to pursue these goals, and to do so successfully. Even the United Nations, which still includes many dictatorships, has been able and willing to take on tasks of democracy promotion.

Multidimensional peace-building efforts involve, in addition to the initial military intervention, policies to reduce drastically the ability of the former combatants to fight again. This requires assistance aimed at disarming and demobilizing former combatants, as well as providing them with the land, relocation, or training needed to integrate them into the civilian economy. It may also involve integrating elements of both sides' forces into a new army under a single civilian command. Finally, these multidimensional efforts also involve providing assistance to build a nation's capacity for democratic governance: forming a transitional government that includes the warring parties, building new political parties capable of competing in elections, reforming the justice system, and securing the conditions for free political expression and guaranteeing a fair electoral process. Nearly all of these activities have been involved in reasonably successful UN peace-building initiatives that have included democratization as a goal; this is true whether the UN has acted alone or with other IGOs and INGOs.[32] As for monitoring, supervising, organizing, and legitimizing free elections, the UN, the EU, and the Organization of American States (OAS) all have substantial experience. Since the end of the cold war made it possible for the UN to support democracy in its member states, its Electoral Assistance Division has done so in 91 countries. Many, though not a majority, followed civil conflicts (http://www.un.org/Depts/dpa/ead/assistance by country/ea_assistance.htm, accessed 10/13/04). In 1990, the OAS formed its Unit for the Promotion of Democracy for the same purpose. IGOs go in, with substantial assistance from International Non Governmental Organizations (INGOs), to help those who want to contest democratic elections rather than fight.[33] If they decide the election is reasonably fair, they give legitimacy to the winner, whether the winner is the government or the opposition.

Conversely, an international organization's refusal to monitor an election—because they don't think it really will be fair, or because they can't get enough access to know what is actually going on—can deprive a dictator of a seal of approval that he seeks by permitting some kind of election. In addition, if external groups monitor the election and conclude it was unfair, their judgment can deny legitimacy to a government seeking international acceptance. Thus, IGO election activities become very important in facilitating democratic transitions under circumstances where many domestic groups want them, or in situations where the government decides, perhaps very reluctantly, that it needs external validation for an election it feels compelled to hold. Sometimes governments are unpleasantly surprised at the outcome of these elections, as happened to the Sandinista regime in Nicaragua. The need for international certification is why independent monitoring of the recent election in Iraq was so important, and why the difficulty in doing so convincingly, because of concern about the ability of Iraqi and U.S. forces to assure basic physical security to civilian observers, was costly.

International organizations' activities are not limited to post–civil war situations. The UN and other IGOs can also help to isolate and eventually remove a dictator who seizes power from a democratically elected government. This eventually happened in Haiti, and the OAS played a major role in preventing or promptly reversing military coups against the elected governments of Paraguay (1996), Ecuador (2000), and Venezuela (2002). Both the OAS and other regional organizations like the EU have the ability to levy severe economic and political sanctions (such as suspension of membership, approval of military intervention by member states) after such a seizure of power.[34] Its June 1991, Santiago Commitment to "defense and promotion of representative democracy and human rights . . . and respect for the principles of self-determination and non-intervention" makes it an important signaler of legitimacy for new governments. For many Latin American governments the greatest military threat has been from within rather than from neighboring states. Thus, the major subregional organization in Latin America—MERCOSUR, consisting of Argentina, Brazil, Uruguay, and Paraguay—was formed in large part to provide means for new democratically elected presidents to control their militaries better. They were able to open up each other's markets and reduce the size of their military establishments under conditions of peaceful international relations. MERCOSUR has a clause that requires its member countries to be democratic.

Understanding the Nonmilitary Effects of IGOs on Democratization

The manner in which international military interventions affect democratization is readily observable and relatively straightforward. The way in which nonmilitary interventions by IGOs influence democratization is not. Among the theories available for helping us understand the interactions among IGOs and nation-states, principal-agent models seem particularly appropriate. They can offer explanations of how IGOs constrain or empower domestic political actors who support democratization, and in turn how domestic actors can use IGOs for their purposes.

As Ikenberry reminds us, nearly all the big global IGOs and many of the important regional ones were established by democracies.[35] For about 25 years, the OAS membership has consisted mostly of democratic states. Its experience illustrates some reasons why democracies cluster geographically. Joining and subsequent membership in regional international organizations composed largely of democratic countries reinforce both democratic transitions and the stability of democracies. The greater the proportion of stable democratic states in the IGO the more credible its guarantees of assistance, the more interested it will be in promoting reforms, the more likely it will set constraining conditions, and the more likely it will enforce them. Thus, IGOs have the capacity to change the cost-benefit perceptions of domestic elites who may not be enthusiastic about democracy.

They can, for example, provide some guarantees of property rights for business and help socialize the military not to interfere in the democratic process. Particularly influential in changing the cost-benefit calculations of reluctant domestic elites are IGOs with serious economic assets to deploy as carrots in inducing attitudinal and behavioral changes. Consider the European Union and its impact on Turkey. Membership in the EU brings many economic benefits and Turkey has sought to become a member of the EU for decades. In order to comply with the stringent governance criteria the EU has established, the Turkish government has worked hard to improve its democratic structures and human rights record.[36] Democratic IGOs can also make continued membership conditional on continued democracy. NATO has such a condition. Though in the past NATO did not eject Greece or Turkey when their governments turned autocratic, its threat is more credible with the end of cold war rivalries that dictators could use to their advantage.

If the threat to punish backsliders is credible, it induces regime leaders to keep their commitments to govern democratically. Moreover, IGOs can become as much an instrument of domestic democracy advocates as those advocates are instruments of IGOs. And this can be extremely important for domestic elites who require credible external support to continue their advocacy of democracy.[37] Thus, newly democratizing states are especially likely to join largely democratic IGOs, and largely democratic IGOs are likely to support democratic transitions and consolidations.[38] The commitment of state leaders to comply with costly conditionalities on governance structures sends a useful signal of their wish for stable cooperative relations.[39]

International organizations that make economic integration among their members a primary goal can be particularly effective as external agents for empowering domestic democracy advocates and stabilizing newly democratic regimes. International trade, as well as external investment and the free movement of persons, carries two kinds of influences.[40] First, a nation's goods and services, and the processes by which they are exported, serve as a carrier of ideas. And basic ideas about desirable forms of political and economic institutions are deeply embedded in the interactions among trading partners. The role of global commerce in spreading Western values, in ways not necessarily intended by either sender or recipient, is well-recognized, whether by applause or derision as "coca-colonization." Second, commercial exchanges create continuing economic interests in access to buyers and sellers of desired goods and services. To the degree that trade benefits consumers and producers broadly throughout a society, its beneficiaries have a stake in the continuation of commerce and in the reliability of institutions that provide continuity.

Most human rights agreements have proved very difficult to enforce, and regimes with little regard for human rights may sign them because the agreements lack institutional "teeth."[41] But outside the well-known Human Rights conventions and other agreements is a class of treaties primarily devoted to fostering economic integration. Preferential Trade Agreements often have human rights provisions. These agreements have been most effective in reducing violent repression when they incorporate "hard" rather than "soft" enforcement mechanisms (i.e., the ability to terminate trade agreements and impose sanctions on repressive member states, rather than mere verbal standards that do not affect membership or market access). Hard enforcement mechanisms empower human rights advocates and coerce elites who would otherwise practice repression. The Lomé Treaties between the EU and states in Africa and Latin America usually have such provisions. Indeed, the Lomé Commission halted benefits after the 1994 Rwanda genocide, forcing the Rwanda army to prosecute some war criminals.[42]

The EU has always had a commitment to democracy and, unlike NATO, has never had a nondemocratic member. Democracy was a condition for membership in Article 237 of the Treaty of Rome that began the integration process in 1950; that commitment was strengthened by the European Parliament in 1962, declaring that to join states must guarantee "truly democratic practices and respect for fundamental rights and freedoms." After the 1967 Greek military coup, the European Commission suspended its Association Treaty with Greece, and threatened to cancel the agreement entirely. As nearly half of Greece's total trade was with the EU, the damage to the Greek economy was widespread and its effects were felt across the political spectrum. Even the junta's conservative supporters began to desert it, contributing to the restoration of democracy in 1974. Rapid defeat of a 1981 coup attempt in newly democratic Spain was assisted by concern in the business community that backsliding would jeopardize their goal of entry into the EU. The democratization process in the Czech Republic, Hungary, and Poland was far advanced by the time their applications to join the EU were considered, but for later entrants the EU's democracy condition probably had a larger effect. Internal forces producing the reversal in 1998 of Vladimir Meciar's movement toward consolidating a one-party dictatorship in Slovakia were strengthened by the European Commission's highly critical report on the situation.[43]

If being densely democratic gives an IGO a willingness to promote democratization, wealth gives it the capability to do so. The EU, populated exclusively by democracies, has enormous resources available for the economic development of its less prosperous members. Its combination of carrots and sticks can deeply affect many constituencies in candidate states. It is surely the most powerful international institution in this respect. Free trade agreements among non-European states lack such strong incentives and resources, though many now typically require a commitment to democracy by their members. MERCOSUR, mentioned above, is probably the most effective. Other trading groups in the Western Hemisphere (CARICOM in Central America, the Andean Pact) and Africa also require a commitment to democracy, but their lesser economic resources and members' less established commitment to democracy raise questions about their impact on domestic politics.

Saving the Democratic Peace, In Concept and Reality

Military interventions have sometimes installed democracies by force, but they have more often failed, and the successes have been immensely expensive in lives and treasure. Sometimes there may be no choice but to defeat a dangerous attacker, and then try to impose a democratic government. Democratization should be a key piece in the consequent responsibility to put the defeated country back together again, with a decent government. I believe that was the case when the United States invaded Afghanistan, whose Taliban-ruled government aided and protected al Qaeda before and after its attack on 9/11. But the need to root out and destroy an attacker is quite different from going to war in order to impose democracy. To justify the Iraq War that way, in retrospect after previous justifications proved wrong, is yet one more distortion to cover a disastrous act. As a general principle, democratization by force is full of practical and moral dangers, depending on many highly unpredictable contingencies, and not to be undertaken as the purpose in a war of choice.[44]

Military interventions are hardly the only factor driving the spread of democracies over the past 60 years. Among the other factors is the relative economic success of democracies. On average democracies may not show higher economic growth rates than dictatorships, but there is less variance. For every dictatorship like China and Singapore that succeeded in producing rapid growth, there are more like Mobutu's Congo or Hussein's Iraq. Most dictators have concluded that their interest is best served by a reliable system to skim off the rents for their personal enrichment and for rewarding the narrow coterie of cronies and security forces they need to stay in power. The people can eat grass so long as they can be repressed. But democratic states promote growth by being more politically stable, educating their population better, providing more stable social spending, and having more equally distributed incomes.[45] The ability of most democracies to produce relatively steady and widely spread growth over time allows those democratic states that have reached a reasonable level of economic development to remain democratic,[46] and to serve as a strong example in an increasingly globalized and transparent world.

Furthermore, democracy thrives best in countries where peoples and governments do not see themselves as under a major external security threat—war and threats of war strain democratic liberties. Democracy is contagious. There appears to be an evolutionary process whereby the percentage of democracies in the system grows, often by regional clusters.[47] Democracies are at peace with one another. They tend spend less of their GDP on the military.[48] Democratic states with democratic neighbors are more stable and feel less threatened than do those with dictatorships on their borders. Democratization is more likely to succeed in a democratic neighborhood.[49]

The better alternative to regime change by force is democracy by example and peaceful incentives. The United States did play a major role in persuading dictators in South Korea and the Philippines to surrender power, and European states, acting individually and especially through regional international organizations, provided similar assistance in Eastern Europe and states of the former Soviet Union. Georgia and the Ukraine showed how semi-authoritarian systems, when the government feels it needs to conduct and then steal an election, can be defeated by a combination of technical assistance to the challenging parties, support of independent media, and support for civil society.[50]

In those peaceful processes international organizations, and particularly those intergovernmental organizations composed primarily of democratic countries, have learned to play a major role. Those organizations have grown in number, functions, and experience. Areas of the world where IGOs are few and weak are likely to lag in democracy without new and stronger organizations. Continued forward movement requires understanding and continued support by international organizations' member governments and peoples.

Notes

Chapter 1　Change and Continuity: Four Decades of Research and Policy

1. Bruce Russett, Harvey Starr, and David Kinsella, *World Politics: The Menu for Choice* (Belmont, CA: Thompson Wadsworth, 2005, 8th edition), Appendix B.
2. Bruce Russett, Steven Jackson, Duncan Snidal, and David Sylvan, "Health and Population Patterns as Indicators of Income Inequality," *Economic Development and Cultural Change* 29:4 (July 1981), 759–79.
3. Hazem Ghobarah, Paul Huth, and Bruce Russett, "Civil Wars Kill and Maim People—Long after the Shooting Stops," *American Political Science Review* 97:2 (May 2003), 189–202, and Hazem Ghobarah, Paul Huth, and Bruce Russett, "The Postwar Public Health Effects of Civil Conflict," *Social Science and Medicine* 59:4 (August 2004), 869–84. These efforts also derive from my effort to understand the implications of long-term effects for any proper application of the just-war criterion of proportionality (see chapter 12, "Ethical Dilemmas of Nuclear Deterrence," this volume).
4. I returned to this topic with a conceptual discussion of measuring dependence, and some conclusions about the need not to exaggerate U.S. dependence, in "Dimensions of Resource Dependence: Some Elements of Rigor in Concept and Policy Analysis," *International Organization* 38:3 (Summer 1984), 481–500.
5. In the run-up to the Gulf War in 1990–91, the first President Bush employed themes combining Saddam Hussein's odious character with his control of oil, antidemocratic rule, and potential access to nuclear weapons (see Bruce Russett, *Grasping the Democratic Peace: Principles for a Post–Cold War World*, Princeton [Princeton, NJ: Princeton University Press, 1993], 126, 165). These themes may seem familiar to those who witnessed the next President Bush's run-up to the Iraq War in 2003.
6. David Sylvan, Duncan Snidal, Bruce Russett, Steven Jackson, and Raymond Duvall, "The Peripheral Economies: Penetration and Economic Distortion, 1970–1975," in William R. Thompson, ed., *Contending Approaches to World System Analysis* (Beverly Hills, CA: Sage, 1983).
7. See our overviews of the literature and our full theoretical model in Steven Jackson, Bruce Russett, Duncan Snidal, and David Sylvan, "An Assessment of Empirical Research on *Dependencia*," *Latin American Research Review* 14:3 (1979), 5–28, and Raymond Duvall, Steven Jackson, Bruce Russett, Duncan Snidal, and David Sylvan, "A Formal Model of 'Dependencia Theory': Structure and Measurement," in Richard Merritt and Bruce Russett, eds., *From National Development to Global Community: Essays in Honor of Karl W. Deutsch* (London: Allen and Unwin, 1981).
8. See principally Bruce Russett, *What Price Vigilance? The Burdens of National Defense* (New Haven, CT: Yale University Press, 1970), and Bruce Russett and Elizabeth C. Hanson, *Interest and Ideology: The Foreign Policy Beliefs of American Businessmen* (New York: W. H. Freeman, 1975). A different kind of

collaborative project on this topic was Bruce Russett and Alfred C. Stepan, *Military Force and American Society* (New York: Harper and Row, 1973), of which all the substantive chapters were written by our Yale graduate students.

9. This organization, now solely at the University of Connecticut, is a publicly accessible archive of opinion surveys, and is not affiliated with the polling organization, Roper Public Affairs.

10. Waltz continues to hold this position. See Scott Sagan and Kenneth Waltz, *The Spread of Nuclear Weapons: A Debate Renewed* (New York: Norton, 2002).

11. Valery Yarynich, *C3: Nuclear Command, Control Cooperation* (Washington, DC: Center for Defense Information, 2003).

12. The most prominent critique was Richard Ned Lebow and Janice Gross Stein, "Deterrence: The Elusive Dependent Variable," *World Politics* 42:3 (April 1990), 336–69. Our response was Paul Huth and Bruce Russett, "Testing Deterrence Theory: Rigor Makes a Difference," *World Politics* 42 (July 1990), 466–501.

13. Paul Huth and Bruce Russett, "General Deterrence between Enduring Rivals: Testing Three Competing Models," *American Political Science Review* 87:1 (March 1993), 61–73.

14. U.S. Conference of Catholic Bishops, *The Harvest of Justice is Sown in Peace* (Washington, DC: USCC, 1993), E.2(b). Save for one advisory session I did not participate in drafting this document, but I approved of these positions.

15. The number three nuclear power, China, had 402 deployed weapons. Hans Kristensen, "World Nuclear Forces," *SIPRI Yearbook 2004 Armaments, Disarmament and International Security* (Stockholm: Stockholm International Peace Research Institute, 2004), 629.

16. Bruce Russett, *Grasping the Democratic Peace: Principles for a Post–Cold War World* (Princeton, NJ: Princeton University Press, 1993); Bruce Russett, ed., *The Once and Future Security Council* (New York: St. Martin's, 1997), and especially Bruce Russett and John R. Oneal, *Triangulating Peace: Democracy, Interdependence, and International Organizations* (New York: Norton, 2001). Also see John R. Oneal, "Confirming the Liberal Peace with Analyses of Directed Dyads, 1885–2001," in Harvey Starr, ed., *Crossing Boundaries: Internal-External Approaches, Levels and Methods of Analysis in International Politics* (New York: Palgrave Macmillan, 2006).

17. Four other very satisfying collaborations spanning more than a decade and multiple publications have been with Paul Huth, David Kinsella, Alex Mintz, and Harvey Starr.

18. I sent Professor Huntington a draft of our critique for comment and correction. His letter of June 14, 1999 refused any substantive comment, but warned, "[I]f you do publish this paper in anything like its current form, I will have no alternative but to write a response detailing in full its deficiencies." We did publish our work, in *Triangulating Peace*, ch. 7 and in Bruce Russett, John R. Oneal, and Michaelene Cox, "Clash of Civilizations, or Realism and Liberalism Déjà Vu? Some Evidence," *Journal of Peace Research* 37:5 (September 2000), 583–608. He responded to the latter in the same issue (Samuel P. Huntington, "Try Again: A Reply to Russett, Oneal and Cox," *Journal of Peace Research* 37:5 [September 2000], 609–10), as did we to him (Oneal and Russett, "A Response to Huntington," 611–12).

19. All the chapters here are reprinted in close to their original form save for correcting typos and other minor errors, and prepared in a common format. They are not doctored to make them look more sensible or more prescient than when they first appeared. I retain thanks to collaborators, colleagues, and funding agencies noted in the original copy both from gratitude and as a piece of history. In addition, I here thank Melissa Joralemon and Yi-Mei Truxes, who worked specifically on preparing this book. I also thank my editor David Pervin for suggesting the book and the directions in which he wisely nudged it.

20. Harvey Starr, ed., *Crossing Boundaries: Internal-External Approaches, Levels and Methods of Analysis in International Politics* (New York: Palgrave Macmillan, 2006).

21. Bruce Russett and Harvey Starr, *World Politics: The Menu for Choice* (New York, W. H. Freeman, 1981), 442–43.

22. The international institutions side of a Kantian perspective is not so well represented in this volume. But for examples see my work with Paul Kennedy and James Sutterlin as staff for the report of the Independent Working Group on the Future of the United Nations, *The United Nations in Its Second Half-Century* (New York: Ford Foundation, 1995), and Russett, ed., *The Once and Future Security Council*. On intergovernmental organizations composed largely of democracies as especially effective in preventing conflict among their members, see Jon Pevehouse and Bruce Russett, "Democratic IGOS Promote Peace," *International Organization* 60 (Summer 2006).

23. These changes epitomize one of what I identify as "five revolutions" in the study of world politics in the past two decades, this one being the revolution "in international relations in the real world." See Bruce Russett, "Four Methods and Five Revolutions," in Alex Mintz and Bruce Russett, eds., *New Directions for International Relations: Confronting the Method-of-Analysis Problem* (Lanham, MD: Lexington, 2005), 22.

24. For early examples see Bruce Russett, "Inequality and Instability: The Relation of Land Tenure to Politics," *World Politics* 16 (April 1964), 444–54, and, on measurement, Hayward Alker and Bruce Russett, "Indices for Comparing Inequality," in Richard Merritt and Stein Rokkan, eds., *Comparing Nations: The Use of Quantitative Data in Cross-National Research* (New Haven, CT: Yale University Press, 1964), 349–72.

25. Russett, "Four Methods and Five Revolutions," in Mintz and Russett, eds., *New Directions* 22–24. All four of these revolutions, some in their early stages (formal analysis in chapters 6 and 10 and chapter 11's verbal discussion of alliances and selection effects subsequently made more persuasive by others' formalizations) can be identified in this book.

Chapter 2   Rich and Poor in 2000 AD: The Great Gulf

This chapter is reprinted from *The Virginia Quarterly Review* 44:2 (Spring 1968), 182–98. It has also been reprinted in German and Japanese. An altered version appeared in my 1974 anthology, *Power and Community in World Politics* (San Francisco, CA: W. H. Freeman, 1974). Here it returns to the 1968 text, allowing a longer time perspective.

Chapter 3 The Marginal Utility of Income Transfers to the Third World

This chapter is reprinted from *International Organization* 32 (Autumn 1978), 913–28, by permission from Cambridge University Press. I am grateful to the Concilium on International Studies of Yale University, the German Marshall Fund, and the National Science Foundation for financial support, and to Steven Jackson, Marguerite Kramer, Miroslav Nincic, Duncan Snidal, David Sylvan, and Michael Wallace for comments.

1. See, e.g., Harold Lasswell and Abraham Kaplan, *Power and Society: A Framework for Inquiry* (New Haven, CT: Yale University Press, 1950); Johan Galtung et al., "Measuring World Development," *Alternatives* 1:1 (1975), 131–58; and Abraham Maslow, *Toward a Psychology of Being* (Princeton, NJ: Van Nostrand, 1968, 2nd edition). Note Amilcar Herrera, Hugo Scolnick, Gabriela Chichilinsky, Gilberto Gallopin, Jorge Hardoy, Enrique Oteiza, Gilda de Romero, Carlos Suárez, and Luis Talavera, *Catastrophe or New Society? A Latin American World Model* (Ottawa: International Development Research Centre, 1976), 53: "Life expectancy at birth is without a doubt the indicator that best reflects general conditions of life regardless of country. Its value is a function of the extent to which the basic needs are satisfied. . . ." For the development of a composite Physical Quality of Life Index including life expectancy at birth, infant mortality, and literacy rate, see John Sewell and all the staff of Overseas Development Council, *The United States and World Development: Agenda 1977* (New York: Praeger, 1977), 147–54.

2. The data in figures 3.1 and 3.2 are from Roger D. Hansen and all the staff of Overseas Development Council, *The United States and World Development: Agenda for Action, 1976* (New York: Praeger, 1976), 132–41. I discussed this procedure in Raymond Duvall and Bruce Russett, "Some Proposals to Guide Research on Contemporary Imperialism," *Jerusalem Journal of International Relations* 2 (Fall 1976), 1–27; and in Bruce Russett, "Hur fattiga maste de fattiga vara?" *Rapport fran SIDA* 6:7 (1975), 3–5. It is basically the same as I employed in Bruce Russett, Hayward R. Alker, Karl W. Deustsch, and Harold Lasswell, *World Handbook of Political and Social Indicators* (New Haven, CT: Yale University Press, 1964), 299–301. The same procedure has been used by Gernot Kohler and Norman Alcock, "An Empirical Table of Structural Violence," *Journal of Peace Research* 13:4 (1976), 343–56, taking off from a suggestion by Johan Galtung and Tord Hoivik, "Structural and Direct Violence: A Note on Operationalization," *Journal of Peace Research* 8:1 (1971), 73–76. Kohler and Alcock, however, are primarily concerned with the number of deaths occurring globally as a result of the deviation of the worldwide income distribution from perfect equality; here we attempt to measure the welfare effects of certain identifiable reductions in income inequality. Also see the careful work of Tord Hoivik, "The Demography of Structural Violence," *Journal of Peace Research* 14:1 (1977), 59–74.

3. This is similar to the coefficient that may be inferred from Kohler and Alcock, "An Empirical Table," allowing for the fact that they are using GNP per capita data for 1965.

4. Here and in the following figure, separate regression coefficients were computed for countries with per capita GNP below $600 and for countries above $1800. At each of these levels, a linear relationship (though different) provides a good fit. Between $600 and $1800, I have joined the two lines with a curve to estimate that portion of the relationship. The linear coefficients are referred to in the text. In computing the coefficients, all OPEC countries were omitted; as explained in the text they are special cases.

5. Income inequality data from Hansen et al., *United States and World Development*, 148–49, show Sweden as less egalitarian than the United States. This does not, however, agree with the opposite (and more generally accepted) conclusion of OECD studies (e.g., M. Sawyer, "Income Distribution in OECD Countries," *OECD Economic Outlook* [July] 1976, 3–36) that show the United States as less egalitarian than all or nearly all of 12 major industrialized countries. I have since replicated part of this analysis on a subset of less-developed countries with very carefully compiled data. It appears that conditions of well-being (life expectancy and infant mortality) can be well predicted ($R^2 = .42$) by a combination of GNP per capita and equality of income distribution, with income inequality contributing roughly one-third of the predictive power.

6. For the two regression lines in figure 3.1, the R^2s were, respectively, .36 and .22; here they are .46 and .25.

7. Evelyn Kitagawa and Philip Hauser, *Differential Mortality in the United States: A Study* (Cambridge, MA: Harvard University Press, 1973).

8. Ibid., 28.

9. Ibid., 180.

10. In a new analysis, Norman Alcock and Gemot Kohler, "Structural Violence at the World Level: Diachronic Findings" (Mimeo, Oakville, ON: Canadian Peace Research Institute, 1977) report that both synchronic and diachronic analyses show virtually the same relationship between wealth increments and life expectancy. The relationship is much stronger for poor countries than for rich ones, but very similar within each subgroup, whether examined diachronically or synchronically. The reasons for the similarity (where we found a stronger diachronic relationship) are not clear, but may be an artifact of their use of GNP per capita in the synchronic analyses and energy consumption as the wealth measure in their diachronic analyses.

11. George H. Gallup, "Human Needs and Satisfactions: A Global Survey," *Public Opinion Quarterly* 40 (Winter 1977), 459–67.

12. John Rawls, *A Theory of Justice* (Cambridge, MA: Harvard University Press, 1971), 114. For further relevant ethical considerations, see Peter G. Brown and Henry Shue, eds., *Food Policy: The Responsibility of the U.S. in the Life and Death Choices* (New York: Basic Books, 1977), esp. the contributions by Peter Singer, Thomas Nagel, Peter Brown, and Victor Ferkiss.

13. Herrera et al., *Catastrophe or New Society?*

14. Jan Tinbergen, Coordinator, *Reshaping the International Order: A Report to the Club of Rome* (New York: E. P. Dutton, 1976), 130.

15. Ibid. and Herrera et al., *Catastrophe or New Society?* 91–94.

16. In 1973 prices; Sewell et al., *United States and World Development*, 67.

17. Here, as elsewhere, we still cannot fully specify the mechanism by which our variables are related. It is clear, for example, that education is related

(negatively) to rates of population increase as it is to life expectancy and low infant mortality. Some of the effects of these variables that we may seem to attribute to income are surely attributable more directly to education. Nevertheless, it is very difficult to sort out the separate effects, and the correlations of such variables as literacy with population growth, life expectancy, and so on are not systematically higher than are the correlations of GNP per capita with population growth, life expectancy, and so on. Note the comment by John Osgood Field and Mitchel B. Wallerstein, "Beyond Humanitarianism: A Developmental Perspective on American Food Aid," in Brown and Shue, eds., *Food Policy*, 239. "Malnutrition, infant mortality and rampant morbidity, illiteracy and ignorance, low productivity and marginal livelihood, large family size and unresponsiveness to family planning programs cohere so strongly that they form a veritable syndrome of poverty, cultural and structural, that is highly resistant to change." For a careful review of evidence on the "child survival hypothesis" suggesting that a drop in infant mortality is a requirement for voluntary reduction of births, see the contribution by Michael F. Brewer in the same volume. Also Robert S. McNamara, "Population and International Security," *International Security* 2 (Fall 1977), 25–55.

18. Rati Ram and Theodore W. Schultz, "Some Economic Implications of Increases in Life Span with Special Reference to India," 1977 manuscript for a festschrift in honor of V. K. R. V. Rao.

19. Arthur Okun, *Equality and Efficiency: The Big Tradeoff* (Washington, DC: Brookings Institution, 1975).

20. Robert Amdur, "Rawls' Theory of Justice: Domestic and International Perspectives," *World Politics* 29 (April 1977), 455.

21. Karl W. Deutsch, Sidney Burrell, Robert Kann, Maurice Lee, Martin Lichterman, Raymond Lingdren, Francis Loewenheim, and Richard Van Wagenen, *Political Community and the North Atlantic Area* (Princeton, NJ: Princeton University Press, 1957), and Edward O. Wilson, *Sociobiology* (Cambridge, MA: Belknap, 1975).

Chapter 4   Comparative Public Health: The Political Economy of Human Misery and Well-Being

Hazem Ghobarah holds a Ph.D. in Government from the University of Texas. He was a postdoctoral fellow at the Weatherhead Center for International Affairs at Harvard, and is now at Mathsoft E&E in Cambridge, Massachusetts.

Paul Huth did his Ph.D. in Political Science at Yale University. He has held positions at the University of Michigan and Harvard, and is now Professor of Politics and Government at the University of Maryland. His most recent book is *The Democratic Peace and Territorial Conflict in the Twentieth Century* (with Todd Allee).

This chapter is reprinted with permission from *International Studies Quarterly* 48:1 (March 2004), 73–94, Blackwell Publishing. We thank the Weatherhead Initiative on Military Conflict as a Public Health Problem, the Ford Foundation, and the World Health Organization for financial support, and Gary King, Lisa Mafti, and Ben Valentino for helpful comments. Data are at http://pantheon.yale.edu%7Ebrusset/.

1. Emmanuela Gakidou and Gary King, "Measuring Total Health Inequality: Adding Individual Variation to Group-level Differences," *International Journal for Equity in Health* 1:3 (2002).

2. Bruce Moon, *The Political Economy of Basic Human Needs* (Ithaca, NY: Cornell University Press, 1991); Adam Przeworski, Michael Alvarez, Jose Antonio Cheibub, and Fernando Limongi, *Democracy and Development: Political Institutions and Well-Being in the World, 1950–1990* (Cambridge, MA: Cambridge University Press, 2000); Andrew Price-Smith, *The Health of Nations* (Cambridge, MA: M.I.T. Press, 2002).

3. Deon Filmer and Lant Pritchett, "The Impact of Public Spending on Health: Does Money Matter?" *Social Science & Medicine* 49:4 (1999), 1309–23; David B. Evans, L. Bendib, Ajay Tandon, Jeremy Lauder, S. Ebenezer, R. C. W. Hutubessy, Y. Asada, and Christopher Murray, "Estimates of Income Per Capita, Literacy, Educational Attainment, Absolute Poverty, and Income Gini Coefficients for the *World Health Report 2000*," Global Programme on Evidence for Health Policy Discussion Paper no. 7 (Geneva: WHO, 2000).

4. In this we respond to the call of Gary King and Christopher Murray, "Rethinking Human Security," *Political Science Quarterly* 117 (Winter 2002), 585–610 for systematic analysis of human misery. Also see Lant Pritchet and Lawrence Summers, "Wealthier is Healthier," *Journal of Human Resources* 31:4 (1996), 841–68 and Bruce Russett, "The Marginal Utility of Income Transfers to the Third World," chapter 3 in this book.

5. David Davis and Joel Kuritsky, "Violent Conflict and Its Impact on Health Indicators in Sub-Saharan Africa, 1980 to 1997," paper presented at the Annual Meeting of the International Studies Association, New Orleans, March 2002.

6. Thomas Zweifel and Patricia Navia, "Democracy, Dictatorship, and Infant Mortality," *Journal of Democracy* 11 (April 2000), 99–114.

7. Przeworski et al., *Democracy and Development*.

8. David Lake and Matthew Baum, "The Invisible Hand of Democracy: Political Control and the Provision of Public Services," *Comparative Political Studies* 34 (August 2001), 587–621.

9. World Health Organization, *The World Health Report 2000: Health Systems: Improving Performance* (Geneva: WHO, 2000), 28.

10. Edward Diener, D. Wirtz, and S. Oishi, "End Effects of Rated Life Quality: The James Dean Effect," *Psychological Science* 12 (March 2001), 124–28.

11. David M.Cutler, Elizabeth Richardson, Theodore Keeter, and Douglas Staiger, "Measuring the Health of the United States Population," *Brookings Papers on Economic Activity—Microeconomics* (1997), 217–82; Christopher Murray and Alan Lopez, *The Global Burden of Disease* (Cambridge, MA: Harvard School of Public Health on behalf of the WHO and the World Bank, 1996); World Health Organization, *World Health Report 2000*.

12. C. D. Mathers, R. Sadana, Joshua Salomon, Christopher Murray, and Alan Lopez, "Estimates of DALE for 191 Countries: Methods and Results," Global Programme on Evidence for Health Policy (GPE) Working Paper no. 16 (Geneva: WHO, 2000).

13. Filmer and Pritchett, "Impact of Public Spending," 1312; Alan Williams, "Calculating the Global Burden of Disease: Time for a Strategic Reappraisal?" *Health Economics* 8:1 (1999), 1–8; Christopher Murray and Alan Lopez,

"Progress and Directions in Refining the Global Burden of Disease Approach: A Response to Williams," *Health Economics* 9:1 (2000), 69–82.

14. Ghanshyam Shah, *Public Health and Urban Development* (London: Sage, 1997); Laurie Garrett, "The Return of Infectious Disease," in Andrew Price-Smith, ed., *Plague and Politics* (New York: Palgrave, 2001), 183–94; Simon Szreter, "Economic Growth, Disruption, Deprivation, Disease, and Death," in Price-Smith, ed., *Plague and Politics*, 76–116.

15. Moon, *The Political Economy of Basic Human Needs*; Bruce Moon and William Dixon, "Basic Needs and Growth-Welfare Trade-offs," *International Studies Quarterly* 36 (June 1992), 191–212; Richard Wilkinson, *Unhealthy Societies: The Afflictions of Inequality* (New York: Routledge, 1996); William Foege, "Arms and Public Health: A Global Perspective," in Barry Levy and Victor Sidel, eds., *War and Public Health* (Washington, DC: American Public Health Association, 2000, 2nd edition), 3–11.

16. Przeworski et al., *Democracy and Development*, ch. 4.

17. Amartya Sen and Jean Dreze, *The Amartya Sen and Jean Dreze Omnibus* (New York: Oxford University Press, 1999); David Evans, Ajay Tandon, Chirstopher Murray, and Jeremy Lauder, "The Comparative Efficiency of National Health Systems in Producing Health: An Analysis of 191 Countries," GPE Discussion Paper no. 29 (Geneva: WHO, 2000).

18. J. P. Pouillier and P. Hernandez, "Estimates of National Health Accounts: Aggregates for 191 Countries in 1997," GPE Discussion Paper no. 26 (Geneva: WHO, 2000).

19. World Health Organization, *The World Health Report 2001: Health Systems: Improving Performance* (Geneva: WHO, 2001).

20. Olson Mancur, "Dictatorship, Democracy, and Development," *American Political Science Review* 87 (September 1993), 567–76; Bruce Bueno de Mesquita, James Morrow, Randolph Siverson, and Alastair Smith, "An Institutional Explanation of the Democratic Peace," *American Political Science Review* 93 (1999), 791–807; Lake and Baum, "The Invisible Hand of Democracy."

21. Sen, *Poverty and Famine*.

22. See also Partha Dasgupta, *An Inquiry into Well-Being and Destitution* (New York: Oxford University Press, 1993); Moon, *The Political Economy of Basic Human Needs*.

23. Zeev Maoz and Bruce Russett, "Normative and Structural Causes of Democratic Peace, 1946–1986," *American Political Science Review* 87 (September 1993), 624–38.

24. Evans et al., "The Comparative Efficiency of National Health Systems." An early effort is Bruce Russett, Steven Jackson, Duncan Snidal, and David Sylvan, "Health and Population Patterns as Indicators of Income Inequality," *Economic Development and Cultural Change* 29 (July 1981), 759–79.

25. See Ted Robert Gurr, *Peoples versus States: Minorities at Risk in the New Century* (Washington, DC: United States Institute of Peace, 2000).

26. Tatu Vanhanen, "Domestic Ethnic Conflict and Ethnic Nepotism: A Comparative Analysis," *Journal of Peace Research* 36 (January 1999), 55–73.

27. Ted Robert Gurr, *Minorities at Risk: A Global View of Ethnopolitical Conflict* (Washington, DC: United States Institute of Peace, 1993).

28. Nicole Ball, *Security and Economy in the Third World* (Princeton, NJ: Princeton University Press, 1988); Alex Mintz, "Guns versus Butter," *American Political Science Review* 83 (December 1989), 1285–93; World Bank, *World Bank Development Report 1993: Investing in Health* (New York: Oxford University Press, 1993); D. W. Fitzsimmons and A. W. Whiteside, "Conflict, War, and Public Health," *Conflict Studies* 276 (Research Institute for the Study of Conflict and Terrorism, London, 1994), 25–26; United Nations Development Programme, *Human Development Report, 1994* (New York: United Nations, 1994); Steve Chan, "Grasping the Peace Dividend: Some Propositions on the Conversion of Swords into Plowshares," *Mershon International Studies Review* 39 (April 1995), 53–95; Francis Adeola, "Military Expenditures, Health, and Education," *Armed Forces and Society* 22 (Spring 1996), 441–55; Julide Yildirim and Selami Sezgin, "Defense, Education and Health Expenditures in Turkey, 1924–96," *Journal of Peace Research* 39 (September 2002), 569–80.

29. We extend data from Diehl and Goertz to recent years from Wallensteen and Sollenberg. See Paul Diehl and Gary Goertz, *War and Peace in International Rivalry* (Ann Arbor: University of Michigan Press, 2000); Peter Wallensteen and Margareta Sollenberg, "Armed Conflict, 1989–99," *Journal of Peace Research* 37 (September 2000), 635–49.

30. Filmer and Pritchett, "Impact of Public Spending;" Evans et al., "The Comparative Efficiency of National Health Systems."

31. Some observations were estimated by multiple imputations from other data on educational attainment. For sources and methods, see Evans et al., "Estimates of Income."

32. For the two equations below the N varies by 1 in either direction because of missing data on expenditures. We also examined instances where collinearity might be a problem, and found none in any of the equations we tested. The highest correlation among any pair of independent variables used in a single equation is only .7, for education and GDP per capita.

33. Since all our hypotheses specify a direction of relationship, the *p*-values are for one-tailed tests.

34. Evans et al., "The Comparative Efficiency of National Health Systems," 24.

35. Nor is there much evidence that they do. Public and private health spending in part substitute for each other. They are weakly correlated, at −.1. In an expanded equation to explain private health spending only two political variables, income inequality and enduring rivalry, are even weakly significant (*p* = about .05). And only those two are significant in an expanded equation for total health spending (*p* = just under .10).

36. While still very good at .50, the adjusted R-square for the allocation of resources to public health in table 4.1 is substantially lower than the .97 for the equation explaining total levels of health spending in table 4.2 and .81 for the equation explaining total levels of health performance in table 4.3. This apparent weakness is largely because the allocation variable is a ratio rather than an absolute level. Imprecise measurement can play a bigger role with ratios, as they are likely to be more volatile in any single cross-section.

37. Filmer and Pritchett, "Impact of Public Spending"; Evans et al., "The Comparative Efficiency of National Health Systems."

38. United Nations, *World Urbanization Prospects: The 1996 Revision* (New York: United Nations, 1998), 132–35.

39. Hazem Adam Ghobarah, Paul Huth, and Bruce Russett, "Civil Wars Kill and Maim People—Long after the Shooting Stops," *American Political Science Review* 97 (May 2003), 189–202, analyze the effect of civil wars more extensively.

40. Paul Collier, "On the Economic Consequences of Civil War," *Oxford Economic Papers* 51 (1999), 168–83; Francis Stewart, "War and Underdevelopment: Can Economic Analysis Help Reduce the Costs?" *Journal of International Development* 5 (July–August 1993), 357–80.

41. On much of the above see Michael J. Toole, "Displaced Persons and War," in Levy and Sidel, eds., *War and Public Health*, 197–212.

42. Fitzsimmons and Whiteside, "Conflict, War, and Public Health."

43. Elizabeth Reid, "A Future, If One Is Still Alive: The Challenge of the HIV Epidemic," in Jonathan Moore, ed., *Hard Choices: Moral Dilemmas in Humanitarian Intervention* (Lanham, MD: Rowman and Littlefield, 1998), 269–86; Helen Epstein, "AIDS: The Lesson of Uganda." *New York Review of Books* 48 (2002), 18–23.

44. Patrick Bracken and Celia Petty, *Rethinking the Trauma of War* (London: Free Association Books, 1998).

45. Dane Archer and Rosemary Gartner, "Violent Acts and Violent Times: A Comparative Approach to Postwar Homicide Rates," *American Sociological Review* 41 (December 1976), 937–63; Arthur A. Stein, *The Nation at War* (Baltimore, MD: Johns Hopkins University Press, 1980).

46. Frederico Gerosi and Gary King, "Short Term Effects of War Deaths on Public Health in the U.S" (Cambridge, MA: Harvard Center for Basic Research in the Social Sciences, 2002).

47. Toole, "Displaced Persons and War," 98.

48. COW data on civil wars website: http://www.umich.edu/ ~ cowproj/; Roy Licklider, "The Consequences of Negotiated Settlements in Civil Wars, 1945–1993," *American Political Science Review* 89 (September 1995), 681–90; Patrick Regan, *Civil Wars and Foreign Powers* (Ann Arbor: University of Michigan Press, 2000); Michael Doyle and Nicholas Sambanis, "International Peacebuilding: A Theoretical and Quantitative Analysis," *American Political Science Review* 94 (December 2000), 779–803; Wallensteen and Sollenberg, "Armed Conflict."

49. Pritchett and Summers, "Wealthier is Healthier."

50. Evans et al., "The Comparative Efficiency of National Health Systems," 13.

51. Two variables that we hypothesized and found to affect public health spending are not included in this output equation. As we noted in discussing the relevant spending hypothesis, the recent literature indicates that democracy's major impact is in raising public health spending, and thus strongly but largely indirectly affects health outcomes. Similarly we hypothesized that the principal effect of an international rivalry short of war would be fiscal, in reducing public health spending. Also, three of the variables we now hypothesize to affect health outputs did not appear in our equations to explain health spending. We encountered contradictory arguments about the probable effect of civil wars (at home, and in neighboring states) on health spending, and no compelling hypothesis that rapid urbanization would significantly affect spending either way. We have, however, run expanded HALE and spending equations not

shown here, and none of these variables, when included, had a statistically significant effect.

52. Suppose civil war kills all but one person in a country during the war, yet that last person is very healthy and is expected to live long. HALE would then drop in the first year due to all the war deaths, but rise in the next year because it is based only on the person alive. In fact, however, we see low HALEs for several years after a war, reflecting new deaths and disabilities.

53. Theory does not tell us just what the correct lag should be. For most infectious diseases—which we hypothesize as the principal cause of indirect civil war deaths—the lag time would seem short. Effects of damage to the health care system would probably last longer, and the lag for cancers would be too long and varied for us to reasonably test for it. Experimentation with the lag structure indicates that the coefficient for wars in the 1977–90 period is only about one-fourth as large as for the 1991–97 period in our basic equation, and not statistically significant. If we make a break between 1991–95 and 1996–97 the impact of the coefficient for the latter period is higher, but the standard error is very much higher. Eliminating all countries whose civil wars extended past 1997 reduces the impact of wars in 1996–97, but not that of earlier wars. Until more detailed data are available the 1991–97 lag to the 2000 HALEs seems about right.

54. The metrics are only approximately comparable between the continuous civil war variable and the dummy variable for presence of a civil war in an adjacent state. One death from civil war per 100 people represents the 95th percentile of civil war deaths (34 countries out of 177 experienced civil wars, of which 9 were at or above this level of severity, so the comparison is reasonable but underestimates the effect of very severe civil wars at home).

55. If a variable for the adult HIV rate in 1999 is added, it is highly significant and raises the predictive power of the equation. The explanatory variables that lose power do offer some hints as to what may be behind the AIDS effect: the rate of urbanization becomes statistically insignificant, and the significance level of income inequality drops to $p = .08$. Inequality and rapid urbanization may well promote HIV/AIDS, but we cannot establish a causal effect here.

56. While we intend in future work to use simultaneous equations to estimate these effects, we currently lack the instrumental variables needed to ensure the effects estimated by 2- or 3-Stage Least Squares are reliable and robust to different instrumental variables and moderate changes in model specification. The advantage of 2- or 3-Stage Least Squares would be to increase the efficiency of the estimated standard errors (i.e., to reduce the standard errors). As a result, the findings we report in this chapter are based on a conservative test of our central hypotheses linking political variables to public health. We are encouraged therefore by the generally strong results we have uncovered despite a conservative approach to statistical testing.

57. Ghobarah et al., "Civil Wars Kill and Maim People."

Chapter 5   Security and the Resources Scramble: Will 1984 be Like 1914?

This chapter is reprinted from *International Affairs* 58 (Winter 1981–82), 42–54, Blackwell Publishing. I am grateful to Stephen Krasner and Patrick McGowan who generously shared their thoughts when I was first formulating this chapter, and to William Foltz and H. Bradford Westerfield who offered later comments.

1. Arguments that the necessary conditions for successful large-scale price increases by international cartels are rare include Davis Bobrow and Robert Kudrle, "Theory, Policy, and Resource Cartels," *Journal of Conflict Resolution* 20 (March 1976), 3–56, and Stephen Krasner, "Oil is the Exception," *Foreign Policy* 14 (Spring 1974), 68–83.
2. In the discussion on the pre-1914 period, I have drawn heavily on the theory and findings of Nazli Choucri and Robert C. North, *Nations in Conflict* (San Francisco, CA: W. H. Freeman, 1974), and in my subsequent remarks on the applicability of these ideas to the contemporary era on Richard K. Ashley, *The Political Economy of War and Peace* (London: Frances Pinter, 1980).
3. For the comparative study of many arms races, see Michael Wallace, "Arms Races and Escalation: Some New Evidence," *Journal of Conflict Resolution* 23 (March 1979), 1–16. Other works providing, in one way or another, evidence supporting periods of "power transition" as especially dangerous are A. F. K. Organski and Jacek Kugler, *The War Ledger* (Chicago, IL: University of Chicago Press, 1979), ch. 1; Bruce Bueno de Mesquita, *The War Trap* (New Haven, CT: Yale University Press, 1981); and Charles Doran and Wes Parsons, "War and the Cycle of Relative Power," *American Political Science Review* 74 (December 1980), 947–65.
4. Previous analyses have approached the topic from a variety of perspectives. Michael Tanzer, *The Race for Resources: Continuing Struggles over Minerals and Fuels* (New York: Monthly Review Press, 1980), stresses the role of private economic interests. Alfred Eckes, Jr., *The United States and the Global Struggle for Minerals* (Austin: University of Texas Press, 1979), emphasizes national strategic interests, and Stephen Krasner, *Defending the National Interest: Raw Materials Investments and U.S. Foreign Policy* (Princeton, NJ: Princeton University Press, 1978), argues that most actions have been taken in light of a national interest as interpreted in the traditional "liberal" perspective of the foreign policy bureaucracy.
5. J. A. Miller, D. I. Fine, and R. D. McMichael, eds., *The Resource War in 3-D: Dependency Diplomacy Defense* (Pittsburgh, PA: World Affairs Council, 1980).

Chapter 6   Conflict and Coercion in Dependent States

Steven I. Jackson took his Ph.D. in Political Science at Yale University, and is now Associate Director of the Cornell University Center in Washington, DC.

Duncan Snidal did his Ph.D. in Political Science at Yale University, and since then has taught at the Harris School of Public Policy Studies and the Department of Political Science at the University of Chicago.

David Sylvan earned his Ph.D. in Political Science at Yale University, and taught at the University of Minnesota and Syracuse University. He now is Professor of Political Science at the Graduate Institute of International Studies in Geneva.

This chapter is reprinted from *Journal of Conflict Resolution* 22 (December 1978), 627–57. We are grateful to the National Science Foundation and the German Marshall Fund for support.

1. For two volumes containing representative articles, see James Malloy, ed., *Authoritarianism and Corporatism in Latin America* (Pittsburgh, PA: University of Pittsburgh Press, 1977) and Alfred Stepan, ed., *Authoritarian Brazil: Origins, Policies, Futures* (New Haven, CT: Yale University Press, 1973). Some of the most influential case studies include Luigi Einaudi, "The Military and Government in Peru," in Clarence Thurber and Laurence Graham, eds., *Development Administration in Latin America* (Durham, NC: Duke University Press, 1973) and Julio Cotler, "Political Crisis and Military Populism in Peru," *Studies in Comparative International Development* 6:5 (1971), 95–113, on Peru; Robert Kaufman, *Transitions to Stable Authoritarian-Corporate Regimes: The Chilean Case? Sage Professional Papers in Comparative Politics* (Beverly Hills, CA: Sage, 1976) on Chile; Guillermo O'Donnell, *Modernization and Bureaucratic-Authoritarianism: Studies in South American Politics* (Berkeley, CA: Institute of International Studies, 1973) on Argentina; Alfred Stepan, *The Military in Politics: Changing Patterns in Brazil* (Princeton, NJ: Princeton University Press, 1971) on Brazil; and Juan Linz, "An Authoritarian Regime: Spain," in Erik Allardt and Yrjo Littunen, eds., *Cleavages, Ideologies and Party Systems* (Helsinki: Westermarck Society, 1964) on Spain.
2. Raymond Duvall, Steven Jackson, Bruce Russett, Duncan Snidal, and David Sylvan, "A Formal Model of 'Dependencia' Theory: Structure and Measurement," in Richard Merritt and Bruce Russett, eds., *From National Development to Global Community* (London: Allen and Unwin, 1981).
3. A full representation of our arguments is in Duvall et al., "A Formal Model."
4. Raoul Prebisch, *Towards a Dynamic Development Policy for Latin America* (New York: United Nations, 1963); Celso Furtado, *Economic Development of Latin America* (London: Cambridge University Press, 1970).
5. Theotonio Dos Santos, "The Structure of Dependence," *American Economic Review* 60 (1970), 231–36.
6. Oswaldo Sunkel, "Capitalismo transnacional y disintegracion nacional en la America Latina," *El Trimestre Economico* 38 (1971), 571–628; Anibal Pinto, "Naturaleza e implicaciones de la 'heterogeneidad estructural' de la America Latina," *El Trimestre Economico* 37 (1970), 83–100.
7. Fernando Henrique Cardoso and Enzo Faletto, *Dependencia y Desarrollo en America Latina* (Mexico City: Siglo Veintiuno Editores, 1969); Samir Amin, *Accumulation on a World Scale: A Critique of the Theory of Under-Development* (New York: Monthly Review Press, 1974).
8. Anibal Quijano, *Nationalism and Capitalism in Peru: A Study of Neo-Imperialism* (New York: Monthly Review Press, 1971); Colin Leys, *Underdevelopment in Kenya: The Political Economy of Neo-Colonialism, 1964–1971* (Berkeley: University of California Press, 1975).
9. See Ted Robert Gurr, *Why Men Rebel* (Princeton, NJ: Princeton University Press, 1970) for a review of the concept and a highly refined treatment of it.
10. At very high levels of manifest conflict, regimes may feel that the costs of coercion are so high that they have no choice but to abdicate power. This would lead to a downward shift in the desired level of authoritarianism, and hence to a sharp decline in the level of coercion. The fall of the junta in Thailand several years ago may be a case in point. In later work, we shall try to explore this possibility.

11. Sec A. C. Chiang, *Fundamental Methods of Mathematical Economics* (New York: McGraw-Hill, 1974), chs. 16, 17, for details on the solution and analysis of difference equations.

12. The solution to the first difference equation for CA_t is $CA_t = [CA_0 - (c + da) / (1 + db)] (-db)^t + (c + da) / (1 + db)$ where $db \neq -1$ and $CA_t = CA_0 + (c + da)^t$ where $db = -1$.

13. We constrain the parameters for the following reasons:

    $MC' = a_1 + 2a_2 CA$. At a maximum, $a_1 + 2a_2 CA = 0$, or $CA = a_1/2a_2$. If a maximum MC is to occur where $CA < 0$, then a_1 and a_2 must be of opposite sign. Further $MC'' = 2a_2$. Since we wish there to be a contrast deceleration; therefore $a_2 < 0$, which implies $a_1 > 0$. To analyze equation (6), we must use the general solution to a third degree equation given by *Cardan's formulas* (as found, e.g., in L. E. Dickson, *New First Course in the Theory of Equations* [New York: John Wiley, 1939], ch. 5). In order to ensure that the function has only one real root (i.e., that CA, is a "single valued function" of MC_t), we rely on the condition that $b_1 - b_2^2 > 0$, which is a sufficient condition for ensuring a positive radical with a single root. Thus, we get the constraint that $b_2^2 > 3b_1$. These calculations presume that $b_3 = 1$ (which we assume, without consequence for the present analysis).

14. These interpretations would be strictly true only if extremely simple forms were assumed for each of the individual arguments. Nonetheless, it is instructive to rely on these interpretations in discussing the substantive implications of the analysis.

15. Solving equations (5) and (6) in terms of CA, we get $b_1 CA_1 + b_2 CA_t^2 + b_3 CA_t^3 = (a_0 - b_0) + a_1 CA_{t-1} + a_2 CA_{t-1}^2$.

16. O'Donnell, *Modernization and Bureaucratic-Authoritarianism*.

17. Antonio Gramsci, *Selections from the Prison Notebooks of Antonio Gramsci*, Quentin Hoare and Geoffrey Nowell Smith, trans. and eds. (New York: International Publishers, 1971); see also on Mexico, e.g., Gabriel Almond and Sidney Verba, *The Civic Culture* (Princeton, NJ: Princeton University Press, 1963).

18. We should also note that under some circumstances pressures from outside the dependent state may work toward a relaxation of internal coercion. Possibly the current U.S. emphasis on human rights may have this effect; perhaps West European pressures played a significant role in the relaxation of coercion in post–World War II Spain. (Certainly other influences were at work in Spain as well. And Spain is only arguably a "dependent" state in the most common sense in which that term is used.)

19. Latent conflict may also decline over the long run from a combination of highly effective coercion and pervasive ideological indoctrination. If controls over communication (indoctrination) can be maintained, a regime may ultimately decide that overt coercion can be significantly relaxed.

20. We have until now treated the opposition as largely a unitary actor. This was necessary for the model as built, and we justified it partly by specifying a longer reaction time for the opposition (in part not only because it must operate mainly in secret, but also because oppositions are in fact fragmented) than for the regime. On the other hand, an opposition can be so divided that well-organized,

highly motivated, secretive groups are not deterred by moderate levels of coercion. A regime that recognized this, and thought it could keep such opponents politically isolated by a pattern of liberalization, might well be willing to accept violent manifestations of conflict from such a fragment of the opposition.

Chapter 7   Islam, Authoritarianism, and Female Empowerment: What Are the Linkages?

This chapter is reprinted from *World Politics* 56:4 (July 2004), 582–607 with permission by Johns Hopkins University Press. We thank M. Steven Fish for sending us his data; Charli Carpenter, Joshua Goldstein, Ellen Lust-Okar, Alex Mintz, and Kenneth Scheve for helpful comments; and the Ford Foundation for research support. Our data and supplementary tables are available at http://pantheon. yale.edu%7Ebrusset/.

1. M. Steven Fish, "Islam and Authoritarianism," *World Politics* 55 (October 2002), 4–37. Specific page references to Fish's article are embedded in the text.
2. In the political science literature, Adam Przeworski, Michael Alvarez, Jose Cheibub, and Fernando Limongi, *Democracy and Development: Political Institutions and Well-Being in the World, 1950–1990* (New York: Cambridge University Press, 2000) provide perhaps the most persuasive evidence, particularly for the ability of reasonably developed states to sustain democracy once it has been established.
3. See Paul Collier and Anke Hoeffler, *Greed and Grievance in Civil War: Justice Seeking and Loot-Seeking in Civil War* (Washington, DC: World Bank, 2001); James Fearon and David Laitin, "Ethnicity, Insurgency, and Civil War," *American Political Science Review* 97 (February 2003), 75–90. The idea of a "resource curse" is often traced to Jeffrey Sachs and Andrew Warner, "Natural Resource Abundance and Economic Growth," Development Discussion Paper no. 517a (Cambridge, MA: Harvard Institute for International Development, 1995). Michael L. Ross considers fuel (mostly oil and natural gas) and other mineral exports separately but gets somewhat stronger results for fuel; Ross, "Does Oil Hinder Democracy?" *World Politics* 53 (April 2001), 325–61. That also seems more relevant for our focus on Islamic countries, for which petroleum products are more often the principal export. We use the measure of fuel exports as a percentage of GDP; it is more highly correlated with authoritarian government than is OPEC membership.
4. World Bank, *World Development Indicators*, http://devdata.worldbank.org/ dataonline (accessed May 2003). We use the average measure of fuel exports as a percentage of GDP from the period 1991–2000. Data from earlier years were used for Afghanistan, Cambodia, Chad, Democratic Republic of Congo, Cuba, Guinea-Bissau, Guyana, Iraq, Liberia, Myanmar, Rwanda, Sierra Leone, Somalia, and Vietnam.
5. Data for 1990 are mostly from Tatu Vanhanen, "Domestic Ethnic Conflict and Ethnic Nepotism: A Comparative Analysis," *Journal of Peace Research* 36 (January 1999), 55–74.
6. Samuel P. Huntington, *The Third Wave: Democratization in the Late Twentieth Century* (Norman: University of Oklahoma Press, 1991), 46, 273–74.

7. Zeev Maoz, *Domestic Sources of Global Change* (Ann Arbor: University of Michigan Press, 1996).

8. Kristian Skrede Gleditsch, *All International Politics Is Local: The Diffusion of Conflict, Integration, and Democratization* (Ann Arbor: University of Michigan Press, 2002); Jon Pevehouse, *Democracy from Above? Regional Organizations and Democratization* (New York: Cambridge University Press, 2005).

9. Democracy in the neighborhood is the average Polity score of contiguous states 1991–2000; Monte Marshall and Keith Jaggers, *Polity IV Dataset, 2000.* Polity is used more often in the international relations literature than are Freedom House rankings, which begin only in 1973; and the rankings for the 1970s were rather controversial. The difference is nevertheless not consequential, as one would expect by comparing Fish's Tables 2 and 3 with his Tables 4 and 5. Contiguity is coded as either directly contiguous by land or contiguous by sea within ISO miles; Douglas Stinnett, Jaroslav Tir, Philip Schafer, Paul Diehl, and Charles Gochman, "The Correlates of War Project Direct Contiguity Data, Version 3," *Conflict Management and Peace Science* 19 (Fall 2002), 59–68.

10. A classic statement is Harold Lasswell's concept of the garrison-police state, in his *National Security and Individual Freedom* (New York: McGraw Hill, 1950). There is little evidence of an "autocratic peace" corresponding to the peace between democracies. See Mark Peceny and Caroline Beer, with Shannon Sanchez-Terry, "Dictatorial Peace?" *American Political Science Review* 96 (March 2002), 15–26; Mark Peceny and Caroline Beer, "Peaceful Parties and Puzzling Personalists," *American Political Science Review* 97 (May 2003), 339–42; Dan Reiter and Allan C. Stam, "Identifying the Culprit: Democracy, Dictatorship, and Dispute," *American Political Science Review* 97 (May 2003), 333–37.

11. Huntington, *Third Wave*, 270–71.

12. Przeworski et al., *Democracy and Development*; Maoz, *Domestic Sources.*

13. Previous experience with democracy is measured as the average Polity IV Political Competition component score 1970–90. Transitional authority codes were deleted from the analysis. Zero is the lowest level of political competition and 10 is the highest. This index focuses on the presence and fairness of elections.

14. On how an unbalanced sex ratio for unmarried young males may disrupt civil order and encourage autocratic government, see Valerie M. Hudson and Andrea Den Boer, "A Surplus of Men, a Deficit of Peace: Security and Sex Ratios in Asia's Largest States," *International Security* 26 (Spring 2002), 5–28. Similarly, powerful men in polygamous societies control not only women but also the lower-class men who have no wives; see Laura Betzig, *Despotism and Differential Reproduction* (New York: Aldine, 1986). Our analysis below, however, does not find that an imbalanced sex ratio produces authoritarian government generally.

15. Women in parliament is an imperfect measure, since some states with rubber-stamp parliaments have high female participation. We drop the Gender Empowerment Index, which was available to Fish for only 92 countries, of which just 20 are Islamic, as compared with 153 to 156 (up to 47 of them Islamic) for the other empowerment variables. Moreover, we think it preferable to assess the effect of specific women's rights rather than of such an aggregated

measure. It performed less well in Fish's Table 10 and not better than specific measures in his Table 9. Similarly we do not use the Gender Development Index in United Nations Development Programme, *Human Development Report 2002* (New York: Oxford University Press, 2002). An indicator of violence against women would be desirable, but we know of no adequate cross-national database. Low fertility rates might be used as an indicator of female reproductive rights, but they could also reflect coercive population policies enforced on women. Our data are primarily from the *Human Development Report*. See the website appendix for precise definitions and information about missing data. We have changed some signs for consistency, so that all measures of the status of women equate higher values with higher status.

16. "Education shall be free, at least in the elementary and fundamental stages. Elementary education shall be compulsory"; rights "to a standard of living adequate for . . . health and well-being [and] medical care"; "to take part in the government"; and "to just and favorable remuneration insuring an existence worth of human dignity." The declaration, reflecting the usage of 1948, frequently refers to persons with the masculine pronoun.

17. See Hisham Sharabi, *Neopatriarchy: A Theory of Distorted Change in Arab Society* (Oxford: Oxford University Press, 1988) and others cited in Fish's fn. 34 (p. 24). See also Elizabeth Fernea, *In Search of Islamic Feminism: One Woman's Global Journey* (New York: Doubleday, 1998); and essays in Charles Kurzman, ed., *Liberal Islam: A Sourcebook* (Oxford: Oxford University Press, 1998).

18. Alfred Stepan, with Graeme Robertson, "An 'Arab' More Than 'Muslim' Electoral Gap?" *Journal of Democracy* 14 (July 2003), 30–44.

19. Ellen Lust-Okar, "Why the Failure of Democratization? Explaining Middle East Exceptionalism" (Manuscript, New Haven, CT: Yale University Political Science Department, May 2004).

20. Arab League members are Algeria, Bahrain, Comoros, Djibuti, Egypt, Iraq, Jordan, Kuwait, Lebanon, Libya, Mauritania, Morocco, Oman, Qatar, Saudi Arabia, Somalia, Sudan, Syria, Tunisia, UAE, and Yemen.

21. See Rafael Reuveny and Quan Li, "The Joint Democracy-Dyadic Conflict Nexus: A Simultaneous Equations Model," *International Studies Quarterly* 47 (September 2003), 371–94. Pevehouse, *Democracy from Above?* (fn. 8) finds that *internal violence* often precedes transitions to democracy. Arab and MID involvement are only moderately correlated (.43). For data source, see the appendix on our website. The period corresponds to that used for democracy in the neighborhood.

22. The Freedom House civil liberties checklist does include the following item (D.4): "Are there personal social freedoms, including gender equality, choice of marriage partners, and size of family?" But it is only 1 item out of the 14 that constitute the civil liberties scale, which in turn is only half of the total Freedom score, so it does not seriously contaminate use of that score as a dependent variable. We retain Fish's preference for measuring regime as a continuous rather than a dichotomous variable—as Przeworski et al., *Democracy and Development*, do—despite some reservations about the truly interval character of Freedom House and Polity scores; see James Vreeland, "A Continuous Shumpeterian Conception of Democracy" (Manuscript, New Haven, CT: Yale University Political Science Department, April 2003).

23. He surprisingly omits OPEC membership from this table.
24. This was a hard test, and even if Islam proved insignificant here it might well be that Islam had reduced democracy in the earlier period.
25. Another variant of the MID measure—uses of military force over a longer preceding period (1970–90)—leaves Islam statistically insignificant and Arab statistically significant in all equations, but that analysis omits many successor states to Yugoslavia and the Soviet Union. To lean against our own hypothesis and in favor of Fish's, we do not present it in the main text.
26. A correlation matrix in the website appendix includes most variables. Many variables of female empowerment not shown are highly correlated with one another (but only one appears in any equation) and with Islamic population (as Fish hypothesizes). To check for multicollinearity we entered the independent variables in this sequence: economic development, Islamic population, a measure of female empowerment, fuel exports, neighborhood, previous democracy, Arab League, and MID. Four female-empowerment measures (sex ratio, women in parliament, education ratio, and life expectancy) *were* insignificant in the presence of only economic development and Islamic population. Economic activity ratio became insignificant when fuel exports were added, as did literacy when Arab League was added. Only women in government stayed significant in the full model. A more systematic check computed the Variance Inflation Factor (VIF) for each model of our tables. It increases our confidence that multi-collinearity is not distorting coefficient estimates. The mean VIF for the models of table 7.1 did not exceed 2.09, nor 1.79 in table 7.2; the highest VIF for an individual variable never exceeded 2.32. In table 7.3 only economic development possibly warranted concern, with a VIF ranging from 5.52 to 5.56 (but well below 10.0 for a definite problem). To be sure, we reran those equations without economic development and found few changes. The effects of Islamic population and Arab League remained the same; democracy became nonsignificant for the sex ratio after being marginally significant in table 7.3.
27. Our variable measures the percentage of women serving in government at the ministerial level in 1996. See the website appendix to compare our measure with that of Fish.
28. Huntington, *Third Wave*, 72–85. See also Scott Mainwaring, *The Catholic Church and Politics in Brazil, 1916–1985* (Stanford, CA: Stanford University Press, 1986); "Democratic Survivability in Latin America," in Howard Handelman and Mark Tessler, eds., *Democracy and Its Limits: Lessons from Asia, Latin America and the Middle East* (Notre Dame, IN: University of Notre Dame Press, 1999); Eric Hanson, *The Catholic Church in World Politics* (Princeton, NJ: Princeton University Press, 1987); and Daniel Philpott, "The Catholic Wave," *Journal of Democracy* 15 (April 2004), 32–36.
29. It is impossible to reproduce the full model from column 4 of table 7.1, because not all the necessary data are available and sufficiently reliable. For democracy we use Polity scores (averaged over the decade in question), since Freedom House began its coding only in 1974. Measures of economic development and MID involvement are readily available for the earlier decades. So is previous experience with democracy, except we omit it for the 1960s because there were so many recently independent former colonies. Economic development and previous experience are averaged over each decade to maximize the number of

observations. MID involvement is taken as a count over each decade. Lacking data on fuel exports we revert to OPEC membership as a proxy. Islamic and Catholic population percentages are relatively constant. Arab League membership changes, but the 2000 membership is still appropriate as a proxy for Arab population. We drop democratic neighborhood because it would require too much new data gathering on changes of borders and sovereign status. Measures of female empowerment in these years suffer from too many problems of data availability and quality—and they show hardly any impact in table 7.1 anyway.

30. The relationship remained positive in the 1990s, but only at $p < .05$ as democracy spread to Asia and elsewhere.

31. See Adam Przeworski, Jose Cheibub, and Fernando Limongi, "Culture and Democracy," *World Culture Report: Culture, Creativity and Market* (Paris: UNESCO Publishing, 1998). The authors identify three sets of views on whether democracy requires certain cultural preconditions: nonculturalist, weakly culturalist, and strongly culturalist.

32. Level of education is measured by the combined primary, secondary, and tertiary gross enrollment rates as percentage of population for 1999. The source is United Nations Development Programme, *Human Development Report*; missing observations filled in with 1996 data from World Bank, *World Development Indicators*.

33. Percentage of population living in urban areas in 1997. Sources as in fn. 32. Education and urbanization are highly correlated with development and each other (see website appendix table), though not with democracy. We include all for the sake of identifying any remaining contribution of Islam, even though it may be hard to identify from the separate contributions.

34. Although we suggest this possibility, its correctness is not obvious. Agrarian production often requires women's full participation in the fields with men, getting them out of the house in ways that may be less available in urban society.

35. "Comparative Public Health," ch. 4 in this book.

36. As military conflict seems to be bad news for democracy, it may also be bad news for women's rights, as much feminist writing suggests. See Cynthia Enloe, *The Morning After: Sexual Politics at the End of the Cold War* (Berkeley and Los Angeles: University of California Press, 1993); Ann Tickner, *Gendering World Politics: Issues and Approaches in the Post–Cold War Era* (New York: Columbia University Press, 2001); V. Spike Peterson and Anne Sisson Runyon, *Global Gender Issues* (Boulder, CO: Westview, 1999, 2nd edition); Melvin Ember, Carol Ember, and Bruce Russett, "Inequality and Democracy in the Anthropological Record," in Manus Midlarsky, ed., *Inequality, Democracy, and Economic Development* (Cambridge: Cambridge University Press, 1997); Joshua Goldstein, *War and Gender* (Cambridge: Cambridge University Press, 2001); and Mary Caprioli, "Gendered Conflict," *Journal of Peace Research* 37 (January 2000), 51–68. But when we added MIDs to the equations for women's rights, it was never significant (equations not shown here).

37. We used a Durbin-Wu-Hausman test to check for possible endogeneity of democracy to women's status and vice versa. We found indications that democracy is endogenous to three of our measures of women's status at most: women in government, education ratio, and economic activity ratio. No measures of women's status were endogenous to democracy. This weak evidence of endogeneity indicates little need to create simultaneous equation models.

38. The sex imbalance may result from Arab countries' relative denial of education, health care, nutrition, and economic independence to women. It is unlikely, however, that it results from practices of infanticide or sex-selective abortion. The former is uncommon in Islamic societies, and the latter is more likely to be practiced by nontraditional secular individuals.

39. Nor are the results different when Catholic is substituted for Islamic, except that democracy falls just short ($p < .06$) of the $p < .05$ level, which was barely reached by Islamic.

40. The matter of women's participation in high levels of the political system is nonetheless complex. We created an interactive variable, GDP x regime score. For women in parliament and our measure of women in government, the individual terms were significantly negative and the interaction significantly positive, meaning women did worse in wealthy autocracies and low-income democracies. Nepal, Central African Republic, and Papua New Guinea are examples of low-income democracies with poor representation of women in parliament and government, and Singapore and most oil-rich Arab states are high-income autocracies with almost no government posts occupied by women.

41. For example, Przeworski et al., *Democracy and Development*. It is worth noting that no relationship between female empowerment and political freedom in Arab states is found in the *Arab Human Development Report 2002* (New York: United Nations Development Programme, 2002), ch. 2.

42. For example, Iraq in 2003 was a very unpromising field in which to plant democracy. All the negative influences in table 7.1, in addition to Islamic and Arab population, were present: fuel exports, low income, bad neighborhood, no history of democracy, and many MIDs.

Chapter 8 The Mysterious Case of Vanishing Hegemony, or, Is Mark Twain Really Dead?

This chapter is reprinted from *International Organization* 39 (Spring 1985), 207–31 with permission by Cambridge University Press. I am grateful to the Netherlands Institute for Advanced Study where I wrote this, to the General Service Corporation and the Yale Center for International and Area Studies for financial support, and to Robert Keohane, Stephen Krasner, Jim Lindsay, Susan Strange, William R. Thompson, and H. Bradford Westerfield for insightful comments.

1. For example, Susan Strange, "Cave! Hic Dragones: A Critique of Regime Analysis," *International Organization* 36 (Spring 1982), 299–324.

2. See Richard Rosecrance's "Introduction" to his edited volume, *America as an Ordinary Country* (Ithaca, NY: Cornell University Press, 1976), 1; Kenneth A. Oye, "The Domain of Choice," in Kenneth A. Oye, Donald Rothchild, and Robert J. Lieber, eds., *Eagle Entangled: U.S. Foreign Policy in a Complex World* (New York: Longman, 1979), 4–5; and George Liska, *Career of Empire* (Baltimore, MD: Johns Hopkins University Press, 1978), ch. 10.

3. See Robert Gilpin, *U.S. Power and the Multinational Corporation: The Political Economy of Direct Foreign Investment* (New York: Basic Books, 1975), and

Robert Gilpin, *War and Change in the International System* (Cambridge: Cambridge University Press, 1981), 231: "By the 1980s the Pax Americana was in a state of disarray"; Stephen Krasner, "Transforming International Regimes: What the Third World Wants and Why," *International Studies Quarterly* 25 (March 1981), 119–48; Charles Kindleberger, "Systems of International Economic Organization," in David Calleo, ed., *Money and the Coming World Order* (New York: New York University Press, 1976); and also many of the contributors to the special issue of *International Organization* 36 (Spring 1982). Robert O. Keohane's *After Hegemony: Cooperation and Discord in the World Political System* (Princeton, NJ: Princeton University Press, 1984) represents a special case. His is the most sophisticated version of hegemonic stability theory, and he explicitly argues against equating a decline in power base with an equivalent decline in the characteristics of a regime. Nevertheless he repeatedly uses such phrases as "a post-hegemony world" (p. 216) and "the legacy of American hegemony" and "hegemony will not be restored in our lifetime" (p. 244), justifying the book's title. The only strong emphasis on the continuity of American power that I have been able to find is Susan Strange, "Still an Extraordinary Power: America's Role in a Global Monetary System," in Raymond E. Lombra and William E. Witte, eds., *Political Economy of International and Domestic Monetary Relations* (Ames: Iowa State University Press, 1982).

4. Keohane, *After Hegemony*, identifies four criteria by which to judge a hegemon of world political economy: a preponderance of material resources in raw materials, capital, markets, and production of highly valued goods. A broader view of hegemony, however, requires inclusion of military, scientific, and other resources.

5. For example, Mark E. Rupert and David P. Rapkin, "The Erosion of U.S. Leadership Capabilities," in Paul Johnson and William R. Thompson, eds., *Rhythms in International Politics and Economics* (New York: Praeger, 1985).

6. See, for instance, Kenneth Waltz, *Theory of International Politics* (Reading, MA: Addison-Wesley, 1979), esp. ch. 7, who regards the United States as more autonomous, and hence stronger, than more internationally involved states.

7. Karl W. Deutsch, *The Analysis of International Relations* (Englewood Cliffs, NJ: Prentice-Hall, 1978, 2nd edition).

8. Robert O. Keohane and Joseph Nye, *Power and Interdependence* (Boston: Little, Brown, 1977), 44, and Stephen Krasner, "Structural Causes and Regime Consequences: Regimes as Intervening Variables," *International Organization* 36 (Spring 1982), 199.

9. Timothy J. McKeown, "Tariffs and Hegemonic Stability Theory," *International Organization* 37 (Winter 1983), 73–93, and Keohane, *After Hegemony*, 37.

10. Duncan Snidal, "Public Goods, Property Rights, and Political Organization," *International Studies Quarterly* 23 (December 1979), 532–66.

11. Stephen Krasner, "State Power and the Structure of International Trade," *World Politics* 27 (April 1975), 314–47, and John Ruggie's review of Krasner's book in *American Political Science Review* 74 (March 1980), 296–99.

12. Joe Oppenheimer, "Collective Goods and Alliances: A Reassessment," *Journal of Conflict Resolution* 23 (September 1979), 387–407.

13. George Modelski, "The Long Cycle of Global Politics and the Nation-State," *Comparative Studies in Society and History* 20 (April 1978), 214–35.

14. Karl W. Deutsch, Sidney Burrell, Robert Kann, Maurice Lee, Martin Lichterman, Raymond Lingdren, Francis Loewenheim, and Richard Van Wagenen, *Political Community and the North Atlantic Area* (Princeton, NJ: Princeton University Press, 1957).

15. Giovanni Arrighi, "A Crisis of Hegemony," in Samir Amin, Giovanni Arrighi, Andre Gunder Frank, and Immanuel Wallerstein, eds., *Dynamics of Global Crisis* (New York: Monthly Review Press, 1982), 77.

16. I am aware that much of the hegemonic stability literature; e.g., a "founding father," Charles Kindleberger, *The World in Depression, 1929–1939* (Berkeley: University of California Press, 1973), is concerned with very specific issue-areas and goods rather than with such broader achievements or "goods" as "peace and prosperity." Focus on narrow issue-areas makes the thesis of a decline in American hegemony more plausible—at least for those selected issue-areas. Nevertheless, issue-areas are usually selected because they are assumed, implicitly or explicitly, to be symptomatic of a broad decline in U.S. ability to maintain the conditions of global prosperity. "Peace" among industrial capitalist powers (and containment of the Soviet Union) is one of those conditions. Thus, while some hegemonic stability writing can escape the strictures of my critique, a general evaluation of the state of American "hegemony" and its consequences—an evaluation that is both common and necessary—must carry the discussion beyond selected, rather narrow issue-areas. Gilpin, *War and Change*, and many of the contributors to the Spring 1982 special issue *of International Organization* would surely agree.

17. See Bruce Russett and Harvey Starr, *World Politics: The Menu for Choice* (New York: W. H. Freeman, 1981, 1st edition), ch. 15, and Michael Doyle, "Kant, Liberal Legacies, and Foreign Affairs, parts 1 and 2" *Philosophy and Public Affairs* 12 (Summer and Fall 1983), 205–35; 323–53.

18. The terms are, respectively, from Deutsch et al., *Political Community*, and Kenneth E. Boulding, *Stable Peace* (Austin: University of Texas Press, 1978).

19. See Melvin Small and J. David Singer, "The War-Proneness of Democratic Regimes, 1815–1965," *Jerusalem Journal of International Relations* 1:1 (1976), 50–69.

20. Not to me the most persuasive explanation, though see Erich Weede, "Extended Deterrence by Superpower Alliance," *Journal of Conflict Resolution* 27 (June 1983), 231–53.

21. Krasner, "Structural Causes," 185.

22. Robert Jervis, "Security Regimes," *International Organization* 36 (Spring 1982), 371.

23. See Arend Lijphart, *The Trauma of Decolonization: The Dutch and West New Guinea* (New Haven, CT: Yale University Press, 1966), ch. 11; and Townsend Hoopes, *The Devil and John Foster Dulles* (Boston, MA: Little, Brown, 1973), 384.

24. See Zalmay Khalilzad, "Islamic Iran: Soviet Dilemma," *Problems of Communism* 33 (January–February 1984), 1–20.

25. Keohane, *After Hegemony*, 34.

26. Melvin Small and J. David Singer, *Resort to Arms* (Beverly Hills, CA: Sage, 1982), 134.

27. For the comparative data on trade, I am indebted to Susan Strange, "Protectionism and World Politics," *International Organization* 39 (Spring

1985), 235–59. Helen Hughes and Jean Waelbroeck, "Foreign Trade and Structural Adjustment—Is There a New Protectionism?" in Hans-Gert Braun et al., eds., *The European Economy in the 1980s* (Aldershot: Gower, 1983), reply that the increase in protectionism during the 1970s was very small. There is some evidence that protectionism rises during periods of cyclical economic downturn, but those increases must not be mistaken for long-term trends. On the collapse of the Bretton Woods fixed-exchange-rate system see Hugh Patrick and Henry Rosovsky ("The End of Eras? Japan and the Western World in the 1970–1980s," paper presented at the Japan Political Economy Research Conference, Honolulu, July 1983, 38): "In our view, despite excessively wide swings in real rates among currencies, the flexible exchange rate system was a way of maintaining the liberal international economic order rather than being a cause of its demise." Also see Keohane, *After Hegemony*, 213: "Substantial erosion of the trade regime . . . has occurred, but . . . what is equally striking is the persistence of cooperation even if not always addressed to liberal ends. Trade wars have not taken place, despite economic distress. On the contrary, what we see are intensive efforts at cooperation, in response to discord in textiles, steel, electronics, and other areas." On liberalization of the Japanese economy see Raymond Vernon, *Two Hungry Giants: The United States and Japan in the Quest for Oil and Ores* (Cambridge, MA: Harvard University Press, 1983).

28. Arrighi, "A Crisis of Hegemony," 65. One could quarrel with the use of "national interest," and qualify it by reference to the interests of the ruling classes, but on the whole I am not inclined to do so—major qualification would require some near-heroic assumptions about false consciousness.

29. Hedley Bull, *The Anarchical Society* (New York: Columbia University Press, 1977).

30. Robert O. Keohane, "The Demand for International Regimes," *International Organization* 36 (Spring 1982), 348. Keohane's discussion is reminiscent of Karl W. Deutsch, *The Nerves of Government* (New York: Free Press, 1963).

31. Robert Axelrod, *The Evolution of Cooperation* (New York: Basic Books, 1984).

32. Keohane, *After Hegemony*, 270: "So the United States farsightedly made short-term sacrifices—in growing financial aid, and in permitting discrimination against American exports— in order to accomplish the longer-term objective of creating a stable and prosperous international economic order in which liberal capitalism would prevail and American influence would be predominant." The proposition that the burdens of empire almost inevitably outweigh its benefits is of course a common one. Note Mark Elvin, *The Pattern of the Chinese Past* (London: Methuen, 1973), 19: "The burdens of size consist mainly in the need to maintain a more extended bureaucracy with more intermediate layers, the growing difficulties of effective co-ordination as territorial area increases, and the heavier costs of maintaining troops on longer front lines further removed from the main sources of trustworthy manpower and supplies."

33. See Russett and Starr, *World Politics*, ch. 18.

34. Bruce Russett, *What Price Vigilance? The Burdens of National Defense* (New Haven, CT: Yale University Press, 1970), ch. 4.

35. Karen Rasler and William R. Thompson, "Global Wars, Public Debts, and the Long Cycle," *World Politics* 36 (October 1983), 489–516, carefully recognize

the particular private benefits, to the commercially extended hegemon, of providing defense and deterrence for others. This should be set against the more familiar argument that military expenditures become a private "bad" by inhibiting capital formation and growth in the hegemon. For evidence, see Karen Rasler and William R. Thompson, "Defense Burdens, Capital Formation, and Economic Growth: The Systemic Leader Case," *Journal of Conflict Resolution* 32 (March 1998), 61–86.

36. Arthur A. Stein, "The Hegemon's Dilemma: Great Britain, the United States, and the International Economic Order," *International Organization* 38 (Spring 1984), 355–86. For the argument that free trade is not necessarily a collective good, see John Conybeare, "Public Goods, Prisoners' Dilemma, and the International Political Economy," *International Studies Quarterly* 28 (March 1984), 5–22.

37. Arrighi, "A Crisis of Hegemony," 57.

38. Edward R. Tufte, *Political Control of the Economy* (Princeton, NJ: Princeton University Press, 1980); Daniel Ellsberg, *Papers on the War* (New York: Simon and Schuster, 1972); and Leslie Gelb and Richard Betts, *The System Worked: The Irony of Vietnam* (Washington, DC: Brookings, 1979).

39. In his brilliant article, Duncan Snidal, "Hegemonic Stability Theory Revisited," *International Organization* 39 (Autumn 1985), 579–614, notes that both Krasner, "State Power," and Gilpin, *War and Change*, fully recognize the degree to which the postwar regimes benefited the United States in particular, and that Gilpin particularly argues that the United States was significantly able to extract contributions as a quasi-government.

40. See Keohane, *After Hegemony*.

41. That is, persuading someone to do something he or she would not otherwise do; see Robert A. Dahl, *Modern Political Analysis* (Englewood Cliffs, NJ: Prentice-Hall, 1984, 4th edition).

42. According to Robert W. Cox and Harold K. Jacobson ("The United States and World Order: On Structures of World Power and Structural Transformation," paper presented at the Twelfth World Congress of the International Political Science Association, Rio de Janeiro, August 1982, 7) "World hegemony is founded through a process of cultural and ideological development. This process is rooted mainly in the civil society of the founding country, though it has the support of the state in that country, and it extends to include groups from other countries." Also see Norbert Elias, *The Civilizing Process*, vol. 2: *State Formation and Civilization* (Oxford: Blackwell, 1982): "Just as it was not possible in the West itself, from a certain stage of interdependence onwards, to rule people solely by force and physical threats, so it also became necessary, in maintaining an empire that went beyond mere plantation-land and plantation-labour, to rule people in part through themselves, through the moulding of their superegos. . . . The outsiders absorb the code of the established groups and thus undergo a process of assimilation. Their own affect-control, their own conduct, obeys the rules of the established groups. Partially they identify themselves with them, and even though the identification may show strong ambivalencies, still their own conscience, their whole superego apparatus, follows more or less the pattern of the established groups." Neither of these statements is meant to deny some reciprocal role of elites in the periphery in helping to shape the dominant world culture.

43. They form, for instance, a key element in Hayward Alker's conception of power. See his "Power in a Schedule Sense," in Alker, Karl W. Deutsch, and Antoine Stoetzel, eds., *Mathematical Approaches to Politics* (San Francisco, CA: Jossey-Bass, 1972).

44. Arthur A. Stein, "Coordination and Collaboration: Regimes in an Anarchic World," *International Organization* 36 (Spring 1982), 324.

Chapter 9   Theater Nuclear Forces: Public Opinion in Western Europe

Donald R. DeLuca holds a Ph.D. in Sociology, and when the Roper Center had an office at Yale he directed its Office of Teaching and Research.

This chapter is reprinted by permission from *Political Science Quarterly* 98 (Summer 1983), 179–96.

1. For example, see John P. Robinson, *Polls Apart* (Cabin John, MD: Seven Locks Press, 1982).

2. *Gallup Political Index* 268 (December 1982), 20; and Elisabeth Noelle-Neumann, ed., *The Germans: Public Opinion Polls, 1967–1980* (London: Greenwood Press, 1981), 490.

3. *Eurobarometre* 13 (June 1980), 20.

4. These fears of the United States are greatest in Britain. In January 1983, the following question was posed: "Who is more likely to initiate a nuclear attack in Europe, the United States or the Soviet Union?" The results were 28 percent for the United States and 48 percent for the Soviet Union. In West Germany, the division was 20 to 45 percent, and in France 12 to 65 percent. (The remainder in each country had no opinion.) See *Newsweek*, International Edition, 31 (January 1983), 11.

5. Opinion Research Limited survey, *New York Times*, February 16, 1983.

6. *Gallup Opinion Index* (Britain) 267 (November 1982), 14.

7. Gallup Poll news release, February 3, 1983, for the American data.

8. Noelle-Neumann, ed., *The Germans*, 420.

9. Four surveys taken between 1977 and 1981 asked respondents' preference for working more closely with each (or both) of the two superpowers. About one-half (49 to 56 percent) chose "prefer to work more closely with the U.S.," while about one-third (32 to 41 percent) indicated that they "prefer to work equally closely with U.S. and U.S.S.R." See Elisabeth Noelle-Neumann, "Breite Mehrheit," *Capital* (August 1981), 90.

10. This analysis is of data from *Eurobarometre* 14 (December 1980), including a cross-tabulation of two items from that survey: military alliance policy preference against preferred levels of spending on defense.

11. Albert Du Roy, "Montee du Neutralisme," *Samedi*, November 21, 1981.

12. Thirty-six percent said they did believe in the Russians' sincerity in July 1981, as compared with 48 percent who expressed disbelief. The break was 17 to 57 percent in April 1959. Elisabeth Noelle-Neumann, "Are the Germans 'Collapsing' or 'Standing Firm'?" *Encounter* (1981), 76–81.

13. U.S. International Communication Agency Surveys, April 21, 1981 and June 1, 1981. The USICA, now the USIA, and other organizations have continued to

ask questions regarding the emplacement of cruise missiles. They have obtained similar results whenever the question is asked in a form that is at all unbiased. Three British surveys in January and February 1983 showed clear majorities against cruise missile deployment in that country. See *The Guardian*, January 24, 1983, the *Sunday Times*, January 23, 1983, and *New York Times*, February 16, 1983. The five-year trends in virtually all of this material, moreover, are definitely unfavorable to deployment.

14. Noelle-Neumann, "Are the Germans 'Collapsing'?" and Noelle-Neumann, "Breite Mehrheit," 88.

15. Noelle-Neumann, ed., *The Germans*, and Noelle-Neumann "Breite Mehrheit," 88.

16. Alain Enthoven and Wayne Smith, *How Much is Enough* (New York: Harper and Row, 1971), discussed the reality behind contemporary evaluations of the European military balance. In strategic missiles, we now know the United States had a ten-to-one superiority at the time of the Cuban missile crisis.

17. Harris surveys as reported in Connie DeBoer, "The Polls: Our Commitment to World War III," *Public Opinion Quarterly* 45 (1981), 129.

18. Earlier surveys demonstrating the same point are found in United States Advisory Commission on Information, *28th Report to Congress* (Washington, DC: U.S. Government Printing Office,1977), 122.

19. Michael Howard, "Reassurance and Deterrence: Western Defense in the 1980s," *Foreign Affairs* 61 (Winter 1982–83), 309–24.

20. MARPLAN survey, November 1980, conducted for *Weekend World*, and survey conducted by National Opinion Polls, reported in *Political, Social, Economic Review* 34 (December 1981), 24.

21. Leo Crespi, "West European Perceptions of the U.S.," paper presented to the Convention of the International Society of Political Psychology, June 1982.

22. The most prominent advocacy of a "no-first-use" posture in Europe is by McGeorge Bundy, George Kennan, Robert McNamara, and Gerard Smith, "Nuclear Weapons and the Atlantic Alliance," *Foreign Affairs* 60 (Spring 1982), 753–68. This view has been criticized by Karl Kaiser, Georg Leber, Alois Mertes, and Franz-Josef Schulze, "Nuclear Weapons and the Preservation of Peace: A German Response," *Foreign Affairs* 60 (Summer 1982), 1157–70. General Bernard Rogers, "The Atlantic Alliance: Prescriptions for a Difficult Decade," *Foreign Affairs* 60 (Summer 1982), 1145–56, presents a strong case that at least a "no-early-first-use" policy is feasible for NATO. See also John Mearsheimer, "Why the Soviets Can't Win Quickly in Central Europe," *International Security* 7 (Summer 1982), 3–39, for a good argument that a "no-first-use" policy is militarily attainable.

Chapter 10 Away from Nuclear Mythology

This chapter is reprinted from Dagobert L. Brito, Michael D. Intriligator, and Adele E. Wick, eds., *Strategies for Managing Nuclear Proliferation* (Lexington, MA: Lexington Books, 1983). It was written as a commentary on a chapter by Kenneth Waltz in the same book.

1. Kenneth N. Waltz, "Toward Nuclear Peace," in Dagobert L. Brito, Michael D. Intriligator, and Adele E. Wick, eds., *Strategies for Managing Nuclear Proliferation* (Lexington, MA: Lexington Books, 1983), 117–33. All quotations from Waltz are indicated by page numbers in the text.

2. The orthodoxy on this issue has recently been broken by several academic writers (not to mention earlier breaks by the governments that have themselves moved to acquire weapons). Waltz himself has upheld this theme for several years, as have Dagobert Brito and Michael Intriligator; e.g., their "Proliferation and the Probability of War: Global and Regional Issues," in Dagobert Brito, Michael Intriligator, and Adele Wick, eds., *Strategies*, 135–44. Where Brito and Intriligator share some of Waltz's unfortunate assumptions, I include them in my criticism. But because their chapter is considerably more restrained in its claims I concentrate on Waltz's contribution. Also see Bruce Bueno de Mesquita and William Riker, "An Assessment of the Merits of Selective Nuclear Proliferation," *Journal of Conflict Resolution* 26 (June 1982), 283–306.

3. David Garnham, "Dyadic International War, 1816–1965," *Western Political Quarterly* 29 (June 1976), 231–42; Garnham, "Power Parity and Lethal International Violence," *Journal of Conflict Resolution* 20 (September 1976), 379–94; A. F. K. Organski and Jacek Kugler, *The War Ledger* (Chicago, IL: University of Chicago Press, 1980); R. J. Rummel, *The Dimensions of Nations* (Beverly Hills, CA: Sage, 1972); Erich Weede, "Overwhelming Preponderance as a Pacifying Condition among Contiguous Asian Dyads, 1950–1969," *Journal of Conflict Resolution* 20 (September 1976), 395–411.

4. Wayne Ferris, *The Power Capabilities of Nation-States* (Lexington, MA: Lexington Books, 1973).

5. David Singer, Stuart Bremer, and John Stuckey, "Capability Distribution, Uncertainty, and Major Power War, 1820–1965," in Bruce Russett, ed., *Peace, War, and Numbers* (Beverly Hills, CA: Sage, 1972); Bruce Bueno de Mesquita, "Risk, Power Distributions, and the Likelihood of War," *International Studies Quarterly* 25 (December 1981), 541–68.

6. See Randolph Siverson and Michael P. Sullivan, "War, Power, and the International Elephant," paper presented at the Annual Meeting of the International Studies Association, Cincinnati, OH, 1982.

7. He refers to this mistakenly as "a different kind of reasoning." He means only that nuclear weapons radically change the probabilities and utilities, not the rational process.

8. Paul Bracken, *The Command of Strategic Forces* (New Haven, CT: Yale University Press, 1983).

9. Harvey Starr and Benjamin Most, "A Return Journey: Richardson, 'Frontiers' and Wars in the 1946–1965 Era," *Journal of Conflict Resolution* 22 (September 1978), 441–67.

10. International Institute for Strategic Studies (IISS), *The Military Balance, 1969–1970* (London: IISS, 1969).

11. Brito and Intriligator, "Proliferation and the Probability of War," in Brito, Intriligator, and Wick, eds., *Strategies*.

12. See Organski and Kugler, *The War Ledger*, for a comparative analysis of cases that suggests nuclear weapons did not play a significant role in preventing war.

13. McGeorge Bundy, "To Cap the Volcano," *Foreign Affairs* 48 (October 1969), 10.

14. Experts include also see Desmond Ball, *Can Nuclear War Be Controlled?* Adelphi Paper no. 161 (London: International Institute for Strategic Studies, 1981); Bracken, *Command of Strategic Forces*; John Steinbruner, "Nuclear Decapitation," *Foreign Policy* 45 (Winter 1981–82), 16–28; McGeorge Bundy, George Kennan, Robert McNamara, and Gerard Smith, "Nuclear Weapons and the Atlantic Alliance," *Foreign Affairs* 60 (Spring 1982), 753–768. The quotation is from General Arthur S. Collins, Jr., "Theatre Nuclear Warfare: The Battlefield," in John F. Reichart and Steven R. Sturm, eds., *American Defense Policy* (Baltimore, MD: Johns Hopkins University Press, 1982, 5th edition), 359–60.

15. Brito and Intriligator, "Proliferation and the Probability of War," in Brito, Intriligator, and Wick, eds., *Strategies*.

16. Steinbruner, "Nuclear Decapitation."

17. David Jodice and Charles L. Taylor, *World Handbook of Political and Social Indicators*, vol. 2: *Political Events*. (New Haven, CT: Yale University Press, 1983, 3rd edition).

18. Jonathan Schell, *The Fate of the Earth* (New York: Knopf, 1982).

Chapter 11   What Makes Deterrence Work?
Cases from 1900 to 1980

This chapter is reprinted from *World Politics* 36:4 (July 1990), 496–524 with permission from Johns Hopkins University Press. For comments and assistance, we thank Robert Axelrod, Roy Behr, Bruce Bueno de Mesquita, Mark Hanson, Paul Kennedy, Jeffrey Klugman, Ed Lazarus, Richard Ned Lebow, Patrick Morgan, Yoshitaka Nishizawa, Steven Rosenstone, and Yagil Weinberg.

1. Patrick Morgan, *Deterrence: A Conceptual Analysis* (Beverly Hills, CA: Sage, 1983, 2nd edition), 11.

2. Ibid., 30.

3. Bruce Russett, "The Calculus of Deterrence," *Journal of Conflict Resolution* 7 (March 1963), 97–109. The logic of this analysis was extended, and difficulties in comprehending the reasons for success and failure delineated further, in Bruce Russett, "Pearl Harbor: Deterrence Theory and Decision Theory," *Journal of Peace Research* 4 (1967), 89–105.

4. Morgan, *Deterrence*, 38, also used a fourth criterion requiring that the leaders of the attacker state desist primarily because of the retaliatory threat. Such a judgment cannot be made definitively. But in all the cases that met our other criteria, we are satisfied that a failure to attack was largely because of the defender's threat.

5. See especially the argument in Bruce Bueno de Mesquita, *The War Trap* (New Haven, CT: Yale University Press, 1981), 27–29.

6. Decisions to threaten a smaller state with attack usually are the result of substantial premeditation (resulting from previously perceived opportunities or provocations), even when they are triggered by a short-term crisis. Similarly, decisions to counter such a threat are usually (though less often) presaged by deliberation or contingency planning.

7. Thomas C. Schelling, *The Strategy of Conflict* (Cambridge, MA: Harvard University Press, 1960), 3–20.
8. Formally, the attacker will fight if $U_{a1} (p) + U_{a2} (1 - p) > U$ where U_{a1} is the utility of attacking if the defender resists, U_{a2} is the utility of attacking if the defender does not resist, U_{a3} is the utility of no attack, and p is the attacker's subjective probability that the defender will resist. If the defender had full freedom of action to decide whether to resist or not only after attacker had committed himself, the utility calculation would be simple: fight only if $U_{ta} > U_{rb}$, where U_{ta} is the utility of resisting an attack and U_{rb} the utility of not resisting. But since much of deterrence consists in committing oneself to irreversible acts (with which one might in the end wish one did not have to follow through), the defender too must calculate from the beginning the probability that the attacker will indeed attack, and the defender's own utilities from the "attacker's' nonattack (if deterrence succeeds) as well as from attack. Hence the symmetrical formula for the defender in deciding whether to commit himself to fight: $U_{r2} (q) + U_{r2} (1 - q) > U_r$ where q is the probability that deterrence will fail. In deciding on the probability the other will fight, each must estimate the other's utilities. In doing so each must make some judgment about whether the other is risk-averse or risk-acceptant. We include a measure for that element in the analysis below. This presentation assumes cardinal calculations of utility and probability; of course few if any political decision makers attach such firm calculations to decisions they make. Nevertheless a rational decision maker has to operate in some crude approximation of this fashion, with estimates of more and less, and our ultimate conclusions do not depend on our assumption being a perfect representation of reality.
9. The systematic evidence on this point is against attributing great importance to the military balance. Erich Weede, "Extended Deterrence by Superpower Alliance," *Journal of Conflict Resolution* (June 1982), 231–54, reports evidence that *mutual* nuclear deterrence prevents war not only between the superpowers, but between their allies across the alliance divide. A. F. K. Organski and Jacek Kugler, *The War Ledger* (Chicago, IL: University of Chicago Press, 1980), ch. 4, find nuclear powers prevailed in only about half of the deterrence crises studied, though local conventional superiority did seem to help. Jacek Kugler, "Terror without Deterrence," *Journal of Conflict Resolution* 28 (September 1984), 470–506, reports similar results, and that even nuclear monopoly (much less if both powers have a nuclear option) brought a favorable outcome only half the time. Russett, "Calculus of Deterrence," reports the irrelevance of both conventional and strategic superiority, and both he and Bueno de Mesquita, *The War Trap*, ch. 5, report the inferior predictive power of the military balance as compared with a full expected-utility model. Randolph Siverson and Michael Tennefoss, "Alliance, Power, and the Escalation of Conflicts: 1815–1965" (Mimeo, Davis: University of California, 1982), find that minor powers with major-power allies are less likely to be the targets of threat than are minor powers without such allies, and that minor powers with major-power allies are less likely to have those threats escalate to war. Nevertheless, all these studies (least *The War Trap*) suffer from challengeable decisions about case selection or measurement, and the results are hardly definitive. More broadly in the literature, there is some evidence that wars are more likely between states of near-equal

power than between states of very disparate power. But it is still not clear whether that statement merely says that states very different in power are unlikely to go to war (they don't "need" to, because it is clear who would win), and whether the war-among-near-equals phenomenon is really a result of changing power relationships in the region of near equality. On this see Bruce Russett and Harvey Starr, *World Politics: The Menu for Choice* (San Francisco: W. H. Freeman, 1981), 119.

10. Alexander George and Richard Smoke, *Deterrence in American Foreign Policy* (New York: Columbia University Press, 1974), 52.

11. This is not to imply that it will have the *same* value on both sides of the equation, only that a more valuable protégé will have greater value on both sides than would a less valuable protégé. Western Europe is a case in point. Presumably its value is much greater (prosperous, industrially intact, willingly allied) to the Western alliance than it would be (economically chaotic, devastated, sullenly occupied) to the Soviet side after a successful Soviet attack. Nevertheless, we imagine that Western Europe is of sufficient intrinsic value that the Soviet Union *might* under some circumstances pay costs to acquire it that it would never pay to acquire, say, only Finland.

12. See Michael Altfeld and Bruce Bueno de Mesquita, "Choosing Sides in Wars," *International Studies Quarterly* 23 (March 1979), 87–112. For a good discussion on the matter of deriving generalizations from a deterrer's past behavior, versus the context-bound meaning of the behavior, see Robert Jervis, "Deterrence and Perception," *International Security* 7 (Winter 1982–83), 3–30, esp. 8–13.

13. H. K. Tillema and J. R. Van Wingen, "Law and Power in Military Interventions by Major States after World War II," *International Studies Quarterly* 26 (June 1982), 220–50, report that ties of formal alliance, and defender's military bases on the territory of the protégé are associated with successful deterrence. Russett, "Calculus of Deterrence" (fn. 4), found no such association with alliance but did with various ties of economic and political interdependence and military cooperation. Bruce Russett and Miroslav Nincic, "American Opinion on the Use of Military Force Abroad," *Political Science Quarterly* 91 (Fall 1976), 411–32, report that among the general American public, willingness to aid other states militarily is stronger the greater the geographical proximity of the protégé and the level of foreign trade. Neither formal alliance nor similarity of political system (save for the protégé's not having a communist government) seemed to matter much.

14. This classification is taken from Charles Gochman and Zeev Maoz, "Serious Interstate Disputes, 1816–1976: Empirical Patterns and Theoretical Insights," *Journal of Conflict Resolution* 28 (December 1984), 585–616.

15. The full data set with all variables is available from the authors. The sources used to identify and select cases of attempted deterrence were Melvin Small and J. David Singer, *Resort to Arms* (Beverly Hills, CA: Sage, 1982); Randolph Siverson and Michael Tennefoss, "Interstate Conflicts: 1815–1965," *International Interactions* 9 (July 1982), 147–78, particularly the appendix listing the data for the article; Glenn Snyder and Paul Diesing, *Conflict Among Nations* (Princeton, NJ: Princeton University Press, 1977), particularly the case summaries in the appendix, 531–70; George and Smoke, *Deterrence in*

American Foreign Policy, 105–500; Robert Butterworth, *Managing Interstate Conflict, 1945–1975* (Pittsburgh, PA: University Center for International Studies, 1976); *Keesing's Contemporary Archives* (London: Keesing's Ltd., 1933–80); *Index to The New York Times* (New York: The New York Times, 1900–80); Thomas Ehrlich, *Cyprus 1958–1967: International Crises and the Role of Law* (New York and London: Oxford University Press, 1974); William B. Quandt, *Decade of Decisions: American Policy Toward the Arab-Israeli Conflict, 1967–1976* (Berkeley: University of California Press, 1977); H. Peter Krosby, *Finland, Germany, and the Soviet Union 1940–1941—The Petsamo Dispute* (Madison: University of Wisconsin Press, 1968); and the Correlates of the War Project data set on international disputes, 1816–1980, obtained from tapes made available through the Interuniversity Consortium for Political and Social Research at the University of Michigan. In some other candidate cases we decided either that there was no overt threat by the attacker (e.g., Soviet Union against Iran in 1979), or no previous overt deterrent threat by the deterrer (e.g., United States for South Korea before the North Korean attack, or the United Kingdom over the Falklands/Malvinas before the Argentine invasion). On this last case, see Richard Ned Lebow, "Miscalculation in the South Atlantic: The Origins of the Falkland War," *Journal of Strategic Studies* 6 (March 1983), 5–35. Inevitably a few cases are marginal for one reason or another. Probably the most questionable to many readers will be the characterization of Israel as the attacker to be deterred in 1967 (case no. 49). We did so because of the origins of the situation. PLO forces, with the complicity of Syria, had been attacking Israel, and Israel threatened to make a (limited) strike on Syria to put a stop to the attacks. Egypt rushed verbally to Syria's side with deterrent threats and began to take military steps that, although they may have originated partly as an effort to deter attack on Syria, escalated to the point where they put basic Israeli security at risk. The result was a failure of deterrence manifested by an Israeli strike (possibly preemptive) against Egypt. See Michael Brecher, *Decisions in Crisis: Israel, 1967 and 1973* (New Haven, CT: Yale University Press, 1980), ch. 5.

16. In an alternative analysis we aggregated both sides for most of these events to make single cases (e.g., Russia and France defending Serbia against Austria-Hungary and Germany in 1914), reducing the total number of cases to 47. But save for one minor exception to be discussed below, the values that emerged in our equations were not significantly different in the two procedures. Hence we shall consider only the results of the "unpacked" cases, which we consider the more appropriate mode of analysis.

17. In fact, all cases that were characterized by relatively low levels of fatalities (250–1,000) also qualified as deterrence failures by one of the other criteria (goal achievement or occupation).

18. Richard Ned Lebow, *Between Peace and War: The Nature of International Crisis* (Baltimore, MD: Johns Hopkins University Press, 1981), 270–71. Also see Snyder and Diesing, *Conflict Among Nations*.

19. The raw data for the construction of this variable were obtained from tapes made available through the Interuniversity Consortium for Political and Social Research at the University of Michigan. For the development of the composite national capabilities index, see J. David Singer, Stuart Bremer, and John Stuckey,

"Capability Distribution, Uncertainty, and Major Power War, 1820–1965," in Bruce Russett, ed., *Peace, War and Numbers* (Beverly Hills, CA: Sage, 1972).

20. The formula used was that developed by Bueno de Mesquita, *The War Trap*, 105. The function is a nonlinear one; i.e., the *rate* at which power declines is less over greater distances.

21. Data on military alliances were gathered from Bruce Russett, "An Empirical Typology of International Military Alliances," *Midwest Journal of Political Science* 15 (May 1971), 262–80; J. David Singer and Melvin Small, "Formal Alliances, 1815–1939," *Journal of Peace Research* 3:1 (1966), 1–32; and International Institute for Strategic Studies, *The Military Balance* (London: International Institute for Strategic Studies, 1961–76).

22. Sources used to calculate trade shares were the following: Sir John Scott-Keltle, ed., *The Statesman's Yearbook* (London: Macmillan, 1905–10); *Memorandum on International Trade and Balance of Payments* (Geneva: League of Nations, 1910–39); H. R. Mitchell, *European Historical Statistics 1750–1970* (New York: Columbia University Press, 1975); *Statistical Abstract of the United States* (Washington, DC: U.S. Government Printing Office, 1946–50); *Yearbook of International Trade Statistics* (New York: United Nations, 1950–80); *World Tables 1976* (Baltimore, MD: Johns Hopkins University Press, 1976); Alexander Eckstein, Walter Galenson, and Ta-Chung Liu, eds., *Economic Trends in Communist China* (Chicago, IL: Aldine, 1969), 671–738; and *Communist China's Balance of Payments* (Washington, DC: Central Intelligence Agency, 1966).

23. Sources included Robert E. Harkavy, *The Arms Trade and International Systems* (Cambridge, MA: Ballinger, 1975); Stockholm International Peace Research Institute, *SIPRI Yearbook* (New York: Humanities Press, 1969–80), U.S. Arms Control and Disarmament Agency; *World Military Expenditures and Arms Transfers* (Washington, DC: U.S. Government Printing Office, 1965–80); U.S. Central Intelligence Agency, *Communist Aid Activities in Non-Communist Less Developed Countries, 1954–1979* (Washington, DC: U.S. Government Printing Office, 1980); League of Nations, *Statistical Yearbook, of the Trade in Arms, Ammunition, and Implements of War* (Geneva: League of Nations, 1924–39); League of Nations, *Armaments Yearbook* (Geneva: League of Nations, 1923–39); Ushisaburo Kobayashi, *War and Armament Loans of Japan* (New York: Oxford University Press, 1922); Eugene Anderson, *The First Moroccan Crisis: 1904–1906* (Hamden, CT: Archon Books, 1966); Jean-Claude Allain, *Agadir: 1911* (Paris: Sorbonne, 1976); Firuz Kazemzadeh, *Russia and Britain in Persia, 1864–1914* (New Haven, CT: Yale University Press, 1968); Edward Thaden, *Russia and the Balkan Alliance of 1912* (University Park: Pennsylvania State University Press, 1965); Peter S. M. Tang, *Russia and Soviet Policy in Manchuria and Outer Mongolia* (Durham, NC: Duke University Press, 1959). If there was more than one defender all defenders' military capabilities were included, but linkages were measured from the protégé to the defender that took the diplomatic lead in trying to deter.

24. In fact, all but one of the results we used are at the .05 level or above. A level of .1 is lower than would be appropriate if we had the luxury of a larger number of cases. But here use of a high level would risk too great a chance of rejecting hypotheses that are basically supported (type II error). Significance levels are

given for a one-tailed test where the hypothesis indicates the sign of the expected relationship.

25. Bruce Bueno de Mesquita, "The War Trap Revisited," *American Political Science Review* 79 (March 1985), 157–56.

26. With a t-test of 1.93 it would be significant at the .05 level with a one-tailed test, but, since its sign is the opposite of that which we hypothesized, the level (.1) appropriate to a two-tailed test is applicable.

27. Alone among our variables, there is some problem of collinearity among the various measures of capability. The indicator for local existing military capability nevertheless remains significant even when other power measures are added to the equation, and it is by far the strongest when each of the four capability measures is used alone.

28. This result also is a bit sensitive to the inclusion or exclusion of the case of Vietnam. If Vietnam were to be dropped, the probabilities, especially toward the upper range of defender's superiority, would be markedly higher.

29. It is worth noting that economic and military-political ties are probably among the variables for which we have the least satisfactory fit between theoretical concept and empirical indicator. If so, and the biasing effect is essentially random, then we may be *understating* their true predictive power. One instance (case no. 49) in which our model erroneously predicted deterrence would fail almost surely results from a weakness in our measure of military strength. In common with most other such efforts (see Organski and Kugler, *The War Trap*, ch. 2), our indicator underestimates Israel's capability.

30. Several articles make this point well. See Andrew Mack, "Why Big Nations Lose Small Wars," *World Politics* 27 (January 1975), 175–200; John Mueller, "The Search for a 'Breaking Point' in Vietnam," *International Studies Quarterly* 24 (December 1980), 497–519; and Robert Jervis, "Bargaining and Bargaining Tactics," in J. Roland Pennock and John W. Chapman, eds., *Coercion: NOMOS XIV* (Chicago, IL: Aldine, 1972).

31. Paul Kennedy, *The Realities Behind Diplomacy: Background Influences in British External Policy, 1865–1980* (London: Allen Unwin, 1981).

32. Lawerence Freedman, *The Evolution of Nuclear Strategy* (New York: St. Martin's, 1981), xv.

33. In broad outline these results confirm the earlier conclusions of Russett, "Calculus of Deterrence." They also support George and Smoke's, *Deterrence in American Foreign Policy*, that the attacker's perception of the adequacy and appropriateness of the defender's military capability is neither a sufficient nor an adequate condition for successful deterrence.

Chapter 12   Ethical Dilemmas of Nuclear Deterrence

This chapter is reprinted from *International Security* 84:4 (Spring 1984), 36–54 by permission of the President and Fellows of Harvard College and the Massachusetts Institute of Technology.

1. The hierarchy has adopted "conservative" positions on some social issues, such as school prayer and abortion. But it was a very early proponent of Social

Security, has been progressive on race relations, and is currently one of the most effective critics of U.S. foreign policy in Central America.

2. U.S. Catholic Conference, *Resolution on Southeast Asia* (Washington, DC: USCC, 1971).

3. John Ford, "The Morality of Obliteration Bombing," *Theological Studies* 5 (September 1944), 272–86.

4. It must be clear that in writing this commentary, I am representing myself only, and the U.S. Catholic Conference is in no way responsible.

5. The most complete and best-informed account of the process of producing the Letter is Jim Castelli, *The Bishops and the Bomb* (Garden City, NY: Image, 1983). An excellent set of commentaries on the Letter is Philip J. Murnion, ed., *Catholics and Nuclear War* (New York: Crossroad, 1983).

6. All quotations attributed to the Pastoral Letter are taken from U.S. Catholic Conference, *The Challenge of Peace: God's Promise and Our Response* (Washington, DC: USCC, 1983).

7. On the evolution of policy, see David Alan Rosenberg, "The Origins of Overkill: Nuclear Weapons and American Strategy, 1945–1960," *International Security* 7 (Spring 1983), 3–71; and Desmond Ball, *Targeting for Strategic Deterrence*, Adelphi Paper no. 185 (London: International Institute for Strategic Studies, 1983).

8. "No civilian targets" means no civilian targets *ever*, even in retaliation for attacks on American civilians. This last aspect will not be popular with many strategists, who understandably would like to retain the threat of purely retaliatory strikes against civilians as a means to ensure Soviet good behavior during a "limited" nuclear war.

9. This argument is expressed by Albert Wohlstetter, "Bishops, Statesmen, and Other Strategists on the Bombing of Innocents," *Commentary* 75 (June 1983), 15–35. I responded in a letter in *Commentary* 76 (December 1983), 6–7.

10. Counterforce strategies have, in the past, repeatedly had the effect of enlarging the list of targets (Rosenberg, "Origins of Overkill," 50). That is therefore a trap inherent in contemporary counterforce policies.

11. John Steinbruner, "Nuclear Decapitation," *Foreign Policy* 45 (Winter 1981–82), 22–23. Also see Desmond Ball, *Can Nuclear War Be Controlled?* Adelphi Paper no. 161 (London: International Institute for Strategic Studies, 1981).

12. Thomas C. Schelling, *Arms and Influence* (New Haven, CT: Yale University Press, 1966), 99.

13. Paul Bracken, *The Command and Control of Nuclear Forces* (New Haven, CT: Yale University Press, 1983).

14. Michael Howard, "Reassurance and Deterrence," *Foreign Affairs* 61 (Winter 1982–83), 309–24.

15. The television program "Saturday Night Live" did a comic interview with a mock bishop who, after explaining the "you can have it but you can't use it" position on nuclear weapons, then declared that "as celibates we are familiar with this problem."

16. Most troublesome in this respect was the quotation from Cardinal Krol that said, "not only the *use* of strategic nuclear weapons, but also the *declared intent* to use them involved in our deterrence policy, are both wrong" (Italics in

original). This statement could be taken to refer to any use of nuclear weapons, or only the use or declared intent to use weapons indiscriminately—i.e., against cities. Since counterpopulation warfare was still an element of American declaratory policy (and very possibly of operational policy) at the time of Cardinal Krol's statement, he was not necessarily condemning *any* use or threat. Similar ambiguity arose regarding advice, in the pastoral section at the end of the second draft, to men and women in defense industries: "You also have specific questions to face because your industry produces many of the weapons of massive and indiscriminate destruction which have concerned us in this letter. We have judged immoral even the threat to use such weapons. At the same time, we have held that the possession of nuclear weapons may be tolerated as deterrents while meaningful efforts are underway to achieve multilateral disarmament." I believe that, in context, the operative qualifier is "massive and indiscriminate destruction," but it is understandable how some readers could have taken this passage as a blanket condemnation.

17. It is nevertheless true that some critics, notably Wohlstetter and the *Times* editorial, ostensibly were responding to the third draft or final version. A charitable interpretation of their criticism is that they simply had not read the later versions carefully. McGeorge Bundy, in his "The Bishops and the Bomb," *The New York Review of Books*, June 16, 1983, 3–8, exhibits a much better understanding of the letter.

18. This passage was subject to several changes from the second draft to the final version. The third draft substituted "curb" for "halt," but at the same time broadened coverage to all "nuclear weapons" systems in place of the second draft's reference to "strategic" systems. The changes occurred during the course of some agonized discussions in the committee under conditions when it appeared, after a communication from the Vatican, that the delicately achieved compromise of the document could be upset, with possible public charges that the committee had exceeded its proper role. The majority reluctantly accepted these changes (while still supporting a freeze) in order to retain other parts of the document that constituted its heart. Unfortunately the press, in their first comments on the third draft, concentrated on the "halt" to "curb" change, missed the expansion of "strategic," and largely ignored the other ways in which the letter remained, as it had been through all permutations, profoundly critical of many aspects of official policy. The committee majority therefore was pleased when the plenary body of bishops, in Chicago, immediately voted over-whelmingly to return to the word "halt." This sequence of events had the effect of demonstrating that the majority of all the bishops wanted a freeze, and that this was not something thrust upon them by a drafting committee.

19. The Pastoral Letter cites some participants in this debate. Others include Robert S. McNamara, "The Military Role of Nuclear Weapons: Perceptions and Misperceptions," *Foreign Affairs* 62 (Fall 1983), 59–80; John Mearsheimer, *Conventional Deterrence* (Ithaca, NY: Cornell University Press, 1983); Bernard W. Rogers, "The Atlantic Alliance: Prescriptions for a Difficult Decade," *Foreign Affairs* 60 (Summer 1982), 1145–56; and the Report of the European Security Study, *Strengthening Conventional Deterrence: Proposals for the 1980s* (New York: St. Martin's, 1983). General Rogers has reservations about whether a full no-first-use policy is feasible, but has been campaigning vigorously for at

least a no-early-first-use posture. For evidence of widespread European public support of a no-first-use policy, see Bruce Russett and Donald R. DeLuca, "Theater Nuclear Forces," ch. 9 of this book.

20. Recall the view of McGeorge Bundy that the explosion "of even one hydrogen bomb on one city of one's own country would be recognized in advance as a cat-astrophic blunder." "To Cap the Volcano," *Foreign Affairs*, 48 (Spring 1969), 10.

Chapter 13   Seeking Peace in a Post–Cold War World of Hegemony and Terrorism

John R. Oneal earned his Ph.D. at Stanford University, and now is Professor of Political Science at the University of Alabama at Tuscaloosa. He was a Fulbright Scholar and Fellow at the Norwegian Institute in 2000.

This chapter was originally "A la recherche de la paix dans un monde d'après-guerre froide caractérisé par l'hégémonie et le terrorisme," *Etudes Internationales* 35 (December 2000), 641–68. Our data are available at http://pantheon.yale.edu%7Ebrusset/.

1. *Perpetual Peace: A Philosophical Sketch* [1795]. Reprinted in Hans Reiss, ed., *Kant's Political Writings* (Cambridge: Cambridge University Press, 1970).

2. John R. Oneal, Bruce Russett, and Michael L. Berbaum, "Causes of Peace: Democracy, Interdependence, and International Organizations, 1885–1992," *International Studies Quarterly* 47 (2003), 371–93; Bruce Russett and John R. Oneal, *Triangulating Peace: Democracy, Interdependence, and International Organizations* (New York: Norton, 2001).

3. Benjamin Most and Harvey Starr, *Inquiry, Logic, and International Politics* (Columbia: University of South Carolina Press, 1989); David Kinsella and Bruce Russett, "Conflict Emergence and Escalation in Interactive International Dyads," *Journal of Politics* 64 (November 2002), 1045–68.

4. A critique of these arguments is Sebastian Rosato, "The Flawed Logic of Democratic Peace Theory," *American Political Science Review* 97 (November 2003), 585–602.

   Defenses of the logic include Dina Zinnes, "Constructing Political Logic: The Democratic Peace Puzzle," *Journal of Conflict Resolution* 48 (June 2004), 430–54, and David Kinsella, "No Rest for the Democratic Peace," *American Political Science Review* 99 (August 2005), 453–57.

5. To extend our previous analyses, we use the expanded trade and GDP data set version 3 compiled by Kristian Gleditsch, with minor revisions.

6. The IGO data set is the Correlates of War 2 International Governmental Organizations Data Version 2.0 compiled by Jon Pevehouse, Timothy Nordstrom, and Kevin Warnke. It improves the set we previously used for the years 1965 to 1991 and extends it to 2000.

7. Nathaniel Beck, Jonathan N. Katz, and Richard Tucker, "Beyond Ordinary Logic: Taking Time Seriously in Binary-Time-Series-Cross-Section Models," *American Journal of Political Science* 42 (October 1998), 1260–88; John R. Oneal and Bruce Russett, "Modeling Conflict While Studying Dynamics: A Response to Nathaniel Beck," in Gerald Schneider, Katherine Barbieri, and Nils Petter Gleditsch, eds., *Globalization and Armed Conflict* (Lanham, MD: Rowman and Littlefield, 2003).

8. Arvid Raknerud and Håvard Hegre, "The Hazard of War: Reassessing the Evidence for the Democratic Peace," *Journal of Peace Research* 34 (November 1997), 385–404.

9. But the lower trade-to-GDP ratio is significant at the .03 level (one-tailed test) if the measure of joint memberships in international organizations is not included in the specification.

10. See Oneal et al. "Causes of Peace." For example, the General Estimating Equation (GEE), taking into account first-order autoregression (AR1), provides unbiased estimates of the coefficients and, with robust standard errors, yields estimates of the coefficients' variances that are consistent even if the correlations among the errors are misspecified: Christopher Zorn, "Generalized Estimating Equation Models for Correlated Data: A Review with Applications," *American Political Science Review* 45 (June 2001), 470–90. Controlling for an AR1 process, GEE explicitly addresses the lack of independence among our observations through time. Errors in prediction are also likely to be correlated across dyads at individual points in time, however. To address this second concern, Patrick Heagerty, Michael D. Ward, and Kristian S. Gleditsch, "Windows of Opportunity: Window Subseries Empirical Variance Estimator in International Relations," *Political Analysis* 10 (Spring 2002), 304–17 offer a correction for spatial correlations that arise because the experiences of dyads at a single point in time are not independent. Interstate conflict is apt to be contagious. The essence of their method is straightforward in that instead of using dyads to define the clusters for producing robust standard errors, the WSEV(Window Subseries Empirical Variance) estimator uses slices of time. When these slices include more than one year, adjustment is also made for autocorrelation. Thus this estimator addresses both spatial and temporal dimensions of dependence.

11. Controlling for past conflicts increases our confidence that we are identifying causal relations, so the strong association of our IGOs measure with peace in the GEE and WSEV analyses may indicate that joint memberships in international organizations are merely correlated with peace and not a cause of it. Past conflict may increase both the likelihood of current conflict and reduce states' joint memberships in international organizations. Also, a close examination (our thanks to Jon Pevehouse for this) shows that fighting is rare both for diplomatically isolated states sharing few or no joint memberships and those sharing many. The problem seems to be with those at the middle levels of membership.

12. All these results are very similar to those summarized by Scott Bennett and Allan C. Stam, *The Behavioral Origins of War* (Ann Arbor: University of Michigan Press, 2004), save that they did not examine the effect of IGOs.

13. Russett and Oneal, *Triangulating Peace*, 173–74.

14. Robert Gilpin, *War and Change in World Politics* (New York: Cambridge University Press, 1981). Power-transition theory also draws attention to the power of the hegemon to constrain states from resorting to military force. A. F. K. Organski and Jacek Kugler, *The War Ledger* (Chicago, IL: University of Chicago Press, 1980); Ronald L. Tammen, Jacek Kugler, Douglas Lemke, Allan C. Stam III, Mark Abdollahian, Carole Alsharabati, Brian Efird, and A. F. K. Organski, *Power Transitions: Strategies for the 21st Century* (New York: Chatham House, 2000).

15. Organski and Kugler, *The War Ledger*; Russett, "The Mysterious Case of Vanishing Hegemony," chapter 8 of this book; John Oneal, "Measuring the

Material Base of the East-West Balance of Power," *International Interactions* 15:2 (1989), 177–96.

16. Douglas Lemke and William Reed, "Regime Types and Status Quo Evaluations: Power Transition Theory and the Democratic Peace," *International Interactions* 22:2 (1996), 143–64.

17. Joane Gowa, *Ballots and Bullets* (Princeton, NJ: Princeton University Press, 1999); Sebastian Rosato, "The Flawed Logic of Democratic Peace Theory," *American Political Science Review* 97 (November 2003), 585–602.

18. Huntington, *The Clash of Civilizations and the Remaking of World Order* (New York: Simon and Schuster, 1996). The quotations in this paragraph are, in order, from pp. 14, 321, 21, 20.

19. Bruce Russett, John R. Oneal, and Michaelene Cox, "Clash of Civilizations, or Realism and Liberalism Déjà Vu? Some Evidence," *Journal of Peace Research* 37 (September 2000), 583–608.

20. The character of different civilizations, rather than directly influencing the likelihood of interstate violence, could shape the political institutions, economic practices, and security arrangements that we have highlighted in our discussion of the Kantian and realist theories. Thus the effect of culture might be an indirect one through these important intermediary influences. Civilizational similarities and differences do help predict alliance patterns; but they make little contribution to understanding countries' political institutions, membership in international institutions, or commercial interactions, as we have shown elsewhere. Consequently, there is no reason to believe that civilizations have major indirect effects on the likelihood of conflict through these variables. See Russett and Oneal, *Triangulating Peace*, ch. 7.

21. Russett and Oneal, *Triangulating Peace*; Oneal et al., "Causes of Peace." For new evidence, see Jon Pevehouse, *Democracy from Above? Regional Organizations and Democratization* (New York: Cambridge University Press, 2005) on international organizations' contribution to democratic transitions and their consolidation, Nathan Jensen, "Democratic Governance and Multinational Corporations: Political Regimes and Inflows of Foreign Direct Investment," *International Organization* 57 (Summer 2003), 587–616 on the greater flows of foreign investment to democracies than autocracies, Erik Gartzke and Quan Li, "War, Peace, and the Invisible Hand: Positive Political Externalities of Economic Globalization," *International Studies Quarterly* 47 (December 2003), 561–86 on investment flows as promoting peace; and Rafael Reuveny and Quan Li., "The Joint Democracy-Dyadic Conflict Nexus: A Simultaneous Equations Model," *International Studies Quarterly* 47 (September 2003), 325–46, and Kelly Kadera, Mark Crescenzi, and Megan Shannon, "Democratic Survival, Peace, and War in the International System," *American Journal of Political Science* 47 (April 2003), 234–47, on the mutual reinforcement of peace and democracy.

Chapter 14   Bushwhacking the Democratic Peace

This chapter is reprinted from *International Studies Perspectives* 6 (November 2005), 395–408, by permission from Blackwell Publications. I am grateful to Mark Peceny for comments.

1. Todd Purdom, "For Bush, No Boasts, but a Taste of Vindication," *New York Times*, March 9, 2004: A10.
2. Below I suggest some reasons why the statement about peaceful democracies in general may be contingent on such influences as leadership attributes and goals.
3. Fred Chernoff, "The Study of Democratic Peace and Progress in International Relations," *International Studies Review* 6 (March 2004), 49–78; David Kinsella, "No Rest for the Democratic Peace," *American Political Science Review* 89 (August 2005), 453–57. David L. Rousseau, *Democracy and War: Institutions, Norms, and the Evolution of International Conflict* (Stanford, CA: Stanford University Press, 2005.)
4. Bruce Russett, *Grasping the Democratic Peace: Principles for a Post–Cold War World* (Princeton, NJ: Princeton University Press, 1993), 135–36; Russett and John R. Oneal, *Triangulating Peace: Democracy, Interdependence, and International Organizations* (New York: Norton, 2001), 303. Also see Lars Erik Cederman and Kristian Skrede Gleditsch, "Conquest and Regime Change: An Evolutionary Model of the Spread of Democracy and Peace," *International Studies Quarterly* 48 (September 2004), 604, fn. 1, who carefully say their results should "not be interpreted as an argument in favor of the Bush administration's efforts to impose regime change in Iraq through military force."
5. Lawrence Freedman, *The Evolution of Nuclear Strategy* (New York: St. Martin's, 1989, 2nd edition), 126–27.
6. Robert Pape, *Dying to Win: The Strategic Logic of Suicide Terrorism* (New York: Random House, 2005), forcefully contends that the U.S. occupation of Iraq is actually encouraging the recruitment of suicide terrorists there and elsewhere. On Bush's arguments for war as varied and unsubstantiated see Chaim Kaufmann, "Threat Inflation and the Market for Ideas," *International Security* 29 (Summer 2004), 5–48.
7. The British intelligence chief's secret report on Prime Minister Tony Blair's July 2002 conversations in Washington declared that "Military action was now seen as inevitable. Bush wanted to remove Saddam, through military action, justified by the conjunction of terrorism and WMD. But the intelligence and facts were being fixed around the policy . . . There was little discussion in Washington of the aftermath after military action." When asked about the report's validity, "British officials did not dispute the document's authenticity" (reported in *The Times of London*, May 1, 2005, on http://downingstreetmemo.com).
8. See John Mearsheimer and Stephen Walt, "Keeping Saddam in a Box," *New York Times*, February 2, 2003.
9. Russett and Oneal, *Triangulating Peace*.
10. Bruce Bueno de Mesquita, Alastair Smith, Randolph Siverson, and James Morrow, *The Logic of Political Survival* (Cambridge, MA: M.I.T. Press, 2003); Dan Reiter and Allan C. Stam, *Democracies at War* (Princeton, NJ: Princeton University Press, 2002).
11. "Machiavelli's Legacy: Domestic Politics and International Conflict," *International Studies Quarterly* 49 (June 2005), 179–204.
12. In the terms of Bueno de Mesquita et al., *Logic of Political Survival*, these are large selectorate but small winning coalition regimes.
13. Kristian Skrede Gleditsch and Michael D. Ward, "Double-Take: A Re-Examination of Democracy and Autocracy in Modern Polities," *Journal of Conflict*

Resolution 41 (June 1997), 231–83 identify just this distinction and examples by breaking down the components of the Polity scale, though their article does not discuss foreign policy behavior.

14. "Warlike Democracies" (Manuscript, Stanford, CA and New Haven, CT: Stanford University and Yale University, 2005).

15. Harald Mueller, "The Antimony of Democratic Peace," *International Politics* 41 (December 2004), 494–520, distinguishes between pacifist democracies which seek a modus vivendi with autocracies and may try to assist their transformation into democracies, and militant democracies which are fundamentally antagonistic to dictatorships and may try to overthrow them by force. He roots this in differences in the prevailing norms in each, and says that which normative tradition prevails in a state may change with the ruling coalition and policy discourse, and external conditions. This does not, however, lead to confident predictions of which set of norms may prevail in a particular state and time.

16. Keller, "Leadership Style, Regime Type, and Foreign Policy Crisis Behavior: A Contingent Monadic Peace?" *International Studies Quarterly* 49 (June 2005), 205–31; Hermann, "Explaining Foreign Policy Behavior Using the Personal Characteristics of Political Leaders," *International Studies Quarterly* 24 (March 1980), 7–46; Hermann, "Assessing the Personalities of Soviet Politburo Members" *Personality and Social Psychology Bulletin* 6 (1980), 332–52.

17. David Dallek, *Franklin D. Roosevelt and American Foreign Policy 1932–1945* (New York: Oxford University Press, 1979), 285.

18. Samuel P. Huntington, *The Third Wave: Democratization in the Late Twentieth Century* (Norman: University of Oklahoma Press, 1991); M. Steven Fish, "Islam and Authoritarianism," *World Politics* 55 (October 2002), 4–37; Daniela Donno and Bruce Russett, "Islam, Authoritarianism, and Female Empowerment," reprinted as chapter 7 of this book.

19. On the less demanding criterion of an occupation designed to produce a reasonably stable and friendly government, not necessarily a democracy, Iraq still was far less promising than Germany, Japan, and many other cases. See David M. Edelstein, "Occupational Hazards: Why Military Occupations Succeed or Fail," *International Security* 29 (Summer 2004), 49–91.

20. Larry Diamond, "What Went Wrong in Iraq?" *Foreign Affairs* 83 (October 2004), 34–56.

21. Thomas Carothers, *Aiding Democracy Abroad: The Learning Curve* (Washington, DC: Carnegie Endowment for International Peace, 1999), 351.

22. Applying the criteria from an earlier exposition, Bruce Russett, *The Prisoners of Insecurity: Nuclear Deterrence, the Arms Race, and Arms Control* (San Francisco, CA: W. H. Freeman, 1983), 140):

    1. *The war must be declared by a legitimate authority.* In 1991, George H. W. Bush thought he needed, in addition to sovereign authority of the United States, explicit approval by the UN. George W. Bush acted without it.

    2. *Those who resort to war must have a right intention.* Hard to tell, given the fog surrounding U.S. intentions.

    3. *The injury the war is intended to prevent must be real and certain.* Doubtful, given the absence of WMDs.

    4. *There must be reasonable hope of success.* The hope was present; the reality remains to be seen, and depends on what "success" means.

5. *The war must be undertaken only as a last resort.* Doubtful.
6. *The measures employed in the war must themselves be moral (for example, the fair treatment of prisoners and respect for the inviolability of noncombatants).* A mixed record, maybe better than in most wars.
7. *The seriousness of the injury to be prevented must be proportional to the damages that are inflicted.* Still to be determined.

23. Mark Peceny, *Democracy at the Point of Bayonets* (University Park: Pennsylvania State University Press, 1999).
24. Mark Peceny and J. Pickering, "Forging Democracy at Gunpoint" (Manuscript, Albuquerque, NM: University of New Mexico, 2004).
25. Peceny, *Democracy at the Point of Bayonets*, 199. Also see James Meernik, "United States Military Intervention and the Promotion of Democracy," *Journal of Peace Research* 33 (November 1996), 391–402; Margaret Hermann and Charles Kegley, "The U.S. Use of Military Intervention to Promote Democracy: Evaluating the Record," *International Interactions* 24:2 (1998), 436–60. Karen Von Hippel, *Democracy by Force: U.S. Military Intervention in the Post–Cold War World* (Cambridge: Cambridge University Press, 2000) critiques U.S. intervention.
26. Peceny, *Democracy at the Point of Bayonets*, 212–16.
27. "Operation Exporting Freedom: The Quest for Democratization via United States Military Operations" *Whitehead Journal of Diplomacy and International Relations* 6 (2005), 97–111. Tures could not report his full statistical analysis in this article, but makes it available by request to jtures@lagrange.edu.
28. On the day of the invasion, I told an inquiring journalist that I felt as though I were living in Athens on the day that city's forces sailed on their expedition to Syracuse, and explained why.
29. Boutros Boutros-Ghali, *An Agenda for Peace* (New York: United Nations, 1992), and Boutros-Ghali, *An Agenda for Democratization* (New York: United Nations, 1996).
30. *Making War and Building Peace: The United Nations after the Cold War* (Princeton, NJ: Princeton University Press, 2006).
31. Peceny and Pickering, "Forging Democracy at Gunpoint," substantially confirm this. Also see Peceny and Pickering, "Can Liberal Intervention Build Liberal Democracy?" in J. Meernik and T. D. Mason, eds., *Sustaining the Peace: War Prevention and Peace-building in Post Conflict Societies* (Routledge: New York, 2006), and Virginia Page Fortna, *Peace Time: Cease-Fire Agreements and the Durability of Peace* (Princeton, NJ: Princeton University Press, 2004). Roland Paris, *At War's End: Building Peace after Civil Conflict* (Cambridge: Cambridge University Press, 2004) is more critical.
32. Russett and Oneal, *Triangulating Peace*, ch. 6; 200–11; also K. Kumar, ed., *Post-Conflict Elections, Democratization, and International Assistance* (Boulder, CO: Lynne Rienner, 2002).
33. Katherine Sikkink, "Human Rights, Principled Issue-Networks, and Sovereignty in Latin America," *International Organization* 47 (Summer 1993), 411–42.
34. The discussion of the OAS draws on Randall Parish and Mark Peceny, "Kantian Liberalism and the Collective Defense of Democracy in Latin America," *Journal of Peace Research* 39 (March 2002), 229–50, and Daniela Donno, *Regional*

Intergovernmental Organizations and the Collective Defense of Democracy, dissertation prospectus (New Haven, CT: Yale University, 2005); see the latter for a more developed analytical typology of various IGO action options.

35. G. John Ikenberry, *After Victory: Institutions, Strategic Restraint, and the Rebuilding of Order after Major Wars* (Princeton, NJ: Princeton University Press, 2001).

36. David Phillips, "Turkey's Dreams of Accession," *Foreign Affairs* 83 (October 2004), 86–97.

37. Conditionality as an enforcement capacity is common to many functional IGOs, both regional and global ones. The best-known examples of domestic elites using an external commitment to strengthen their hands for policies they want to choose anyway are from study of the International Monetary Fund. Many such conditionalities from the IMF, of course, are at best irrelevant to democracy promotion. See James R. Vreeland, *The IMF and Economic Development* (New York: Cambridge University Press, 2003).

38. The above paragraphs draw on Jon Pevehouse, "Democratization, Credible Commitments, and IGOs," in Daniel Drezner, ed., *Locating the Proper Authorities: The Interaction of Domestic and International Institutions* (Ann Arbor: University of Michigan Press, 2003), and Jon Pevehouse, *Democracy from Above? Regional Organizations and Democratization* (New York: Cambridge University Press, 2005); also Dan Reiter, "Why NATO Enlargement Does Not Spread Democracy," *International Security* 25 (Spring 2001), 41–67.

39. Charles Lipson, *Reliable Partners: How Democracies Have Made a Separate Peace* (Princeton, NJ: Princeton University Press, 2003).

40. Russett and Oneal, *Triangulating Peace*, ch. 4.

41. Oona Hathaway, "Do Human Rights Treaties Make a Difference?" *Yale Law Journal* 111 (June 2002), 1935–2042.

42. Emily Hafner-Burton, "Trading Human Rights: How Preferential Trade Agreements Influence Government Repression," *International Organization* 59 (Summer 2005), 593–629.

43. This discussion draws heavily on Nikolay Marinov, "Does Integration Spread Democracy through Ideas or Conditionality?" (Manuscript, New Haven, CT: Yale University, 2004).

44. Immanuel Kant, writing within the just war tradition, would agree. See his *The Metaphysics of Morals*, reprinted in Hans Reiss, ed., *Kant's Political Writings* (Cambridge: Cambridge University Press, [1797] 1970): 168–70, esp. 17, that the victor in a defensive war [no mention of preemption] may then compel an unjust aggressor nation "to accept a new constitution of a nature that is unlikely to encourage their warlike inclinations."

45. Yi Feng, *Democracy, Governance, and Economic Performance: Theory and Evidence* (Cambridge, MA: M.I.T. Press, 2004), David S. Brown and Wendy Hunter, "Democracy and Social Spending in Latin America, 1980–92," *American Political Science Review* 93 (December 1999), 779–90; Ghobarah, Huth, and Russett, "Comparative Public Health," chapter 4 in this book; Joseph T. Siegle, Michael M. Weinstein, and Morton Halperin, "Why Democracies Excel," *Foreign Affairs* 83 (October 2004), 57–71.

46. Adam Przeworski, Michael Alvarez, Jose Cheibub, and Fernando Limongi, *Democracy and Development: Political Institutions and Well-Being in the World, 1950–1990* (New York: Cambridge University Press, 2000).

47. Lars-Erik Cederman, "Back to Kant: Reinterpreting the Democratic Peace as a Macrohistorical Learning Process," *American Political Science Review* 95 (March 2001), 15–31; Cederman and Mohan Penubarti Rao, "Exploring the Dynamics of the Democratic Peace," *Journal of Conflict Resolution* 45 (December 2001), 818–33.

48. Benjamin Fordham and Thomas Walker, "Kantian Liberalism, Regime Type, and Military Resource Allocation," *International Studies Quarterly* 49 (March 2005), 141–57.

49. Zeev Maoz, *Domestic Sources of Global Change* (Ann Arbor: University of Michigan Press, 1996); Kristian Skrede Gleditsch, *All International Politics is Local: The Diffusion of Conflict, Integration, and Democratization* (Ann Arbor: University of Michigan Press, 2002); Gleditsch and Michael Don Ward, "Visualization in International Relations," in Alex Mintz and Bruce Russett, eds., *New Directions for International Relations: Confronting the Method of Analysis Problem* (Lanham, MD: Lexington Books, 2005).

50. Francis Fukuyama, *America at the Crossroads* (New Haven, CT: Yale University Press, 2006).

Index